Lake District
Winter Climbs

Snow, Ice and Mixed Climbs
in the English Lake District

by

Brian Davison

Diagrams by Al Phizacklea

Photographs edited by Nick Wharton

Edited by Stephen Reid

The FRCC and Rock Climbing Guides to the English Lake District

1907–2007

The formation of the Fell and Rock Climbing Club was proposed at Coniston in 1906 at the instigation of Edward Scantlebury and Alan Craig, two of a 'coterie of keen young mountaineers living on the southern confines of the English Lake District'. Before the end of the year the club had over 40 members enrolled and was officially founded in 1907 when Ashley Abraham accepted the office of President. The first Club Journal was produced that same year and many new climbs were reported therein and in further annual volumes.

The Club published its first rock climbing guidebook in 1922 (Doe Crag by George Bower) and since that date has produced a continuous series of definitive guidebooks to Lake District rock climbing. These guidebooks are written and published by volunteers who update the text and check new climbs, many of which have been, and continue to be, pioneered by Club members.

The Club now has over 1000 members and owns several club-huts both in the Lake District and elsewhere. Membership has always been open to applicants of either sex who can demonstrate an ongoing interest and enthusiasm for climbing in the Lake District. Enquiries regarding the FRCC and its guidebooks should be addressed to the current Club Secretary or Guidebooks Editor, whose addresses are available from the Club's website at www.frcc.co.uk or from the BMC.

This guide to the winter climbing of the English Lake District is one of a number of publications and events commissioned to mark the centenary of the FRCC in 2006/7. It is published in conjunction with Cicerone Press, who have for many years published a winter climbing guide to the Lakes.

An early ascent of Skew Gill *(I), Wasdale*
(FRCC Collection; copyright The Abraham Family)

© Fell and Rock Climbing Club and contributors

First edition 2006

ISBN 10: 1 85284 484 1
ISBN 13: 978 1 85284 484 4

Dedication

This guide is dedicated to all past and present Lakeland winter climbers, particularly those early pioneers whose climbs often went unrecorded save for their fleeting footprints in the snow. We follow in their footsteps.

Cover photo: Icicles festoon Dove Crag, Grasmoor, as climbers tackle the excellent *Chicken Out* (V) (Photo: Stuart Holmes)

CONTENTS

Map key

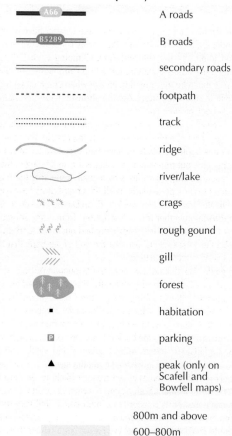

A66	A roads
B5289	B roads
	secondary roads
- - - - - -	footpath
....	track
～～	ridge
	river/lake
	crags
	rough gound
	gill
	forest
▪	habitation
P	parking
▲	peak (only on Scafell and Bowfell maps)

800m and above
600–800m
300–600m
0–300m

FOREWORD

Previous winter climbing guides to the Lake District have been published independently by Cicerone Press. This is the first edition to be produced jointly by the Fell and Rock Climbing Club (FRCC) and Cicerone Press – a new departure for both organisations, and one that should very much be welcomed in an age when commercial interests often seem to ride roughshod over the altruistic nature of traditional club guide-book production.

If writing an accurate rock climbing guide is a difficult task, writing an accurate winter climbing one is virtually impossible. The majority of climbs in this book are likely to have had very few ascents, indeed maybe only one, but true winter conditions are so fleeting in the Lake District that checking descriptions by actually repeating the routes is very difficult to do – particularly as all the contributors have 'proper' jobs and limited free time. Nonetheless, Brian Davison has done sterling work in drawing together route descriptions from many sources and arranging the information into a logically laid out guide (and it will be noted from the 'First Ascents' list near the end of the book that he has the right background for the task).

The guide also includes two articles – 'Mountain Accidents' by Dr John Ellerton, essential and potentially life-saving reading for all climbers, and 'Winter Climbing and Nature Conservation' by Simon Webb of Natural England, which underlines why climbers need to be sensitive to the often delicate ecology of their environment. The 'First Ascents' list near the end of the book is based on considerable historical research by FRCC members Mike Cocker, Colin Wells and Brian Davison, and has resulted in what is as good a stab at a 'First Ascents' list for Lakeland winter routes as we are ever likely to get – no doubt many earlier ascents than those claimed have gone unattributed: there simply wasn't anywhere to record this information until very recently.

A common retort when informed that work is in progress on a new winter guide is 'What's the point? We hardly get a winter these days.' Whilst the evidence shows that winters were often longer and harder in the past (the Solway Viaduct was badly damaged by huge icefloes washed down the River Eden in 1880/1881 for example), a glance at the more recent first ascents will reveal that there is still plenty of 'winter'

Al Phizacklea on thin ice on Mayday Direct *(VI), Scafell,
during the first ascent (Photo: Steve Swindels)*

around, even if you have to make a point of being in the right place at
the right time to catch it.

Best to be prepared then – and this is the guide to help you do just
that. Every known winter climb in the Lake District is covered herein,
and Nick Wharton, aided by use of the FRCC helicopter and a small
army of assistants, has assembled a superb of winter climbing photos
and photo-diagrams, which, together with Al Phizacklea's fine maps,
should make locating your route easier than ever before. The climbs are
there; all you need is this guide – and the weather!

Happy hunting!

Stephen Reid, FRCC Guidebook Editor, October 2006

INTRODUCTION

The Lake District National Park is situated entirely within the county of Cumbria in the north-west of England, not far from the Scottish border. It is a land of dramatic contrasts, with rugged peaks, or fells as they are known locally, rising high over lush green valleys and the deep dark waters that give the area its name. Indeed it contains both the highest mountains and the most extensive lakes in England. However, unlike national parks in many other parts of the world, the Lake District is a populated area, full of working hill farms, villages and market towns. It bears both the ancient scars of mining and quarrying and the modern ones of tourism, and yet is still reckoned to be one of the most tranquil and beautiful areas in the British Isles.

It is unsurprising, therefore, that the Lake District is popular not only with climbers, but also with hill walkers, fell runners, mountain bikers, canoeists and a host of other mountain and countryside users. Furthermore, it has an interesting history (as evidenced by such ancient monuments as the splendidly named Mediobogdum – the Roman fort on Hardknott Pass – and the more recent Borrowdale wad mines), and is also especially renowned as a source of inspiration to many poets and artists, including Wordsworth, Coleridge, Ruskin, Beatrix Potter and three generations of the Heaton Cooper family.

The unceasing efforts of a great number of people over many years have contributed towards keeping the Lake District as a place of great beauty to be enjoyed not only by outdoor enthusiasts, but also by the myriad of other visitors and also the locals, though it has to be said that the interests of these diverse groups do not always coincide. Not least among these efforts were the long and hard campaigns for the area's special status fought by those with the foresight to realise the dangers of unchecked development. Now there are several bodies, statutory and otherwise, like the National Park Authority, the National Trust and the Friends of the Lake District, and their army of wardens, rangers and others, both paid and voluntary, who fight a daily battle to maintain the fragile fabric of this much loved landscape.

The valleys of the Central Lake District are arranged like the spokes of a wheel with the hub in the area of Great End, the northernmost outlier of the Scafell massif. The major valleys of this central area are, in a

clockwise direction, Langdale, the Duddon Valley, Eskdale, Wasdale, Ennerdale, Buttermere, Borrowdale and Thirlmere. East of Thirlmere lies the Helvellyn massif and the parallel valley of Patterdale with its subsidiary valleys of Grizedale, Deepdale and Dovedale. Eastwards again, the Far Eastern Fells have many small and relatively unfrequented valleys. In winter cold air currents from Siberia can bring conditions that in a matter of days can transform this pastoral yet mountainous scene into an arctic wilderness: sadly for winter climbers, it can be transformed back again just as quickly.

This guidebook contains every known winter climb worth recording in the English Lake District. The climbing areas in this guide are generally based on the valleys (as listed above), from where there is access to the various cliffs described. A brief description of the approach to a climbing area is given at the beginning of the valley chapter, with any specific crag approaches being included at the beginning of that crag section. Where not obvious, the descent from each crag is also given. The crag grid reference, altitude and aspect, and, where relevant, an indication of the weather conditions likely to bring the crag into climbing condition, have also been included. For completeness, a few other routes within Cumbria, but outside the Lake District, are also covered.

CONDITIONS

The winter climbing season can lie anywhere between October and April, but good conditions are generally unlikely before the New Year, as until then there are unlikely to have been enough cold days to freeze the ground thoroughly and any snow which falls will have soon melted. While the presence of snow is a must for winter climbing, its presence alone is not enough, as a dump of snow on unfrozen ground merely insulates the soil below and slows down the freezing process. Several days of cold temperatures prior to snowfall are the best indicator that conditions may be suitable on the fells. If you have a particular cliff in mind, then keep an eye on the wind direction and see if it is blowing onto the cliff and thus aiding the freezing process. And while the hills may often be covered with a coating of snow, it takes a few days for fresh snow to consolidate through a freeze–thaw cycle and become better for climbing; and it takes a prolonged period of snowy wintery weather to fill gullies with the snow necessary to build up really good conditions.

John Kelly building up to a Grand Finale *(VI), Great End, during the first ascent in 2006 (Photo: Steve Ashworth)*

However, water ice and turf can freeze and give good climbing after only few days of hard frosts or a longer period of sub-zero temperatures – the important thing here is that it should have regularly been freezing at night. In fact, often some limited thawing during the day is desirable, as long as it freezes again the next night, as this builds the ice thickness up more quickly. With the milder winters of the changing climatic conditions encountered over the last few decades, buttress and mixed routes which come into condition more readily than snow gullies generally provide more reliable climbing.

As well as the regular television and radio weather forecasts, there are a host of other forecasts available by phone and on the internet. A useful forecast for the Lake District National Park, which gives information about snow conditions on the fells, is available on the internet at http://www.lake-district.gov.uk/weatherline/home/index.php, or by telephone 017687-75757.

While arguments will continue to rage over the true definition of a winter climb, in this guide a climb is considered to be 'in condition' if its ascent is largely easier with axes and crampons than without. So when you're climbing, think about the conditions and be honest with yourself (and others). Would progress be easier without your tools? If it would be, then you are doing a cold ascent of a rock route and not a true winter ascent. As far as can be ascertained, all of the climbs described have been done in true winter condition in a single outing. Speculative or incomplete ascents have been omitted, or mentioned as awaiting a true complete ascent. Whilst in Cicerone's previous winter climbing guide only a few of the then new mixed routes had been repeated, now many more have had repeat ascents and new, even harder, climbs have been created. Where possible, descriptions and grades are from a consensus of opinion.

While climatic conditions have not been kind to the winter climber in the decade since the last winter guide, there has been a rise in the standard of climbing, and many new routes – and indeed several new cliffs – are included in this guide. While some claim that winter climbing in the Lakes is dead, and indeed others would say it was never alive, neither statement is correct, and true winter climbing conditions can be found most years, though often they may last only for a few days. All this means that, more than ever, being in the right place at the right time with the right attitude is crucial for success.

Tony Daly launches up steep ice at the start of Dove Crag Gully *(IV/V), Grasmoor (Photo: Martin Armitage)*

Growing environmental awareness and concern over conservation of rare species, both flora and fauna, mean that several ecologically sensitive areas are protected by law, and therefore climbing in these locations is vulnerable to regulation if these areas are abused. It is up to the individual to safeguard access to these sensitive areas by climbing only when they are fully frozen and in true winter condition. Repeated hacking of unfrozen turf can cause serious damage (both to climbs and to flora) and should be considered completely unacceptable. This is particularly true on the crags of the Helvellyn escarpment which are home to especially rare alpine plants, but can applied to the entire district – please read the chapter on 'Winter Climbing and Nature Conservation'. However a neatly placed pick in well-frozen turf causes little damage.

CHOICE OF VENUE

As would be expected, the higher the cliff the greater your chance of finding it in condition. Most of the best crags face north or east and so receive limited sunshine, which allows snow to build up. The aspect and altitude at the base of each crag is noted at the start of each crag section to aid you in choosing a venue.

Facing north-east, and being far from the coast, **Great End** is one of the most reliable crags for collecting snow and tends to retain it for longer than most other areas in the Lakes. The **Helvellyn** coves, while slightly less reliable, can be better if the wind has recently been from the east. Both come with easy access, and the price tag for that can be crowds. In fact in winter a prevailing easterly wind is likely to bring cold air and will help freeze turf and form water ice, but it often does not offer much chance of snowfall, so areas such as **Blea Tarn**, which readily form water ice, can be a good choice if it has been cold and dry. Such conditions used to occur regularly whenever a large high pressure system formed over the North Sea, a common occurrence around February time during the 1980s, and something that has re-established itself in late February during the last couple of winters. Blea Tarn is generally somewhat quieter in terms of numbers: however it is also more limited in choice of routes. In general, if the wind has been from the east then it is often better to choose a cliff on the east side of the district with an easterly aspect to it.

If the winds are from the west or south-west they are more likely to bring snow, and so, providing there has been some cold weather prior to

Winter as it used to be ... Black Crag, *Borrowdale, c.1963, at the time that* Troutdale Pinnacle *had winter ascents (Photo: Ray McHaffie Collection)*

the snowfall to freeze turf and form ice, anywhere can be good. **Scafell** is high enough that it can often rime up on a more westerly wind even if snow has not fallen, and **Gable Crag** is another reliable venue in these sort of conditions. However, areas close to the sea are greatly affected by milder coastal winds, and are seldom worth considering except in exceptional circumstances.

There are many icefalls and gills that freeze given a sufficient period of cold conditions. Some high falls like **Newland's Hause** and **Low Water Beck** come into nick reasonably quickly, but even these take about a week of sub-zero night-time temperatures to form. Strangely enough, for the more seepy sort of climbs periods of intense cold aren't necessarily ideal as the water may freeze in the ground: better to have a slight thaw during the day and a refreeze at night allowing a build-up and thickening of the ice.

So keep an eye on what the weather has been doing for a week or so before you venture out, and that should help you choose somewhere in condition and allow you to make the most of those short winter days.

EQUIPMENT NOTES

For those climbing in the hills in winter a firm grasp of basic winter skills is essential. You should know how to navigate using a map and compass (a GPS, though useful, is no substitute), how to use an ice axe to cut steps and arrest a slip, and how to walk wearing crampons. These are the basics for getting you to a climb and back to the valley at the end of what may be a long day: they should be second nature.

The following notes on equipment may be useful as a guide for those embarking upon their first winter routes.

Clothing: Everyone has their own personal choice of clothing. In general a multi-layer system is most versatile and allows good regulation of heat. It can get very warm walking to a crag and very cold actually on the route (not to mention even colder if you get benighted), so it is important to carry spare clothing so as to stay warm during what could be lengthy belaying sessions. Hypothermia can come on with surprising swiftness and should not be underestimated as a risk. Modern fabrics can be very quick-drying and warm, and, importantly, lightweight, so use these, and in addition try to get clothes that don't ride up when you stretch up during climbing. A waterproof jacket is essential. This

Making the most of good conditions – Andy Atkinson and John Shepherd on a nocturnal ascent of Launchy Gill *(III), Thirlmere (Photo: Al Phizacklea)*

prevents snow sticking to fleeces and thermals and wetting them if it warms up during climbing. Waterproof trousers or salopettes, while performing the same function, can constrict movement, so whether you wear then during the climb may depend on the garment, conditions and individual preference. Modern softshell leggings can be very good and a lot more comfortable in most conditions. An alternative to a layering system is the Pertex/Pile system invented by Buffalo which certainly works well and is relatively cheap, but not perhaps as versatile.

Gloves: For technical climbing, gloves can be a real problem: they need to be warm but not clumsy. Dachstein woollen mitts, whilst warm, may become difficult to use and put on when wet, but they are also a lot cheaper than their modern counterpart and will do fine for easier routes. However, mitts generally, though warmer, lack the dexterity of fingered gloves. A thin inner glove worn inside mitts fitted with securing wrist elastic cords allows removal of the mitt when necessary.

Harder routes often require greater dexterity than mitts allow to enable easier handling and placement of protection, not to mention the occasional use of a rock hold – and for this gloves may be essential. There are commercially available ice climbing gloves that are warm, waterproof and equipped with knuckle protection – and a hefty price tag!

The skint, or thrifty, can experiment with ski gloves or, for improved grip on axes, rubberised garden gloves. Finding the right combination of gloves comes down to personal preference born out of long experience. Many years of climbing have led me to use a combination of thin gloves for technical hard pitches and mitts for general use and, perhaps most useful, to develop a tolerance to pain. Having several pairs of gloves and mitts in your sack is no bad thing, especially if your route is a long one.

Helmet: Whilst many climb without a helmet in summer, only the foolish do so in winter – the risk of ice and rock falling spontaneously or being knocked off the crag by other climbers is just too great. Your helmet should be big enough to fit over a balaclava or hat, and in winter it can be well worth putting it on below the approach slopes as they may avalanche or be prone to falling ice from the crag. The helmet should have some system to enable a headtorch to be fastened to it.

Harness: Step-in leg loops can prove problematical in combination with crampons, especially on steep slopes, so a harness you can put on easily without taking your feet off the ground is recommended.

Amazing ice architecture on Great End (Photo: Ray McHaffie Collection)

Boots: Whilst plastic double boots are lightweight, warm, waterproof and rigid enough take step-in or clip-on type crampons, they can be uncomfortable, and it is worth loosening them for the walk-in and tightening them for the actual climbing. Unlike a leather boot they do not readily give and mould to your foot shape, so if not comfortable straight away they are never likely to become so. The new generation of lightweight leather or leather-substitute boots now on the market are considered more comfortable than plastics and allow a better feel of what your foot (and crampon) is placed on. They do, however, still require drying out at the end of the day and are not generally as warm. If you are camping, bivying or bothying, and no heat for drying is available, you may have to, just as in the Greater Ranges, sleep with your boots to help the drying process: in which case the inners of a plastic boot are much more comfortable to snuggle up with in your sleeping bag than a full leather boot. Gaiters prevent snow entering boots and feet from getting cold. Some newer boot designs have an integral gaiter.

Crampons: Most people use step-in crampons which are convenient and save cold fingers if your boots are rigid enough to take them. Strap-on crampons can be fitted to boots with slightly more bend – modern versions have the bulk of the straps replaced by an excellent enclosing plastic basket system. Monopoints are becoming more popular and are good on both ice and particularly on buttress climbs where the single front point can be inserted into a fine crack without being forced out again by the second point. Whilst completely rigid crampons are good on hard climbs, they are not very comfortable to walk in, and for the Lakeland fells, a semi-rigid crampon is probably the best choice.

Axes and Hammers: While reverse curve (banana pick) tools are better for ice and technical routes, a traditional (alpine) curved pick is better for ice axe braking, and is just as good for easier routes. Sharp axes and crampons work better than blunt ones on ice, but don't stay sharp for long on mixed routes. If you're serious about mixed climbing then get a modular axe which allows replacement of picks and adze and hammer heads. While the basic concept of the reverse curve pick ice tool is unchanged, ice tool design has improved, with ergonomically designed grips and special leashless tools. However, extremely wiggly axes with bulky handrests and thin 'B' rated picks designed for pure water-ice climbing are not likely to be much use in the Lake District – it is better to go for simpler designs with straight or slightly bent shafts and tough 'T' rated picks. It's also worth carrying a spare set of bolts and a pick, and the tools to tighten them up with as well.

Hardware: This is very route dependent. A greater selection of rock gear is needed on mixed routes than on snow and ice gullies, but watch out for camming devices which can easily slide out of icy cracks, though this is not to say that they shouldn't be carried at all. Slings are particularly useful, both for spikes and threads and as extenders. While the placement of pegs is often frowned on, particularly on good rock routes, they may be the only source of protection if a crack is iced up. Drive-in ice screws (Warthogs) are good for both ice and frozen turf, though they are becoming difficult to find in the shops these days; ice-hooks can also be useful for frozen turf. For pure water ice, sharp tubular ice screws, preferably with wind-in handles, are essential. A dead-man may be useful for easy gullies and long snow sections. Ropes should be dry-treated for preference, and double ropes mean you can abseil twice as far if you need to get down quickly. It is also worth carrying several metres of tape or cord and a pocket knife so that abseil slings can be rigged quickly, and although finding ice solid enough to construct one may be rare in the Lakes, you should know how to construct an Abalakov thread. Every member of the party should carry a set of Prussik loops and know how to use them.

Steve Ashworth in 2005, making the first ascent of one of the hardest mixed routes in the Lakes, Evolution *(IX), Great End (Photo: Peter Ashworth)*

Rucksack: A day out in winter requires far more kit than in summer. A 50 to 60 litre sac should allow you to get everything inside if things are to be kept dry.

Refreshments: It is important to replace lost liquids, particularly during the walk-in. A thermos means warm drinks, but may not be worth the extra weight – it's a tough choice! You need sufficient calories for the day and some spare emergency rations.

Headtorch: Should be considered essential, and check the battery and spare bulb before you head for the hills.

Map and Compass: Each person should have their own map and compass – and know how to use them. Incidents of parties splitting up or becoming separated in poor weather are not unknown.

Bivi Bag: If it all goes horribly wrong and you end up spending the night out, a bivouac bag can mean the difference between life and death. Each member of the party should have their own. They can range from a simple body-sized plastic bag to an expensive breathable model. From the climbing point of view, the best are semi-breathable and very light as they will not fill up your rucksack nor weigh you down too much.

First Aid Kit: A small selection of bandages, plasters and pain-killers, together with some antiseptic cream, is well worth carrying. See the section on Mountain Accidents (page 441).

Camera: It's no use moaning about the quality of photos in guidebooks if you don't carry one and use it! If it is digital then make sure it is at least 4 mega-pixels and set on maximum quality.

WINTER GRADES

The open-ended Scottish two-tier system has been used in the guide with a slight modification. Roman numerals are used to indicate the overall route grade (I, II, III etc), and Arabic numerals are applied to the harder routes to signify the technical difficulty of either the hardest pitch on the route or, where known, individual pitches. In this way the system is analogous to the rock climbing grade system where routes with safe or short-lived technical sections may have a higher technical grade than overall grade – eg V (6) where a standard V would be V (5). A more serious route may be less technically demanding but still warrant V – eg V (4). However, just to confuse things, a sustained (albeit safe) route may also be given this grade. The route description should make it apparent which is the case.

For each route the grade is listed after the heading. Pitch lengths are usually given where necessary, but on some of the easier sections only overall lengths are used. The familiar three-star rating has been used to indicate quality, where known, though this is often dependent on conditions. Stars that have been assigned by the first ascentionists may be differentiated by being left hollow: feel free to fill them in, or not, if you do the route, and please let us know of unstarred routes that deserve stars (and vice versa!).

THE NUMERICAL WINTER GRADING SYSTEM

I	Straightforward snow gully around 45 degrees or easy angled ridges; cornices maybe encountered.
II	Gullies with some steep snow or short ice pitches and more difficult ridges; still usually summer scrambles.
III	More sustained than a II with longer ice pitches and some technical sections on buttresses.
IV	Longer steep ice requiring fitness and arm strength or difficult rock or mixed ground which may require axe torquing techniques.
V	Sustained steep ice. Mixed routes with several technical sections.
VI	Vertical ice or serious climbs which may be sustained and technical and also highly technical but relatively well-protected mixed routes.
VII	Longer multi-pitch routes with long sections of vertical or thin ice. Mixed routes with many technical sections requiring fitness, skill and experience to link together.
VIII, XI	The system is open ended, with these harder grades signifying as for VII but even more tenuous, poorly protected and desperate.

DESCRIPTIONS

Many of the routes in this guide have had few ascents, so grades, pitch grades, pitch lengths, stars and, alas, descriptions should all be treated with a healthy scepticism. Such is the fickle nature of Lakeland winters that it is simply not possible to check them in the same way one can summer rock climbs. If you do find any errors, or have any comments to make (comments on individual pitch gradings are particularly welcome), or wish to record a new route of your own, then you can do all these things at the New Routes Bulletin Board of the Fell & Rock Climbing Club at http://www.frcc.co.uk. In the Recent Developments section of the same website you will be able to see any new routes that have been recorded since this guide was published.

Mark Thomas stretched to the limit on thin and technical mixed climbing during the first winter ascent of The Gnomon *(VII), Bowfell (Photo: Dave Almond)*

HISTORICAL

The third edition of Cicerone's *Winter Climbs in the Lake District* (1997) for the first time included a 'first ascents' list or, as was suggested at the time, a 'first claims' list. Since then, many earlier claims have come to light, and Mike Cocker and Colin Wells have delved deeper into the county archives and unearthed numerous records of further early ascents.

Late Victorian and pre-World War I routes were generally well recorded in the journals of the FRCC and Climbers' Club and in other journals, in various 'climbing books' kept at local hotels and club huts, and in early guidebooks. These have all been incorporated into the guide, along with many contemporary accounts which we hope will be of interest. Those wanting to learn more about the remarkably advanced achievements of the early winter climbing pioneers of the Lake District are directed to articles in recent FRCC journals describing their activities in some detail. In addition, a regularly updated 'first ascents' list is maintained on the FRCC website.

Between the two world wars, fewer ascents are mentioned, and those undertaken during and in the years after World War II are very poorly recorded indeed. In the main this was probably because there was no winter climbing guidebook, and therefore no tradition of recording routes. In addition there was the feeling that everything had been done before and therefore the route wasn't new, and often this was very likely the case. The memories of a number of the older climbers, to whom we are profoundly grateful (but will not name here to avoid embarrassment), have been tested in an attempt to fill in the rather large gaps in knowledge of this era, but there is no doubt that many blanks remain.

The ascents of the last two decades or so are generally more reliably documented somewhere – if we can find it – but we can only include the information we are given.

As the conditions and style of historic ascents can no longer be verified we have had to be cautious, and only those known to be climbed in true winter conditions have been included.

The updated 'First Ascents' list has been included at the back of this guide for your interest and amusement, but it still is, and will probably always be, a 'first claimed' list.

'What a great day out!' (Photo: Stephen Reid)

WARNING

Winter climbing can be a dangerous activity carrying a risk of personal injury or death. It should be undertaken only by those with a full understanding of the risks and with the training and/or experience to evaluate them. Whilst every care and effort has been taken in the preparation of this guide, the user should be aware that conditions can be highly variable and can change quickly, thus materially affecting the seriousness of a climb.

Therefore, except for any liability which cannot be excluded by law, neither Cicerone, the Fell and Rock Climbing Club of the English Lake District, nor the author accept liability for damage of any nature (including damage to property, personal injury or death) arising directly or indirectly from the information in this book.

ACKNOWLEDGEMENTS

The author would like to thank the FRCC guidebook production team. Particular thanks must go to Stephen Reid (FRCC Guidebooks Editor) for his help and encouragement, Nick Wharton for his ceaseless efforts in selecting and taking photographs, and Al Phizacklea for drawing the maps to his usual high standard. Jonathan Williams and Cicerone Press have been excellent partners in this enterprise, and the FRCC Committee, and in particular Eileen Clark the current President, deserve much praise for their foresight in backing the project and in allowing the unprecedented use of FRCC funds to hire a helicopter so that the photographic team could avoid over-exerting themselves in taking pictures of the crags in winter condition.

Thanks must also go to all those who have given their help and advice, past and present, during the preparation of this guide. First and foremost are the writers of the previous Cicerone guides on whose work this guide is based: Bob Bennett, Bill Birkett and Andy Hyslop. Contributors to the guide, other than those mentioned above, include Simon Webb of Natural England, himself a keen climber, who wrote the chapter on Winter Climbing and Nature Conservation, and Dr John Ellerton, an icefall fanatic, who wrote the section on Mountain Accidents. On the editing side, Colin Wells and Sally Baxendale contributed a great deal of time and effort; as did Dave Willis and Eric Shaw with the photography; and Vertebrate Graphics very kindly assisted with the Lake District endpaper map. In addition there are those who have provided photographs – their names appear in the text: permission to use the Abrahams photographs was most kindly given by the Abrahams family. Mike Cocker and Colin Wells have unearthed a fantastic amount of historical information, and Iain Whitmey has also delved deep into the FRCC Archives. Others who have helped with information and have not already been mentioned include: Neil Allinson, Steve Ashworth, Bob Bennett, David Birkett, Gareth Browning, Clive Danridge, Dom Donnini, Colin Downer, Jim Fotheringham, J Glynn-Williams, Simon Harvey, Dave Hayward, Pete Hirst, Andy Hyslop, Nick Kekus, Les Kendall, Ron Kenyon, Guy Lee, Rob Lee, Jim Lowther, Mike Lynch, Jim Loxham, Margaret McHaffie, Adrian Nelhams, Martin Panton, Bill Pattison, Keith Phizacklea, Owen Ross, Mark Thomas, Graham Watson, Colin Whornham, Dave Wilkinson, and Stuart Wood. The Rockfax Lake District Winter Routes Database (http://www.rockfax.com) and its contributors have also provided some useful information.

Finally I would like to thank Fiona for her patience in putting up with my endless nocturnal visits to the attic for yet another night of guidebook writing.

To many the Lake District is considered as a bit of a backwater when it comes to winter climbing, somewhere to drive past on the way to Scotland. It is hoped that this guide will serve to show that this is not the case and that, given the right conditions, there is great potential in the area.

Brian Davison, October 2006

WINTER CLIMBING AND NATURE CONSERVATION

by Simon Webb of Natural England (www.naturalengland.org.uk)

INTRODUCTION

The Lake District mountains and fells provide opportunities for climbing, walking and quiet enjoyment of landscape, wildlife and geology. The crags, buttresses and gullies are a rich and sensitive environment full of heathers, rare arctic-alpines, colourful flowering herbs and dwarf trees. If future generations are to continue enjoying the Lake District, it is essential that we all contribute towards its long-term conservation. Climbers (in both summer and winter) can play an important role in protecting the mountain environment. The first step is to be aware that the best places for winter climbing are also the most important locations for upland vegetation and the home to rare plants and ferns. These places are sensitive and vulnerable, and climbers must take extra care to minimise their impact.

WHAT SORT OF VEGETATION IS FOUND IN THE UPLAND CRAGS AND GULLIES?

The most impressive examples of upland vegetation are found amongst the cliffs and gullies of the Lake District high fells. Here, the steep ground provides refuge from grazing sheep, and in many cases offers the specialised soils and climatic conditions favoured by upland plants.

Although the fells and mountains are often thought of as natural or wild, the vegetation has been highly modified by man. For example, the impact of increasing sheep numbers over the past 50 years has led to a huge reduction in the area of heathland vegetation.

The heathery vegetation seen on crags and steeper slopes is simply surviving there away from the hungry mouths of grazing sheep. These areas are important as they are reservoirs of heathers and flowers that can re-colonise the uplands now that conservation organisations are negotiating lower sheep numbers. The best examples of heathland have many different types of heather – ling, bell heather, bilberry, crowberry, cowberry and bearberry can all be found in a mixture of colours and textures.

Mixed heathers are often found in the crags and on steep ground (Photo: Jean Johnston)

Similarly, there are more trees on the crags than on the open fell-side. Young trees are nibbled away by sheep, and only on the steeper slopes (or where grazing pressure is very low) can they get beyond the seedling stage. Some of the Lake District upland trees are rare and specialised. Juniper is probably the most well known. A native conifer, it is evergreen and prickly, with its berries smelling strongly of gin when they are purple and ripe. A specialist dwarf type of juniper inhabits the crags above 500m. Even rarer is the downy willow. This bushy tree, with leaves that are downy white underneath, is restricted to 10 individual plants growing in the Helvellyn Coves.

The Lake District is the English stronghold for arctic-alpine plants. These plants thrive in the cold and harsh conditions of high latitudes and high altitudes. When the last ice age came to an end (some 10,000 years ago) they dominated the Lake District vegetation, but now they are

restricted to the highest ground, especially north- and east-facing coves and gullies. This is also where the most consistent winter climbing is found. The arctic-alpines include purple saxifrage, moss campion, alpine cinquefoil, mountain avens, alpine catchfly and alpine mouse-ear. These species often flourish where the soils are rich in basic minerals. In the high fells this generally equates to the gullies or flushes (water seepages/ice smears),

Juniper clings to the crags and steep slopes (Photo: Simon Webb)

Purple Saxifrage is one of the more widespread arctic-alpines in the Lake District (Photo: Simon Webb)

so again winter climbing locations coincide with the botanically richest areas.

The gully sides and areas with richer and deeper soil are also home to a type of plant assemblage called tall herb ledge vegetation. This looks remarkably like a Pennine hay meadow growing high in the mountains. Tall colourful herbs such as wood crane's-bill, globe-flower, water avens, wild angelica and roseroot cover ledges and gully bottoms in a luxuriant and spectacular show of mountain colour.

The preferred location for winter climbers and vulnerable vegetation is therefore the same place – the steepest ground, north- and east-facing coves, gully lines and damp upland turfs and ledges.

Upland vegetation and rare plants are vulnerable to the impact of winter climbing because their area of growth is restricted (and therefore even a small amount of damage can be significant) and because they are easily damaged – especially in marginal winter climbing conditions. For some of the winter, the plants will be safe beneath a snow cover or frozen deep in a crack. But in a changing climate winter conditions are fickle, and plants will more often be exposed to the impact of axes and crampons.

HOW CAN CLIMBERS CAN HELP PROTECT UPLAND VEGETATION AND RARE PLANTS?

Climbers (or other people involved in outdoor recreation activities) are not generally responsible for the decline in the extent and quality of wildlife habitats in the UK. However the nature of the sport is such that it takes climbers to the most sensitive parts of the landscape, to areas unaffected by grazing pressure, and to the places best suited to rare plants. Climbers need to be aware that they are going to these special places, that there is legal protection in place for Sites of Special Scientific Interest (SSSIs) and beyond (see below), and that climbers must take extra care not to damage or disturb them.

The following **best practice** gives some pointers on how climbers can minimise their impact on the environment:

- If weather conditions are marginal and the snow or ice is thin and melting, then rare plants will be vulnerable. For climbers who have trudged up the mountain with a full sack, it will be tempting to go for it anyway, but this will certainly lead to loss of mountain plants.
- Climbing turf routes is not a trend that will ever be good for upland vegetation. In marginal conditions it could be a disaster, as it often causes loose lumps of turf to slide off. Some rare plants in the Lake District (alpine saxifrage, mountain avens and scrubby cinquefoil for example) are limited in numbers to a few individual plants, so even localised impact is significant.
- Placing protection can also have an impact. Resist the temptation to clean out the cracks with your axe just to see whether you can slot a nut home. Many of these plants die back in winter and grow up again in spring. Cleaning their rootstock from cracks will quite simply kill them.
- Route preparation (or gardening) is more of a feature of summer climbing, but does occur for winter new routes too. Cleaning that crack to get a peg placement or kicking off that loose block may have an unacceptable impact. As detailed below, this vegetation is protected by law, and if route preparation will damage mountain vegetation it should not go ahead.
- Any trees growing above 600m are likely to be really important ecologically, or a rare species, or both. These are not good places for runners, belays, lower-offs or a quick hook and heave with the ice tool. Give the mountain trees the respect they deserve.
- Dry tooling, hooking or torqueing are best reserved for steep and non-vegetated crags. There are aesthetic arguments against this type of climbing on traditional climbing lines (crampon scratches, etc) but there are strong ecological arguments about damage to vegetated crags too.

THE LAW – WHAT DOES IT SAY?

Natural vegetation and birds are an important part of our heritage, and government has enacted strong laws to protect them. These laws apply to both landowners and those enjoying outdoor recreation. This legal framework is part of the UK's national and international obligations towards conservation.

Much of the upland landscape of the Lake District is within SSSIs. Although there is much of interest to conserve outside these sites, SSSIs do form the central core of the statutory conservation system in the UK. This wildlife law doesn't just give powers to designate and protect special sites, it also provides for many positive initiatives to conserve wildlife, including mechanisms for grants, management agreements and action plans, as well as open access provision.

In general terms all wild birds and their nests and eggs are protected by law, with heavy penalties for disturbance. While this is unlikely to be an issue for winter climbers – most birds nest in the spring and summer – ravens do nest as early as the end of February. The voluntary raven bans which are widely advertised should steer climbers clear of the most likely locations for conflict.

Natural vegetation is also protected by legislation both within SSSIs and beyond. Reckless damage to an SSSI carries severe penalties with a £20,000 maximum fine. In addition to general protection there is a suite of the rarer plants and animals that receive additional protection.

These laws are strong, but if you take time to find out about the birds and natural vegetation in the mountain environment you are visiting it is unlikely that there will be conflicts. Following the codes of conduct and best practice is always a better alternative to court cases or permanent climbing bans.

WHERE ARE THE MOST VULNERABLE AND IMPORTANT AREAS?

The vegetation described above (heathers, trees, arctic-alpines and tall herb ledge) is widespread in the uplands of the Lake District and needs conserving across its whole range. It really is so rare and vulnerable that any example of it that is left is important to conserve. The following section describes the most extensive and richest areas we know about, but if a place is not mentioned below it does not mean that it is not important and does not matter.

Without question the **Helvellyn and Fairfield** range is the most important and vulnerable area. This extended north–south ridge has the geology, altitude and aspect that is perfect for rich upland vegetation. The east-facing coves, their back walls and their gullies contain the most important English populations of the plants described above. Here in Red Tarn Cove, Nethermost Cove, Ruthwaite and Cock Coves, in the gullies at Tarn and Falcon Crags and (on the Fairfield side) Sleet Cove to Link Cove (including Scrubby Crag and Hutaple Crag), there are exten-

Red Tarn, Helvellyn (Photo: Simon Webb)

sive stands of tall herb ledge vegetation together with locations for the rare arctic-alpines and mountain willows. The real rarities grow here – alpine saxifrage, scrubby cinquefoil, holly fern and downy willow.

The top of **Honister** pass – the icefall, old mine workings and the crag itself – is also of considerable interest. The tall herb vegetation is so luxuriant that it has been described as the 'hanging gardens of Honister'. The area around Buckbarrow Crag and Yew Crags is also good, but it does not match the colourful splendour of the main Honister Crag.

On the **Scafell range** areas of upland or rare vegetation are much more patchy. The gullies are the most interesting, especially Piers Gill, Skew Gill, Greta Gill and Ruddy Gill. A few of the crags are good – Cam Spout Crags, Horn Crag and Lingmell Crags – and it is quite likely that there are good areas that have not yet been found. **Great End** seems to be less interesting apart from South-East Gully, where the only Cumbrian location for a plant called dwarf cornel is found.

The **Wasdale Screes** are important too – the loose and mineral-rich rock favours arctic-alpine plants. Both the gullies and buttresses are vulnerable to summer or winter visits. Their looseness means that climbing could bring down blocks – amongst which some of the rarities grow.

The crags below **High Street** (including Blea Water Crag and the areas above Small Water) are also strongholds for tall herb ledge vegetation and arctic-alpines. If the icefall is in condition then the plants here will be well buried, but the gullies and crags elsewhere are much more vulnerable.

Lychnis at Hobcarton Crag (Photo: Simon Webb)

The areas around **Pillar and Ennerdale** are very variable – some being ecologically poor others extremely rich. Pillar Rock itself is made of quite acidic rock, and as many plants like a base-rich environment, the main climbs are of lower ecological value. Much of Pillar rock is covered with junipers, though, and great care and respect needs to be shown here. West Waterfall is probably the richest area on the rock itself and is best avoided in poor conditions. Without doubt the main area to avoid is Hind Cove. Here is the healthiest Cumbrian population of Scrubby Cinquefoil. This plant's only UK locations are in the Lake District and Teesdale. This would be really vulnerable to turf climbing or climbing in poor conditions, as Cinquefoil favours the wetter areas (these will be where the ice is).

Another area to avoid is the gully lines and loose buttresses of **Hobcarton Crag** high above Whinlatter Forest. This is the only English locality for Alpine Catchfly (and one of only two UK places where this grows). Again this rare and beautiful plant is vulnerable to winter climbing, although as it grows on loose and short buttresses you would have to be fairly desperate to climb there.

SUMMARY

Winter climbers in the Lake District can play an important role in safeguarding the colourful and vulnerable natural vegetation of the mountains. It is difficult to picture when everything is covered with snow or ice, but you can make a positive difference. Understand that winter climbers and upland vegetation often need the same places, but the two can co-exist if the best practice above is followed.

LANGDALE

Ease of access makes Langdale one of the most popular valleys in the Lake District, both in summer and winter. Bowfell in particular, one of the most accessible mountain crags in the district, has many modern mixed routes and more traditional gullies, and, after a sustained period of cold easterly winds, the seeping wall of *Crinkle Gill* can freeze to form some excellent icefalls. In such conditions, the other gills too provide good routes.

The head of Langdale is split into two branches separated by the **Band**, a ridge running down from Bowfell which provides an excellent path to the summit. The left (southerly) branch is known as **Oxendale** and heads up to *Crinkle Crags*, while **Mickleden**, the northern branch, leads to the *Bowfell Crags* and Angle Tarn.

The climbs are described in a clockwise direction starting in the south with *Blake Rigg* above Blea Water, then heading round into Oxendale and onto Bowfell, before returning eastwards along the northern side of the valley.

Blake Rigg

(NY 287 040)
Alt. 350m East facing

This large broken crag above Blea Tarn, between Great and Little Langdale, has only one recorded route to date. Start from the car parking area on the road, if you've been able to drive up that is (it's less steep from Little Langdale side), and follow a path to the south of the tarn. Strike up the fellside, aiming for the right side of the crag.

Blake Rigg Icefall   100m III 1996

A watercourse falls down slabs on the right-hand side of the crag. The route steepens as you get higher. A harder start may be possible up the corner leading out left from near the start but has yet to be caught in condition.

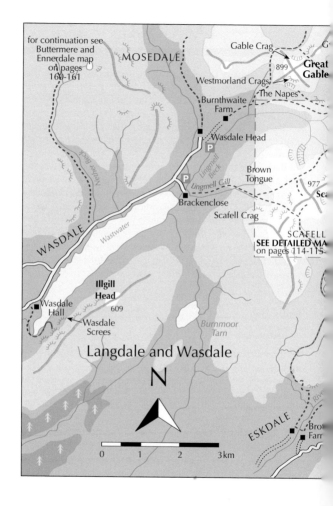

for continuation see
Buttermere and
Ennerdale map
on pages
160-161

MOSEDALE

Gable Crag

Great Gable

899

Westmorland Crags

The Napes

Burnthwaite
Farm

Wasdale Head

P

Brown
Tongue

977

Lingmell Beck

P Lingmell Gill

Brackenclose

Sc

Nether Beck

Scafell Crag

SCAFELL

SEE DETAILED MA
on pages 114-115

WASDALE

Wastwater

Illgill
Head
609

Wasdale
Hall

Wasdale
Screes

Burnmoor
Tarn

Langdale and Wasdale

N

0   1   2   3km

ESKDALE

Bro
Farr

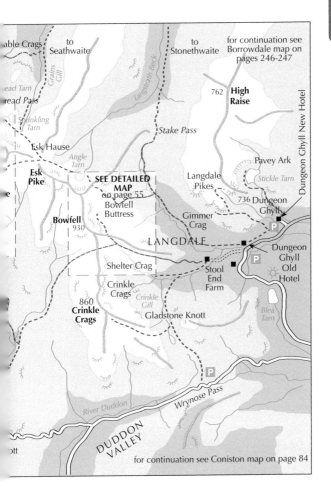

able Crags
to Seathwaite

ead Tarn

ead Pass

Sprinkling Tarn

Esk Hause

Angle Tarn

Esk Pike

e

Bowfell
930

SEE DETAILED MAP
on page 55
Bowfell Buttress

Shelter Crag

Crinkle Crags

Crinkle Gill

860
Crinkle Crags

Gladstone Knott

Grains Gill

Langstrath Beck

to Stonethwaite

for continuation see Borrowdale map on pages 246-247

762 **High Raise**

Stake Pass

Pavey Ark

Stickle Tarn

Langdale Pikes

736 Dungeon Ghyll

Gimmer Crag

LANGDALE

Stool End Farm

Dungeon Ghyll New Hotel

Dungeon Ghyll Old Hotel

Blea Tarn

River Duddon

Wrynose Pass

DUDDON VALLEY

ott

for continuation see Coniston map on page 84

Langdale Overview

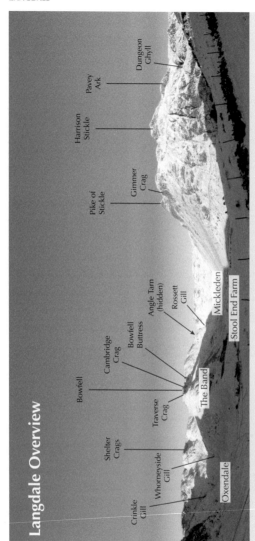

The head of Langdale showing the location of the major crags and features (Photo: Lou Johnson)

OXENDALE

The following routes are found in Oxendale, the left-hand branch at the head of the Langdale valley.

It is best to park in the National Trust car park at the Old Dungeon Ghyll Hotel. Return to the road and take the path through Stool End Farm and along the side of the beck. If heading for *Browney Gill*, cross at the first bridge. For most other routes, continue on the north (right) bank to a second bridge over Buscoe Sike which flows into *Crinkle Gill* at this point. From here many of the climbs can be reached. At this confluence the right fork of the stream leads to the obvious fall of *Whorneyside Force*. (Although the latter is sometimes referred to as *Hell Gill*, that name is properly reserved for the deep ravine on the right, a few hundred metres further upstream from the main waterfall – this can be readily combined to provide an excellent finish to the main fall.) For *Isaac Gill* cross the bridge, then traverse south across *Crinkle Gill*, before contouring round the hillside into the gill. It can also be reached by following *Browney Gill* from its confluence with *Crinkle Gill*. (When approaching from this direction, *Isaac Gill* is the first stream encountered flowing in from the right.) The ice routes adorning the walls of *Crinkle Gill*, meanwhile, may be found in a ravine well upstream.

Great Knott (NY 259 043)

This craggy hill on the south side of Oxendale is bound on its east by *Browney Gill*, a branch of which curves round to the south side. *Isaac Gill* is to the north of *Great Knott*.

Browney Gill (NY 261 040) Alt. 620m South and East Facing

This stream runs up from Oxendale to Red Tarn between Pike of Blisco and Cold Pike. Take the path from Stool End Farm, cross the stream at the bridge, and head up towards Red Tarn. Before reaching the tarn, contour rightwards across the hillside into the right-hand branch of the gill. A 15m Grade II pitch is climbed, before a stream coming in from the left is followed; this has several short icefalls at about Grade II (2003). Continuing up the right fork, a steep rock wall on its right side

Steve Ashworth works his way across Bowfell Buttress on the first ascent of Bowfell Girdle (V) (Photo: Brian Davison)

drops down from *Great Knott* and contains several steep pitches. The right fork of the gill itself ends in a final pitch at the top of the rocks. To its right, and close into the steep rock wall, is an icy, mossy runnel (20m, III, 2003). Three icefalls about 25m long form down the rocks themselves. Only the right-hand one has been climbed (IV, 2003). It has a steep start and finish, with easier ground in the middle.

Isaac Gill is the first gill flowing into *Browney Gill*, upstream of its confluence with *Crinkle Gill*.

Isaac Gill   250m I/III 1993

Rising to *Gladstone Knott* in a series of short ice pitches (I/II) the main pitch (II/III) is met halfway. A steeper pitch, with a left-hand start up a slanting groove, is also possible (IV+). A good approach to routes on *Gladstone Knott*.

Whorneyside Force   70m II/III ★★★

This frozen waterfall can be clearly seen on the approach up the right bank of Oxendale Beck. The fall is climbed in three steps. From above a large pool, the first icefall leads to a recess on the right and a peg belay (30m). The wide middle fall can be climbed on the left, right or centre depending on conditions, preference and crowds. The large pool at the top, which will hopefully be frozen, is furnished with a large flat rock round which a comforting belay may be taken (25m). The final shorter pitch starts from the back of the pool (15m).

Hell Gill   300m III/IV

From the top of *Whorneyside Gill*, *Hell Gill* is found further upstream on the right. Go through the narrow, deep ravine, passing several pools and small falls, to reach the final steep fall. If formed (a rarity) climb it direct (IV). The right-hand exit, up a steep weeping mossy corner/groove, is more reliable (III, 1996).

Gladstone Knott   (NY 256 046)
                                          Alt. 600m East facing

Reached by following *Isaac Gill*, or the ridge between *Isaac Gill* and *Crinkle Gill*, this small vegetated outcrop is found on the left, above a level shoulder on the hillside. The right-hand (east) side of the *Knott* contains a compact buttress possessing five distinctive chimneys. To their left the ground is more broken, offering several easy mixed routes, with *Zero Gully* being the wide easy-angled snow gully to the left of the crag – a good **descent**.

Zero Gully   80m I 1996
Climb the broad gully defining the left side of the crag.

Left Corner   50m I 1996
A shallow corner-line runs up the crag about 10m right of *Zero Gully*. It has a few steeper steps.

Y Route One   50m I 1996
The inverted Y-shaped recess just left of the main compact buttress. The left-hand branch has several ice bulges.

Y Route Two   50m I 1996
The right-hand branch of the inverted Y. Start on the left-hand side of the buttress at the bottom of the gully. The gully at the top is independent of *Y Route One*.

First Chimney   40m II 1996
The leftmost of the chimneys, the obvious gully on the left side of the main buttress.

Second Chimney   40m III ★ 1996
The first of the three gullies on the right half of the main buttress has a tricky exit.

Third Chimney   30m II/III ★ 1996
The middle of the trio slants from left to right.

Fourth Chimney   30m IV (5) ★★ 1996
The deepest and hardest of the chimneys. A steep wall leads up into the chimney. Inside the chimney, face outwards and use small ledges to go directly up to a chockstone at the top of the chimney. It is possible to exit here, up easy turf on the left, or continue up the chimney for a further 15m.

Fifth Chimney   **30m III ★★ 1996**

Right of the buttress is a steep wall, then an iced corner. Climb the ice, stepping left near the top where the corner narrows.

Crinkle Gill

(NY 257 049)
Alt. 400m North facing

The main gill gets more interesting with height. There are three main variations near the top. **Left-Hand Fork** (II/III) provides the longest section of ice, with several short pitches. **Central Icefall Direct** (III/IV) gives a good 40m pitch, while the steeper **Chimney Runnel** to the right is IV/V.

A few hundred metres above the confluence with *Hell Gill*, the gill begins to cut into the steep crag forming a 30m north-facing wall. Fed from the hillside above, continual seepage makes this a reliable venue for steep ice.

The Wrinkled Crinkle   **25m IV/V (4) 1984**

Slightly downstream from the 30m wall is a small crag. *The Wrinkled Crinkle* is the first ice streak to be reached on the left of the crag. It is less frequently in condition than the other routes.

About 12m above the bed of the gill is a large bay to the right of the crag. The next route climbs the centre of this.

Crinkle Cut   **50m III 1981**

Climb into the bay on a steep pitch of ice – easier options are, however, available. Climb the back of the bay to an awkward exit up the wall forming the left corner of the bay.

Further up the gill is the long 30m vegetated wall. This can give some excellent ice pitches. *Whiteout* at the right end is recognisable by its conspicuous 'chandelle'.

Wight-Out   **35m VI (6) 1986**

The second ice smear left of *Whiteout*. Best done by keeping to the left edge and trending leftwards at the top. It forms less often than the other routes here.

Ray of Sunshine   30m V (6) 1986

The ice smear left of *Whiteout* is thicker in its lower section. Climb this to awkward moves at 10m, then thinner ice above, to an exit on turf. Difficult and poorly protected.

Whiteout   30m V (5) ★ 1986

The obvious 'chandelle' of ice at the right end of the wall. Though the most substantial of the icefalls, it can be thin and poorly protected in the lower half. Take the chandelle direct; protection depends on the quality of the ice.

Great Cove at the head of *Crinkle Gill* contains several easy gullies, short buttresses and grooves, all of which can make winter climbs. The following example is just one of many.

Long Walk   50m IV 2005

When approaching up *Crinkle Gill*, a buttress (NY 251 046) with two chimneys/grooves on its left side is clearly visible to the left of the prominent col which has Long Top to its north-west (right). Easy snow leads to the base of the right-hand groove.

1   25m (3). Climb the vegetated corner/groove which steepens at about 20m. Move onto a ledge on the left, and then up a short groove to a ledge and large flake belay.
2   25m (4). Climb back right onto a ledge and into the base of the chimney. Struggle up this to a spike belay on the left-hand side.

The buttress to the right is a very pleasant IV.

Shelter Crags   (NY 251 055)
Alt. 700m East facing

This neglected crag is found in the most northerly of the Crinkle Crag coves, just south of the Three Tarns. The crag is split by *Central Chimney*, which cuts back into its southern section. The latter is the steeper part of the crag and contains several ice lines which are clearly visible when walking up the Band. *Shelter Corner* lies toward the left of the buttress, whilst *Shelter Icefall* climbs a chimney-fault filled (one hopes) by an obvious icefall. The right-hand section of the crag is a continuous vegetated wall which curves round and up the hillside. *Thirty Nine Steps*

Shelter Crags

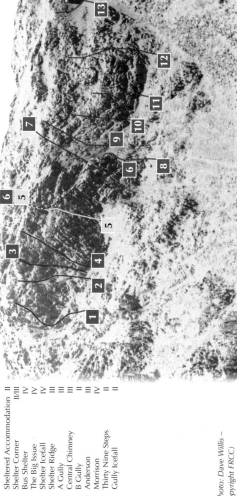

1	Sheltered Accommodation	II
2	Shelter Corner	I/III
3	Bus Shelter	IV
4	The Big Issue	IV
5	Shelter Icefall	III
6	Shelter Ridge	III
7	A Gully	III
8	Central Chimney	II
9	B Gully	III
10	Anderson	III
11	Morrison	IV
12	Thirty Nine Steps	II
13	Gully Icefall	II

*(Photo: Dave Willis –
Copyright FRCC)*

starts where the wall turns uphill into a snow gully and follows an eponymous series of pleasant steps.

Follow the Band (as for Bowfell) to where the path levels out, then strike west across the fell and descend to cross Buscoe Sike before entering the combe. Alternatively, cross the bridge over Buscoe Sike at its confluence with *Crinkle Gill* and head up the ridge on the left bank of Buscoe Sike before trending left to the same point. **Descent** is possible down snow slopes at either end of the crag, though to the left is generally quickest. The routes are described from **left** to **right**.

Sheltered Accommodation 40m II 2003

Well to the left of the corner taken by *Shelter Corner* is an easy-angled turfy buttress at the left-hand side the crag overlooking the descent. Climb this.

Shelter Corner 70m II/III ★★ 1996

The fine turf corner at the left-hand end of the crag can form some easy-angled ice.

1   30m. From right of the corner-line, climb over ledges of iced turf to the base of the corner.

2   40m. It is possible to climb the open corner by many subtle variations.

Bus Shelter 60m IV ★ 2003

About 10m below the turfy start of *Shelter Corner* is a rectangular block lying against the crag.

1   40m (5). Start 5m left of the block and climb up a steep crack which allows a turfy runnel to be reached. Follow this up progressively steeper turf to a steep V-groove and climb this with difficulty to a ledge and block belay on the left.

2   20m (3). Climb the short ramp and mixed ground above to finish.

The Big Issue 65m IV ★★★ 2003

This climbs the next groove to the right. Start 5m down (right) from the rectangular block lying against the crag.

1   45m (5). Climb a steep crack (there is a flake to its right near the bottom) to reach a turfy ledge (this ledge may also be reached from the top of the block by a 2m traverse right). Follow grooves, then make an awkward step left into the main groove. Follow this to its top, then make delicate moves right across the top of a slab

to easier ground and a block belay at a ledge 10m higher.
2   20m (3). Climb the turf ramp at the right side of the ledge.

Shelter Icefall   65m IV ★★★ 1996

A prominent icefall in the narrow chimney fault to the right. It is steepest in its lower section.
1   50m (4). Climb the iced-choked chimney. The crux proves to be a bulge and a step left at about 10m. Above, the ice, though steep, is generally thicker, and leads to a large block-covered ledge.
2   15m (4). From the back of the ledge, continue up a steep iced corner, moving right near the top.

Shelter Ridge   55m III (2003)

The right-hand side of the buttress forms a ridge overlooking *Central Chimney* at a point where it narrows.
1   15m (4). Climb up small ledges to blocks at the end of a ramp-line on the left side of the ridge.
2   25m (3). Go easily along the ramp, with a couple of small steps, to belay to the right of the ledge, near the top of *Shelter Icefall* pitch 1.
3   15m (4). Climb the final iced corner of *Shelter Icefall*.

Central Chimney   80m III ★ 1996

The obvious central gully cutting back left into the crag.
1   40m (2). Easy slopes lead to where the walls of the gully/chimney close: continue to belay at the back of a cave.
2   40m (3). Make awkward moves out right onto steep ice (peg) and gain easier-angled snow and ice to finish.

Variation: Central Chimney Left-Hand Finish   80m IV 2003

1   40m (2). Follow *Central Chimney* pitch 1.
2   30m (5). Climb to the peg at the overhang (where the standard route goes right up the wall). Make an awkward step left onto the left wall of the chimney, then a long step, past two very loose blocks, to a ledge on the left wall of the chimney. Climb a wide crack at the left end of this ledge to a sloping shelf on the right. Go across this and back into the chimney, with an awkward move round a rib to gain a ledge.
3   10m (5). Climb the recess at the back of the ledge, starting up the right crack, and transferring to the left crack at half height.

Right of *Central Chimney*, the crag has a gully wall containing *A and B Gullies*, and a larger front face with a well-defined ledge at its foot.

A Gully 60m III 1996

From the lower part of *Central Chimney*, where the walls start to close together, climb the left-hand of the two shallow gullies leading up the wall.

B Gully 60m II 1996

The shallower right-hand gully has a small rock step at half height.

Anderson 70m III (4) 2003

The first feature at the left end of the front face is a left-slanting corner. Climb this to grass, then climb rightwards to dubious spikes and up to a stance. Climb easily leftwards, then take a steep little wall rightwards to the finishing corner.

Morrison 70m IV (4) 2003

In the middle of the front face is a slim left-facing groove with a good spike at 3m. Climb the groove to ledges, then traverse 2m left, and climb another groove to a stance. Easier grooves and gullies lead to the top.

Where the ledge ends and the wall curves up into a wide gully/snow slope is an easy series of icy steps on the left side of the gully – this is **Thirty Nine Steps** (II, 2003). On the left side, near the top of the easy snow gully, is another easy snow gully with the short stepped **Gully Icefall** (II, 1996).

BOWFELL (NY 245 065)
Alt. 902m

The jewel in the crown of Langdale winter climbing, with the highest climbs in the dale. Many fine mixed climbs can be found on the buttresses overlooking the Mickleden branch of the valley, whilst numerous short gullies cleave the remote *Bowfell Links* overlooking the head of Eskdale.

Bowfell Buttress, and neighbouring crags, are usually reached via Stool End Farm and the Band. *Neckband Crag* is low down on the north-east side of the Band, where the path starts to level – a vague

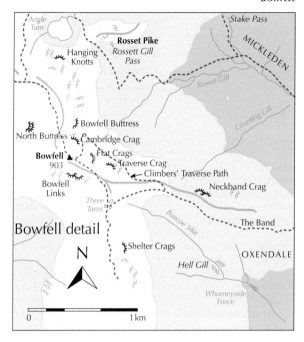

path leading off to the right will take you there. Continuing up the Band, a narrow path, the **Climbers' Traverse**, leads off to the right at a point where the main ridge from Bowfell comes down to the path. For *Bowfell Links*, however, keep on the main (left-hand) track, and continue onto the col and the Three Tarns. From the tarns follow the path up Bowfell for a few hundred metres before traversing west across a scree and snow slopes to the *Links*. The Climbers' Traverse itself leads to the main Bowfell crags, *Traverse Crag*, *Flat Crags*, *Cambridge Crag*, *North Buttress* and *Bowfell Buttress*. These crags can also be reached by taking the Mickleden path to part way up Rossett Gill before striking up to the base of the crags. This is a better approach in deep snow, and also allows you to view the climbs en route.

The crags are described as approached along the Band, starting with *Neckband Crag*, followed by the isolated *Bowfell Links*, and finally the main group of Bowfell crags facing north into Mickleden.

Neckband Crag
(NY 256 062)
Alt. 550m North facing

More correctly known as *Earing Crag*, this low-lying, steep and compact crag overlooking Grunting Gill is perhaps better suited to summer activity than that of winter, but has had some recent additions on its easier-angled right-hand side.

The mossy corner and wall between the summer routes of *Virgo's* big corner and *The Gizzard* has been climbed as far as the roof (**Master of Torquing** 25m, VI 6, 2000), but still awaits a complete ascent to the top of the crag.

Salvation
60m VI ☆ 2006

Start at the right-hand side of the crag at the lowest part of the buttress, right of the large corner and the arete of the summer line of *Flying Blind*, in a shallow bottomless groove (not the first corner to the left of the right-hand arete).

1   40m (8). Climb the bottomless groove on small hooks and tiny torques until it is possible to place big nut runner on the left (first gear after 5m). Pull over the corner to a semi-rest below a vegetated steep corner-crack. Climb it (well protected but strenuous) and pull out over the top to a resting spike, then move up and left to little ledges and left again to three cracks in the top wall. Climb the two that form a triangle, then follow these to the top to reach a large flake belay.

2   20m Follow meandering easier climbing to the top.

The Neckband
70m IV (5) 2000

The slabby rib bounding the right-hand side of the crag is climbed with minor diversions.

1   35m. Climb the rib, passing a ledge, and continue to a horizontal ledge. Traverse left to find a belay.

2   35m Continue directly above by the easiest line.

Groove and Ramp
100m II 2000

Climb the shallow groove/gully bounding the right edge of the crag. A turfy start leads to snow and a finish up a narrow left-trending ramp on the left wall. A cornice may form at the top.

Bowfell Links   (NY 246 063)
                                          Alt. 785m South facing

This remote crag on the south side of Bowfell is split into numerous gullies and buttresses. The routes are often in condition, but a clear sunny
day soon strips the crag of snow due to its southerly aspect. As the routes
are short it is possible to climb several in one visit. The routes are
described from **right** to **left** as one approaches the crag from the Three
Tarns. **Descent** is usually on the right of the crag, but is possible to the
left.

No. 1 Gully   50m I 1996
The **descent** gully – when there's snow in it. This is the first gully line: it
bounds the right end of the crag.

Hidden Gully   50m I 1996
To the left of *No. 1 Gully*, climb up easy-angled rocks until *Hidden
Gully* is gained higher up the buttress. Climb the gully, passing a few
short steps before the angle eases.

Chimney Crack   30m II 1996
The buttress left of *No. 1 Gully* has a prominent off-width crack splitting
its left-hand side. Scramble over turf-covered rocks to its start and climb
the crack, passing several helpful jammed blocks, to exit onto easier
ground.

Pitch and Putt   50m II/III ★ 1996
The next gully to the left. A large chockstone gives a 10m pitch before
easy climbing gains the top. (With sufficient snow this can be banked
out.) It is also possible to pass the chockstone by the easy buttress on the
right before making a precarious step left, back above the chockstone
into the gully.

Two Under Par   70m II 1996
The next gully left again. Easy until the end, where a grassy corner on
the left is taken.

Direct Finish   20m II 1996
Climb the icy corner at the top.

Tower Buttress   60m III (4) ★ 1996

The buttress to the left has a small col near its top. From lowest rocks of the buttress, climb two short steep walls. Follow the crest of the buttress to the col. An easier line of turf on the left side of the crest is also possible. A short wall leads to easier ground.

Hole in One   70m III ★★ 1996

The next gully left again provides a good struggle over two short chockstone pitches.

Twisting Turf   70m II ★ 1996

The buttress to the left. Climb an obvious turf-covered ramp up its centre. A steep wall is passed on its right near the top.

The next feature is the obvious gully with a chockstone at half height, *Great Gully*.

Great Gully Wall   80m III 1996

A shallow groove/crack in the right wall of *Great Gully* leads to a position on the wall level with the chockstone in the gully. Continue up a shallow scoop in the buttress above.

Great Gully   100m IV (4) ★★ 1996

The chimney contains a large chockstone at half-height which forms a cave. This is best climbed on its right.

Vulcan Buttress   45m II/III ★ 1996

The next buttress to the left has a distinctive inverted V at the top. Start up a mossy ramp slightly right of centre, and follow the ramp leading onto easy turf-covered ledges. Finish up the inverted V.

The next large gully to the left (*Sunday Special*) has a cleft (*The Caddy*) running up the wall to its right, and a shallow groove-line up the right wall, starting just below the chockstone in the main gully.

The Caddy   70m II 1996

Climb the obvious narrow cleft on the right at the bottom of the large gully of *Sunday Special*.

Half Way Up   60m IV (4) 1996
A few metres below the chockstone in *Sunday Special* is a groove.
Climb the groove to finish near *The Caddy*.

Sunday Special   70m III ★ 1996
Climb the chimney to the chockstone (crux at 15m). Easy climbing
above leads to the top.

Green Buttress   80m II ★ 1996
The buttress left of *Sunday Special* has an initial steep start before easing
off.

The remaining Bowfell crags all overlook Mickleden and can be
approached from the Band via the Climbers' Traverse or from the Rossett
Gill path.

After crossing a steep scree-covered section of fellside, the Climbers'
Traverse goes under some broken outcrops (*Traverse Crag*) to *Flat Crags*
and the other buttresses of Bowfell.

Traverse Crag   (NY 250 064)
Alt. 720m East-north-east facing

The first outcrop passed on the *Climbers' Traverse* has a series of broken
grooves and ramp-lines on its right-hand side and is ideal for winter
climbing, although none of the routes are very long. The left side of the
crag is marked by two easy gullies. **Left Gully** is a straightforward snow
slope (70m, I, 2004) and a useful **descent**. To its right and close into the
buttress is the more interesting *Buttress Gully*.

Buttress Gully   70m II 2004
The narrow gully tucked into the left side of the buttress. Follow this to a
block and pass it via a snow runnel on the left. Above, follow easy turf
to the left or, for a more challenging finish, follow the continuation of
the chimney to the right.

The right side of the crag is marked by a pinnacle.

Into the Groove   65m VI 2005

There are three obvious grooves towards the right side of the crag with a
pinnacle to their right. This climb takes the leftmost of them and begins
at a large chockstone.

1   15m (6). Climb awkwardly past the large chockstone, step left to a
     large block, and continue up the blunt arete to a ledge below a wall
     at the foot of the groove.
2   50m (7). Difficult and poorly protected moves up the wall lead to
     turf at the bottom of the V-groove. Exit this up and rightwards to a
     ledge and continue up a further series of grooves to the top.

Big Groove   65m V 2005

The next groove to the right, and most prominently defined of the three,
starts up a V-groove.

1   15m (3). Climb the obvious V-groove to the right of the large chock-
     stone-filled chimney/groove of *Into the Groove*, and belay below
     twin grooves.
2   50m (6). Start up the left-hand of the two grooves, move into the
     right-hand groove, and up to a ledge. Follow the groove above to
     another ledge and then yet another groove to a ledge. When you're
     bored with grooves, climb the final wall past a prominent thread
     runner to the top.

Band on the Run   70m IV (5) 2005

The right-hand groove is, by way of blessed contrast, almost more like a
series of corners. A pinnacle marks its right side.

     Climb the corner where the pinnacle meets the broken groove on
its left-hand side. From the top of the corner, cross the groove-line and
climb a short steep chimney. From the top of the chimney, climb the
short wall on the left to a big grassy ledge. Climb the corner above and
move along the broad grassy ledge to join a wide gully. Climb up this
and exit underneath a chockstone.

Chockstone Gully   50m II ★★ 1995

The gully round the corner to the right faces *Flat Crags*. Climb a vegetated groove followed by a chockstone to belay below another chockstone and cave. Finish through a hole at the back of the cave.

Flat Crags
(NY 249 064)
Alt. 750m East-north-east facing

When approaching along the Climbers' Traverse, *Flat Crags* can be recognized by an obvious large bay in the middle of the crag and also by a leftward-sloping terrace that runs up beneath the main crag. The routes are described from **right** to **left**.

Crack Magic
60m VII 1999

A steep and technically demanding climb, following a line from the Climbers' Traverse to a leftward-sloping terrace and then up the main corner (the summer climb of *Flat Crags Corner*) in the centre of the large bay.

1 20m (5). Start 20m to the left of the junction between the ramp and the Climbers' Traverse. Climb the open corner to a gap in the rock, then move up and right to a steep wall and bulging crack. Climb this to belay on the terrace in the centre of the bay.

2 20m (7). Step up onto a rightward-trending ramp leading into a steep corner. Climb this to an awkward step left onto a big ledge and belay.

3 20m (7). Another awkward step and a steep crack lead to a strenuous pull over some wedged blocks and the top.

B.B. Corner
40m VII 2005

A winter version of the summer line which climbs a prominent mossy corner in the back of the large bay in the centre of the crag.

1 25m (7). Climb the corner right of the ramp-line start of *Crack Magic* to belay on a ledge.

2 15m (8). Continue up the corner passing an awkward bulge.

Mary Ann
40m IV (5) 1999

The less steep left-hand side of the crag at the top of the sloping terrace has a small cave which lies to the left of a slabby bay of rock. Either follow the first pitch of *Crack Magic* to the bay, or climb more directly, well to its left, or scramble to this point via the terrace. Start at a flake about 6m right of the cave.

The route follows the summer route in the lower half. Climb up right to a crack on the edge of a slab and follow it to below a band of overhangs. Move left under the overhangs and up into a grassy/snowy

North Buttress and Cambridge Crag

1	Professor	V
2	Left-Hand Route	IV
3	Rib and Groove	V
4	Right-Hand Route	V
5	Misty Mountain Hop	IV
6	Cambridge Crag Climb	II
7	Riboletto Groove	V
8	No Way Out	IV
9	Siamese Chimneys	IV
10	The Gnomon	VII
11	Soul Vacation	VIII
12	The Flying Gimp Trick	IV
13	Cambridge Girdle	IV

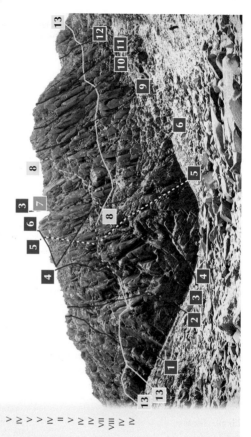

(Photo: Steve Ashworth)

bay. From the top of this, move up to a short corner and make an awkward move up and right onto a block-covered ledge on the right. A further short corner leads to the top.

Cambridge Crag

(NY 246 066)
Alt. 775m North-east facing

The next crag in the group lies higher up the hillside than *Flat Crags* and to the north. A spring (the **Waterspout**) flows from the base of the crag and is a good landmark. The crag is home to many mixed routes but they do tend to catch the sun. They are described from **left** to **right**.

Professor   85m V 2004
Start on the right side of a shallow bay which is the fourth obvious bay located to the left of, and about 50m uphill from, the Waterspout.
1   40m (5). A steep awkward bulge leads into a very prominent leftward-slanting, parallel-sided, shallow chimney. Follow this line to an awkward move at the top and then belay.
2   45m (3). Continue more easily up and leftwards, via an obvious V-groove and open gully. An iced-up slab and more mixed ground lead to the top.

Left-Hand Route   80m IV 1986
Starting about 40m left of the Waterspout, at the third groove, this climb approximately follows the summer route of *Borstal Buttress*.
1   35m (5). Assault the layback crack and groove to arrive, with luck, in a snow bay. Belay behind a huge boulder.
2   45m (3). Climb several short grooves to gain the top.

Rib and Groove   140m V 2006
Start 10m left of the Waterspout at the foot of the crag in an open vegetated groove, Right-Hand Route Direct Start, just left of the ramp taken by *Right-Hand Route* and 30m right of *Professor*.
1   50m (5). Climb the groove for 5m and follow it as it trends back left and up to a recess with a steep back corner bounded on the left by a smooth wall. Climb the corner and pull out right passing through a bulge on the right with a dagger of rock in the back (good nut placement). Pull out of this and follow a snowy bay right to a short corner step, and above to a broad snowy ledge and belay.

2   35m (6). Climb the corner on the left of the belay, mantle a turf step and balance up to hook thin moss and turf with a crack for protection, then pull over the top to snowy terraces. Traverse right for 25m passing behind a 'gendarme' to arrive at the belay of *Riboletto Groove*.

3   55m (6). Follow pitch 2 of *Riboletto Groove* to the summit, passing under the wedged block!

Right-Hand Route   110m V 1986

Starting at a broad slab about 10m left of the Waterspout, this climb roughly follows the line of the summer route *Cambridge Crag Climb* (but should not to be confused with the winter line to the right of the crag with the same name).

1   35m (4). Climb the rightward-slanting slab to a thread. Continue diagonally right, around two aretes, to reach the foot of a stepped groove. From the top of the groove, move back left to belay by another large groove.

2   20m (5). The groove above leads to a leftward-trending chimney which is followed onto a large arete. Climb this to a belay.

3   15m (6). Climb a steep groove on the left (crux, one nut was used for aid on the first ascent – it is not known whether it has since been climbed free) to easier ground.

4   40m (2). An easy gully on the left leads to the top.

Variation: Right-Hand Route – Direct Start   50m IV (5) 1991

The central groove used as the first pitch of *Rib and Groove* is followed for 35m to the bulge and a hard leftward finish. The belay at the top of pitch 2 on the ordinary route is gained by moving back right.

Misty Mountain Hop   120m IV (4) 2005

This climbs the broad buttress line to the left of the gully (*Cambridge Crag Climb*). Climb the ridge on the left side of the gully linking short corners and easier mixed steps to where *Cambridge Crag Climb* traverses left. Follow this and take any easy independent line to the summit.

Cambridge Crag Climb   75m II ★ 1979

This takes the shallow gully starting just right of the toe of the buttress. It should not be confused with the summer climb of the same name.

1   30m. Follow the shallow gully, keeping to the centre where it branches.

2   20m. From a block belay under the headwall, follow a leftward-sloping ramp to another large block.

3   25m. Pass the block on the right, then go diagonally right across snow to finish up a short groove.

Riboletto Groove   95m V (6) 2006

Really an alternative finish to *Cambridge Crag Climb*, finishing up the steep turfy groove/chimney to the right of *Riboletto*.

1   40m (2). Follow *Cambridge Crag Climb* to belay at the headwall below prominent arete, the summer route of *Riboletto*.

2   55m (6). Climb the groove to the right of the arete passing a large wedged block. Above this, the groove narrows to a chimney. Thrutch up this, and make some hard moves to gain the turfy continuation groove. Step right and climb a short steep corner to gain easy ground.

No Way Out   130m IV 2005

Yet another alternative finish to *Cambridge Crag Climb*, taking a groove in the headwall where the parent route takes the easy leftward traverse option.

1   40m (2). Start as for *Cambridge Crag Climb* and follow it for 40m to a spike and nut belays on the right side of gully.

2   30m (3). Bear up and right, and then traverse right under a prominent rock arete (summer route of *Riboletto*). Belay on a wall on the right.

3   30m (3). Continue up and right over a couple of steep walls to a belay just left of a large pinnacle.

4   30m (5). Climb a steep turfy groove to a terrace, and then the continuation groove above to the top with some trying moves.

North Buttress   (NY 246 066)
Alt. 790m North-east facing

North Buttress lies to the right of *Cambridge Buttress* and at a slightly higher altitude. The left-hand side of the buttress has a number of short broken walls and ribs which extend down to *Cambridge Crag*.

The buttress at the far left side of the crag is separated from the grooved right-hand portion by broken ground. The routes are described from **left** to **right**. The first route, *Siamese Chimneys*, starts on the north-facing

North Buttress – Gimps Wall Area

1	Skint and Single	VI
2	Die Another Day	IV
3	Gimps to the Left of Them	IV
4	The Flying Gimp Trick	IV

(Photo: Steve Ashworth)

wall on the left of the crag. *Soul Vacation* is a winter version of *Sword of Damocles*, the prominent right-hand of the three grooves in the steepest area of the buttress. The other routes take the right side of the buttress and more broken ground further right.

Siamese Chimneys   90m IV 1986

The obvious chimney-line to the left of the prominent grooves is climbed to half-height where a second higher chimney is followed.

1   20m (4). Climb easily to the base of the chimney proper. Follow this to a large overhang where it is possible to move right and upwards to a ledge.

2   30m (5). Move right to the corner with a cleft on its left: use both these features to make upward progress to a ledge, and move right to the bottom of the second chimney.

3   40m (3). The final chimney leads to a small headwall and the top.

The Gnomon   65m VII (8) ☆☆☆ 2006

To the right of *Siamese Chimneys* are three prominent groove systems: this climbs the leftmost groove. Easy scrambling leads to a spike belay at the bottom of the groove.

1   40m. Follow a crack in the corner up into a niche and protection. Step down and make a wild traverse left and climb a short wall to a ledge on the left rib. Make another committing swing right past an old peg to a groove and follow this to the top. Scramble up and belay below a tower.

2   25m. From the centre of the tower move up and right around to the top of the tower then follow cracks in the final wall to the top.

Soul Vacation   60m VIII (8) ☆☆☆ 2004

This, the right-hand of the three prominent grooves, follows the summer line of *Sword of Damocles*, an oft-eyed line that many failed to find in true winter condition over the past two decades. It is now safer without the hanging flake that gave the summer route its name. There is sufficient protection, although it can be strenuous to place.

1   25m. A crack leads rightwards into the base of the groove. Move up behind a pinnacle and continue up the groove to an awkward step right to gain a ledge at the edge of the buttress. Move up and traverse left across the groove to belay at the base of the main groove.

2   15m. The main pitch: climb the groove, passing a bulge on the left to a belay.

3   20m. Climb the flake crack above. This proves strenuous but there's a rest at the end. Continue up the crack until it is possible to move right to easier ground near the top.

Scabbard   30m IV (5) 1987

To the right of the three grooves, climb steep ice and turf at the back of the bay to the right of the summer line of *Scabbard* and left of the gully.

To the right of *Soul Vacation*, approximately 50m up the hill, the wall becomes easier angled and more broken.

The first two climbs start at the base of the same icy groove, on the left side of an easier-angled bay.

Skint and Single   40m VI (7) 2002

Start up a smaller groove immediately to the left of the more prominent corner-groove of *Die Another Day*. Climb the icy groove to a block, and surmount this to a small grassy ledge. Delicately step left for a metre to a verglassed, overhanging groove (crux). Climb this, and the broken groove above to the top.

Die Another Day   50m IV (6) 2003

Start in the same place as *Skint and Single*, but climb the more prominent corner-groove with an icicle at its bottom. From its top, trend left up turf steps to a ledge which is about 5m below the left-hand of two overlaps. Step steeply up and right into a groove right of the left overlap, and continue more easily to good belays.

Gimps to the Left of Them   50m IV (5) 2003

This line links up the two most obvious ice features on this part of the crag. A thin smear forms low down this is gained by using turf from the right. Continue up the line of least resistance to the ice umbrella above, climb it, and finish up a turfy corner.

The Flying Gimp Trick   50m IV (5) 2003

Climb the corner feature on the right-hand side of the crag, trending left up turfy cracks to finish. Alternatively move left on the obvious ledge at about 15m, and follow the most obvious turf line back rightwards (at an easier grade).

Continuing up the hillside the wall steepens for the next 50m or so until it is split by an icy chimney with an awkwardly steep section about halfway (**Icy Chimney** 30m, III, 2004). Starting at the foot of the chimney is a ramp-line running up rightwards. This gives some excellent mixed climbing up a series of turfy holds and steep steps (**Ramp Line** 30m, II, 2004).

Cambridge Girdle   200m IV (4) 2006

A left-to-right traverse of *Cambridge Crag* and *North Buttress*. Start at the left-hand side of *Cambridge*. An obvious rising traverse line is visible crossing both buttresses and going under the start of *Soul Vacation*. The true length is uncertain and no pitch lengths or grades are given as the route (bar the final 10m) was soloed.

A series of starts are possible: either begin up a short prominent right-facing corner-line to an easy shelf; or to the left of the corner and round an arete is a groove that leads to the same place; or from further up the *Great Slab* it is possible to walk easily onto the start of the traverse line. From the top of the corner go up and right and round an awkward step to easy snow.

Brian Davison pauses briefly above Langdale on the first ascent of Bowfell Girdle *(V) (Photo: Steve Ashworth)*

Bowfell Buttress

1	Plaque Route	IV
2	Sinister Slabs	VI
3	Central Route	VI
4	Bowfell Buttress	V
5	Ledge and Groove	IV
6	North Gully	I/II
7	Bowfell Girdle	V

(Photo: Brian Davison)

70

A further rising traverse leads to a short descent into the gully of *Cambridge Crag Climb*. Cross this, followed by some difficult moves up to ledges at a higher level. Go round these to the bottom of *Sword of Damocles/Soul Vacation*. Climb down slightly and round an arete to the base of a groove. Traverse across the base of the wall. As it was in the beginning, so it is in the end with a choice of finishes. Either walk easily right onto the hillside, or finish up the obvious corner above *The Flying Gimp Trick*, or continue traversing up a ramp-line until it is possible to climb a stepped groove about 3m before *Icy Chimney*. At last, the day is done.

Bowfell Buttress

(NY 245 066)
Alt. 750m North-east facing

Bowfell Buttress, the large crag to the right, and separated from the other crags by a wide scree run, is the most extensive of the buttresses in this area. It is bordered by *South* and *North Gullies* on its left and right sides respectively. This impressive buttress is tilted slightly off-vertical and is seamed by corners and grooves. It has the highest concentration of quality winter routes in the valley.

South Gully   150m I 1870

This is the broad slope to the left of the buttress and is of considerable historic interest as the first recorded winter climb in Britain. It can be used as a **descent**, but is often heavily corniced, and terminates in a boulder field below: not perhaps the best place to practise glissading.

Plaque Route   100m IV (4) ★ 1986

This starts near a large boulder that may be seen poking out of the snow at the left side of the crag and follows the left edge of the buttress. The route lacks any real line; just progress upwards over grassy ledges trending slightly leftwards. The final section contains some loose rock so it may be advisable to move further left onto more vegetated ground.

Sinister Slabs   115m VI ★ 1986

This follows a similar line to the summer route and holds snow well. Start by a rib 5m to the left of the bottom of the crag.

1   40m (4). Follow the rib on the right, past a block at 10m, and move left to a ledge below a slanting chimney. Follow the chimney to a corner and belay.

2   30m (6). A leftwards-slanting slab leads past blocks to a rib. Continue to a groove on the right and a tricky exit onto a belay ledge.

3   45m (3). The chimney above gives easy climbing up to continuation gullies, which in turn lead to short walls and the top.

Bowfell Buttress   110m V ★★★ 1937

One of the technical test pieces of the Lakes and a futuristic achievement at the time of its first ascent which was long overlooked. Fine mixed climbing leads up the nose of the buttress. Start 3m left of the edge of the smooth wall forming the base of the crag, at a ridge in an open left-facing corner system.

1   25m (4). Follow the ridge and then a chimney on the right leading to a ledge on the right.

2   30m (5). Move diagonally left to a slim right-facing groove/chimney system, which leads to ledges and a large snow terrace.

3   30m (6). The 5m iced crack above on the right leads with difficulty to a ledge. Move up and leftwards, over a tricky slab (this can be difficult if poorly iced) to a pinnacle. An exposed traverse left leads to a groove and chimney.

4   25m (5). Follow the groove/chimney to a wall. Either move left to easy ground, or, if you haven't had enough, step right and follow the icy groove to the top.

Central Route   90m VI (8) ★ 1991

A direct and harder line to the left of *Bowfell Buttress* which starts just to its right and crosses it after 15m.

1   15m. Start at a broken groove 5m to the right *Bowfell Buttress*, and climb the groove and the slabby walls to the top of the rib, as for *Bowfell Buttress* pitch 1.

2   15m. Enter the steep chimney with difficulty and follow it strenuously to a tricky exit right to the arete near the top.

3   20m. Climb up leftwards to a large block and belay.

4   40m. Surmount the block somehow, and move up a shallow groove to a rib and slab. Follow this leftwards to easier ground.

Ledge and Groove   115m IV ★ 1991

This attempt to follow the right edge of the buttress tends to wander, and is escapable to the right at several points. Start 5m left of *North Gully*.

1   20m (3). Climb the wall to a large snowy ledge and continue to a second ledge.
2   25m (4). From the right-hand side of the ledge follow a series of steps to an overhang. This is bypassed by a traverse, left then back right, to a belay on the edge of the buttress.
3   30m (5). Follow grooves on the right to a chimney that leads to a ledge.
4   40m (5). Start up a groove on the right, then continue up short walls, trending leftwards, to the top.

North Gully   125m I/II ★ 1910

The gully bounding the right side of the crag. A steep pitch at the bottom leads to straightforward snow to the top. The steep starting pitch can be avoided by interesting climbing up broken ground on the right.

The continuation of *North Gully* cuts off the buttress from the hillside above and then drops down into *South Gully* (I). It is **not** recommended as a descent as any error in route finding will lead parties onto steep ground.

Right Wall Eliminate   65m V (6) 1994

A climb based on the E1 summer line of the same name, starting at an obvious corner on the left about 20m above the steep pitch of *North Gully*.
1   20m. Follow the corner to a ledge and spike belay.
2   25m. Move right a few metres, past a crack in the wall to where the angle eases, and follow turf placements to the right-hand end of a ramp-line. Traverse left up the ramp until below an inverted bottom-less V-groove. Climb this to a large ledge and spike belay.
3   20m. Climb a turf-filled groove to the right of the belay to a small roof at 10m. Here the groove splits into two grooves. Follow the left one.

Corner and Rib   45m IV (4) 1995

Start at a wide shallow corner near the top left side of the *North Gully*, about 40m past the steep first pitch.
1   20m. The corner is followed until it becomes an obvious V-groove after about 20m.
2   25m. Move right onto the rib and follow it more easily to the top.

Bowfell Girdle 170m V 2006

A girdle traverse of the buttress starting from the large grassy shelf on the left of the buttress and finishing at *North Gully* on the right. Best preceded via the *Cambridge Girdle* – especially if you are feeling a bit crabby.

1 50m. Traverse easily to the large grassy shelf on the left of the buttress.

2 20m. (3) Downclimb about 5m to a narrow ledge and move right to belay a few metres short of a shallow corner.

3 50m (6). A wandering pitch. Traverse right to the corner, then downclimb a few metres, until it is possible to go round the base of an arete into a groove. Climb the groove for 5m to a ledge on the right. Move to a wide crack at the end of the ledge and downclimb this awkwardly to a narrow ledge. Shuffle along the ledge to the start of another large ledge running across the buttress.

4 50m. (4). Cross the ledge. This can be continued with a short piece of downclimbing into *North Gully* between the two steep chockstone pitches. Or, as on the first ascent, about 10m before the gully is reached, the wall above the ledge is climbed to a higher ledge. This is then followed easily into *North Gully* above the second chockstone pitch. Either finish up the gully, or, if you have a plentiful supply of energy and provisions, keep on traversing to link in with the *Great End Girdle* in a *grande enchainement*.

The final route starts about 200m below *Bowfell Buttress* where an obvious drainage line spills over slabs which are located about 200m above a major right-hand bend halfway up the Rossett Gill path (a useful approach route).

Gimpsuit Fall 30m III/IV 2004

Head for the obvious ice pillar. Climb up the slab and finish direct up the short steep pillar of ice at the top.

Angle Tarn and Hanging Knotts (NY 243 075)
Alt. 620m North facing

The area around Angle Tarn contains much broken rock and short buttresses that often freeze to give short icefalls that have provided a reliable winter playground for generations of climbers. Whilst each individual pitch of ice does not warrant a separate description, many of the icefalls can be linked together to weave a route to the top. *Hanging Knotts* is the scrappy crag at the back of Angle Tarn. Its top buttress resembles a V of rock and is taken by *Evening Buttress*.

The best approach is from Langdale via Rossett Gill, though it is possible, but longer, to go from Borrowdale via Esk Hause.

The routes are described in a clockwise order around the tarn, starting from the Rossett Gill approach.

Evening Buttress   IV (6) 65m 1993

This route is to be found on *Hanging Knotts*. It climbs the iced-up right-hand end of the buttress, with the crux short and low down. Best approached via *Angle Tarn Gully* (see below) or the icefalls.

Angle Tarn Gully   100m I Pre-1909

This obvious gully runs up the fellside close to the left side of the tarn and right of *Hanging Knotts*. Usually a straightforward snow slope.

Angle Tarn Icefalls   30m III/IV ★★ 1930s

In a good year there are many to choose from, but the best lie near the top of Rossett Gill. About 100m right of the gully, at the back of the tarn, a short rock buttress about 15m high provides two falls most winters. Another pitch above can be combined to give a good route to the top.

About 100m to the right of the *Tarn Icefalls* is a broad easy snow gully. The lower left wall of this gully provides several pitches up to 45m long (III). When you've finished on these, 200m further right is a frozen stream containing a 20m vertical pillar of ice in its upper reaches (III/IV). Further right again is an easier 15m ice runnel (III).

LANGDALE PIKES   (NY 278 073)

Having a southerly aspect, the remaining routes described in this area of the valley can soon be stripped of any snow on a cloudless sunny day. The greatest concentration of climbs is to be found on *Pavey Ark*, though the low-lying gills are fun if you can find them frozen.

David Birkett in wild conditions on first winter ascent of The Crack Direct *(VII), Gimmer Crag (Photo: Mark 'Ed' Edwards)*

North-West Gully (300m, I/II*, 1995) is the obvious gully (NY 272 072) splitting the west side of **Pike of Stickle**, overlooking Mickleden. It provides an interesting way to the summit if heading up from the valley. The gully is clearly seen from further north up the valley. Ramble up easy fellside to the ill-defined lower portion of the gully. Follow a stream bed in the middle of the rocky pike. The gully walls start to close in and a short wall bars the way to the top section of the gully. This can be passed on the left. Alternative left or right finishes are possible past a chockstone.

Gimmer Crag

(NY 277 070)
Alt. 525m South-east facing

Being south facing and at a relative low altitude *Gimmer* is not known for its winter routes. However, sheltering in north-west-facing *North-West Gully*, both **The Crack** (1962) and **Hiatus** (1926) high up in the gully have seen winter ascents of a sort. A more recent ascent of *The Crack* which continued directly up the corner is described here. The reader is referred to the FRCC Langdale guide for full descriptions of the other climbs.

The Crack Direct   75m VII ☆☆☆ 2006

This winter ascent follows throughout the true line of the prominent corner cleaving the wall overlooking the gully. Start just above the huge chockstone in the gully at the foot of an easy-angled corner which leads to the corner proper.

1   30m (7). Follow the corner-crack of the summer route until that route traverses left. Continue up the true corner above until overhanging rock forces a short rising traverse on to the left wall and up to a block below a rib. Stand on the block to turn the rib and enter a turf groove. Climb the groove for 4m to a spike belay.

2   22m (8). Step up to gain the left-leaning undercut crack. Make difficult moves up and left to gain the base of a turf groove/corner. Follow this corner and make strenuous moves to gain the haven of the *Bower*.

3   23m (7). The deep corner crack of the summer line is followed to the top, giving a sustained pitch.

The **South Face of Harrison Stickle** (NY 281 073) is the home of **South Face Route** (150m, II/III) which starts up a slight depression in the middle of the face before making a traverse right to the crest up which it finishes.

Dungeon Ghyll   III/IV ★ 1985/6

Perhaps best to forget about this one unless it's a serious winter freeze; the last time it was in full condition was during the 1980s. As further deterrent it should be noted that the gill is important as the home of rare alpine plants, especially the canyon bit at the top under Harrison Stickle – please climb here only in truly frozen conditions, and please read the section 'Winter Climbing and Nature Conservation'.

Starting almost from the New Dungeon Ghyll Hotel, the lower section seldom forms. When it does, the bottom fall rising from *The Dungeon*, beneath the great capstone that spans the gill, provides the crux (IV). The portion above (NY 287 068, alt. 320m) has several short pitches and one longer one (III/IV). Approaching Harrison Stickle the upper section gives several short pitches and one longer at 30m as the scenery becomes more impressive.

Stickle Ghyll   I/II

This open, low altitude gill (NY 292 067, alt. 180m) is actually in condition more often than one might imagine, and makes an enjoyable approach to *Pavey Ark* if you're not rushing up for something harder thereabouts.

Pavey Ark in an icy grip (Photo: Alastair Lee)

Pavey Ark
(NY 286 079)
Alt. 570m South-east facing

Being south-facing, this large crag strips of snow quickly, though it can produce some very good climbs after a period of severe frost and/or build-up of snow, in which case it is worth making an early start. It is very accessible from Langdale.

Follow the path alongside *Stickle Ghyll* from the New Dungeon Ghyll car park to Stickle Tarn. The crag is at the back of the combe, at the far side of the tarn. It is split diagonally from bottom right to top left by the scramble of *Jack's Rake*.

The deep-cut gully on the far left is *Little Gully*, with *Great Gully* divided from it by a large buttress. The diagonal break crossing the main crag from right to left is *Jack's Rake*. *East Gully*, to the right of the crag, is the best **descent**. The routes are described from **left** to **right**.

Pavey Ark

1	Little Gully Left Branch	II
2	Little Gully Right Branch	III
3	Middling Buttress	III
4	Great Gully	III
5	Stony Buttress	III
6	Crescent Climb	III/IV
7	Deception	IV
8	Gwynne's Chimney	IV
9	Cook's Tour	IV
10	Stoat's Crack	VI
11	Jack's Rake	I
	East Gully (descent)	- - - ▶

(Photo: Eric Shaw)

Little Gully   110m 1930s

The first 60m has 15m of mixed climbing in it then a further 50m of easy snow leading to a choice of branches.

Left Branch   55m III ★★

The most reliable route on the crag. A 25m icefall leads to a ledge and belay on the right or left (30m). Continue up 20m of steepening ice with easy snow above and a belay further back (25m). Continue up easy snow to the top.

Right Branch   50m II

The gully on the right. Climb behind the top chockstone and bridge out above it. Climb to *Jack's Rake* and finish up this.

Middling Buttress   100m III ★ 1986

The well-protected buttress between *Little Gully* and *Great Gully* is climbable under almost all frozen conditions.
1   50m. Start just left of centre of the buttress and head straight up for the tree belay at mid-height which is gained on rope-stretch.
2   50m. Continue straight upwards.

Great Gully   105m III ★ 1901

Good climbing, but sadly not often in condition.
1   50m. Mixed climbing up the gully leads to a belay below the huge chockstone.
2   30m. Your mate's lead! The chockstone is best turned by the right iced wall. Easy snow leads to a cave.
3   25m. A choice of a through-route or over the cave, then up steep ice to reach *Jack's Rake*. Finish up or down *Jack's Rake*, or via a gully on the right which leads to the summit of the mountain.

Stony Buttress   110m III

The buttress to the right of *Great Gully*. Start as for *Great Gully* but move right onto the buttress and follow the left edge of the buttress overlooking the gully. After 20m move right to a series of corners and grooves and follow these to *Jack's Rake*. The rock quality is poor.

The next feature is a crescent-shaped slab and wall bounded by *Crescent Climb* on its left and the corner of *Deception* on its right side.

Crescent Climb   100m III/IV

A companion route to *Deception*. Best climbed when the slab is iced.

1   55m. Climb to an overhang at the left side of the slab taking the line of least resistance.
2   15m. Traverse right to the end of the overhang and a stance. With careful rope work this can be combined with the next pitch.
3   30m. Turfy slabs lead to *Jack's Rake* which is followed to the top or bottom.

Deception   60m IV ★ 1986

The obvious corner-line of the summer route *Deception* which starts at the right end of the slab taken by the summer route *Arcturus* is hopefully distinguished by ice smears.

1   20m (3). Follow a right-slanting turfy line to a holly.
2   20m (4). Continue in the same line to belay below a steep corner.
3   30m (3). Follow the corner to *Jack's Rake*.

Jack's Rake   450m I

The prominent right-to-left diagonal line running across the face is a popular summer scramble and an interesting winter route. It is also a possible descent for the competent, but care should be taken when it is iced up.

Gwynne's Chimney   55m IV (5) ★ 1979

Approach by scrambling up *Jack's Rake* to below the start of the chimney and summer line at a tricky step at the left end of the first level section in *Jack's Rake*, the top of *Crescent Climb*.

1   25m. Follow the chimney over steps and bulges to level with a gorse bush on the left of the chimney at 15m. Move up and right and make delicate moves right to exit the chimney and gain a snow ledge. Traverse the ledge for 2m and ascend blocky ground for 7m to a ledge and belay.
2   30m. Follow a groove above the belay to an exposed rib. Trend left, climb over a steep blocky step, and follow the turf groove above to the top.

Direct Finish   50m IV (5) ☆ 2006

Follow the chimney as for the standard route until it makes a traverse right at about 17m. Instead continue up the narrow chimney with a tight squeeze but some good axe placements in a crack on the right wall and turf to finish: breathe in again at the top.

Cook's Tour   100m IV ★ 1981

Starting halfway up *Jack's Rake*, just after a steep section, and just down from the top of *Deception*.

1   30m. Start at a short chimney just opposite a large rowan tree, and head up rightwards over easier vegetated mixed ground.
2   35m. Move left and follow an open gully, then a chimney to belay.
3   35m. Follow the easiest line up cracks and broken walls to finish.

Stoat's Crack   150m VI ★ 1976

The buttress at the right side of the crag, starting where it curves round into *East Gully* from near the bottom of *Jack's Rake*, and passing to the left of the prominent overhang halfway up the cliff.

1   60m (4). Climb a slanting corner trending left. Continue up corners to a spacious ledge below the overhang. A careful choice of runner placements and a 60m rope are useful, though intermediate belays are possible at several places.
2   30m (6). From the left-hand end of the ledge, climb an icy open groove to below a slabby wall.
3   30m (4). Strategically positioned turf allows progress up icy slabs to a large block belay.
4   30m (2). Continue easily to the top.

White Ghyll   (NY 298 072)
Alt. 400m West facing

This steep crag, high up on the eastern flank of White Gill, normally holds little interest for the winter climber.

Approach from the New Dungeon Ghyll car park by either following the road east a few hundred metres to the footpath signpost on the left, and then taking the obvious path up to the gill, or follow the *Stickle Ghyll* path until it crosses the gill, then continue along the path by the wall at that level to enter *White Gill*.

White Ghyll Chimney   75m IV 1982

High up the gill, near the left end of the crag, the transition of the crag from steep grooves and overhangs to a steep slab is marked by an open chimney/fault-line. Climb the chimney/fault to a chockstone, step left onto the slabs and continue to the top, belaying where appropriate.

CONISTON

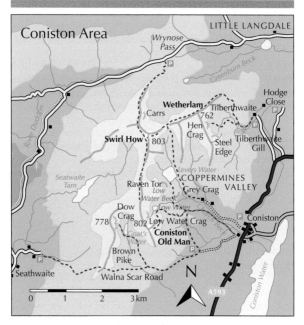

Coniston Area

LITTLE LANGDALE

Wrynose Pass

Greenburn Beck

Hodge Close

Wetherlam · Tilberthwaite

Carrs

762

Hen Crag

Swirl How · 803

Steel Edge

Tilberthwaite Gill

River Duddon

Levers Water

Seatwaite Tarn

COPPERMINES VALLEY

Raven Tor

Grey Crag

Low Water Beck

Dow Crag

Low Water

778

802 Low Water Crag

Coniston

Goat's Water

Coniston Old Man

Brown Pike

N

Seathwaite

Walna Scar Road

A593

Coniston Water

0   1   2   3 km

With its proximity to the coast and an open south-westerly aspect, Coniston and the surrounding fells are greatly affected by milder coastal winds and so tend to be less frequently in condition than most other areas in this guide. Best conditions result from a long spell of easterly or northerly winds followed by snow. When such conditions do arise, however, a visit to *Dow Crag* can provide a wonderful mountain day with relatively easy access. Many of the other routes in this section are isolated icefalls, such as those in the slate quarries, or frozen gills, which are often low lying and so require a prolonged period of cold weather to form.

The climbs are described starting with those on the Old Man of Coniston and the mountains around Coniston village before moving to the outlying crags.

Dow

Brown Pike
(SD 262 966)
Alt. 600m East facing

To the south of *Dow Crag* is Brown Pike with its small combe containing Blind Tarn on its east flank. Approach as for *Dow Crag* but continue on for another kilometre past the *Dow* turning to where cairns mark the start of a quarry track on the right. Follow this round the hillside into the cove.

North-East Gully   150m I
This follows the slanting gully above and to the left of *Blind Tarn* at the back of the corrie. It takes a nice line to the summit ridge.

Dow Crag
(SD 264 977)
Alt. 610m East facing

This wonderful mountain crag has a series of five prominent buttresses named A to E, separated by imposing gullies.

Dow Crag is easily accessible if you can drive up the steep (and often icy) Walna Scar road out of Coniston village. However, even if you have to walk, the going up the road is easy, and it's only 1.5km to a gate where the metalled road ends – park here (SD 288 971). Take the left-hand track and continue in the same direction, along the bridleway, to a large cairn which marks the junction with the track from Torver. Take the right-hand branch, going initially up a steep grassy slope, and contour round in 1.5km to Goat's Water below the cliff (2 hrs). From the tarn, for routes on *'A'* and *'B' Buttresses*, slog up steep scree to the mountain rescue box under *'B' Buttress*. For *Easter Gully* and routes further right, follow sheep tracks across diagonally below *'B' Buttress*, or skirt around its base from the rescue post.

The routes are described from left to right.

Dow Crag

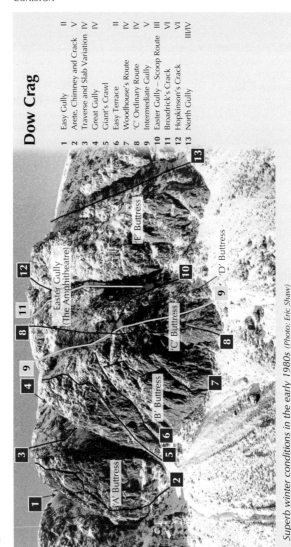

Superb winter conditions in the early 1980s (Photo: Eric Shaw)

Easy Buttress

Easy Gully Left Branch   120m I
The first gully/rake at the left-hand end of the crag does not give any real difficulties and is often used as a descent.

Easy Gully   120m II
This deep gully marking the left side of *'A' Buttress* is straightforward in its lower section with a chockstone to pass. The larger chockstone near the top can be bypassed by an exposed traverse onto the left wall or can be climbed direct.

Easy Gully Right Branch   120m ★ III
Start up *Easy Gully*. The right-hand branch is a smaller gully-line and leads right up the side of *'A' Buttress* to its crest.

'A' Buttress
The leftmost major buttress.

Arete, Chimney and Crack   110m V (5) ★★★ 1996
This classic route starts at the bottom left of the buttress and takes a long rightward-arching line up the face, ending directly up the centre top of the buttress. On the first ascent, ledges were covered in neve and cracks choked with ice.
1   20m. Start at the lowest point of the left side of the buttress and climb the *Arete* to a ledge. Continue up the steeper wall above to gain an overhung ledge.
2   10m. Make a move left and climb a crack to blocks.
3   20m. Move diagonally right to a blocky recess and continue traversing right to belay below the *Chimney*.
4   10m. The *Chimney*: climb it passing an awkward chockstone.
5   25m. Traverse right along the exposed ledge to beneath the chimney-crack.
6   25m. And finally the *Crack*. This is sustained and exposed and is followed right to the top. A fitting finale.

Eliminate 'A' received a winter ascent in the 1970s. It is very rarely in true condition and the reader is referred to the FRCC Dow guide for a description.

Spectacular wreathes of winter snow mist creep up Dow Crag
(Photo: Eric Shaw)

Great Gully   120m IV 1911

The deep gully bounding the right side of 'A' Buttress. A hard route for its day.

1   15m. A straightforward snow slope leads up to the chockstone.

2   30m (4). Generally hard unless banked out – and that doesn't happen often. Continue up for 15m to where the gully narrows to become a chimney. Climb this and surmount the capping chockstone.

3   75m. Easy snow leads to a slabby exit rightward. It is also possible to finish easily direct.

Traverse and Slab Variation   120m IV 1986

2   70m (4). From the amphitheatre above the third chockstone, follow a system of ledges left across the left wall of the gully into a groove which leads to a shallow cave. From the cave, climb the obvious slab (good protection) to the corner. Layback this to an impressive block belay above 'A' Buttress. The pitch can be split at several places depending on rope drag.

3   50m. Easier scrambling leads to the top.

'B' Buttress

The next great buttress to the right – it is easily distinguished by the mountain rescue box at its foot.

Giant's Crawl, the obvious slabby gangway which cuts up across the buttress, has reputedly been climbed in winter but details are unknown.

Easy Terrace   250m II 1907

The line of the summer descent route from 'B' Buttress. Once the terrace is gained, traverse along ledges for 75m, then follow the easier continuation of *Intermediate Gully* to the summit.

Woodhouse's Route   105m IV ★★ 1912

The route follows a diagonal line across 'B' Buttress from the foot of the very impressive *Central Chimney* which bounds the right side of the buttress.

1   30m. Start below a wide groove, below the large pinnacle at the bottom left of *Central Chimney*. Climb the groove to the base of the pinnacle then take the wide crack on the left to the crevasse behind the pinnacle.

2   35m. Step left and enter the chimney, and follow this to a ledge and possible belay after 10m. Traverse left to a deep recess. The deep rock cleft above leads to a ledge on the left in another 10m. Continue directly to a terrace, and traverse right to a block beneath a steep crack.

3   40m. Depending on ice conditions climb the crack, or the slab running diagonally right below the wall for 15m. A crevasse leads right to a steep wall with a projecting block. Climb the wall to its left and up to easier ground. Trend left, or straight up, to reach *Easy Terrace*.

'C' Buttress

The lowest of the *Dow* buttresses is slabbier than the others.

'C' Ordinary Route   255m IV (5) ★★★ 1919

An impressive line up the buttress. It follows the summer route throughout, but misses out the *Easy Terrace* descent by continuing directly up the buttress on easier-angled ground directly to the top of the crag. Start just left of the toe of the buttress, the lowest point of the crag.

1   30m. Climb onto the front of the buttress to a ledge on top of a large flake. Continue to a smaller ledge and climb the scoop above.

Easier-angled ground and ledges lead to a good ledge with a fallen flake.

2   25m. From the left end of the ledge, climb an open scoop to gain a ledge up to the right. Follow easier-angled ground leftwards to a ledge on the corner of the buttress.

3   25m. The groove on the right leads to a ledge. Move right and go up to a slab which is followed to a large ledge. Move up right again to a ledge and better belays.

4   15m. Traverse 3m left then climb the wall above, left of the crack. Move left to beneath a small cave then climb the wide crack to the top of a large flake lying to the left of a cave. From the top of the flake, move left then back right to a small stance and belay only 3m above the flake.

5   20m. Traverse rightwards across slabs to a good ledge. Continue rightwards along a gangway to a ledge. A short wall on the left leaves you level with *Easy Terrace* which is over to the left.

6   140m. The summit ridge is gained up easier-angled ground by a fairly direct line.

Intermediate Gully   225m V (4) ☆☆ 1919

The imposing deep-cut crack between 'C' and 'D' Buttresses. The grade is a bit of a guesstimate as it is seldom in condition and has had few winter ascents: with reasonable icing it is thought it would make a good gully climb, but it will be found much tougher as a mixed route.

1   30m. Follow the gully easily until the walls close in.

2   20m. Continue up the crack and chimney to a recess (possible belay). This section can also be passed by a groove on the right then a traverse back left into the gully. Continue up and over the chockstone.

3   20m. The steep crack above leads to easier ground, then steepens before reaching a recess below a large chockstone.

4   15m. Climb over the chockstone to a cave, then move right and up and left into crack in the left wall. Follow the crack until level with *Easy Terrace* over to the left.

5   140m. As for 'C' *Ordinary*: easier-angled ground leads directly to the summit ridge, or the continuation of the gully can be followed with one more awkward chockstone – best passed a few metres lower on the left wall.

Easter Gully (The Amphitheatre)

Easter Gully – Scoop Route   **180m III ★★ 1918**

The next gully right is *Easter Gully* with its preliminary short chockstone pitch leading into *The Amphitheatre*. This can be tricky if not banked out and is best taken on its left (15m). From here several routes may be taken, but under snow and ice the best exit at an easy grade is by a system of ledges and a scoop which starts just right of the deep chimney of *South Chimney* on the left wall. A crack, then ledges, lead to a block. Overcome the block and take the scoop above to *Easy Terrace* (25m). Traverse left and finish up the easy upper section of *Intermediate Gully*. A slightly harder finish, requiring better conditions, is to wind a way directly up the buttress above (140m).

The next two routes are gained by following *Easter Gully* to the *Amphitheatre*, whose steep back wall has cracked corner-lines at either side – *Broadrick's Crack* on the left and *Hopkinson's Crack* on the right. **Blizzard Chimney** (1914), the first chimney on the left in the *Amphitheatre*, and **South Chimney** (1914) to its right, have both been climbed in heavy snow conditions, but their grades are unknown. They are both graded Difficult in summer.

Broadrick's Crack   **195m VI ★★ 1996**

The left-hand crack. A demanding main pitch which is nevertheless escapable at a few places.

1   15m (3). Climb *Easter Gully* to the *Amphitheatre*.
2   30m. Easy mixed ground leads to the base of the steep crack/corner on the left side of the *Amphitheatre*.
3   50m (8). This is the meat of the route, originally climbed in one 50m pitch, though it would be possible to split the pitch at a number of points. Hard and strenuous climbing leads to where the crack widens in 20m. Pass a chockstone on its right side and belay on the right at the base of an easy snow gully.
4   50m. Climb the snow gully to a col and then downclimb into the main gully above *Hopkinson's Crack* on the right. Follow the left-hand gully where it splits.
5   50m. Follow the gully to the top.

Jones's Route (1914) follows *Broadrick's Crack* to *The Bandstand*, and continues, crossing *Hopkinson's Crack* and traversing rightwards 5m to finish up a deceptively easy-looking scoop. It has received an ascent under heavy snow. The grade is unknown – it is Very Difficult in summer.

Hopkinson's Crack   **260m VI ★★★ 1995**

The crack and corner on the right of the back wall of the *Amphitheatre*. It has been climbed in mixed conditions, and also with a ribbon of ice down the main corner-line.

1   15m (3). Follow *Easter Gully* to the *Amphitheatre*.
2   15m (2). Move up to the base of the corner-crack, at the back right of the *Amphitheatre*.
3   30m (7). The wide icy crack is poorly protected in its lower part. Pass several difficult steep sections and a final strenuous move (crux) to a large belay ledge on the left (*The Bandstand*), and move left to a block belay.
4   20m (5). Return back right into the corner-line and follow the crack more easily to belay where the crack widens to a snow gully.
5   50m (4). Follow the right-hand chimney-line where the gully splits, passing an awkward chockstone to enter it.
6   100m. Easy snow curves round to the right near its top to be barred by a small rock wall.
7   30m (3). Climb a rock rib on the right to the top.

Black Chimney (25m, 1912), the dark short deep chimney on the right wall of *The Amphitheatre* has received an ascent under snow. The grade is unknown, but it is Difficult in summer.

'E' Buttress
The final buttress.

North Gully   **55m III/IV 1912**

The gully at the right side of the crag. Climb the gully, passing the cave to the right and the top overhangs to the left.

   Descent is possible by abseil or down a terrace on *'E' Buttress* to the left.

THE OLD MAN OF CONISTON
(SD 272 978)
Alt. 803m

The highest summit in this southern part of the Lake District has a few climbs around the mountain tarns of *Low Water* and *Levers Water*, and several frozen gills when temperatures drop low enough. *Low Water Beck* comes into condition more often than you'd imagine, and if some sections are a bit too damp, you can always wander up the side until you find an icier bit.

Low Water
(SD 275 983)
Alt. 547m

If you can get up the often icy Walna Scar Road from Coniston, park beyond the gate where the surfacing ends (SD 288 971). Take the right-hand track and follow it north, as per the main tourist route, taking the left fork until a further track branches right into the cove below the obvious fall.

Low Water Beck
90m III ★★★ 1940s

This is the beck running past the left side of *Cove Crag*. It falls from the high mountain tarn of the same name. It freezes quickly and is easily accessible, so making it popular, and it can be combined well with the icefalls above. The fall is best climbed on its left side up to a chockstone. Exit left on iced slabs or more steeply up the curtain of ice to the right (***Direct Finish***, IV). In a good winter the beck can continue to give easier climbing up to (and even over!) the tarn to the crag at the back of the corrie.

Low Water Crag
(SD 272 982)
Alt. 670m East facing

This small crag nestles at the back of the cove above *Low Water*. It can be approached by climbing *Low Water Beck* in suitable winter conditions, or via the tourist track, as for the beck. The climbing extends across the whole fellside.

Summit Route   140m II 1962

Follow snow patches and mixed ground, to the left of the main crag, directly to a satisfying finish at the summit cairn.

Mulled Wine   140m II 2004

The slim buttress to the left of *South Gully*. A good little route, similar in character to *Summit Route* further across the corrie. Start 30m to the left of *South Gully*. Climb initially up broken ground (slabs and steps) to the bottom of a steep 30m pear-shaped buttress. Turn this on either left or right at the same grade (left is better) to return to the top of the obstacle, and enter an obvious V-groove in the centre of the buttress. Go up this to more broken ground and onto the slopes above *South Gully*.

Spring Route   150m IV 2006

Really a left-hand variation finish to *South Gully*, breaking out left where the gully becomes better defined, but an independent start is possible. Start as for *South Gully*.

1   50m (3). Climb the icefall, then head slightly right up a snowfield before turning left into a gully.
2   20m (2). Enter the gully and belay before the narrowing (good spike).
3   50m (3). Climb the narrowing (crux), then enter the first gully on the left.
4   30m (2). Continue up the gully and easier ground to the top.

South Gully   140m III ★ 1962

This is the gully bounding the left side of the crag. Chockstones and boulders provide small ice pitches to be turned, and these lead to the upper exit slope, which is followed to the ridge.

Wild World   150m IV (5) ★ 2003

This route takes a straight line up the steep bit of buttress, just right of *South Gully*.

1   50m. Start just right of *South Gully* and trend right to the bottom of a steep corner. Climb this, then step right onto an exposed arete and spike. Bold climbing up steep turf directly above leads to a belay below a V-groove.
2   50m. Step right, and ascend up two right-angled corners. Step left from the top of the second corner and climb to a belay below an overhanging wall.

Coniston Old Man

II
II
IV
III
IV
III/IV
I
III

Low Water

Low Water Beck

Low Water

1 Summit Route
2 Mulled Wine
3 Spring Route
4 South Gully
5 Wild World
6 Percy's Passage
7 North Gully
8 Low Water Beck

*(Photo: Dave Willis –
Copyright FRCC)*

95

3   50m. Move round to the left, then over a chockstone and scramble
     to the top.

Percy's Passage   150m III/IV ★★ 1967

This lies to the left of *North Gully*, on the right side of a subsidiary buttress which lies up and right of the main buttress containing *South Gully*.
An obvious line of icefalls comes down the buttress in three or four short
pitches which are open to several variations depending on the conditions. The most enjoyable route links the many icefalls on the lower section of crag to a series of short steep walls and rightward-trending ramp-
lines higher up.

North Gully   150m I 1919

The shallow snow gully to the right of the crag is straightforward apart
from one small step.

To the right again is a small hanging valley which can provide several
short pitches, some of them difficult. Several discontinuous variations
are possible.

Levers Water   (SD 279 993)
                                         Alt. 413m

To the north of *Low Water* lies *Levers Water*. The two crags here are best
approached from the Copper Mines Valley, above Coniston village. The
small crag of the local landmark of **Simon's Nick** (SD 281 989), easily
seen from the path up to *Levers Water*, is said to give a Grade III. It rarely
receives drainage since the mine workings have closed, and no ice now
forms.

Grey Crag   (SD 282 987)
                       Alt. 330m South-east facing

This long crag bounds the hillside above the water works in the Copper
Mines Valley. Approach via the YHA track from Coniston.

Hazel Allen heading for the light on Low Water Beck *(III), Coniston
(Photo: Colin Wells)*

Grey Crag Icefall   **30m IV (4) 1964**

A good icefall usually forms at the left side of the crag. A thin sliver of ice leads to a tree belay. Climb a short 5m wall of ice, and then a rocky ice chimney (often thin on ice), to the top of the crag.

Module   **30m IV 1981**

The thin ice smear on the right of a prominent wall at the far right end of the crag.

Raven Tor   (SD 277 988)
           Alt. 550m North facing

This is the large broken buttress above *Levers Water*. Its northerly aspect means it is often in condition. Approach up the Copper Mines Valley via the Water Works track to *Levers Water*. Although only one route is described, the gully on the right-hand side of the crag is similar to *Central Gully* (II), and the buttress between the two gullies gives some of the best climbing (II). The remaining broken buttresses present many other possibilities for good climbing at Grade II.

Central Gully   **100m II 1959**

Situated to the left of centre, this is largest gully line on the crag. Rather indefinite initially, it becomes deeper nearer the top, with a steep exit providing the crux of the route – right where it should be, at the top!

WETHERLAM   (NY 288 011)
           Alt. 762m

Sitting to the north of the Old Man of Coniston, *Hen Crag* and *Steel Edge* are worth a visit, whilst the slate quarries around the foot of the mountain contain some interesting water ice on the rare occasions that they freeze.

From the car park at Tilberthwaite Cottages (NY 306 010), follow the path by *Tilberthwaite Gill* and head north into the combe to reach *Steele Edge* in just over an hour.

Steel Edge
(NY 294 005)
Alt. 500m North-east facing

Steel Edge defines the southern edge of the north-east facing combe of Wetherlam. The icefalls described are enjoyable and form quite readily. Ascend the *Edge* to half-height, then drop down onto its north side: the routes lie above.

Close to the Edge
40m III ★ 2002

This icefall forms on the north side of *Steel Edge* near its top where the edge joins the bulk of Wetherlam. Thick ice forms down a steep slab coming from a groove above. A good climb that is more often in condition than *Low Water Beck*.

Further from the Edge
35m IV ★★ 2003

An excellent ice pitch to the right of *Close to the Edge*. Climb up the steep nose for 10m then up the slab straight above to the top.

South Hen Crag
(NY 293 006)
Alt. 520m North-east facing

Further rightwards round into the combe, this large, rambling crag is a dispersed jumble of walls and short buttresses to the south of *Hen Crag*. It offers many possibilities in the lower grades which do not warrant individual description. The following routes are two of the better ones.

South South Gully
200m I ★ 2002

The notable gully in the centre of the crag gives good climbing throughout. A bit vague lower down but more obvious and better defined in its upper half.

South South Groove
200m II ★ 2002

Branching right from halfway up *South South Gully* is an open turfy corner leading onto easier slopes above.

Hen Crag
(NY 290 008)
Alt. 600m North-east facing

Situated on the east side of Wetherlam, this large crag overlooks *Tilberthwaite Gill*. In winters with a build-up of snow some excellent winter climbing can form quite quickly.

Take the track which leads from the car park beside Tilberthwaite Cottages.

If conditions are suitable, **descent** is possible down *North Gully*.

South Gully   200m I
This gully bounds the left side of the crag and leads to the summit ridge of Wetherlam. To the left of *South Gully* are many other climbs of a similar grade.

Hen's Teeth   200m II/III 2002
Parallel to but easier than *Hen Crag Buttress*. Start in a bay 20m left of *Hen Crag Buttress*. Follow a turfy/heather groove straight up for 90m. Climb up an easy shelf into a V-corner on the right (20m). Trend right on slabby rocks to the top.

Hen Crag Buttress   250m III/IV ★★★ 1970
An excellent mountaineering route requiring a good build-up of snow to cover the heathery ledges. It follows a diagonal line crossing the buttress from left to right. Start up an icy groove in the back of an open bay just to the left of the toe of the buttress, and continue along a natural line of weakness. Difficult moves on the second pitch lead to a heather ledge, and from there further pitches lead more easily to the top right of the crag. Belay as required.

Left-Hand Finish   250m III ★ 1980
Follow the original route for a couple of rope lengths until good ice leads out left. Finally a diagonal ramp leads up left to the summit.

Direct Finish   50m III 2000
From where the original route joins the heathery ledge, instead of traversing right to easy ground, go straight up stepped grooves and ledges at a similar grade to the climbing below.

Direct Start   **60m VI (5) 1993**

Starting right of the toe of the buttress, climb short walls and heathery ledges until it is possible to move left to the crest of the buttress. From here, follow turf to the large snow field and join the original route.

Hen Pecked   **200m II 2004**

The blunt ridge at the far right side of the buttress, overlooking *North Gully*. Start at the base of *North Gully*. Climb the ridge, up a small initial steep step, then steep heather (50m). Keep right, looking steeply down into *North Gully*, and continue in the same line all the way. Belay as required (150m).

North Gully   **200m I**

The gully on the right side of the crag. This finishes at a point near the summit of Wetherlam and can serve as a useful descent route.

North Buttress   **200m III 2002**

Start immediately right of *North Gully*. Good climbing up the obvious buttress, mostly via turfy grooves, steepening near the top.

TILBERTHWAITE AND THE SLATE QUARRIES

When sub-zero temperatures grip the area give the slate quarries a thought if you're looking for water ice. Several steep pitches giving excellent climbing have been climbed when conditions prevail.

Tilberthwaite Gill (NY 303 007, Alt. 240m, East facing) itself can offer a few short ice steps after a good freeze, and a more interesting approach to the next route.

Tilberthwaite Trundle   **23m IV 1982**

From the car park ascend *Tilberthwaite Gill* or (quicker) the path through the quarries on the left bank, cross the bridge, and follow the right bank to a landslip level with a right-angle bend in the gill. An icefall forms on the left bank of the gill at this point. Follow the right side of the fall to a platform at about 10m – above where the icefall steepens. Step left onto the main pillar (which drops down from a groove above) and follow this to a tree belay on the right. This route can easily be combined with some of the nearby quarry icefalls.

Hodge Close Quarry
(NY 316 017)
Alt. 150m

The one route recorded here has not been ascended since a major rock-fall (1996) removed a deep skin of rock above, and extending rightwards from, the cave. The whole area now looks extremely unstable and **dangerous** and is not recommended.

Side Show Icefall   50m V (5) 1982
Pass through the cave to the wall of the quarry overlooking the pond.
1   20m. At the mouth of the cave climb the slab to belay in a niche on the right.
2   30m. Move left, and follow grooves and ice to the top.

At the southern end of the quarry, the summer line of **Sasquatch** has been top-roped (8).

Adjoining **Parrock Quarry** (NY 317 018) often forms a fan of slabby ice on the east side about halfway down the entrance incline. Various 30m pitches can give quality entertainment at Grade II/III (1982).

Tranearth Quarry Icefall   20m IV (6) 1982
This quarry above Torver, at the lowly altitude of 240m (SD 280 960), can give a 20m icefall where the waterfall enters the quarry, but it rarely forms.

Carrs
(NY 273 012)
Alt. 550m East facing

To the south of Wrynose Pass, this extensive broken east-facing crag overlooks Greenburn and Little Langdale. It offers several easy gullies and buttress routes.
    Little and Great Carrs are easily accessible from the Three Shires Stone on Wrynose Pass. Follow the ridge of Wet Side Edge, then drop

down to the foot of Great Carrs. If Wrynose is blocked with snow, approach from Little Langdale via Greenburn, or go somewhere else. **Descent** is best down the snow basin at the left end of the crag. In poor visibility, locating the correct route is difficult.

The gullies are obvious and do not warrant individual descriptions but are worth a visit. The two longer gullies start at the same point at the lowest point of the buttress. The slightly longer **Left Gully** (I/II, 200m) curves left, while the right-hand **Middle Gully** (I/II, 190m) is more direct. **Right Gully** (I/II) is the shorter distinct gully starting higher to the right.

Various options are also possible up the buttresses. The two outlined here give some unimaginative climbing without any real difficulties. **Left-Hand Buttress** (I, 180m, 1998) is followed from its lowest point without any real problems. **Central Buttress** (I, 180m, 1998) takes a nondescript line up the central buttress. Several other similar routes have been climbed.

Rob Jones on the first ascent of **Further from the Edge** *(IV), Steel Edge (photo: Richard Jones)*

ESKDALE

Situated in the south-west corner of the Lake District, Eskdale has little to interest the winter climber unless Arctic conditions grip the region, in which case some water courses freeze. However, if that is the case, you probably won't be able to get to the valley! Please see the map 'Langdale and Wasdale' on pages 42–3.

The first two falls are found in north-facing gills on the south side of the valley. They are easily reached from the main road along the valley bottom, and are both only about a kilometre from the Woolpack Inn at Boot.

Stanley Force   **60m IV (4)** ★ **Early 1970s**
This lies above Dalegarth Station at a lowly 140m. When approaching from the west, use a car park south of the main road (NY 171 002). Follow the track up to the waterfall (NY 174 995). During a prolonged freeze this gives three pitches, the first being the crux, with 15m of vertical ice. A further 35m of climbing can be had if the gill is followed a little further.

Birker Force   **60m III (4)** ★★ **Early 1970s**
Further along the south side of the valley from *Stanley Force* (NY 188 999, alt. 200m), this waterfall has been known to freeze in exceptional conditions.

East of *Birker Force*, and due south of the cattle grid at the foot of Hardknott Pass, is a gill that is not named on the map. This is **Harter Fell Gill** (200m, II/III, early 1970s), the first gill which is encountered on the left when following the Harter Fell track from Jubilee Bridge (the bridge situated just west of the cattle grid). There is a lot of good ice bouldering on the fellside just west of this gill.

Heading north into Upper Eskdale, **Scale Force** (early 1970s, NY 213 024, alt. 150m) can give nearly a kilometre of falls in steps with easier ice between them (II/III).

Cam Spout Crag

(NY 215 055)
Alt. 520m East facing

A rambling crag overlooking the Great Moss in Upper Eskdale. It can be approached from Eskdale by following the path by the river, starting at the foot of Hardknott Pass. Alternatively a shorter, but steeper approach may be made from Wasdale, over Mickledore and down to the Great Moss. Either way is quite a trek.

Cam Spout Crag is home to rare alpine plants – please climb here only in truly frozen conditions (see the chapter 'Winter Climbing and Nature Conservation').

Peregrine Gully
130m I/II

The gully bounding the crag on its right. Snow for a short way leads to ice pitches up the gully bed before a final steepening. Avoid some of this by climbing onto a rib on the left leading to the summit ridge.

Slightly further north is the waterfall of:

Cam Spout
45m II/III

This fall on How Beck lies next to the Mickledore path (NY 217 058, alt. 520m) and comes into condition after a longish freeze. The main pitch can be linked with a route on Scafell if you've walked up from Eskdale and are quick (or don't mind a return in the dark!).

Dave Rogers having a wonderful day out on Cam Spout *(II/III), Eskdale (Photo: Dave Rogers Collection)*

LITTLE NARROW COVE

This secluded little cove is found at the head of Eskdale, between *Ill Crag* and Scafell Pike. Although it faces south-east over Eskdale, from which it can be approached, it is in fact easier to approach it from Wasdale over the Scafell Pike, dropping down to the head of the cove (only 200m from the summit of Scafell Pike).

Chambers Crag
(NY 217 072)
Alt. 850m North facing

Chambers Crag is situated at the head of Little Narrow Cove towards its western (Scafell Pike) side. An easy Grade I gully leading to the left-hand side of the crag may contain good neve if you are lucky. The crag has a large sloping ledge system running about 7m above its base and slanting rightwards to a pinnacle on the right-hand side of the crag.

Ema Ho   100m IV (4) ★ 1996
A route following a prominent turfy break in the centre of the crag and a snow bay slightly to the left of its centre. The name is Tibetan meaning 'It is sacred' and it has been touted as the highest route in England.
1   40m. A compact wall guards the approach to a long ledge running the length of the lower section of crag; surmount this and belay in the centre.
2   60m. The steep break is climbed to an obvious snow bay; belay where possible, then reach the top.

Chambers Pinnacle   110m IV 2006
A traverse of the ledge system running along the lower portion of crag and up behind the pinnacle.
1   30m. Climb easily up through the lower wall to gain the ledge system.
2   40m (4). Follow the ramp rightwards to a steep rocky step 10m below the top of the pinnacle and belay behind it. (It is possible to escape easily by traversing off at this point.)
3   40m (4). From the belay behind the pinnacle, traverse about 10m right to below a large flake. Climb up to the flake, which marks the

start of a rising right-to-left traverse on ledges across the wall. Climb until right of a bottomless groove and then follow a fainter turfy groove for 15m to the top of the crag.

Chambers Ramp   80m I 2006

An obvious ramp-line rising from left to right across the base of the crag, with one small step in the middle. With care this makes a useful **descent** from the right side of the crag.

Ill Crag   (NY 221 072)
Alt. 740m South-west facing

Ill Crag is situated near the head of Little Narrow Cove on its east side, situated opposite to but lower than Chambers Crag.

Big Question   150m IV (4) 1996

The line is shaped like an eponymous question mark. Answer it by starting from snow at the highest point of the base of the crag, just to the right of a gully on the left side of the crag.

1   20m. Climb the steep gully on the left of the crag.
2   20m. Traverse right and climb up through a rock barrier.
3   40m. Move up to a pillar and corner on the right, and make easy moves to a belay further right.
4   30m. Steep turf leads to a belay.
5   40m. The final curl of the question. Move gradually up and left to finish.

Big Answer   130m III 1999

This rather vague response starts to the right of the *Big Question*, between it and more broken ground. Follow the line of least resistance up turf and ice, avoiding the *Big Question* on its right for its entire length.

Ill Gully   130m II 2006

The prominent gully on the right-hand side of the crag. Apart from an awkward chockstone at about one-third height and a choice of finishes, there is little else to tax mind or body.

WASDALE

Situated in the western Lake District, Wasdale provides the easiest access to *Scafell* and its excellent winter climbing. *Scafell* is described in the current FRCC rock climbing guide as 'A cold, wet crag that's miles from the road.' What more could one ask for in a winter venue? And being the highest climbing in England, the main crag on *Scafell* produces some of the most reliable winter conditions in the district in the form of classic gullies and more modern mixed routes. Please see the map 'Langdale and Wasdale' on pages 42–3.

But though *Scafell* may be the jewel in the crown, there are other good crags accessible from the valley. The gullies of *Wasdale Screes* in particular can give some of the longest water-ice climbs in the region.

In summer, most people approach Wasdale over the passes of Wrynose and Hard Knott, but even in a mild winter this is not really an option, though Ulpha Pass is often drivable if the steep road out of Ulpha village is ice free. A safer but longer alternative is to take the A595 coast road, leaving it before or after Holmrook for Stanton Bridge, Nether Wasdale, then go along Wast Water to the head of the valley. If travelling from the north, leave the A595 at Gosforth.

The crags are described anti-clockwise around the valley.

Wasdale Screes

(NY 155 043)
Alt. 260m North facing

These large broken crags above the screes at the foot of the south-eastern end of Wast Water are seamed by a series of gullies named alphabetically from left to right. As the climbs start at a low altitude, a prolonged period of frost is required before they come into condition, but when they do, they give classic water-ice routes.

The shortest approach is by the footpath from opposite Woodhow Farm (NY 140 042), at the west end of the lake. There is limited parking here or at the YHA at Wasdale Hall (NY 145 045) further along the road.

Wasdale Screes are very important for rare alpine plants – there are really rare things here, especially on the south-west end nearer Whin

Wasdale Screes

1	Great (B) Gully	III
2	Right-Hand Branch	V
3	The Ramp	II
4	The Ramp Left-Hand	II/III
5	C Gully	IV
6	D Gully	II
7	E Gully	II

(Photo: Al Phizacklea)

Wasdale

Rigg; generally they can be found on the most unstable and loose bits. Please only climb here in truly frozen conditions (climbing on the buttresses is to be discouraged at any time – see the chapter on 'Winter Climbing and Nature Conservation').

The climbs are described from **right** to **left** as approached from the west, with the pump house at the end of the lake serving as a convenient reference point. (NB the gullies have been wrongly identified in a number of previous summer and winter guides and have now been named correctly.) The easiest **descent** is to gain the path running along the top of the crag and follow it south-west, over Whin Rigg summit, and continue down the east side of *Greathall Gill* to the west (right, looking up) of the main crag.

Greathall Gill   Early 1970s
Situated well to the right of the main crags, this tree-filled gully occasionally freezes to give two steep ice pitches of 10 to 15m about halfway up the gill, with tree belays at the top.

The iced slabs below the west end of the *Screes* offer a good place for beginners to practise technique.

E Gully   130m II Early 1970s
The rightmost of two shallow gullies at the west end of the crag, directly above the pump house. This tends to take less drainage than the major lines so can be a bit thin.

D Gully   130m II Early 1970s
Approximately 30m left is another, slightly better defined gully. Both these gullies open out to easy ground well before the top of the crag is reached.

C Gully   230m IV ★★ 1963
The prominent deep cleft originally named by the Victorian pioneers: the first of the major gullies reached from the right.
1   50m. Short ice pitches lead to a steep corner.
2   35m. Take the corner direct, or alternatively traverse right to a ramp which leads back to the gully bed after 10m. Continue to below the big ice pitch and belay on the left.
3   20m. Climb the centre of the ice, moving left at the top.
4   20m. Amble easily up the gully bed and climb a short crack; this

can be avoided on the left. Continue up to belay in the amphitheatre.

5   30m. The frozen waterslide; climb this, and easy snow, to a peg belay below the final pitch.

6   25m. The final steep ice pitch. Surmount a bulge near the top to pull into the gully above.

7   50m. Easy snow leads to a belay.

The Ramp   230m II Early 1970s

Starting just right of *Great Gully*, and approximately 70m to the left of *C Gully*, a steep ramp curves up through the buttress to the right of *Great Gully*. It forms several ice pitches interspersed with snow and old bits of aeroplane wreckage, and finishes near the top of *C Gully*: the first pitch is the steepest. The route has been used as a descent by those competent, but is not recommended.

The Ramp Left-Hand   230m II/III Early 1970s

Follow *The Ramp* for 2 or 3 pitches until a hanging gully forming an obvious drainage line appears on the left (120m). Climb the short icefall into a narrow chimney (crux), and follow this into the deeper gully bed. Follow the gully to the top (110m).

Great (B) Gully   240m III ★★ 1892

This, the biggest of the gullies, contains the huge *Amphitheatre* in its upper part. Most of the pitches are interspersed with scrambling.

1   35m. Two short icefalls and scrambling lead up to where the subsidiary gully runs up right.

2   20m. Steepening ice leads to a bulge and a final pull over to belay.

3   45m. More scrambling leads to the *Waterslide Pitch*, and sometimes a further small pitch.

4   25m. Easy ground leads into the *Amphitheatre*.

5   50m. Continue up to the left branch, passing two more ice pitches, to where the gully narrows once again.

6   10m. Steep ice is bridged to belay below the final crack.

7   55m. The final steep 10m pitch leads to a snow slope which is followed to the summit.

Right-Hand Branch   100m V (4) ★★★ 1978

The magnificent icefall to the right of the *Amphitheatre*, if complete, gives a stupendous 90m of continuous ice. After the first pitch, rock

belays are available but are poor in the upper reaches where ice screws may be preferable. Once in the *Amphitheatre*, the route can be seen.

1   30m. An easy gully line leads up to the start. Follow the steepening ice cone towards the overhang which is turned on the left; belay on the left.
2   40m. Move back right to the centre of the icefall and climb straight up over bulges. A poor rock belay can be found on the left, or use ice screws.
3   30m. Climb diagonally right for 15m then up to where the angle eases.

Chimney Finish   **65m II/III 1984/5**

This lies to the right of the *Great Gully* ordinary finish, between this and the finish of the *Right-Hand Branch*. It is best approached from the foot of the *Right-Hand Branch*, passing over vegetation and an icy groove. Struggle your way up the steep chimney.

A Gully   **160m II Early 1970s**

The next gully lies 150m left of *Great Gully* and immediately left of the largest buttress. This wide open scree gully contains just two awkward steps, and may be used as a descent if care is taken.

Seven Pitch Gully   **260m II Early 1970s**

About 150m left of *A Gully*, this is the furthest left (east) of the gullies and gives several interesting short steep ice pitches in magnificent scenery. The route is obvious in its lower reaches: at the top go left for the normal finish, or take the wide gully to the right for a pleasant alternative ice pitch.

Variation Icefall   **III Early 1970s**

At about half-height, steep ice on the right wall leads to a traverse left. An awkward descent then allows the main gully to be rejoined. Alternatively continue on up rightwards to the summit. A sheep track can also be traversed right at this point, and a descent down an icy ramp leads to *A Gully*.

The small crag of **Low Adam Crag** (NY 158 047) lies below the *Screes* at an altitude of about 260m and faces north-west, opposite the

Eileen Clark on Great Gully *(III), Wasdale Screes (Photo: Syd Clark)*

point where the upper road into Wasdale reaches the lakeside. The following climb is located about 100m above it.

Juniper Ridge   **130m I/II Early 1970s**
The climb starts in a gully left of, and below, a big pinnacle. Under good snow conditions it provides an interesting corniced ridge route. From the gully, gain the ridge and pass the large pinnacle on its right. Continue up the meandering ridge to the summit.

SCAFELL MASSIF

Scafell and its associated crags are best approached from the car park at the north end of Wast Water, passing Brackenclose (FRCC hut) and ascending Brown Tongue. This route passes *Black Crag* (to the right of the path) before reaching the north-west facing combe of Hollow Stones. *Pike Crag* stands on the left-hand (east) side of this combe under Scafell Pike. The main crag of *Scafell* is on the right-hand (west) side, with the distinctive *Shamrock Buttress* lower down to its right. The *East Buttress of Scafell* is hidden round to the right, over Mickledore, the col at the back of combe.

All of these mountain crags can be gained from other valleys, but such approaches are much longer and harder. From **Borrowdale** take the Corridor Route via Styhead Tarn. From **Eskdale**, go via *Cam Spout*, and from Langdale via Angle Tarn and the summit of Scafell Pike.

Black Crag   (NY 201 070) Alt. 600m North-west facing

Most people dash past this crag in a headlong rush for greater things on *Scafell*. As such it is usually quiet, while its larger neighbour can see queues forming for routes. It will be seen to the right of the path at the top of Brown Tongue, the steep part of the approach from Wasdale. Due to its westerly aspect and lower altitude it is less often in condition than *Scafell*, but little time need be lost in ascertaining this either on the

*Mark Hill on Black Crag Grooves (IV), Black Crag, Wasdale
(Photo: Colin Wells)*

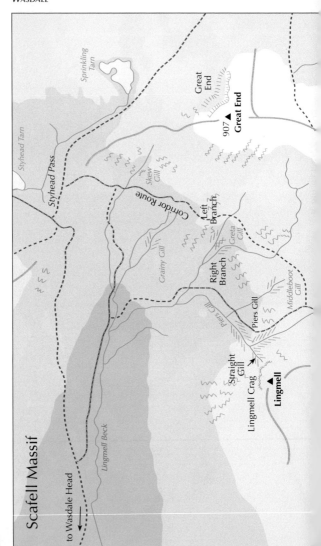

Scafell Massif

to Wasdale Head

Lingmell Beck

Sprinkling Tarn

Styhead Tarn

Styhead Pass

Corridor Route

Skew Gill

Great End

907 ▲ **Great End**

Grainy Gill

Left Branch

Greta Gill

Right Branch

Middleboot Gill

Piers Gill

Piers Gill

Straight Gill

Lingmell Crag

▲ **Lingmell**

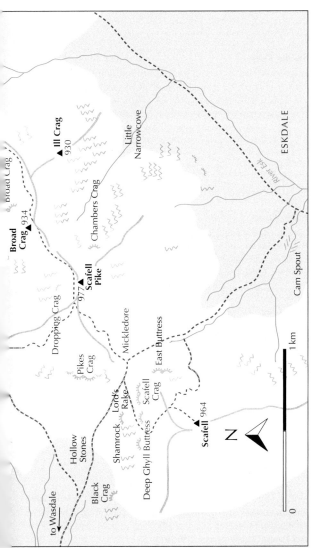

ascent or on the descent, if another route is fancied.

The routes are described from left to right.

Sinister Ridge 150m III (4) ★★ 1984

Leave something in reserve; the difficulties are at the top. Start about 15m up and right of the lowest point of the left-hand ridge.

1   25m. Climb a short wall with difficulty (if you're in luck it may be banked out) to easier ground and a belay at the foot of a groove.
2   30m. Follow the groove and continue up in the same line.
3   20m. Continue up the wall above the leaning flake (not as bad as it looks) to the foot of another wall.
4   25m. Make a traverse left, crossing a groove with some difficulty (crux).
5   50m. Climb up a shallow gully on the left to finish.

Black Shiver 50m III 1998

Start at a well-hidden gully/chimney tucked in on the right of *Sinister Ridge* and down and left of an obvious pinnacle high on the crag, from which an abseil descent to the foot of the route can be made.

1   25m. Climb the gully which has a steep right wall.
2   25m. Climb the ice smear on the left.

Black Crag Grooves 130m IV (4) ★ 1996

This route follows the line of grooves running down from the summit of the crag. As the route is mainly on vegetation it is only worth trying if fully frozen.

1   45m. Easy-angled turf leads to where the crag steepens.
2   25m. Follow a turf-lined groove to a chimney which is quit for a leftward-slanting ramp, then go up over a rock outcrop to a poor belay.
3   20m. Follow ice in the back of a steep groove and surmount the bulge to easier ground and a spike belay.
4   20m. Move left to another steep grassy groove, with the bulge at half height this time.
5   20m. Follow easy ground to the summit.

First of Many 120m III (3) 2005

This route starts right of the central line of *Black Crag Grooves* and crosses that route. Start at a leftwards-slanting groove near the centre, and about 50m left of the start of *Dexter Slab*.

1   30m. Follow the obvious groove, hard at first, to gain the leftwards-slanting turf groove which traverses to a large belay ledge. Poor anchors.

2   25m. Climb the wall behind the belay to a large stepped groove which goes first leftwards and then rightwards to a large ledge. Bomber belay.

3   25m. Climb the short awkward corner behind the belay and move easily to a left-slanting snow rake leading to a good belay in a large bay.

4   35m. Climb the weakness in the wall behind the belay to gain a groove system which is followed for 30m to a poor exposed belay.

5. 35m. Step left into another groove which narrows at about 15m and which provides some thin moves before the groove funnels out and is followed to the top of the crag. Good belays.

Dexter Slab   60m III 1984

Up on the right flank of the crag is a prominent gully below a buttress. This route takes a line up the centre of the slab below the gully, starting from the bottom of the gully. The difficulties can be avoided.

1   30m. Move right to some blocks after 5m, then climb the slab by the best line.

2   30m. A traverse leads up and right over a large flake to a terrace. The wall above is turned on the right.

Black Crag Gully   30m I/II 1984

A descent route in summer, the gully runs up diagonally left from the foot of *Hole and Corner Gully*, the short prominent gully up on the right of the crag.

Variation   IV

A vertical column of ice about 15m high can form about halfway up the gully.

Hole and Corner Gully   50m II

The obvious gully up on the right side of the crag.

Hole and Corner Gully Icefall   30m III ★

The curtain of ice forming on the left wall and running up left out of *Hole and Corner Gully* gives a good pitch.

SCAFELL

Two of the finest Lakeland mountain crags are to be found on the east and north sides of this mountain, *East Buttress* and *Scafell Crag* itself. The rounded shape of the *East Buttress* does not encourage good winter climbing conditions, and little has been done in the way of complete ascents on the crag. *Scafell Crag* to the west of Mickledore has two contrasting sections. The main crag gives some intimidating modern mixed routes on the buttresses, with classic gullies in between. The three gills are *Deep Ghyll* (the easiest on the right), with the Scafell Pinnacle between it and *Steep Ghyll* (the central of the three), and *Moss Ghyll* to its left.

The more broken ground of *Scafell Shamrock* to right of this area is separated from the main cliff by *Lord's Rake* which starts at the right end of the main crag and runs up diagonally right to a small col. Running off left from this first section is the impressive gap of *Deep Ghyll*. After crossing another small col, *Lord's Rake* emerges from a steep slope onto open fellside. This used to provide a convenient descent route but, at the time of writing (2006), it has suffered a series of rockfalls, and is probably best avoided at present. The ground to the right of the *Shamrock* takes much drainage, which can form easier climbs which complement those on the main crag. These generally consist of good ice pitches separated by easy-angled snow. The lines described can often be combined in a number of ways.

The best approach is from Wasdale, up the obvious path on the right-hand side of Brown Tongue. For other approaches see above.

Descent: If descending back to the base of the climb there are a number of choices. The safest but longest are described first. For routes finishing near Mickledore or on the *East Buttress*, descend via Fox Tarn or, more carefully, via *Broad Stand*. This latter requires a certain amount of zigzagging past rocky steps. When just above Mickledore, move to a large boulder perched over to the left. A thread can be found at its base which allows the short abseil to Mickledore to be made. For routes finishing on the main crag, either descend as described above, or downclimb *Deep Ghyll* – the steep chockstone in the middle section generally gives the only real difficulties. Alternatively, part-way

Bryan McGowan at the start of the steep ice on Hole and Corner Gully Icefall *(III), Black Crag, Wasdale (Photo: Glenn Wilks)*

Wasdale

121

down *Deep Ghyll* below *Great Chimney* follow the exposed *West Wall Traverse* into the lower part of *Lord's Rake* (but see warning above) and descend this, or go over the col and carefully descend the broken ground to the right of *Scafell Shamrock*.

Scafell Crag

(NY 209 068)
Alt. 790m North facing

The routes are described from left to right. The routes start from **Rake's Progress** (I, 1908), a narrow shelf running along the base of the crag about 10m up, which can give Grade I climbing and can be easily gained from the foot of *Moss Ghyll*, or by a more exposed traverse from Mickledore.

North Climb   10m III 1899
A short scrappy climb starting 10m right of the highest point of *Rake's Progress*. A short wall leads to a square-cut recess; move left to abseil off, or continue up chimneys and across slabs to the summit.

Keswick Brothers' Climb had an ascent in winter (1910) but its grade is not known. It is VD in summer and its description is in the FRCC Scafell guidebook.

Tricouni Slab   75m IV 1986
This section of the crag has a series of right-facing slabs. This is the left-most slab, to the left of *Botterill's*. Well-protected technical climbing. Start from *Rake's Progress*.
1   20m (4). From an overhung recess, ascend the narrow slab to a ledge on the summer route of *Keswick Brothers' Climb*. The left edge of the slab (*Keswick Brothers' Climb*) has also been climbed to the same belay.
2   15m (3). Climb the chimney at the left end of the ledge.
3   40m (4). Continue over ledges up rightwards to a hollow, and finish up the chimney/gully.

Botterill's Slab   95m V (6) ★★★ 1984
A modern classic which is often in condition. The obvious leftward-

Impressive winter conditions on Lord's Rake, *Scafell*
(Photo: Martin Armitage)

Scafell

1a	Rake's Progress	I
1b	Lord's Rake	
2	Botterill's Slab	V
3	Moss Ghyll	IV
4	Steep Ghyll	V
5	The Girdle Traverse	VII
6	Deep Ghyll	I/II
7	Deep Ghyll Integrale	III
8	West Wall Traverse	I

*(Photo: Dave Willis –
Copyright FRCC)*

slanting slab starts from *Rake's Progress*. The slab is actually climbed via the corner on its right, the ascent being facilitated by icy and mossy remnants, with protection available on the right wall. Difficulties depend on the amount of ice.

1   20m. Climb the short chimney to the base of the slab.
2   25m. Climb the corner of the slab above, the meat of the climb.
3   30m. The short wall above leads to a wide chimney. Move up to an open gully on the left.
4   20m. Climb the open gully.

Before the loss of the *Great Flake* chockstone an ascent of **Central Buttress** was claimed (1986). The *Flake Crack* was climbed without crampons, and the ascent took place over two consecutive days with the climbers returning to warm beds in the valley overnight. Whilst this was a good effort by the climbers involved, the consensus is that it can not really be considered a true winter ascent if crampons were unnecessary and the route was not completed in one single push, even if over only two days. In any event, the loss of the *Flake* chockstone has completely altered this section of the climb, possibly rendering it unclimbable in winter. Aspirant single-day ascentionists are referred to the FRCC Scafell guidebook for a full description.

Moss Ghyll Grooves   105m V (6) ★ 1985

Not being a natural drainage line, heavy ice build-up is never going to be likely on this summer classic, and time has shown that it doesn't come into condition often. The route starts out of *Moss Ghyll*, the obvious major gully right of the large sweep of walls that contains *Central Buttress*. It is the lowest of the major diagonal lines to the right of *Central Buttress*.

1   20m. From *Rake's Progress*, climb about 20m up *Moss Ghyll*, or easier via the wall to the right, to the first large ledge at the start of the sloping ramp/groove on the left of the gully.
2   20m. Climb the groove, passing a bulge.
3   20m. Continue up the corner above and up the narrowing slab, then pull right into the next groove. Regain the corner of the groove when possible, and follow this to a traverse right onto the ledge at the start of the next groove.
4   25m. Climb the second slab, making the most of iced cracks.
5   20m. Move left, and step up to follow the easier gully to the summit ridge.

Harvest Crunch   **120m VII (9) ★★ 1987**

One of the hardest routes in the area, and still unrepeated. The summer line was freed of aid only after the first winter ascent. It follows the second diagonal line running left out of *Moss Ghyll*, about 50m up the gill, and opposite *Tennis Court Wall*. It takes a line up the right side of the prominent slab of the summer route *Slab and Groove*.

1   50m. Climb *Moss Ghyll* to a ledge at the start of the second diagonal line running out of the left side of the gill.

2   25m. Follow the right corner of the slab to the first roof. The climbing really starts now! Make a long reach with axes and a hard pull over the roof on ice. Climb to the second roof, and step left with difficulty under the roof to thin moves on the slab leading to the belay (crux).

3   45m. If you've anything left, follow the groove, the second pitch of the summer route *Slab and Groove*. This becomes easier with height.

Moss Ghyll   **135m IV (5) ★★★ 1893**

This is the large gully line dividing the *Central* and *Pisgah Buttresses*. The route follows the gully to an amphitheatre from where several alternative exits are possible, the *Collie Exit* being the classic of the district. The route is graded for well-iced conditions which have not occurred readily in recent years. It will probably feel a grade harder in lean conditions; then again you may just be climbing badly.

1   30m. Starting from *Rake's Progress*, climb the gully to a cave pitch after 10m. This is turned on the right by a short chimney, before traversing back into the gully bed.

2   20m. Climb up on the right of the narrow chimney/crack and continue up steep snow to belay below *Tennis Court Wall*.

3   25m. Climb the cracked wall on the right to a ledge. A delicate traverse leads back left and up to belay below a massive chockstone.

4   20m. In exceptional climbing conditions it is possible to climb the wall on the left and go diagonally left into an amphitheatre. More usual, however, is to follow the summer route under the chockstone to an exit through a 'window' on the left. Make a delicate traverse across the wall, the infamous *Collie Step*, and up into the amphitheatre. Belay and decide on which exit you want (see below).

Collie Exit   **40m IV 1893**

The standard finish at the same grade. Climb directly up the slabs on the left for about 10m to a traverse left to a short chimney. This leads to the ridge.

Barton's Exit   **40m V (4)**

Follow the *Collie Exit* to where it traverses left then continue up the steep slabby corner above the overlap.

Mechanical Orange   **80m VIII (8) 1987**

This poorly protected climb follows the summer line of *Clockwork Orange* from the amphitheatre of *Moss Ghyll*. On the first ascent the second unclipped from the belay and stood on the chockstone ready to jump to take up slack in the event of a leader fall. Still unrepeated.

On the left of the amphitheatre, and roughly parallel with the slabs of the *Collie Exit*, a thin slab runs out left from *Collier's Chimney*.

1   40m. From 2m up *Colliers's Chimney*, follow the slabby groove left to where the wall steepens. Move left along a narrow ledge, or a flake below this, to a belay in the corner.

2   40m. Follow the corner to the top, taking a line on the left wall to avoid the thrutch where the gully narrows.

Collier's Chimney   **35m V (5) ★★★ 1984**

The true continuation finish to *Moss Ghyll* is much harder.

Follow the line of the deeply cut chimney on the right of the amphitheatre with some difficult chockstones. Under good conditions the wall right of the chimney gives an excellent bold pitch rejoining the chimney near the top.

Pisgah

Pisgah Buttress has *Moss Ghyll* on its left and *Steep Ghyll* to its right.

Pisgah Buttress Direct   **155m V (5) ★★★ 1937**

This classic summer Severe also makes an excellent winter route and is one of the first of the mixed climbs to come into condition. Start at a chimney on the right of the buttress (the start of the summer route *Bos'n's Buttress*).

1   20m. Climb the chimney and step onto a ledge on the left. A more direct start up the front of the buttress is also possible.

2   30m. Climb the walls above, trending right to a belay on the large crevasse overlooking the lower part of *Steep Ghyll*.

3   15m. Make a difficult traverse left to a large ledge close to *Moss Ghyll* with an open corner above.

4   30m. Climb the corner to a belay behind a pinnacle overlooking *Steep Ghyll*.

Wasdale

Scafell – The Pinnacle Area *(Photo: Bert Jenkins)*

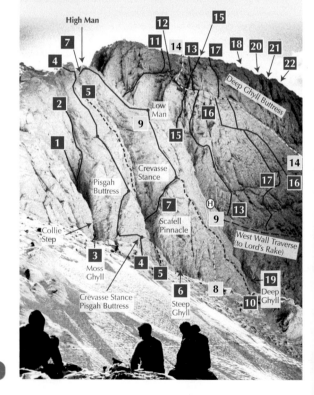

5   30m. Climb the pinnacle above, and trend left to gain a large snow-field.

6   30m. The buttress above is slightly easier than that below.

Restless Natives   125m VI (6) 1986

This route takes the line of slabs and ramp systems on the right-hand edge of the buttress, following approximately the summer line of *Bos'n's Buttress*. Start up the chimney of *Steep Ghyll Direct Start*. An overall sustained route.

1   30m. Climb the chimney to the deep crack-line on the left. Follow this with some difficult moves onto the ledge.

2   15m. Move right from the ledge, and climb the steep crack to the right of the arete (hard) and the ramp above to a belay.

3   20m. Move up and right to a twisting crack and follow this, and a short wall, to belay behind a pinnacle.

4   30m. Climb the wall above to a leftwards-trending gangway leading to a belay below the headwall.

5   30m. Move to easy ground on the left.

Bridge of Sighs   175m V (5) 1986

This climb follows the continuous corner system which runs up left from the easy snow at the top of pitch 1 of *Steep Ghyll*.

1   50m. Climb the first pitch of *Steep Ghyll* to the easy-angled snow. Belay in the top left corner of the large sloping ledge.

2   25m. The slabs on the left lead to a belay on thin blade pegs level with the top of the gully on the right.

3   35m. Bridge across the gully, rather wildly, and continue up steeply in a direct line to the ridge.

4   65m. Easy ground leads to the top.

Steep Ghyll Grooves   115m V (6) 1986

The grooves overlooking the narrow gully of *Steep Ghyll*.

1   50m. Climb *Steep Ghyll* and belay where the gully walls close in near the start of the main pitch.

2   15m. Climb the left wall of the gully to a niche (blade peg runner). Move right 5m and up to a ledge at the bottom of a chimney, using a peg for aid to gain the ledge.

3   50m. The chimney and groove lead to easy slabs at the top.

Steep Ghyll   **210m V (4) ★★ 1891**

Probably the first Grade V in the British Isles, if not the World! The main pitches give fine sustained climbing with just adequate protection – if you can find it. Either start up a groove from *Rake's Progress* in line with the gully or, slightly easier, traverse right from the start of *Moss Ghyll* to reach the start of the first pitch.

1   60m. Easy climbing on snow leads to a large snowy ledge or snow-field and the narrowing gully walls of the main pitch tucked in on the top right-hand side.

2   60m. The ice pitch on the left leads to easy snow leading up between the constricting walls of the gully to a stance at the foot of a bottleneck chimney.

3   55m. The crux pitch and a long lonely lead. Climb the chimney for 12m (possible poor stance for those with 50m ropes – buried wide crack up on left) and continue up the steep groove, passing two bulging sections, to the shallow gully leading to the *Jordan Gap* between the *Pinnacle* and the rest of the mountain.

4   35m. From the gap, move left to easy ground.

Direct Start   **55m V (5) ★★ 1963**

To the left of the normal start to *Steep Ghyll* is a deep chimney, steep at its top.

1a   20m. A steep icy step leads to the back of the chimney, where the gully steepens.

2a   35m. The wall is climbed on frozen vegetation and cracks. Step right at the top to easy snow at the start of the main pitch of *Steep Ghyll*. Finish up *Steep Ghyll*.

Scafell Pinnacle

This buttress to the right of *Steep Ghyll* forms the pinnacle which towers over the cleft of *Deep Ghyll* to its right. The majority of the routes here reach the top of the main buttress known as the *Low Man*. The fine *Knife Edge Arete* leads to *High Man*, the true summit of the buttress. **Descent** from here is possible by descending a short wall on the left to the *Jordan Gap*, from where a traverse left leads one to the Scafell summit plateau.

Low Man by the Right Wall of Steep Ghyll   **230m V (5) 1995**

This starts high up in *Steep Ghyll* where the gully narrows and twists left. The route follows a parallel line of grooves and slabs to the right of *Steep Ghyll*.

1 & 2 120m. The first two pitches of *Steep Ghyll* – to where the chimney narrows.

3   35m. Follow a short wall on the right to a good ledge, then a short chimney on the right of some slabs to a belay.

4   35m. Make difficult moves right to gain the groove, which is followed to easier ground and the *Knife Edge Arete*.

5   40m. Follow the *Arete* to *High Man*.

Slingsby's Chimney Route   245m IV (5) ★★ 1899

Many of the routes up the *Pinnacle* meet at the base of *Slingsby's Chimney* and must climb it to gain the summit. This route offers the quickest and easiest approach to the chimney for those eager to get to grips with it.

1 & 2 120m. The first two pitches of *Steep Ghyll* – to where the chimney narrows.

3   40m. Follow *Low Man by the Right Wall* to the ledge, then traverse across to the crevasse at the foot of the chimney.

4   45m. Climb a short wall, then grapple up the difficult bulging chimney (crux) to easier ground – front crawl seems to offer the best approach.

5   40m. Finish up the *Arete* to *High Man*.

The next feature is the shallow but defined corner of *Hopkinson's Gully*, which starts up the centre of the *Pinnacle*.

Hopkinson's Gully   155m VI ★★ 1986

Start about 10m to the right of *Steep Ghyll*, at a groove.

1   30m (6). Climb a short wall with difficulty to gain access to the groove. Sustained climbing up the groove (Friend at half-height) eases, with a move right just before the belay.

2   40m (4). The groove leads to the deep crack gained by an awkward step. Climb up this to belay below *Slingsby's Chimney*.

3   45m (5). Thrutch up the chimney to easier ground and follow this to the top of *Low Man*.

4   40m (3). The *Knife Edge Arete* to *High Man* with a descent to the gap.

Moonbathing   140m VI ★★★ 1986

The route follows a line up right of *Hopkinson's Gully* to a ledge overlooking *Deep Ghyll*, the site of the historic *Hopkinson's Cairn*.

Wasdale

Duncan Richards on first ascent of Moonbathing *(VI), Scafell, in 1986
(Photo: Al Phizacklea)*

1 30m (6). Follow the first pitch of *Hopkinson's Gully* to the belay.
2 30m (5). Start up the groove on the left for 2m (*Jones's Route
   Direct*). From a runner placement, traverse right nearly 15m to a
   ledge below a corner. Climb this to the ledge of *Hopkinson's Cairn*
   with a poor belay, best on the left.
3 40m (4). The arete above is climbed on its left-hand side to a block.
   Move right up a ramp, then back left, to an easier line running left
   across the buttress. Easier ground above leads to *Low Man*.
4 40m (3). The arete to *High Man*.

Jones's Route Direct   **65m (to the crevasse below
                                   Slingsby's Chimney) VII (7) ★★ 1984**
Starting from a slab overlooking *Deep Ghyll*, at the bottom right-hand
side of the *Pinnacle*, this route reached the crevasse at the bottom of
Slingsby's Chimney. The only known ascent to date was not complete to
the top of the pinnacle as the first ascentionists abseiled into the easier
lower pitches of *Steep Ghyll* from the crevasse. Sadly the route is rarely
in condition.

1   25m. Climb the slab on the right-hand side of the pinnacle to gain the gangway above with difficulty. Follow the thin slab diagonally left with some tenacious moves.
2   25m. The corner above leads to a traverse left to a belay in *Hopkinson's Gully*.
3   15m. As for *Hopkinson's Gully*. Follow the corner above to belay at the crevasse below *Slingsby's Chimney*.

Deep Ghyll   200m I/II 1886

This large gully, starting a few metres up *Lord's Rake*, cuts deeply back into the mountain. Two large chockstones must be overcome in the lower pitches, but a snowy winter can see these pitches all but obliterated. If they are impassable, an alternative start giving access to routes higher up the gill is via the **West Wall Traverse** (I, 1906/7). The start to this lies up *Lord's Rake,* at the col behind *Shamrock Buttress,* and traverses into the *Deep Ghyll* above the chockstones. Although a popular path in summer it can be difficult to locate under heavy snow. Great care should be taken as the traverse line passes between difficult ground both above and below, so needs to be located correctly. Also see comments above (page 121) about the dangerous state of *Lord's Rake*.

To climb the gully direct, climb snow to the cave below the first chockstone. Surmounting this on the right is usually the easiest option (15m). Above, straightforward snow slopes lead to a smaller chockstone (65m). The easy ground above this is where the *West Wall Traverse* comes in from the right.

Age Concern   110m VI ★★ 1986

This thin and technical climb is really a winter ascent of *Jones's Route Direct from Deep Ghyll*, which follows the obvious curving crack on the left wall of *Deep Ghyll*, starting from just above the second chockstone and following a line to *Low Man*.
1   10m (2). Climb easily up to the foot of the crack.
2   30m (5). The crack is entered with difficulty and climbed to a snowy niche. Delicate moves left across slabs, and upwards, lead to a good spike runner and possible belay, or traverse left to another stance and belay on the arete.
3   20m (6). Move right and climb *Gibson's Chimney*, the continuation of the crack to the ridge.
4   50m (3). Climb the ridge with one awkward step to the top of *High Man*, then descend to the gap.

Centre Route   60m VI ★★ 1996

High up *Deep Ghyll*, the left wall below *High Man* forms an impressive slab topped with some overlaps. Starting from the junction *Deep Ghyll* and *Professor's Chimney*, this route follows the right-to-left rising diagonal summer line of *Jones and Collier's Climb* from *Deep Ghyll* to the large grassy recess, then ascends the overhung slab and the grass corner above to the summit of *High Man*. It catches the afternoon sun on clear days, so an early start is recommended. Start at the right corner of the slabs.

1   30m (6). From just above the right corner of the slab, make difficult and poorly protected moves to a diagonal leftwards traverse up the slabs and belay in the snowy recess at the top left of the slabs.

2   30m (4). *Low Man* can be easily reached up a short corner at the back of the recess: follow the *Knife Edge Arete* to *High Man*. But more fun can be had by following the overhung slabs up right to a ledge. Follow the grass corner (*Woodhead's Climb*) to the top of *High Man*.

There is a choice of exits from the head of *Deep Ghyll*. The main gill continues up easy snow slopes leading straight to the summit plateau. To the left are the following finishes:

New Professor's Chimney   50m II/III 1891

Start up the left-hand gully at the top of *Deep Ghyll*. Where this steepens, take the left fork, cutting steeply up behind the pinnacle to finish at *Jordan Gap*. Traverse left and round to the right to gain the summit.

Old Professor's Chimney   50m II ★ 1891

The true continuation finish to the chimney. Where the previous route takes a gully on the left, continue up to finish at a small bulge.

Slab Finish   35m II ★★

From below the bulge in *Old Professor's Chimney*, traverse right to an exposed finish up an iced slab.

Impunity Slabs   40m III ★ 1986

To the right of the *Slab Finish* to *Old Professor's* is a shallow corner: climb it.

The Girdle Traverse **275m VII ★★★ 2005**

Although this girdle starts at *Botterill's Slab*, as is traditional, it is described at the end of the relevant section. As it crosses *Central Buttress*, *Pisgah Buttress* and *Scafell Pinnacle*, you certainly get your money's worth. Although never technically desperate, the route contains a lot of sustained climbing, with several hard pitches towards the end, and – being a traverse – has to be protected for both leader and second, which can be time consuming. The only ascent to date was done with good neve on the ledges and took nine hours, with the ascentionists being rewarded with a fine sunset from the top of the pinnacle.

1   35m (6). Climb *Botterill's Slab* for 6m to a line of ledges on the right which lead diagonally to a narrow ledge. From its left end, climb a shallow corner to the left end of the *Oval*, the large ledge at the base of the *Great Flake*, which is reached by a delicate traverse right to where the ledge widens.

2   35m (5). From the right end of the *Oval*, downclimb and traverse right round a corner, then make a move up a slabby wall to a large turfy ledge. A short traverse right round an arete leads to the top of pitch 1 of *Moss Ghyll Grooves*. Downclimb this to the bed of *Moss Ghyll*.

3   35m (6). Climb the turfy wall to the right of the gill, heading for a prominent corner in the middle of the buttress. The lower portion of the corner is climbed to belay on a ledge, below the steep upper corner, which contains several good chockstones.

4   15m (5). Move rightwards along a block traverse line. Follow this to the right side of the buttress, and step down to a spike belay on the right of the buttress overlooking the *Direct Start to Steep Ghyll*.

5   10m (3). Move up snowy slabs and traverse right to belay at the top of the *Direct Start to Steep Ghyll*.

6   50m (4). Cross *Steep Ghyll* easily and climb to the start of its steep pitch. Climb the right wall of the gill to the *Crevasse*. Climb to the top of this and downclimb the other side to its base.

7   15m (7). Go back up the *Crevasse* to the first large chockstone and make a delicate traverse right (*Sansom's Traverse*) to *Hopkinson's Cairn*.

8   30m (8). Climb the corner to the left of the arete and step right onto a sloping shelf leading to a corner (*Bad Corner* of the summer rock route *Moss Ledge Direct*). Climb the corner with difficulty to a spike belay on the arete overlooking the corner of the summer line of *Jones's Route from Deep Ghyll*.

9   20m (8). From the belay, step down and climb across the thin wall above *Bad Corner* to the arete. Once round the arete, follow a wide crack and easier ground to *Low Man*. These are the summer lines of *Gibson's Traverse* and *Low Man from Hopkinson's Cairn*.

10   30m (3). Climb the *Knife Edge Arete* and continuation ridge to the top of *High Man*.

Deep Ghyll Buttress

This buttress bounding the top right-hand side of *Deep Ghyll* possesses some of the highest climbs in England. It is deeply cleaved by the prominent *Great Chimney*.

Upper Deep Ghyll Route   65m II ★ 1986

Start at a shallow groove 50m higher than the cleft of *Great Chimney*. Gain a left-to-right diagonal line running across the crag. The first 10m are the hardest.

Great Chimney   20m IV (4) 1986

The obvious wide cleft below the upper buttress. The chockstone at half-height is passed on the right by difficult but well-protected moves to easier climbing in the gully above.

Jacob's Ladder   70m V (6) 1999

The corner-groove to the right of *Great Chimney*.

1   35m. From just below *Great Chimney*, climb to a ledge on the right of the arete. Climb the corner at the back of the ledge to a sloping ledge overlooking *Great Chimney*.

2   35m. Use a flake to make a balancy move right and up to below an overhang, then back left into a sentry box. Climb the wall above overlooking the chimney.

The next two routes are on the section of buttress below *Great Chimney*. This has a deep chimney-crack in its lower section and a prominent left-facing corner running up its centre. The routes follow these lines.

West Wall Climb   70m IV (4) ★★ 1986

Start some 20m down to the right of *Great Chimney*, below a deep chimney on the lower section of the buttress.

Jon Westaway in deep snow on West Wall Traverse *(I), Scafell (Photo: Colin Wells)*

1   40m. Enter the deep chimney-crack with difficulty and wiggle upwards. From the top of the crack, move diagonally rightwards over short steep steps to belay in a vague bay.

2   30m. Climb a crack/groove on the left of the thin arete situated at the back of the bay. Move right and up to a steep wall. A swing right across the blank slab leads to an arete. Follow this, and the short wide crack above, then follow easier ground to finish.

Great Western   95m IV (4) ★★★ 1995

Start below the prominent wide crack of the summer route *Gobsite*. This route takes the prominent left-facing corner, left of the wide crack.

1   20m. Climb the corner below the prominent wide crack and belay to the left, below a large pinnacle.

2   20m. Follow another corner on the left to a ledge and belay at its left-hand end.

3   20m. The ramp above leads to a larger ledge. Follow the corner on the right to belay by a large detached flake.

4   35m. Head for two perched blocks which form an arch on a ledge up and right of the belay. From the ledge, follow a corner-line a few metres to the left of the arched blocks to finish overlooking *Great Chimney*.

The steep wall above *West Wall Traverse* has a steep grassy break on its right-hand side.

Sod's Law   90m VI (6) ★★ 1984

This follows the grassy break.

1   25m. The shallow open groove leads to a large flake belay.

2   35m. A short steep corner on the left leads to thin slabs, which are taken directly to gain the ledge of *Deep Ghyll Integrale*.

3   30m. A short overhang on the right leads to finishing chimneys.

Sodom   110m V (6) ★ 1990

Start at a ramp and groove to the right of the grassy break of *Sod's Law*.

1   25m. Climb the easy ramp and V-groove and belay at the flake as for *Sod's Law*.

2   45m. Move to a ramp above the belay. This leads leftwards to a ledge above the short steep corner of *Sod's Law*. A long traverse left along the ledge, and some awkward climbing, leads up to the ledge on *Deep Ghyll Integrale*.

3   40m. Finish as for the *Integrale*, traversing left along the ledge until overlooking *Great Chimney*, then up the arete.

Sod All   50m III (4) 1986

A long diagonal rake (*Deep Ghyll Integrale*), rather like *Jack's Rake*, is situated to the right of *Sod's Law*. This runs from right to left just below the top of the cliff, and is gained from between the two cols on *Lord's Rake*. Follow this rake leftwards for some distance, past a narrow chimney, to a shallow groove on the right. Climb the groove and a narrowing chimney to the top.

To the right of *Sod All*, and above the start to the *Integrale* (between the two cols on *Lord's Rake*), are three short but interesting chimneys.

Eye Spy   40m V (4) 1997

The first of the three chimneys is steep and insecure in its lower section, but has a pleasant through-route at the first chockstone.

About 20m to the right is a large sloping ledge slightly lower than the start of *Eye Spy*: the other two chimneys start from here.

Dharma Armour   45m III 1997

The middle chimney line trends leftwards.

Chimney Stack   45m IV 4 1997

The chimney at the right-hand end of the ledge. Pass a chockstone near the start and squeeze through several narrow restrictions before moving left at the top; beware of several loose blocks.

Deep Ghyll Integrale   140m III (3) ★★★ 1990

Follow the rising diagonal line leftwards from between the two cols on *Lord's Rake* (this ledge system crosses the higher part of *Deep Ghyll Buttress*). The ramp is easy, but becomes narrow and exposed as the corner of *West Wall Climb* is crossed. Continue to a belay overlooking *Great Chimney* (100m). The final pitch gives airy climbing up the exposed arete. Move up a flake, then across a short slab, to a final delicate exposed step right.

Castor   100m II/III 1984

This route starts 3m right (west) of the second small col of *Lord's Rake* when approached from the pinnacle. The main difficulties are in the first pitch, with several variations possible thereafter.

1   20m. Cross the short wall to reach the right edge of the ridge and climb this.
2   35m. The wall on the left is turned by a chimney. Continue up to a pile of blocks.
3   45m. Climb the wall behind the blocks, and continue up two slabby ribs to the top.

Pollux   70m III 1987

Start left of a prominent pillar of rock projecting from the main cliff, 40m down to the right of the second col of *Lord's Rake*.

1   10m. Climb the corner on the left side of the pillar. Head for a groove up to the left, and belay just below the groove.
2   25m. Climb the groove to a niche which is exited by the left wall to gain a grass ledge.
3   35m. Follow the rib to the right to the top.

Scafell Shamrock   (NY 205 070)
                                    Alt. 720m North facing

This is the area of rather broken rock below *Lord's Rake*. It is the first buttress to come into view when walking up from Wasdale, hence the name. The broken ground to the right of the *Shamrock* proper also has some climbing, and a large rambling buttress with a prominent icefall down its centre (*Cascade*) is situated up and right of the broken ground.

The routes are described from **right** to **left**.

Cascade   215m II/III ★ Early 1963

This starts at the toe of the rambling buttress system and continues over three interesting ice pitches with a series of easy snowy ramps in its upper reaches.

1   40m. Follow an icy groove for 16m to easier ground.
2   40m. The ice pitch above steepens towards the top. Continue to an easy-angled snowfield.
3   20m. Cross the snowfield, trending up rightwards.
4   50m. Follow a shallow ice gully to a belay.
5   40m. Move up, and follow a leftward-slanting ramp for 12m to gain a small col.

6   25m. Continue diagonally left, up a similar ramp system, to easy
     ground just west of the finish of *Lord's Rake*.

An ill-defined buttress marks the right end of the area of broken ground
on the right of the *Shamrock Buttress*. Above this buttress, an open snow
slope runs up into a gully, **Red Gill** (I/II), which continues up (with a
small pitch in lean conditions), to cross *Lord's Rake* past the second col,
and continues to the top. This can make a useful **descent** from *Scafell*
under a big snow build-up.

The Direct Route   165m II/III ★★ 1969
This follows the line of the stream draining down the middle of the broken ground, and climbs the mass of ice that builds up in the centre of
this area.
1   25m. Either climb the obvious icefall at the bottom of the shallow
     gully or turn it on the left.
2   30m. Easy-angled ice leads to another steeper ice pitch out of a
     gully on the right.
3   30m. Climb the icefall to belay on easier ground.
4   35m. Above, easy snow leads to a leftward-slanting rake below icy
     cascades.
5   45m. Climb the ice cascade from the bottom of the rake for 25m,
     then snow, to finish at the second col of *Lord's Rake*.

Pillar Variation   45m IV Early 1970s
A vertical pillar of ice sometimes forms at the left end of the icy cascade,
near the top of *The Direct Route*. Climb the pillar direct, and its continuation ice bulge.

The Lost Arrow Traverse   75m II 1972
From the left-slanting rake below the final ice cascade of *The Direct
Route*, traverse a system of ledges and grooves across the buttress above
Easy Gully to emerge onto *Lord's Rake*, opposite *Deep Ghyll*.

Easy Gully   170m I/II
This broad leftward-slanting gully/rake cuts into the top of the
Shamrock. Take the easiest line into the gully, and exit right from its top
onto *Lord's Rake*. A more exacting start can be made immediately right
of *Tower Buttress*. Combined with a finish up *Deep Ghyll*, this provides
300m of easy climbing to the summit of *Scafell*.

Wasdale

Drainage from the rock nose below the *Shamrock* often forms some exciting looking icicles to 'boulder': sadly they seldom extend to ground level.

Twisting Gully   150m IV (4) 1996

On the right side of the *Shamrock*, between the summer lines of *Rampart* and *Silk Cut Slab*, is an obvious S-shaped gully. The lower pitches involve climbing steep icy chimneys, before finishing up the last 50m of *Easy Gully* to the top of the *Shamrock*.

Intermittent Chimneys   100m IV 1985

On the left side of the *Shamrock*, this series of three stepped chimney pitches starts some 60m down from the bottom of *Lord's Rake*.

Scafell East Buttress   (NY 210 067)
Alt. 800m East to south-east facing

This spectacular convex-shaped buttress east of the col of Mickledore rarely forms ice to its base; the few winter climbs here are generally steep, and hardly any complete ascents have been made. However, the upper sections of several routes have been climbed after an abseil approach. Whilst this makes for an exciting day out in an impressive setting, the climbs themselves still await complete ascents.

Mickledore Chimney   115m III ★ 1891

This distinctive deep rift starts some 50m down from Mickledore. Steep snow between the steep walls leads to a prominent chockstone pitch (65m). This can be bypassed by escaping out right. If you opt not to, then climb the double chockstone pitch (15m) and continue up steep snow to finish up a short chimney on the right (35m).

Icefall Start   30m III/IV 1960

Just right of the start of *Mickledore Chimney*, a groove gives a short ice pitch with a hard start.

Icefall Finish   15m IV ★ 1960

The ice pitch which forms on the left side of the upper gully.

Tia Maria   **50m V (6) 1996**
This route follows the first crack system up the left wall of *Mickledore Chimney*, where the wall steepens.
1   30m. Start up the lowest of the parallel cracks. Difficult and poorly protected climbing leads to a recess and block belay.
2   20m. From the left side of the recess, climb the continuation of the crack.

A low stone wall bivouac site can be found several metres downhill from *Mickledore Chimney*. This makes a useful reference point. *Overhanging Wall* is the only route to have had a complete ground-up ascent on this section of the crag; the other routes can be used as variation finishes to the start of *Overhanging Wall*, and as such are included here. A clean ascent is still awaited, however, as the only ascent to date employed some aid and tension points. While the author (and many others) has been watching ice formation in this area for over 20 years, he has yet to see it reach the ground.

The first pitch of the summer route **SOS** (XI 10, 2006), the mossy groove adjacent to the walled shelter, has been climbed to the first belay and junction with *May Day Direct*. This offers a possible mixed direct start to *May Day Direct*, but has yet to be linked with it in winter to form a complete route to the top of the buttress. The top pitch of the summer line of **May Day Direct** (VI 6, 1984) has been climbed with an abseil approach. See the FRCC Scafell guide for a description.

Overhanging Wall   **25m V (6) 1985**
Start at an overhung ledge containing a large boulder, about 10m left of, and several metres lower than, the bivvy wall.

Climb up a corner to the left of the ledge: this leads to a small ledge. A traverse up and right leads to a rib and the crack to its right, reached with some aid. Follow this to a ledge. Move to a mossy crack on the right, and surmount a bulge with aid. Continue up and right to another ledge. A traverse leads to a corner on the left: climb this to a belay. A choice of three finishes are possible from here depending on the conditions. These top pitches come into condition more regularly than the lower pitch and have been approached by abseil.

Minotaur   **50m VI (5) ★★★ 1984/85**
This finish was used on the first ascent of *Overhanging Wall*: the other pitches mentioned have to date only been approached by abseil. *White*

Slab is followed until a move right is possible onto an iced ramp-line. This is followed to its top. It can be climbed in one 50m pitch or split.

1   25m. Follow *White Slab* to belay just below the iced ramp-line.
2   25m. Climb the corner to a slab on the left, this is followed to easier ground.

White Slab   40m III (3) 1984

In summer this is a distinctive white-coloured slab: hopefully it is in winter as well. Often thinly iced, this obvious white slab on the left of the belay contains a large block in its centre. Climb the ice.

Overhanging Wall – Original Finish   45m IV (5) 1994

From the belay, climb the right-facing corner, right of the prow overlooking *White Slab*. Step right, and climb the iced corner running up to a chimney. Climb this – a series of awkward bridging moves lead to easier ground.

Great Eastern Route   125m V 1960

A winter ascent of one of the easier *East Buttress* routes. One exposed move on the crux pitch is far harder than anything else on the climb. Start at an opening 5m to the right of the lowest part of the crag.

1   5m (3). Easy rocks are followed by a walk to the left.
2   25m (6). Ascend the cracked slab/ramp-line slanting up to the left. At the top of the ramp an exposed move leads to a ledge and good spike.
3   35m (4). Continue up the corner to a slab below a large overhang. Go diagonally right across the slab and up a short step to a peg belay.
3   40m (4). Continue right to another awkward step up, then continue along the ledge to a deep cleft. Step up onto a grassy ledge and use the offwidth corner-crack and wall to gain the ledge above.
4   20m (3). Climb up and round from the left end of the ledge, and move up to easier ground.

Direct Start   V (6) 1999

A direct start up the icy first pitch of *Gold Rush*, about 12m left of *Great Eastern Route*.

1   30m. Climb the icefall that forms at the start of *Gold Rush*: if it is thick enough, follow it to the ramp-line *Great Eastern*; otherwise follow an overhung ledge, trending right to join the ramp-line at a lower point.

The wide crack at the extreme left-hand side of the main crag is *Slime Chimney*.

Slime Chimney   131m IV (4) 1984

The winter route roughly follows the summer line.

1   65m. Climb easily up mixed rock and snow steps to beneath the three parallel chimney cracks on the extreme left side of the buttress: belay.
2   15m. Move left onto the blocks, traverse left, then delicate diagonally left to belay in a bay.
3   35m. Climb the narrow chimney-crack at the back of the bay, then the easier ramp system.
4   16m. Move to easy ground on the left, then finish up an easy gully on the left.

SCAFELL PIKE

The highest point in the country doesn't offer as much climbing as its neighbour, but there are some interesting coves and gullies tucked away on both sides of the mountain. For those crags on the southern (Eskdale) side of the mountain, see the Eskdale section.

Pikes Crag   (NY 210 071)
                                      Alt. 750m West facing

Pikes Crag overlooks Brown Tongue and is visible from the road in Wasdale. The crag is south of the col to Lingmell. Looking left from Mickledore, the crag is seen as a series of short slabby buttresses which catch the sun. Further round, the most extensive buttress is known as *Pulpit Rock*. This is separated from the rest of the mountain by a deep cleft. Left of the *Pulpit* are several gullies (lettered for convenience, see below), while the final long gully marking the left end of the crag is imaginatively named *Long Gully*. The crag generally gets more sun than its larger neighbours, so an early start or a cloudy day can help find the best conditions. The routes are described from left to right to keep the ordering of the alphabet gullies.

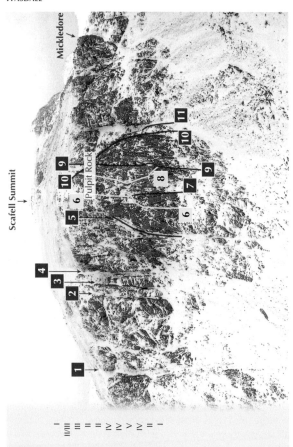

Pikes Crag

1	Long Gully	I
2	A Gully	II/III
3	B Gully	III
4	C Gully	II
5	D Gully	II
6	Left of Centre	IV
7	Right of Centre	IV
8	Grooved Arete	V
9	Slanting Groove	IV
10	Crenation Ridge	II
11	Descent Gully	I

(Photo: Dave Willis – Copyright FRCC)

Long Gully   250m I

The long gully to the left of the crag. There are no real difficulties but it makes a pleasant route to a small col, and then to Scafell Pike's summit.

Buttress Route   100m II

The buttress between *Long Gully* and *A Gully*. A left-sloping ramp leads to a few short pitches before the top.

A Gully   150m II/III

The first of the three gullies lying close together in the centre of the crag.

1   45m. A short chimney leads to steep snow, then a belay below a small chockstone.
2   20m. Bridge up past the chockstone to further steep snow and a belay below a large capstone.
3   50m. Struggle past the capstone on the right wall for 10m and belay at a small chimney.
4   35m. Follow easy snow to the top.

The buttress between the two gullies (**AB Buttress**, 1908) has been ascended in heavy snow and ice conditions, but its grade is not known.

B Gully   175m III

The most difficult letter in the alphabet – in fact, a bit of a B! A steep chimney/gully with a through-route for the thin.

1   35m. Follow ever-steepening snow slopes to a buttress splitting the gully: belay on the left.
2   40m. Follow the right branch past several ice bulges to a vertical chimney. Climb the chimney with difficulty and either belay below the chockstone or climb another 10m via the 'through' route on the right (or, for the more substantial climber, go via the outside of the chockstone) to easier snow above.
3   100m. Continue in the gully line to the top.

C Gully   180m II

The next gully in the alphabet.

1   30m. Follow the steepening concave snow slope to a belay in a cave below a large chockstone.
2   20m. Pass the chockstone by a traverse onto the left wall. Climb awkwardly back right to gain snow slopes above the chockstone.
3   130m. Easy snow leads to the top.

Wasdale

Horse and Man Rock   165m III ★★ 1983

A varied climb with an awkward finish; take care with the rock on the
Horse and Man. Start at a groove 15m down and left from the huge
chockstone in *D Gully*.

1   50m. Climb the groove.
2   20m. From the groove, traverse left round two corners.
3   50m. A series of chimney pitches lead to a belay in a cave.
4   45m. Traverse over easier ground to finish up *Steeplechase Groove*,
     on the right.

Steeplechase Groove   115m II/III 1983

A good climb; the grade varies with conditions. Start at the groove of
Horse and Man Rock.

1   50m. Take a direct line up to the right of the cracked wall to a peg
     belay.
2   35m. Head for the cave above.
3   30m. Easier ground leads to the top.

D Gully   140m II

The gully behind *Pulpit Rock*, on its left side. The imposing chockstone at
the bottom of the gully can be passed by a short groove on the left. Move
up to a small slab on right, before traversing back into the gully. A choice
of finishes: the subsidiary gully on the left poses few difficulties, or, more
interestingly, continue up to the ridge between *Pulpit Rock* and the Pike.

Pulpit Rock

Some of the best climbing on the crag is to be found on *Pulpit Rock*. The
buttress immediately right of *D Gully* is known as *Mare's Nest Buttress*.
To its right, and separating it from *Pulpit Rock*, is a grassy or snowy gully,
the next route. All the routes here require a short abseil descent to reach
the top of *D Gully* and *Descent Gully*: this runs down the Scafell (south)
side, with *D Gully* dropping down from the col on the north side.

Mare's Nest Gully   40m I/II 1905

A steep wall bars entry to easier snow at the start of the depression.
Above the gully narrows, giving more interesting climbing. Finish on
snow at the summit of *Pulpit Rock*.

The next distinctive feature is a depression in the centre of the *Rock*. This
is taken by *Urchin's Groove*. To its left, the corner-line running the

height of the crag is *Central Line,* which has left and right starts.

Left of Centre   95m IV (4) ★★ 1987

The clean buttress left of the depression is split by the crack of *The Citadel,* a summer VS. Start to its left.

1   30m. Climb the groove on the left of the buttress to belay on the right at a large ledge.
2   35m. Follow the large slabby corner on the right to belay at the top.
3   30m. The chimney above is undercut and awkward to enter; follow it to the top.

Right of Centre   90m IV (5) ★ 1989

Start up the corner to the right of the clean buttress.

1   25m. Climb the corner leading to the right end of the large ledge at the top of the first pitch of *Left of Centre*. The steep offwidth crack near the top of the corner proves the crux of the route.

2 and 3 65m. Follow *Left of Centre* to the top.

Urchin's Groove   100m V (4) ★★ 1984

This follows a series of disconnected grooves up the shallow depression to the right. The first pitch benefits from a good build-up of snow.

1   35m. Start near the centre of the depression. Back and foot to a peg belay above a traverse line.
2   35m. Climb the slab above, then a short icy wall to a stance; peg protection useful.
3   35m. A difficult traverse left leads to a finish up a well-iced wall.

Grooved Arete   130m V (5) 1970

An entertaining climb starting from a V-groove below a large overhang to the right of the prominent arete at the right-hand side of the crag. There are some loose blocks.

1   10m. Climb up a left-sloping grassy groove to a steep crack below the overhang.
2   25m. Climb a crack on the left then make a step left to the arete. Follow this to belay at a grass ledge.
3   30m. Climb the chimney above to grassy/snowy ledges and a belay at a rectangular corner.
4   50m. Follow the corner until it is possible to move right onto the arete. This is followed past a large block on the right.
5   15m. Slabs lead to the summit of the *Pulpit.*

Slanting Groove   130m IV (5) ★ 1987

The obvious corner on the right of the crag. Start as for *Grooved Arete*.

1 45m. Follow the grassy groove as for *Grooved Arete* to the steep crack. Move right to a small overhang which is passed with difficulty. The crack above leads into the corner-line.

2 45m. Follow the corner-line passing an overhang: several belay options.

3 40m. Continue up the corner to the large block on *Grooved Arete*. This is followed to the top.

Southern Cross   145m IV ☆ 2006

Essentially a direct line on *Southern Corner*. The climbing is more in keeping with the first pitch of that route and provides a direct line up this part of the buttress, taking in the groove immediately left of *Slanting Groove* on pitch 2.

1 40m (4). Start as for *Southern Corner* and climb the initial groove of that route. Where *Southern Corner* moves rightwards, continue up and slightly left to a good ledge beneath a steep wall.

2 30m (5). Climb the wall for 3m until it is possible to move left around the edge. Trend leftwards into an open groove and climb this to where it steepens beneath another rock wall.

3 25m (5). Climb the wall above for a few metres, then move rightwards via a series of cracks to gain a precariously perched block, just below the right arete. Follow the arete to good ledge and belay where *Southern Corner* comes up from the right.

4 50m (3). Follow *Southern Corner* to the top of *Pulpit Rock*.

Southern Corner   155m IV (4) 1979

The corner and groove system right of the clean wall to the right of *Slanting Groove*.

1 50m. Start at a shallow groove 10m right of *Grooved Arete*. Follow this to easier ground. Move into a corner on the right and follow a grassy ramp to the belay.

2 45m. A groove above leads to cracks. Follow these leftwards to a pedestal and so into the base of a chimney.

3 45m. From the top of the chimney move left to broken ground.

4 15m. Continue more easily to the top.

Crenation Ridge   110m II 1983

Good climbing up the left arete of *Descent Gully*. Start from *Descent*

Gully, where its walls are only a few metres apart. A good build-up of snow is required to get past the difficulties on the first pitch. Keep to the arete where possible, and belay as required until you reach the top.

Descent Gully   120m I

The obvious gully on the right-hand side of *Pulpit Rock* dividing it from the mountain. The gully curves up and left behind *Pulpit Rock*: take what difficulties you can find direct. A straighter right-hand finish leads up through some narrow gully walls to the path above Mickledore.

Vestry Wall   20m III 1998/1999

This name has been given to the broken wall overlooking *Descent Gully* at the rear of *Pulpit Rock*. Start approximately in the mid-section of the wall (a broken chimney-line lies further down to the right). Ascend via short icy corners and ledges passing a block/flake on the left.

Dropping Crag   (NY 215 074)
Alt. 880m North facing

Found to the east of *Pikes Crag*, and lying just north of the summit of Scafell Pike, this is probably the highest crag in England. It has several short groove lines on its left side.

Drop Out   50m III 2005

Start below the left-hand groove and climb the left side of a block to a stance. Swing left to easier ground which leads to a short headwall. Finish directly up a shallow groove.

Broad Crag   (NY 220 077)
Alt. 850m North facing

Broad Crag, the mountain to the north-east of Scafell Pike, contains this broken crag of the same name on its north side. This steep but small buttress has a snow slope running up towards its right-hand end, and the buttress is split by a gully.

Left Ramp   50m I/II

Follow the aforementioned snow slope on the right-hand side of the buttress to below steep ice. A leftward traverse below the buttress leads to an icy ramp. Follow it to the top.

Broad Crag Gully 50m II/III ★★

The gully splitting the buttress is short but perfectly formed and gives a good ice pitch – and all above 850m! Start up the snow slope as for *Left Ramp* to a peg belay.

1   25m. Steep ice leads to a stance on the right.
2   25m. Easier climbing leads to a finish on the mountain summit.

Broad Crag Gully Left Wall 45m IV (4) 1991

From the peg belay of the gully, start up steep ice in the gully, then move onto the icefall on the slabby left wall. This is followed steeply to the top with a belay well back.

LINGMELL (NY 209 082) Alt. 802m
North-west and North-east facing

The isolated summit of Lingmell, situated to the north of Scafell, has some exciting gills to climb on its north-east flank. Despite the height of the peak, however, many of the climbs start at only around 300m.

One route has been recorded on the north-west flank.

Lost World Gully 200m II/III Early 1970s

The obvious gully high up at 500m and cutting up into the face that looks over to the *Napes* (NY 207 086).

Moving round to the east side of Lingmell, the main line is the distinctive deep gorge of *Piers Gill* with its right-angled bend, but there are many other gills. Previously there has been some confusion over the names of these becks and gills which has led to them being climbed and claimed on several occasions. Where possible grid references will be used to locate the exact position on the map: it's then up to you to find it on the ground! Lingmell Beck, to the north of the mountain, is formed from Spouthead Gill, which flows east to west, and *Piers Gill* which cuts a deep path in a roughly north to south direction.

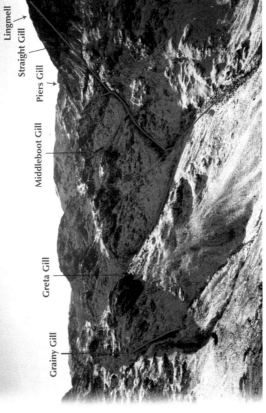

Piers Gill

Grainy Gill	II/IV
Greta Gill	III
Middleboot Gill	IV
Piers Gill	II/III
Straight Gill	II/III

(Photo: Al Phizacklea)

Facing upstream the gills are, from left to right:

- *Skew Gill* flowing into Spouthead Gill and described in the Borrowdale section.
- The two branches of *Grainy Gill*, separated by a narrow ridge: these flow into Spouthead Gill further downstream.
- Two hundred metres to the right are the two branches of *Greta Gill* that flow into *Piers Gill*; *Middleboot Gill* and *Piers Review* flow into *Piers Gill*; and *Straight Gill* which flows into *Piers Gill* from the west side.

Follow Lingmell Beck round the north side of the mountain towards Styhead Tarn, but, once round the spur of the hill, turn south and follow *Piers Gill* which flows into Lingmell Beck at (NY 212 092). *Piers Gill* and the routes directly connected to it are described first from right to left. These routes generally start at a low altitude and need consolidated snow for the best conditions.

Lingmell Crags and all these gills are home to rare alpine plants – please only climb here in truly frozen conditions, and please read the chapter 'Winter Climbing and Nature Conservation'.

Piers Gill   II/III 1936/7

This deep ravine forms three ice pitches which can be buried after heavy snow. More an outing than a climb, it finishes just below the path of the *Corridor Route*. Keep to the gill.

Straight Gill   265m II/III

Starting out of the right side of *Piers Gill*, this route climbs the side of Lingmell to end at the summit. For the full experience follow *Piers Gill* to *Bridge Rock* above the second waterfall. Alternatively traverse the slopes of Lingmell on the right bank of the gill until *Straight Gill* is reached, coming down from Lingmell on the right.

At the convergence of the two gills, climb a steep ice pitch out of *Piers Gill* for 15m. Continue for another 200m up fairly steeply angled snow, passing several small pitches and a cave formed by a chockstone, passed on its left. Another 50m leads to the summit cairn, possibly passing via a cornice.

Antarctic Monkeys   220m II/III 2006

This route takes the gully-line north of *Straight Gill* and south of the ridge of *Straight Gill Right-Hand Arete*, with its prominent pinnacle at one-third height.

Climb easily up the widening gully to a small amphitheatre with a corner on its right. The corner can be climbed at Grade III or avoided by climbing turf on the left, then traversing back right into the main gully. Climb easily until the gully forks. Take the left fork up steepening turf, then onto steepening ice until the gully widens near the top. Follow broken ground to the plateau. Belays as you find them.

Straight Gill Right-Hand Arete   200m III (4) 1984

Mixed climbing up the right side of *Straight Gill* leads to a gap. Either continue up the ridge and drop with difficulty into another gap or reach this point by a detour into *Straight Gill*. Various finishes are possible. Either keep to the ridge passing over a rock tower or avoid the difficulties of the ridge by an awkward step up to easy snow, heading back to the final section of the ridge; or climb an icy groove on the left of the tower to a col below the final section of the ridge.

The area to the right of the *Straight Gill Right Hand Arete* contains several short gullies (II/III). The large snowfield on the left-hand bank of *Straight Gill* leads to **Curving Gully** (I/II) and the summit.

The next route downstream leaves the left side of *Piers Gill*.

Pier Review   300m V (4) 1996

Approach *Piers Gill* from Lingmell Beck and bear right into the impressive deep gorge of the main gill. At the point where further progress up *Piers Gill* becomes difficult due to deep water and steep rock at each side, look up left and you will see the way up into the gill of *Pier Review*. The route up keeps on the right of the water but then follows the general line of this branch gill. After some 70m the main gill takes a right turn and here you have the option of taking the slightly steeper line straight ahead, with a short but interesting icefall, joining the original gill a little higher; or, alternatively, following the gill rightwards then back left. Just a little higher, following the general water line, an icefall forms on a slab that ramps up on the left: climb this and easier ground to meet the corridor route close to *Piers Gill Crag*.

Midway between *Greta Gill* and the upper portions of *Piers Gill* is an impressive waterfall formed by a small beck falling over Middleboot Knotts (NY 214 082) at an altitude of about 600m.

Middleboot Gill   25m IV ★★ 2005

Middleboot Gill drains into *Piers Gill* downstream of the narrow gorge. The lower part of the gill gives three short Grade III pitches to the icy top pitch. This is an icy slab leading into a cave on the left (peg) where the top 10m is almost vertical: a good pitch.

From the Corridor Route, *Greta Gill* drains down to the west (right) of the small *Stand Crag* (NY 219 088) and into *Piers Gill*. Below *Stand Crag*, the right branch forms an impressive icefall clearly seen from the approach.
    Greta Gill starts with two short icefalls, 5m and 10m pitches above pools, before splitting into a right and left branch.

Right Branch of Greta Gill   (NY 217 085) 50m III

From the top of the second short icefall, the right branch gives a series of short ice steps leading to an impressive top pitch and, above that, the Corridor Route.

Left Branch of Greta Gill   65m III 1991

From the top of the second short icefall, the left branch follows the easy gill bed past two steeper sections to the final headwall. A steep wall to the right of the final headwall offers two variation finishes on steep ice.

Left Branch Variation Exits

At the top of the gill, just before the final steep exit pitches of the standard *Left Branch* route, an impressive icefall forms down the right wall, *Greta Garbo*. A less steep fall forms lower down to its right, *Silver Screen*.

Silver Screen   40m III 1996

Start from the bed of the gill, just upstream from a small ice cave, and a few metres right of *Greta Garbo*. Climb the thinly iced wall and slab above before moving right into a narrow gully exit. (The lower wall can bank out.)

Greta Garbo   40m V 1997

The impressive icefall just upstream on the right. Follow ice to a natural break midway (peg in place and very large nut or Friend placement under the roof). Move out onto the icicle and ascend in a fine position, steep at first but then easier, to finish in a small amphitheatre (the

Dressing Room). Continue up a couple of short icy walls. Nut and tree belay up and round on the left of the *Dressing Room*.

About 200m left of Greta Gill, past *Stand Crag*, are the distinctive parallel streams of *Grainy Gill*.

Grainy Gill   II to IV 1890

To the left of *Stand Crag*, the twin branches of this gill are separated by a narrow ridge (NY 218 089). The left branch is II, with the right branch a more interesting IV with two pleasant icefalls. During the snowier winters of Victorian times the gill was considered a useful approach to *Great End*.

Due to their proximity to *Great End*, **Skew Gill** (NY 219 092) and **Spout Head** (NY 223 092) are described in the Borrowdale section.

MOSEDALE

This valley, the left-hand branch of the valley at the head of Wasdale, runs north by north-west from the Wasdale Head Inn towards Steeple and Pillar. On the west flank, the crags below Red Pike (NY 165 104) are split, right of centre, by the wide **Mosedale Gully** 120m (1985). It has **Left-** and **Right-Hand Starts** and numerous mixed **Variations** at II–IV, including the steep **Chimney Pitch** (III/IV) halfway up the gully.

WESTERN WASDALE

Returning to western Wasdale, on the opposite side of the lake from the *Wasdale Screes* is **Overbeck** (NY 169 077, alt. 320m, marked as **Dropping Crag**), a low-lying and south-west-facing crag that is seldom in winter condition nowadays. Access is from *Overbeck Bridge* on the north of the lake, from where an obvious path heads up to the crag. In the centre of the crag are the three obvious **Overbeck Chimneys** (30m, III/IV, 1913) – from left to right, **B**, **Central** and **Ash Tree**.

Wasdale

Dave Bodecott nonchalantly solos up Green Ledge Icefall *(II), Pillar Rock, on the first ascent (Photo: Stephen Reid)*

ENNERDALE

This secluded valley, running east to west, has no recorded winter climbing on its north side, nor much likelihood of any. The south side, however, is a different matter, playing host to a series of high north-facing venues including Steeple, Scoat Fell, Pillar, Kirk Fell and, at the head of the valley, Great and Green Gables. The last two crags, and to a lesser extent Kirk Fell, have become increasingly popular in recent years due to their reliable conditions and ease of access from *Honister Pass*. However, since this approach is less suitable for the other crags in Ennerdale, these Upper Ennerdale crags are described in the following chapter on Great Gable and Kirk Fell.

Due to access restrictions in the Ennerdale valley, vehicles are not allowed past the Forestry Commission car park at *Bowness Knott* (NY 109 154). For the crags lower down the Ennerdale Valley, either approach from *Bowness Knott* car park in **Ennerdale** (a mountain bike is useful) or from **Wasdale** or **Buttermere**. All of these approaches make for a long day in winter.

The summit of Steeple has a cove to either side, Mirklin to the west and Mirk to the east.

From Bowness Knott in **Ennerdale** the best approach is to cross the concrete ford on the River Liza before Gillerthwaite and take the path up onto Lingmell; follow this path eastwards to Low Beck and cross it to continue up onto the crest of the spur running north from Steeple. It is possible to contour into either combe from Long Crag (2hrs 30mins – 3hrs, although this can be reduced to 1hr 30mins by using a mountain bike).

The crags can also be reached in about 2hrs 30mins from **Wasdale Head**. Follow Mosedale Beck to Wind Gap between *Pillar* and *Black Crag* on Scoat Fell. From here *Black Crag* is easily reached. For the other crags, continue along the ridge westwards to Scoat Fell, from where various descents can be made into either combe.

From Gatesgarth Farm in **Buttermere** take the path to Scarth Gap, and on the Ennerdale side follow the path west through the clear-felled forest to cross the valley opposite the memorial footbridge. Cross the bridge and turn right (west) and take the upper track, eventually crossing

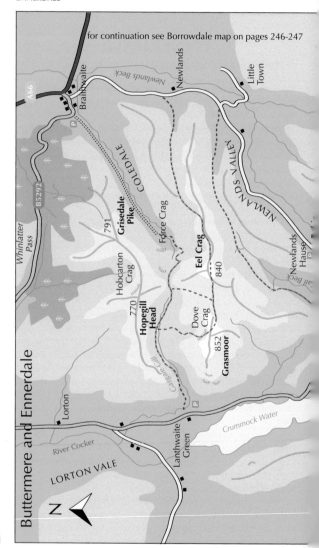

for continuation see Borrowdale map on pages 246-247

Newlands Beck

A66

Brathwaite

Newlands

Little Town

P

B5292

Whinlatter Pass

COLEDALE

Grisedale Pike

791

Force Crag

Eel Crag

840

NEWLANDS VALLEY

Newlands Hause

Hall Beck

P

Hobcarton Crag

770

Hopegill Head

Dove Crag

Grasmoor

852

Cassdale Gill

Buttermere and Ennerdale

Lorton

River Cocker

P

Lanthwaite Green

Crummock Water

LORTON VALE

N

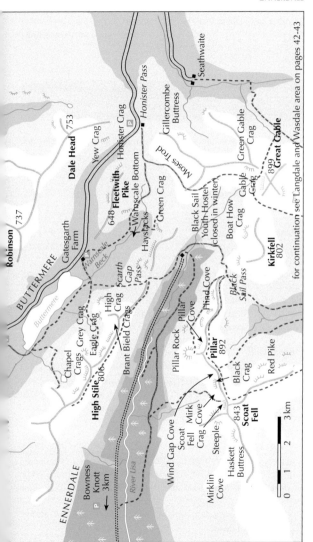

for continuation see Langdale and Wasdale area on pages 42-43

Western Crags

a bridge, until a path leads through the trees and up the west bank of High Beck into lower Mirk Cove. By contouring round under Long Crag, Mirklin Cove can also be reached (3hrs).

MIRKLIN COVE
(NY 154 115)
Alt. 700m West facing

The cove contains a number of easy snow gullies (I) mainly on its west (right) flank. While the gullies have been climbed they have not been described or recorded and are left to the individual to explore. From a distance the two steeper buttresses, *Steeple West Buttress* and the more impressive and central *Haskett Buttress*, are the main features.

Haskett Buttress
(NY 155 114)
Alt. 700m North-west facing

An obvious feature situated at the back of the cove. The main buttress is bounded on its left by the vegetated *Haskett Gully* and on its right by *Western Gully*. To the left of *Haskett Gully* is a tiered vegetated buttress with an easy 100m snow gully to its left (**Left Gully**, I , 1970s) which can be a useful **descent**.

Haskett Gully   90m IV (5) 2004
The deep cleft defining the left side of the buttress. Follow the gully to within a few metres of the steep jammed blocks where it narrows. Climb turfy ledges on the left wall for about 5m until it is possible to move right into the back of the gully. A few more metres of steep climbing lead to easy ground which is followed to the top.

Western Gully   90m I/II 1970s
The gully immediately right of *Haskett Buttress* is followed to the top with a choice of finishes. The right-hand and easiest one leaves the main gully bed and continues up on turf and rock, where it steepens at about two-thirds height. The central finish continues up the gully, where it steepens at a small ice step. The left-hand finish climbs a slightly steeper ice step from this point.

Mirklin Cove
showing Haskett Buttress and Steeple West Buttress

1	North Gully	IV
2	West Buttress	II/III
3	West Chimney Route	II/III
4	Left Gully	I
5	Haskett Gully	IV
6	Western Gully	I/II

(Photo: Dave Willis – Copyright FRCC)

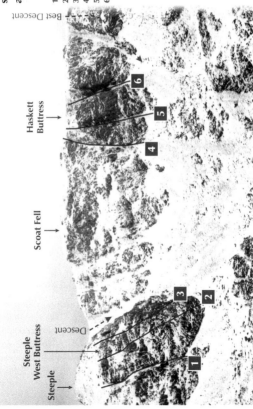

Best Descent

Haskett Buttress →

Scoat Fell →

Steeple West Buttress →

Steeple

Descent

163

Steeple West Buttress
(NY 156 117)
Alt 700m West facing

Directly below the summit of Steeple, this buttress faces west into Mirklin Cove. It is bounded on its right (south) side by a wide easy-angled scree gully (a useful **descent**) and on its left (north) by a gully with a cave at about one-third height.

About 20m to the left of the crag some pleasant 10m pitches of steep ice form. The easier turfy buttress above can be followed to the top.

North Gully   100m IV (5) 2004
The gully is a straightforward snow-plod except for a steep cave pitch about a third of the way up – best climbed on its right where ice tends to form; the more there is, the easier the climbing! An easier alternative is to bypass the cave altogether by traversing right onto the buttress about 5m below it, then climbing easy steps up the buttress until past the cave before traversing back into the gully above at a grade more in keeping with the rest of the climb (II).

Due to insufficient information the following two routes may cover similar ground (or indeed be the same route!). The lines on the diagram therefore should only be regarded as providing an approximate indication.

West Buttress   100m II/III 1986
A line to the left of the band of continuous rock running up the centre of the buttress. Aim for a snow patch in the middle of the buttress and continue on up.

West Chimney Route   100m II/III 2004
The right side of the buttress contains a continuous rib of rock. To its left is what, from below, looks like a shallow chimney curving left at its base. From the lowest point of the crag, climb a turfy corner on the left to reach the base of this shallow curving chimney-line. (When viewed from close-up this is not obvious, and then appears more like a wide turf-covered depression running up the crag.) Follow this to the top.

MIRK COVE AND WIND GAP COVE

(NY 160 116) and (NY 164 118) Alt. 700m East Facing

The coves on the east side of Steeple are really one large cove divided by a vague rocky spur that lies to the west (right) of *Black Crag*. Wind Gap Cove lies left of this; Mirk Cove to its right. **High Beck** flows out of Wind Gap Cove. It gives a 15m Grade II/III pitch (1997) and can make a good alternative approach to the crags. The crags are described from **right** to **left**.

Steeple East Buttress
(NY 158 117)
Alt 700m East facing

Western Crags

At the right-hand side of the cove near the top, and leading to the summit of Steeple, is the *East Buttress*.

Steeple East Buttress   150m III ★★ 1986
Follow a shallow gully line to the left of a rock rib. Climb the rib, taking belays where required, to finish on the summit.

Scoat Fell Crag
(NY 159 115)
Alt 750m North-east facing

Whilst *Scoat Fell Crag* can sometimes be a miserable summer venue being high up, north facing, turfy and slow to dry, these qualities make it an excellent winter climbing ground that comes readily into condition. In recent winters some plum lines have been picked, but there is still scope for exploration. For those without mountain bike, an approach from Wasdale might save a little time. In this case, follow a bridlepath up the west bank of Nether Beck until a subsidiary path branches off at NY 1520 0985 north-westwards to Scoat Tarn. From the tarn follow a small stream (with an intermittent grass trod) north up to a shallow col between Great Scoat Fell and Little Scoat Fell. From here the remains of a substantial dry stone wall are followed north-eastwards to a prominent cairn. The descent gully lies to the right of the crag (looking up) and just beyond this about a dozen yards away. In

Scoat Fell Crag

1 Turf Wars — IV
2 East Gully — IV
3 Scoathanger — IV
4 Sod this for a Lark — IV
5 Scoating for Boys — II
6 Serendipity Ridge — III

(Photo: Colin Wells)

poor visibility (not uncommon) follow the wall until NY 15817 11419 just before a marked break in direction of the wall. The head of the **descent** gully is a few metres directly opposite this point at NY 15829 11447. If you encounter a sudden change in direction of the stone wall from north-east to south-south-east, you have gone too far. Retrace your steps back to the break in direction and then a little further beyond that.

The crag is divided just left of centre by a huge square-cut gully (*East Gully*) flanked by fine rock towers.

Turf Wars   55m IV ★ 2005

Based on the summer line of *Travesty Cracks*. Start 4m left of *East Gully*, at a short wide chimney, the left-hand of two.

1 15m (3). Climb the chimney, and easy ground above, to belay at a crack in a block down and left of an impressive vertical corner.
2 20m (4). Starting several metres down and right of the corner, traverse horizontally rightwards on turf ledges, and then follow a left-wards-slanting groove-line up leftwards (crux) to a large ledge.
3 20m (4). Climb slightly up the groove above, then traverse left to gain a small ledge on the arete on the left. Drop down off this into a hanging gully on the left of the arete, and battle with rope drag up this to the top.

East Gully   80m IV ★ 1995

The major square-cut central gully is harder (and better) than it looks from below. Start under the right-hand rib defining the gully, just left of a short chimney.

1 25m (4). Climb up turfy steps and then step right over the top of the chimney before climbing back left under the rib and into the gully (can be climbed direct but is rather bold). Continue up the gully with interest to a belay on the right below a short wall.
2 20m (5). Overcome the wall with difficulty, and move up to a bigger square wall that completely blocks the gully. Surmount this via a narrow cleft on the right (crucial ice-hook runner), and belay in the bay above. This pitch may bank out under good snow cover.
3 15m (3). Climb diagonally leftwards (almost to the crest); spike belay.
4 20m (3). Step down, traverse right and pull up a short corner to gain a rising snow traverse line. Follow this up rightwards to the top. A harder finish looks possible up the obvious crack system leading directly out of the bay.

Western Crags

To the right of *East Gully* is a clean grooved tower, and on the right of this a rightward-rising chimney fault-line separates the tower from more broken vegetated ground to its right.

Scoathanger   80m IV ★ 2005

Start directly under the chimney fault-line.

1   50m (4). Climb easily up to the right wall of the tower. Move up right to the first chimney and climb this. The second chimney proves more awkward and is entered from the right. A difficult exit leads to a large platform.

2   30m (4). Climb steep and not too well-protected turf up the wall above, with a hard move left to gain easier ground, and move up to the ridge. Avoid a steep slab by striding left into a hanging chimney, and climb this awkwardly to easier ground (the climb originally finished via *Scoating for Boys*).

Sod this for a Lark   70m IV ★ 2005

Twenty metres to the right of *East Gully* is a bay, at the back of which easy-angled ground leads up to a prominent steep dark chimney. Start from this bay.

1   30m (2). Follow a vague chimney-line up the centre of the bay to below the steep chimney.

2   20m (4). The chimney is technically sustained but well protected.

3   20m (2). Follow a turfy groove just left of the rock rib above (and just right of a smooth wall), moving out left at the top.

Scoating for Boys   75m II 2004

Start 30m to the right of East Gully.

1   25m (2). Climb easy leftward-sloping ground to gain a ledge system and follow this leftwards, passing underneath the deep square-cut chimney of *Sod this for a Lark*.

2   20m (3). The chimney is avoided by a rising groove/ramp-line on the left which leads to a platform and a junction with *Scoathanger*.

3   30m (2). Follow the fault-line up rightwards onto an easy-angled slope, then move right round a rib into an easy gully and so to the top.

Serendipity Ridge   115m III ★ 2004

A very enjoyable climb. Many variations can be made to the first pitch: the one giving the most exciting climbing is described. Start at the lowest point of the crag, a few metres left of the descent gully.

1   40m (3). Trend rightwards to gain a short chimney overlooking the descent gully. Go up the chimney to a ledge and then follow the obvious horizontal traverse line leftwards round the buttress to a block belay under a roof.

2   35m (3). Just left is a short open groove: climb it to a platform. The steep wall ahead is avoided by traversing left and ascending an exposed rib. Follow the rib above, and then easier ground, to belay on a block under a steep wall barring access to the final rib.

3   25m (4). A slim groove just left of the block leads to a narrow ledge. Traverse rightwards along this and make an awkward and exposed step down and around the rib on the right to gain easier ground. Straightforward climbing up the broad ridge leads to block belays below a short step.

4   15m. Surmount the step and continue easily to the top.

In the centre of the two coves, and slightly lower than *Black Crag*, and 250m to its west, the low rocky dividing spur which curves up to join the main Scoat Fell ridge makes a pleasant winter outing.

Black Crag   (NY 165 117)
Alt. 650m North-north-west facing

Black Crag is situated high in the middle of the cove. It is lower than and well to the left of *Scoat Fell Crag*, and just to the left of the top of the vague ridge that separates Wind Gap Cove from Mirk Cove.

Easy Gully   120m I 2003
Follow the wide gully between *Black Crag* main buttress and the smaller one to its left. The left side is a little steeper, and various interesting exits can be followed at the top.

The Main Ridge Climb by the
Lower Slabs Ordinary Route   115m IV 1997
Generally follows the summer line with the some variations. Start from a snow basin above and right of the start of *Easy Gully* (this may be reached by following *Easy Gully* to the chimney then traversing right at its start, or by traversing right under the crag for about 50m then back left until about 10m from the start of the chimney).

Western Crags

Black Crag

1 Easy Gully — I
2 The Main Ridge Climb by the Lower Slabs Ordinary Route — IV
3 West Gully Cave Route — IV
4 West Gully Tunnel Route — IV

(Photo: Adrian Clifford)

1   35m (3). Follow the turf ramp leftwards for 5m to a ledge before climbing a shallow groove up and leftwards to a short arete and a rock platform.

2   15m (5). Gain the steep cracked buttress on the right and climb straight up to thin and committing moves to gain a small footledge on the left and the top of the buttress.

3   50m (3). Climb the easy-angled turfy ridge to a short awkward wall to a ledge below a chimney.

4   15m (4). Follow the chimney strenuously to a sloping rock platform. Escape left on easy turf ledges.

Variation to Pitch 4: Gully Finish   2003

4   60m. Avoid the final strenuous chimney at the top of the route by continuing up towards a short buttress, and up the ridge beyond this to the huge rock glacis. Walk across this and go left around the base of the upper buttress and briefly into *Easy Gully* before following the shallow gully which curves right along the edge of the buttress to the summit.

West Gully Cave Route   60m IV 2003

Start at the right-hand side of the crag by the deep gully.

1   25m. From the foot of the gully go up into the lowest cave. Exit via the left wall, aiming for the small chockstone and grassy ledge. Pass the large block on the left then go up to the next cave and belay in the back of this.

2   15m. Traverse out on the left wall, then go straight up to the next cave, but belay at its mouth.

3   20m. Go straight up the gully, keeping left of a small block, to the top.

West Gully Tunnel Route   45m IV 2003

Start as for *West Gully Cave Route*. Go up towards the lowest cave but take the ramp to the right from just below it, then go left to the ledge below the slab which leads to the chimney of the summer climb *Crack, Chimney and Slab Route*. Climb the slab corner-crack to the right of this up to the chimney. Bridge up this for about a metre then cross over to the groove on the buttress to the right. Go up the wide crack for 2m then step right to the flake-crack, which is climbed to a big ledge on the left. Go into the cave at the end of this and exit from a gap at the top of the cave. Easier ground leads to the top.

PILLAR

There are several possible approaches to Pillar, all of them long.

From **Ennerdale** take the right fork in the forest track about 2.5km beyond Gillerthwaite (YHA) which leads directly to a concrete bridge across the River Liza. Cross the bridge, turn left, and after 50m some small wooden steps mark the start of a good path which ascends diagonally through the forest, crossing an upper forestry road and continuing again in a diagonal direction before emerging, with fine views, at the base of the combe below the *Rock*. If on a bike, the upper track can be reached by cycling on up the valley, past the first path to a junction where you turn sharp back right for 600m (1hr 30mins with a mountain bike, otherwise 2hrs).

The traditional approach from **Wasdale Head** takes the path to Black Sail Pass. Head north-west past Looking Stead to pick up the well-marked track known as **The High Level Route**, which contours the northern slopes of Pillar Mountain. Follow this route to Robinson's Cairn, where *Pillar Rock's* magnificent eastern profile can be seen. Continue the traverse to the base of the *Rock* (about 2hrs 30mins).

From Gatesgarth Farm in **Buttermere**, follow the path to Scarth Gap. Do not descend to Black Sail Youth Hostel, but follow a path which starts a short distance down on the Ennerdale side and heads diagonally down in a westerly direction to reach the valley bottom opposite the memorial footbridge. Cross the bridge and turn right (west), take the upper track, and, after 600m, follow a diagonal path back leftwards and then ascend steeply to the combe beneath the *Rock* (about 2hrs 30mins).

Winter sun casts a glow over Pillar with Scafell in the background
(Photo: Alastair Lee)

West Cove
(NY 172 125)
Alt. 750m North facing

West Cove Gullies
100m I

There are two very obvious gullies that start above the steeply sloping ground immediately west (right) of *Pillar Rock*. Both run up to the summit of Pillar Mountain.

Pillar Rock
(NY 172 123)
Alt. 600m East, north and west facing

Once a centre for classic rock climbing, the long approach seems to deter all but the keenest in summer and winter nowadays, and so this is a good choice of venue for those seeking solitude. Many of the classic gullies were climbed in winter nearly a century ago, but a trickle of routes have been done over the last few decades and there is still scope for further development.

Pillar is a complex crag comprising of two cones stuck together, one higher than the other, termed *High Man* and *Low Man* respectively. In plan it runs longitudinally north and south at right angles to Pillar Mountain, on the north slope of which it lies.

Pisgah and East Face of High Man

The *East Face of High Man* is the short face of *Pillar*, well seen from the top of the *Shamrock Traverse* and overlooking the scree funnel at the top of *Walker's Gully*. *Pisgah* is the small summit immediately south of *High Man* and separated from it by the *Jordan Gap*.

Pisgah from Jordan Gap (6m, IV, 1933) follows the summer line up short wall on the north side of *Pisgah*. On *High Man* itself, **Central Jordan** (15m, III, 1913) has been climbed under heavy snow conditions. It follows the corner to the right of the highest point of the *Jordan Gap* which leads to a large sloping ledge. A crack on the left takes you to the top of *High Man*. **West Jordan** was also descended the same day – its description is in the FRCC's Pillar guidebook.

Pillar Rock

1 Great Doup Buttress — II
2 Shamrock Traverse — II
3 Shamrock Gully — IV
4 Photon Corner — IV
5 Shamrock Chimneys — V
6 Walkers Gully — V
7 Savage Gully — V
8 Savage Gully Direct Finish — VI
9 North Climb — II
10 Green Ledge Icefall — II
11 North-West Climb — V
12 The Old West Route — III
13 West Waterfall Gully — IV
14 Slab and Notch Climb — III

(Photo: Dave Willis – Copyright FRCC)

Western Crags

Slab and Notch Climb 50m III (4) 1890

On the east side of the *High Man* this route provides the easiest way to the top, as well as being the best **descent**. There are numerous belays and pitches can be split. Start near the foot of *East Jordan Gully*.

1 20m. Climb up right and onto the big *Slab*, descend slightly and continue right along the base of the *Slab* to a step. Climb the step to a corner and gain the *Notch* above.

2 30m. Move 4m right then go up an arete to a ledge. Step right and climb the stepped slab to a chimney above and right. Follow this to a deep notch and up to the top of the *High Man* (the easy gully descending from the *Jordan Gap*).

The variation humorously known as **The Easy Way** is considerably harder unless clad in tweed and nails. Beyond the *Slab*, instead of climbing up to the *Notch*, make an exposed traverse rightwards along the *Ledge* to round the *Curtain*, and descend slightly to the *Steep Grass* in *Great Chimney* (a summer D that will almost certainly have been climbed in winter though it is unrecorded). Go up this and struggle up a short chimney to rejoin the standard route.

The Curtain and the Arete (1899) has been climbed in winter. It is the ridge that *Slab and Notch* crosses – the full description is the FRCC's Pillar guidebook.

Shamrock

This is the large area of rock containing many grooves and aretes left (east) of the main rock and divided from it by *Walker's Gully*. The usual track up Pillar Mountain via the *Shamrock Traverse* goes up scree on its left-hand side and then traverses across just above its summit. It is divided into an *Upper Tier* and a *Lower Tier* by the *Great Heather Shelf* which runs diagonally up rightwards across its centre and is reached by easy scrambling from the left. Up on the left side of the *Great Heather Shelf* is an obvious groove and corner-line, which gives the summer route of *Photon*. The routes are described from left to right.

Shamrock Gully 160m II 1890

The obvious gully bounding the far left side of the *Shamrock*, to the right of the path and to the left of a long low overhang. In summer it is a loose and vegetated gully; wait for it to freeze and fill with snow and it becomes more interesting.

Photon Corner   **135m IV (4) 1983**

This follows the summer line of *Photon* to the top of pitch 4 then descends into *Shamrock Gully*. Start by scrambling 60m up the Great Heather Shelf to the foot of a clean groove on the left.

1   65m. Climb directly up the groove to below main corner/groove on the right.
2   25m. A ribbon of ice often forms in the corner – follow this to a poor belay.
3   25m. Move left and continue on steep mixed ground up the corner above.
4   20m. Traverse left for 15m to a belay overlooking *Shamrock Gully*. Descend or ascend the gully.

Shamrock Chimneys   **160m IV (4) ★ 1985**

1   30m. About 5m right of the groove of *Photon Corner*, start up the narrow chimney on the left, breaking out left at 15m. Follow the slab, then the chimney on the right.
2   20m. Continue up the chimney, passing chockstones and a cave.
3   25m. Easier ground leads to a V-chimney then further easy ground.
4   85m. Follow the easiest line up the shallow gully to the top.

Walker's Gully   **140m V (4) ★★ 1914**

First climbed by Siegfried Herford in an age of snowier winters, this gully divides the *Shamrock* from the *North Face of Low Man*, but is seldom in condition, particularly the steep top pitch which is the crux of the climb.

North Face of Low Man

Right of *Walker's Gully* is *Green Ledge*, a long grassy terrace which traverses under the main crag, separating it from easier ground below.

Green Ledge Icefall   **60m II ★ 2004**

This takes the buttress under *Green Ledge* on its left-hand side. Climb a short steep groove to exit onto scree. Follow very easy-angled ice up rightwards to a steeper left-slanting ice runnel which exits onto *Green Ledge* at the start of *North Climb*.

Savage Gully   **104m V ★★★ 1997**

This follows the obvious gully/groove line from the left end of *Green Ledge*. Start as for the summer line of *North Climb*, from the very left end

Western Crags

Steve Prior, on the first major pitch of Savage Gully *(VI), Pillar Rock, during the second ascent (Photo: Stephen Reid)*

of *Green Ledge* where a short wall leads to a square platform. The first two pitches are as for *North Climb*.

1   10m (3). Climb onto the square platform and traverse left to the foot of the main groove.

2   25m (4). Climb the groove into the gully line proper and continue past a chockstone to a spike belay below a steep groove with a thin crack in its right wall, on the left, and the deep *Twisting Chimney* of *North Climb* on the right.

3   25m (6). Climb the groove on the left to a grassy ledge and large thread.

4   20m (6). Continue up the groove then move left to the continuation of a shallow chimney. Follow this to a steep bay and dubious block belay just below the final overhanging headwall.

5   24m (6). On the first ascent, a steep corner/groove/chimney just to the left of the dubious block belay was taken with a rock belay in a small rock outcrop well back.

Direct Finish   **VI ★★ 2004**

5   24m (7). Follow the original summer line up the undercut square chimney on the right of the dubious block belay.

To get off the mountain, return to the gully bed and then make a rising traverse left over steep heather to gain the scree above *Walker's Gully*.

North Climb   101m IV ★★ 1913

Start from the very left end of *Green Ledge* where a short wall leads to a square platform.

1   10m (3). Climb onto the square platform and traverse left to the foot of the main groove.

2   25m (4). Climb the groove into the gully line proper and continue past a chockstone to a spike belay below a steep groove on the left and the deep *Twisting Chimney* on the right.

3   34m (3). Climb *Twisting Chimney* and then trend leftwards up an open groove. Scramble up to a belay on a small ledge at the meeting of two narrow chimneys.

4   9m (4). *The Stomach Traverse*. Climb the right-hand chimney which curves to its right in the upper half.

5   18m (3). The be-chockstoned corner is climbed via a capstone, followed by a walk of 6m to the *Split Blocks*. These are climbed by the obvious chimney. Traverse to the left, crossing the *Strid*, to a ledge below and right of the *Nose*.

6   5m (5). The *Nose*. From the corner, work out left to stand on the tip of the projecting flake. Hard moves up and left gain better holds and a ledge just above. Move up without further difficulty to belay 5m higher on the right wall of the grassy *Stony Gully*, which leads to *Low Man*.

North-West Climb   130m V (6) ☆☆☆ 1960

Climbed under exceptional conditions, the like of which will probably not be seen again during the life of this guidebook. A tour de force – and quite probably harder than it is graded!

For a full description the FRCC Pillar guide will need to be consulted. The route was started by following the slabs of *Nor'-Nor'-West Climb* which were banked out with snow. The short tricky groove at the start of pitch 3 of that route led to the top of the *Bounding Buttress*. From that point, *North-West Climb* was followed (via *Lamb's Chimney*) with only *Oppenheimer's Chimney* being free of ice.

West Waterfall Gully   220m IV (5) ★★ 1969

This is the deep cleft that bounds *Low Man* on its west side. It is home to rare alpine plants and should only be climbed in truly frozen conditions

(please read the chapter 'Winter Climbing and Nature Conservation'). Start on the right of the broken crag under *Green Ledge* at a well-defined gully. Short pitches lead up to the final main 30m pitch. This is very steep (often overhung) and usually much harder than its grade in anything but good conditions. Climb it to finish on the *Western Scree* under the *West Face of Low Man*: a magnificent pitch (but it has been known to bank out). If the final pitch is not formed there are several possibilities: you can quit the gully on the right some 30m below it by ice that forms where the summer scramble from *Green Ledge* crosses it (III 4); or quit it on the left at the same point and following the summer line of **Waterfall Climb** (50m, III 4), up a groove system in the rocks which bound the gully on its left side to gain the *Western Scree* – or indeed traverse leftwards and then descend slightly at this point to gain *Green Ledge* and walk off.

West Face

The Old West Route   165m III ★★ 1913

A route following a line of weakness running up diagonally left across the *West Face of Pillar Rock*, effectively dividing *Low Man* from *High Man*. From the top of *Low Man*, it runs up the front (north) of the rock to its summit via the well-worn summer scramble. With a good banking of snow the lower section is not without interest, whilst the upper part can be awkward in icy conditions. **Descent** is either by abseil into *Jordan Gap* or, more traditionally, by downclimbing *Slab and Notch Route*. *High Man's* imposing *West Face* contains a prominent groove-line on its left-hand side.

Gomorrah   85m VII (7) ☆☆ 1986

The summer VS gives a fine hard route that has yet to see a second ascent. Start directly below a huge triangular roof (at the start of the summer route of *Vandal*).

1.   45m. As for the summer *Direct Start*, climb a corner to the roof, then traverse left to the foot of a crack. Climb this steeply and the ledges above to a loose block belay.

2.   40m. Traverse right to a crack-line and climb cracks, a chimney and a groove direct to the top. On the only ascent to date a peg was used for aid at mid-height.

Stephen Reid is rewarded with fantastic conditions on the big icefall of West Waterfall Gully *(IV), Pillar Rock (Photo: Colin Wells)*

New West Climb   87m IV (4) ★★ 1903

A fantastic lead for its time but rarely in condition these days. Start just above a big embedded block, 25m or so down the scree from *West Jordan Gully*.

1   20m. Follow easy rocks in a shallow chimney, trending slightly to the left, to a rib which leads to a small corner. Follow a steep staircase to belay on a good ledge.

2   10m. Climb a wide, shallow chimney which leads to a small platform, and traverse horizontally left for 4m to step down to a good belay.

3   17m. Climb the obvious groove to ledges and make an awkward traverse left to the foot of a chimney (chockstone belay).

4   20m. The imposing chimney above is followed to a chockstone at 9m. Avoid the chimney beyond by traversing horizontally right and around a rib with difficulty. Continue rightwards, then up, to surmount a pile of blocks which form a magnificent belay.

5   20m. Climb the crack up the slab above to a small ledge. Finish via a block-filled grassy groove on the right or, better (if iced), the slab on the left.

West Jordan Gully, which bounds the *West Face of High Man* on the right, separating it from *Pisgah*, has been climbed under snow but does not appear to come into proper winter conditions.

Pillar Cove   (NY 173 121)
                                     Alt 750m   North facing

The cove immediately east of *Pillar Rock*, sometimes called **Great Doup**, sports two or three short Grade I gullies which finish steeply on the mountain ridge. These have been climbed on since 1887.

Great Doup Buttress   120m II 1972

The ridge forming the left side of the cove generally offers easy-angled climbing with the odd steeper section near the top, where it is joined to the main ridge by a horizontal section behind a small tower.

Hind Cove
(NY 178 122)
Alt 600m North-east facing

Further east is *Hind Cove*, which is crossed by the High Level Route just before it ascends to Robinson's Cairn.

From the ecological point of view, Hind Cove is potentially one of the most sensitive areas to climb in the Lakes in marginal conditions, for here is the healthiest Cumbrian population of scrubby cinquefoil, a plant whose only British locations are in the Lake District and Teesdale. Cinquefoil is really vulnerable to turf climbing or climbing in poor conditions as it favours the wetter areas (and these will be where the ice is). Please read the chapter 'Winter Climbing and Nature Conservation'.

Hind Cove Gully   100m II 1999
From the path below the cove just east of Robinson's Cairn, the dark cleft of the gully can be seen about 100m above the path. A through-route passes the jammed blocks, and one further step poses the only other obstacle to the easy top section.

Rib and Gully Climb   120m I/II 1999
The rib on the left side of the cove (with a scree-filled gully on its right) offers a pleasant route to the top with difficulties avoided if desired.

Western Crags

GREAT GABLE AND KIRK FELL

Though mostly located in Ennerdale, the crags of Great Gable, Green Gable and Kirk Fell are more easily approached from Honister Pass, Borrowdale or Wasdale. *Napes Needle,* situated on the south side of Great Gable, is traditionally considered to be the birthplace of British rock climbing, but the *Napes* cannot be recommended as a winter climbing venue, particularly given the trend towards warmer, less snowy winters. By contrast, however, north-facing *Gable Crag* on the other side of the mountain is home to many splendid modern mixed routes which are often in condition and relatively accessible. Please see the map 'Buttermere and Ennerdale' on pages 160–61.

GABLE SOUTH

The first routes described on Great Gable are located on the south side of mountain and best approached from either **Borrowdale** via Styhead Tarn or from **Wasdale**.

South-west-facing **Kern Knotts** (NY 215 096, alt. 520m) is hardly worth considering as a winter climbing venue. However, a party attending the popular FRCC Easter meet of 1913 ascended **Kern Knotts Chimney** in wintery conditions – so you never know.

On the south-west-facing **Napes** (NY 210 101, alt. 700m), the historically resonant rock climbs of **Napes Needle** and its popular extension, **Needle Ridge**, have both seen ascents under heavy snow conditions (1896 and 1891 respectively), as has **Arrowhead Ridge Direct** (1911). None of these hold snow or ice well in winter. **Needle Gully** behind the *Needle* was likewise the scene of early activity (1899), as was **Eagle's Nest Gully** to its left (1890). **Tophet Bastion** (II, 1960), the left-to-right diagonal line up the left arete on *Tophet Wall*, has also been climbed in snowier times.

Great Gable and friends meet above the clouds (Photo: William Barnes)

Westmorland Crags

(NY 211 102)
Alt. 800m South facing

As with the other climbs described on this side of Great Gable, an early start or a cloudy day are advantageous for these routes. Although it is south-facing, the crag is high, being situated just below the summit, and as such can offer some good (if fleeting) winter climbing, with the best being on the buttresses (the gully lines are turfy and can hold neve, but not normally ice). Only two routes have been recorded here in winter and the descriptions are a little vague. The rock climbs mentioned are currently recorded on the FRCC website, but will soon appear in a new edition of the FRCC Gable guide which will need to be consulted. There is plenty of scope for further routes.

The crag lies directly above the the *Napes* and below the summit of Great Gable. From Wasdale it is best approached from Beck Head between Great Gable and Kirk Fell; from Borrowdale take the climbers' path under *Kern Knotts* and cut up Hell's Gate Screes past *Tophet Wall* to the crag above; from Honister Pass, it is best to approach from above via Green Gable, Windy Gap and the summit of Great Gable to Westmorland's Cairn at the top of the crag.

Western Crags

Butterfingers 70m III (4) 2005

A line up the central buttress, starting just to the left of the small pinnacle, some 15m right of *Sparrow Fart Rib* and some 20m right of the lowest part of the crag below a steep wall. This route is basically the broken lower part of *Flake Gully Buttress* (and this climb appears to be mainly via *Chockstone Chimney*) finishing around the *Cairnbrian*. It is climbed in three pitches of decreasing difficulty, with the trickiest stuff on the first pitch. Some caution should be exercised due to the presence of large loose blocks.

Follow Your Nose 90m V 2005

The steep gully to the right of the buttress containing *Butterfingers*.

1   50m. Start at a steep groove/gully line 5m left of small pinnacle at lowest point of crag. This is followed at around Grade III through a couple of steep narrow sections to a block belay. Traverse left to right and climb a further steepening to a large ledge.

2.   40m (4). The crux pitch involves delicate hooking.

GABLE NORTH

Even though they stand at the head of Ennerdale, *Gable Crag* and Green Gable (and to a lesser extent Kirkfell) are most easily approached from **Honister Pass**, which, if not ice bound, offers convenient access. (Drivers should beware of snowfall during the day which can quickly close the pass.) It is also possible to approach from Seathwaite in **Borrowdale** (or from **Wasdale**), via Styhead Tarn and over the col of Windy Gap, whence *Green Gable Crag* is only a few minutes away on the right (north-east), with *Gable Crag* to the left (west).

Gable Crag (NY 213 105)
Alt. 800m North facing

Located on the north side of the mountain, this remote high crag is really a collection of buttresses with the weaknesses between them giving obvious winter lines, while the buttresses themselves provide classic high standard mixed routes in the modern idiom.

Gable Crag

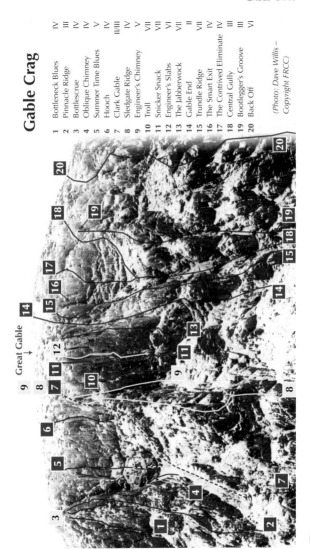

1	Bottleneck Blues	IV
2	Pinnacle Ridge	III
3	Bottlescrue	IV
4	Oblique Chimney	IV
5	Summer Time Blues	V
6	Hooch	IV
7	Clark Gable	II/III
8	Sledgate Ridge	IV
9	Engineer's Chimney	V
10	Troll	VII
11	Snicker Snack	VII
12	Engineer's Slabs	VI
13	The Jabberwock	VII
14	Gable End	II
15	Trundle Ridge	VII
16	The Smart Exit	IV
17	The Contrived Eliminate	IV
18	Central Gully	III
19	Bootlegger's Groove	III
20	Back Off	VI

(Photo: Dave Willis –
Copyright FRCC)

When approaching from Windy Gap the first route to be encountered is *Windy Ridge*, which has a wide gully on its left and a narrower gully to its right separating it from the main crag. A path traverses under a series of isolated buttresses, with the *Bottle-Shaped Pinnacle* high up on the right and then, high up, the distinctive wall of *Engineer's Slab*, with *Engineer's Chimney* on its left-hand side. Approximately up the middle of the crag, and serving as a good reference point, is *Central Gully*. *Moses's Back Door* starts up the obvious wide gully on the right side of the crag. **Descent** is possible at either end of the crag. The routes are described from left to right, in the order in which they are most likely to be approached.

Windy Ridge   40m III 2002

This buttress at the left of the crag stands on its own, isolated by a wide scree gully on its left and a narrower gully to its right separating it from the rest of the crag. Start up a turfy corner at its lowest point.

1   40m. From the lowest point of the buttress climb a turfy corner to a large snowy bay. This can also be easily entered from the wide scree gully to the left. Choose a groove above (the left-hand one is probably the easiest) and follow this onto the easier-angled ridge.

Either ascend or descend the wide gully easily reached from the top of the ridge, or:

Variation Finish   80m III 2003

2   30m. Move right across the top of the gully to the ridge above the right-hand side of the gully and the prominent slab above.

3   50m. Follow the crest of the ridge to pop out just by the tourist path.

Late Season Flurry   200m II 2006

Start in the narrow gully immediately right of *Windy Ridge*. An interesting easier route which gains from its impressive surroundings.

1   80m. Start up the gully, but move right and climb the left edge of a buttress until almost level with the top of *Windy Ridge*. Follow a ramp up to the right, then traverse right to gain a gully line.

2   25m. A short ice pitch and mixed ground leads to the foot of *Aaron's Slab*.

3   25m. Go left into the icy gully and follow it past another short ice pitch to an upper amphitheatre.

4   70m. The ramp on the right leads to the summit slopes.

Pinnacle Crack 70m V (6) 2000

This turf and snowed-up rock route lies up the wall immediately to the right of the narrow scree gully that marks the left edge of the crag.

1   40m. Climb a rib to the base of the *Upper Buttress* (left of the summer routes of *The Slant* and *Mallory's Left-Hand Route*).
2   30m. Climb the crack up the slabby wall and exit behind the pinnacle.

Torquers Are No Good Doers 50m VII (7) 2002

This route, whose name arguably holds the trophy for the most awkwardly contrived pun in the book (and there's quite some competition), follows the crack-line of the summer route *The Serpent*. High up on the left end of the crag is an obvious slab with a crack running through it (*Mallory's Left-Hand Route*). To its right is a prominent corner/groove (*Mallory's Right-Hand Route*) and, between, some very steep crack-lines. This route takes the second crack-line left of the slanting ramp-line of the summer route *The Slant*. Scramble up and right to the start.

1   30m. Move right off the belay onto a slab and steeply into a hanging niche on good hooks. Pull right out of the niche round a blunt arete and climb a shallow groove above to a belay. (The first pitch of the summer route *The Serpent*).
2   20m. Follow the continuation crack above to the left side of a detached block pinnacle. Climb the left side of this to easy ground.

Access to the next few routes can be gained by a variety of enjoyable pitches on the broken lower tier. A bay with a big slab forming its left side acts as a good reference point. The right-hand side of the bay is marked by the mixed line of *Pinnacle Ridge*. The slab can be climbed via a right-to-left weakness at V (6), 20m, or direct at VI (6), 20m (thin). The chimney at the back of the bay can be climbed over the chockstone V (7), 20m. Above, an easy ridge or turfy grooves lead to the foot of *Mallory's Buttress* which is bounded on its right by the corner of *Bottleneck Blues* and the slabby wall of *Pinnacle Crack* on the left.

Mallory's Corner 75m IV (6) 1997

The route follows part of the summer climb of *Mallory's Right-Hand Route* which takes the next groove system to the right and the large grassy corner above. Start at a crack right of a glacis.

1   25m. Climb the crack on excellent placements and follow the continuation flake rightwards into the main line of the corner. Two

steep steps lead to a corner with belays at the foot of a chimney.
2   50m. Take the fine corner on the right to the summit.

Direct Start   IV 1999
1   30m. Ascend ledges diagonally rightwards to the undercut crack of
    the summer line. Climb this and the groove above to a big ledge
    and belay. (This is the summer line of *Mallory's Right-Hand Route*).

Bottleneck Blues   45m IV (4) ★ 1997
Superb well-protected mixed climbing up the huge corner to the left of
Pinnacle Ridge. Start at the base of the open corner.
1   25m. Move up to a flake and step right into the right-angled corner.
    Follow this direct past a hollow flake (crux), then traverse right to an
    obvious block belay on the ridge overlooking the bottle-shaped
    pinnacle.
2   20m. Follow the continuation grooves to the top (various options
    depending on conditions).

Pinnacle Ridge   200m III ★★ 1947
The ridge to the right of the huge corner of *Bottleneck Blues* has a repu-
tation for coming into condition very rapidly. Follow the obvious curving ridge from the left to the top of the pillar on *Oblique Reference*.
Make an awkward step up and left on the wall behind the pillar (crux),
then follow easy ground to the top.

The wide gully between *Pinnacle Ridge* and *Sledgate Ridge* to the right
is the base of the summer descent route from climbs on *Engineer's Slab*,
and the next climb roughly takes this line.

Clark Gable   130m II/III 1960
Start up the corner-line right of the ridge and follow the gully to the
amphitheatre below the headwall. Move diagonally right round the rib
to gain the top of *Engineer's Chimney*.

The next five routes are all reached by following *Clark Gable* to the
amphitheatre. For *Hooch* continue up *Clark Gable* to a large block belay
above *Clark Gable*. For the remaining routes move left towards the obvious *Oblique Chimney*.

Oblique Reference 120m IV (4) ★ 1995

Start at a pillar 10m down from the foot of *Oblique Chimney*.

1   30m. Follow a groove on the left of the pillar to its top.

2   90m. As for *Pinnacle Ridge*: make an awkward step up and left on the wall behind the pillar, then follow easy ground to the top.

Oblique Chimney 55m IV (5) ★ 1893

The prominent leftward-slanting chimney-line on the left, above the amphitheatre. Cave belay at half-height.

Bottlescrue 75m IV (5) 1995

A right-to-left line diagonal starting 10m up right from the toe of the buttress and finishing in *Oblique Chimney* above the difficulties.

1   20m. Follow *Summer Time Blues* to the belay.

2   30m. Ascend leftwards over ledges and ice smears to belay at a snow ledge.

3   25m. A crack at the left end of the ledge leads up to a large ledge and continues left to a flake. A traverse left under the flake leads into *Oblique Chimney*.

Summer Time Blues 70m V ★★ 1995

A route originally ascended on the first day of British Summer Time. It takes a shallow chimney-line in the left side of the headwall immediately above the amphitheatre and to the right of *Oblique Chimney*.

1   20m (5). The chimney is guarded by a small steep buttress. From the amphitheatre, move up 10m over steeper ground to a ledge below slabs, just left of the chimney proper. Belay in the corner just left of the shallow chimney.

2   50m (6). Follow the steep chimney with improving protection as it becomes more defined. A through-route finish is available for the slim.

Hooch 40m IV (6) 2000

A mixed climb with reasonable protection, taking the wall just right of the summer route of *Moonshiner* in the area left of *Engineer's Chimney*. Overhead near the crag top is a prominent groove with a protruding block. *Hooch* takes the next groove left of this. Start at a large block.

Follow the corner behind the block, then step left to a spike on the arete. Take the prominent bulging rib on the left to a good ledge below the smooth top wall, which has a groove on its right-hand side. Climb the wall using cracks to grasp a block in the groove, then continue straight up. Pinnacle and chockstone belays are available up to the left (but beware of loose boulders).

A protruding buttress can be seen below the line of *Engineer's Chimney*; this is *Sledgate Ridge*.

Sledgate Ridge   80m IV (5) 1985

A useful approach to the routes higher up on *Engineer's Slab* as well as a route in its own right. The start of the ridge is just above the path at the base of the crag, below and left of the prominent buttress containing *Engineer's Slabs*.

1   20m. Either start up a hard crack or, if you're going for bigger things higher up the crag, use the easier chimney on the right and continue up the iced grooves to a ledge.
2   20m. Ascend a wall at the left end of the ledge, moving diagonally rightwards over slabs to a large grassy platform.
3   40m. Ascend the chimney, or (if your arms are up to it) any of the other routes around this area.

The prominent buttress with *Engineer's Slab* up its centre, and *Engineer's Chimney* on its left side, is found up and left of the start of *Central Gully*. The best approach is leftwards over broken ground from a snow bay just left of the start of *Central Gully*.

Engineer's Chimney   50m V (4) ★★ 1910

Bounding the left side of the big wall containing *Engineer's Slabs* is an obvious chimney. The chimney does not hold a lot of snow, and the crux may be on verglassed rock. The original ascent, in very icy conditions, was a futuristic achievement.

1   15m. Start up snow to a fork in the chimney.
2   25m. Follow the left branch, the difficulties easing where the chimney widens. Pass a chockstone to finish up an iced crack.
3   10m. Easier ground leads to the top and a belay.

Troll   60m VII ★★ 2003

To the right of *Engineer's Chimney*, a block overhang can be seen about half-way up the crag. The route climbs this feature.

1   30m (8). Start right of *Engineer's Chimney* and climb the wall to

the overhang. Surmount this using a crack on the right and belay on a ledge.

2   30m (4). The summer line moves right and climbs a steep slab to a break, then traverses right to the flake on *Snicker Snack*, which is followed for a few metres before moving into a groove on the right to finish. However, this was not in condition on the first ascent, so the team went straight up on stepped ledges following the obvious snowiest line.

Snicker Snack   60m VII ★★★ 2003

The classic summer E3 crack-line in the wall left of *Engineer's Slabs*.

1   45m (9). Start up the wall as for *Engineer's Slabs* but continue up thin cracks to belay at a huge flake.

2   15m (7). Climb the flake and traverse right to a small overhang. Gain a thin crack above and follow this to the top.

Stuart Wood following the main pitch of Snicker Snack *(VII), Great Gable, on the first ascent in 2003 (Photo: Steve Ashworth)*

Engineer's Slabs 65m VI ★★★ 1985

This summer classic has become a modern winter test piece in recent years and gives excellent mixed climbing. It starts up cracks in the middle of the big face: the belays are somewhat cramped.

1   25m (7). Follow cracks, then a chimney leading to a sentry box.
2   25m (7). A difficult traverse right (crux) for 10m on iced cracks leads into a vertical crack, which is followed to some strenuous moves onto a belay ledge.
3   15m (6). Follow the steep groove above.

Arete Finish 20m VI ★★ 1997

3   20m (7). From the belay below the final groove, follow the stepped crack to a spike on the arete and make a few delicate moves up this to easier ground and the top.

The Jabberwock 75m VII ★★★ 2003

This follows the crack system on the right-hand side of the prominent steep headwall, approached by scrambling from the right.

1   20m (5). Climb the cracked wall to a ledge on right of a large flake.
2   30m (7). Climb a crack to a large ledge at 20m and continue to a ledge and shattered block belay.
3   25m (6). Follow the exposed groove above to the top. It is also possible to finish further left.

Gable End 150m II ★★ 1960

Start up easy slopes to the left of *Central Gully* and head to a gully and corner-line running directly up the crag immediately right of the main rock buttress of *Engineer's Slab*.

Trundle Ridge 140m VII ☆☆ 2003

A climb following the left ridge overlooking *Central Gully*; if you stray too far left you'll end up on *Gable End*.

1   40m (7). From the lowest rocks of the ridge, climb a grassy corner to a saddle in the ridge. Climb a short wall and steep off-width crack to the top of a pinnacle.
2   10m (4). Step down from the pinnacle and cross a chimney using a jammed block to gain a ledge.
3   30m (7). Climb the steep crack directly out of the gap to gain a shallow corner. Follow this, and the short wall when it runs out, to a large stance.

4   60m (3). Easier climbing leads to the top via *Gable End* or one of the *Central Gully* finishes.

Central Gully   225m III ★★ 1891

An interesting outing with avoidable lower steep pitches and several alternative exits. The traditional route is described first. All of the variations start up this and go to the headwall after the second pitch.

1   35m. Climb the chimney direct (if iced), or the arete on the left.
2   20m. Climb the second chimney direct, or a smaller easier chimney on the left, over a chockstone. Traverse back to the gully bed.
3   50m. Continue up easier snow to small stance at the gully headwall.
4   20m. On the right is a small steep corner-chimney leading onto a large terrace.
5   30m. Head easily up to the right to steeper rock at the right end of the terrace. Climb a small pitch above the *Smuggler's Retreat* then follow the easy gully which runs out into a rake.
6   100m. The rake leads easily to the summit.

The Contrived Eliminate   50m IV (5) 1960

5   (20m). From the headwall in the main gully, climb directly up an iced crack for 5m to a large snow slope. Cross this to a belay below a slabby stepped headwall.
6   (30m). Take the line of least resistance through the wall to summit snow slopes.

The Smart Exit   73m IV (4) ★★ 1937

5   (18m). From the stance at the headwall, follow the left-slanting groove to the left end of a large snow slope.
6   (16m). Ascend the snowfield easily up left to the gully-chimney at the top left.
7   (45m). Climb 10m of steep ice and exit onto snow leading to the summit plateau.

Less than Smart Exit   60m III ★ 1996

5   (20m). Follow *The Smart Exit* to the snow slope, but traverse left for about 15m to a lower gully with a small chockstone.
6   (40m). This leads to the exit slopes above the ice pitch of *The Smart Exit*. The gully steepens at a detached pinnacle on the left. Pass this to easier ground and a corner at the top of *Gable End*.

Bootlegger's Groove   150m III ☆ 1999

Excellent mixed climbing up the big corner right of *Central Gully*. Start at the base of *Central Gully*.

1   40m. Climb up rightwards to an overhanging block at 12m. Pull over (first crux), then straight up the corner to a belay below a left-leaning corner-crack.

2   40m. Climb the crack (second crux) to easy ground, then continue straight up a prominent groove. Pull out to easy snow and follow this for 15m to a large block and thread belay.

3   40m. Move right and finish up the ridge, or traverse right into the easy top part of *Smuggler's Chimney* or *Central Gully*.

4   30m. Easy snow to the top.

The next obvious feature is a steep crack/chimney, the summer route *Smuggler's Chimney*. The next two routes take a fairly similar line up the groove system midway between this and *Moses's Back Door*.

Back Off   65m VI (7) 2003

This follows a natural winter line based around the summer route of *Smaug*. Start in the first snow bay to the right of *Central Gully*.

1   40m. Start up an iced corner to belay below an obvious rib.

2   25m. Move right to a thin crack to the right of the rib and follow this to a steep crack. Avoid the overhanging crack and go right. Follow *Moses's Back Door* to the top (a further 125m).

Gone with the Wind   60m IV 1997

A climb which takes the buttress and groove system located between *Smuggler's Chimney* and the start of *Moses's Back Door*. This and the previous route possibly share the 'steep ice groove' variation (described as part of *Moses's Back Door*) to give a more direct line. To the right of *Smuggler's Chimney* is a small buttress. Start at the foot of the buttress below a wide open gully. From the start a vertical crack and block are visible high up on the left edge of the buttress.

1   25m. Ascend the buttress to a large ledge. From the left-hand end of the ledge, move up to the edge, ascend the crack and surmount the block (crux), pulling up onto a ledge. Move up into a large bay directly below a groove (the same point can be reached by going directly up from the right-hand end of the large ledge).

2   20m. Ascend the groove system to emerge near the top of *Smuggler's Chimney*.

3   15m. The short corner direct to the large terrace below the head-wall. Easier ground leads up and left to the summit.

Moses's Back Door   190m II 1960

From the wide open gully on the right of the crag, gain a ramp which leads left to a snow bay. Cross the snow bay and traverse left again to a groove which leads to the *Smuggler's Retreat*. Finish as for *Central Gully*. A steep ice groove also leads from the snow bay to the same place.

In Her Mouth   90m V (6) 2003

Below *Doctor's Chimney* and above the grassy gully of *Moses's Back Door* is an obvious rock ramp running from right to left with a chimney/groove at its base. Start at the chimney/groove, which is the start of the summer route *Sundowner*.

1   30m. From a spike on the left, traverse right into a chimney/groove and climb directly to a belay on a large ledge above.
2   60m. Climb the corner to the right of the belay until a traverse left is possible along a narrow ledge. Follow this to its end and swing round an arete. Climb direct to the top of crag.

Doctor's Chimney   130m III ★ 1962/3

Start up the wide gully at the right side of the crag and after 50m ascend the obvious chimney on the left. Follow this (30m) then continue easily to the top.

Great Gable Traverse   600m II 1960

Also known as the **Traverse of the Gods**. The traverse follows a great bow-shaped natural weakness starting from the foot of the easy gully near Windy Gap. From the foot of *Oblique Chimney*, the line runs along the base of *Engineer's Slabs* to cross *Central Gully*, beyond which it dips to reach easy slopes below *Doctor's Chimney*. It is not without interest in its own right and is a useful approach to many of the routes on the face.

Western Crags

Green Gable Crag

(NY 214 106)
Alt. 750m West facing

This crag sits on the West Face of Green Gable at the head of Ennerdale and faces across to the more imposing *Gable Crag*. It can be reached in about an hour from Honister Pass. Access is also straightforward from Borrowdale via Styhead Tarn and up Aaron Slack to Windy Gap, whence the crag is to be seen immediately on the right. If travelling from Wasdale, follow the path to Beck Head to the west of Great Gable, then skirt along the path under *Gable Crag* to the head of the valley, and thence contour round to *Green Gable Crag*. Although short by traditional winter standards, several routes may be climbed in a visit, making it a worthwhile venue.

The climbs are described from **right** to **left**.

Turfed Out
70m II (3) 2006

Start up and right of *Calculator*.

1   30m (3). Follow a wide crack to gain a ledge. Move right and up a short awkward wall to reach iced slabs. Follow these up left to the top of the buttress.
2   40m. Pleasant mixed ground leads to the top.

Calculator
72m IV (4) ★ 1995

From the lowest point of the buttress climb to a large ledge. From the centre of the buttress move diagonally left to the base of a V-groove above a shattered overhang at the left edge of the buttress. Follow the V-groove to the top. A further 30m of easy climbing leads to the summit.

Sod-U-Like
75m II 1995

Start at the lowest point of the buttress, next to *Calculator*, and climb up and left of *Calculator* to pass the shattered overhang on its left side. Climb a V-groove left of the buttress to its top and then follow *Calculator* to the top.

Parallel G
80m II/III 1995

The parallel-sided gully to the left of the buttress. Follow the gully to the point where it widens above and finish to the right of the next buttress.

Green Gable

1	North Gully	I/II
2	Garden of Eden	III
3	East of Eden	IV
4	Ride the Wild Turf	III
5	Epsilon Chimney	III
6	Gully of the Plods	I/II
7	Beta Hammer Belter	III
8	Parallel G	II/III

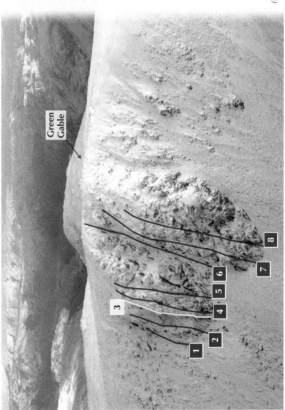

Green Gable

(Photo: Steve Ashworth)

Western Crags

199

Beta Hammer Belter   75m III 1995

The lowest point of the crag is characterised by a deeply cut chimney.
Start in a recess, to the left of the chimney, at a turf-filled gully. Climb the
gully to more open ground, then steeper iced rock above, turning an
overhang on its left.

Mutley's Icy Wait   90m II 2002

Start up ice on the right side of the gully wall just below the short rock
step at the start of *Gully of the Plods*. Frozen turf leads to a short cleft at
10m. Continue up easier ground, and at 60m climb a short icy chimney
with a large chockstone in it. Follow easy ground to the top.

Gully of the Plods   120m I/II 1978

An obvious gully which effectively separates the crag into two sections.
It is climbed via the right-hand branch. The left-hand branch gives some
steep moves on turf at a similar grade.

Epsilon Chimney   57m III ★★ 1995

To the left of *Gully of the Plods* are some slabs with a chimney on their
left. Climb the chimney.

Ride the Wild Turf   45m III (4) 1995

About 10m to the left of *Epsilon Chimney* is a small detached buttress.
Start on its left and continue up a grassy corner right of some rocky ribs
to finish up grooves.

East of Eden   60m IV (5) ★ 1995

This route follows the wall just left of and below the broken ribs of the
previous route.

1   10m. Climb the wall and go up leftwards at its top to a recess on the
     right.
2   30m. Turn the slab and short steep wall to the left to a ledge below
     the overhang (crux). Move right under the overhang and enter the
     chimney above. Belay at the back of the chimney.
3   20m. Climb the corner above and finish up and right.

Stuart Allinson on Beta Hammer Belta *(III), Green Gable Crag
(Photo: Harry Worsnop)*

Western Crags

Garden of Eden
80m III ★★★ 1995

Follow easy ground to the grass-covered recess of *East of Eden*. Continue up the icy corner to the top.

Green Gable End
80m IV (4) ★ 1995

Start up the easy ground as for *Garden of Eden* but belay at the left-hand side of the recess to the left of the largest slab, below a grassy corner groove. Continue up the corner and move right into the continuation groove at the top.

Arjuna
43m III (5) 1995

Start a few metres up the descent gully at the left-hand side of the crag. Follow a corner-line filled with turf to an overhang and chockstone. Pass this (crux) and follow a groove above to the top.

North Gully
30m I/II 1995

The wide shallow gully between the left edge of the buttress and the smaller buttress to its left.

North Face
20m I 1995

Easy climbing up the buttress left of *North Gully*.

KIRK FELL
(NY 195 105)
802m

Kirk Fell is the shapely hill immediately west of Great Gable. It can be most easily approached from **Honister**, or from **Wasdale** via Blacksail Pass or Gavel Neese.

On the south (Wasdale) side of Kirk Fell is *Ill Gill*.

Ill Gill
265m II/III 1963

A prominent long gash seen on the Wasdale side of the mountain close to the path up to Styhead. After a period of hard frost, the gill gives an excellent mixed route which, in a good season, can be followed to the summit of the mountain.

All of the remaining climbing on Kirk Fell is on the north (Ennerdale) side.

The path leading under Boat Howe from Great Gable via Beckhead Tarn crosses **Boat Howe Gill** at (NY 204 109, alt. 580m) just before *Boat Howe* is reached: it can give 150m of water ice in a sharp freeze (II).

Boat Howe

(NY 199 110)
Alt. 700m North facing

This crag is situated high on the Ennerdale side of Kirk Fell and is best approached from Wasdale by Beck Head or, slightly longer, via Black Sail Pass. It is also possible to approach from Honister Pass following the approach to *Gable Crag*. The crag has a number of obvious gullies at Grade I/II. The climbs are described from left to right.

The broken easterly buttress contains **Esplanade Climb** (II/III) up the centre – follow your nose. Further right is a steep pillar of rock, *The Boat*, with the obvious cleft of *Starboard Chimney* to its right.

Starboard Chimney   40m IV (5) ★★ 1990

To the right of the main buttress is a short cleft. Climb it if you like that sort of thing. Strenuous.

To the right of *The Boat* across a scree gully is the *West Buttress*.

Horizon Climb   100m IV (4) 1989

A good mixed route that is often in condition. Start up a corner to the right of a series of slabs.

1   40m. Climb up the corner right of slabs and move right to broken rock and a series of ledges.
2   20m. Follow the corner-line on the left to a ledge.
3   40m. Follow a series of ledges trending right to finish up a ridge.

Black Sail Buttress

(NY 194 111)
Alt. 620m North facing

This crag is found high up on the north-west side of the mountain, above Black Sail Pass, and is best approached from the Wasdale side. It is marked on the map as *Kirkfell Crags*.

Kirk Fell Gill   165m II/III ★ 1963

Marked as *Sail Beck* on the map, *Kirk Fell Gill* (NY 194 113) is approached from the *Black Sail* path via upper Ennerdale or Wasdale. The northerly aspect and high altitude produce some good and relatively long-lasting ice.

The climbing in the gill actually starts where it enters a cleft a hundred metres or so below the buttress itself. The stream crosses the old smugglers' track between *Black Sail* and *Beck Head* at the lowest point of the path. From this point, several minor pitches lead to a large ice pitch, all of which are escapable.

The remaining climbs lie on the crag itself. The first two may in fact be one and the same.

Central Groove   100m II/III 1984

Start at a steep vegetated groove to a terrace. Move up the mixed ground above via the easiest line. From the terrace it is possible to go right and descend into the easy gully or traverse left to easy ground.

Ignition Buttress (100m, III, 1963), the buttress just right of *Kirk Fell Gill* offers some steep mixed ground leading to a snow terrace. Above, a large icefall can be followed to the top.

Black Sail Gully   180m II (3)

This pleasant gully marks the right side of the crag and finishes almost on the summit of Kirk Fell.

BUTTERMERE

Tucked away in the north-west corner of the Lake District is the remote valley of Buttermere, a noticeably quieter area than many other parts of the National Park. Access to the valley from the north and east is usually via Honister or Newlands passes, and from West Cumbria via Lorton Vale to the north-west (the latter is often passable when other roads are closed due to ice). Please see the map 'Buttermere and Ennerdale' on pages 160–61.

Buttermere runs in a south-east to north-west direction and contains the lakes of Buttermere and Crummock Water. The head of the valley is dominated by Fleetwith Pike, which has Honister Pass to its north and Warnscale Bottom to its south-west. There is climbing on both sides of the valley. The south side contains the low-lying crag of *Haystacks* and its various gullies. To its west, between the summits of High Crag and High Stile, is Birkness Combe, with a number of classic winter climbs such as *Birkness Chimney* and *Birkness Gully*. West again lies Bleaberry Combe and *Chapel Crags*. The gills on the north side of the valley can hold good ice in prolonged cold spells, with additional, more reliable climbing being found on the mountains of Hopegill Head and Grasmoor. Fleetwith Pike itself arguably contains the best pure icefall climbing in the Lakes, only a short walk above Honister Pass.

The Newlands Valley, Coledale and Whinlatter Pass, which lie to the north-east of Buttermere, are also described in this section.

HONISTER PASS (NY 225 135)

From Honister Pass a number of winter climbs are easily accessible, the greatest concentration being the icefalls which form on *Honister Crag*. This north and north-east facing crag lies immediately above the pass on its south side. Fed by drainage from the old mine workings, great curtains and chandeliers of ice form to create a superb collection of routes up to 150m in length within 20 minutes walk from the car.

The road on the west (Buttermere) side of Honister Pass has a gentler incline than the east (Seatoller) side, from which most people usually approach. Unfortunately this is readily prone to icing. However if the pass is thereby rendered inaccessible by car, an approach by foot, especially on the Buttermere side, is not too arduous.

The first two routes described are found on the **north** side of the pass.

Yew Crags
(NY 219 147)
Alt. 350m South-west facing

Yew Crag Gully is the only major gully in the broken crag on the northern slopes of the upper Buttermere Valley. Being south facing, it is seldom in condition – an early start is worthwhile when it is.

Yew Crag Gully
140m IV (4) ★

The gully is best approached directly from the road to its foot.
1   30m. Easy snow to the first chockstone, which is passed on the right.
2   20m. A small chockstone pitch leads to the foot of a big icefall.
3   30m. The bulging icefall leads to easier snow, above which it is possible to escape to the right.
4   60m. For a fuller mountaineering experience, continue up the gully for several short pitches. It is then possible to continue to the summit ridge.

Buckstone How
(NY 223 143)
Alt. 400m South-west facing

Situated just to the north-west side of the summit of Honister Pass, *Buckstone How* is easily reached by taking an old quarry track that contours northwards from the road just past the pass summit opposite the youth hostel and slate mine works. (NB This is not to be confused with 'Buckstone Hows', which is marked on the 1:25,000 OS map occurring much further north.) Descend diagonally across slate spoil to the crag. It is rumoured that the summer VS **Sinister Grooves** has been climbed in winter, though no further details are known. A description will be found in the FRCC Buttermere guide.

The remaining climbs are located on the **south** side of the pass.

Quarry Fall   25m IV (5)

This free-standing icefall is located just behind the quarry and youth hostel car park in a small stream basin to the right of the fence, about five minutes' walk from the road. The steep bit is short, and the route ends abruptly in the stream bed above.

FLEETWITH PIKE – NORTH FACE

The mountain, as well as containing arguably the best pure ice climbing in the Lake District on *Honister Crag*, also has some climbing on its west flank, overlooking Warnscale Bottom.

Honister Crag Icefalls   (NY 217 140)
Alt. 350m North-east facing

A long period of cold northerly or easterly winds are required to bring this fine collection of icefalls into condition. Many of these routes, which are draped over the old slate workings of *Honister Crag*, were climbed in the last quarter of the 20th century when conditions were on occasion quite fantastic. Unfortunately the recent resumption of working at the quarry seems to have reduced drainage down the crag, with the consequence that these icefalls form less frequently and less densely than they used to.

The line of the icefalls, the old mine workings and the crag itself are home to rare alpine plants – please climb here only in truly frozen conditions and read the chapter 'Winter Climbing and Nature Conservation'.

The first route is reached by taking the lower of two inclines from the Honister Mine car park at the top of Honister Pass, marked as the 'Monkey Shelf' on a slate inlaid on the track. Follow it to the fourth bridge, about 5 minutes from the car park. The icefall is above the bridge.

Incline Fall   25m II/III 2004

A nice short pitch narrowing steadily all the way to an awkward finish. Limited rock protection can be arranged on the left. There is a tree belay set back at the top.

The remaining icefalls are all reached from an incline running off the Honister to Gable track. From the top of the Honister Pass take the main track towards Gable, but after a short distance branch off on the quarry incline to the right, and where this divides take the lower fork. This exposed renovated railway incline, which follows occasional tunnels, strikes a rightward-rising diagonal line across the Honister Face of Fleetwith Pike. (The incline is a useful general reference point, and the three main climbing areas described below are described relative to it.)

After a few hundred metres the incline enters a tunnel, access to which is barred by large gates (the other end is a few hundred metres away). It is necessary to traverse, on the downhill side, before scrambling back up to the incline over slate scree on the other side. Alternatively, follow a rising ramp containing spikes to the right of the tunnel entrance (awkward in mountaineering boots) around a rock bluff to emerge at a gully adjacent to *Upper Left Gantry Crag*, which is gained by scrambling across the gully. This aptly named crag usually holds three steep icefalls. The other end of the tunnel emerges beyond *Upper Left Gantry Crag*. To the right the incline now continues above a slate buttress topped by an old iron gantry standing on the incline. This gantry, obvious from the road, serves as a useful landmark amidst the complex slate-strewn surrounds. *Gantry Crag*, which lies below it, is bounded on the left by *Cable Gully* and on the right by *Quarryman's Gully*, a wide gully filled with slate scree.

Tunnel Vision   30m III/IV 1997

The icefall to the left of the tunnel entrance. Climb a groove to a bay, passing an overhang and an iron spike (if the icefall has failed to form down to the incline this bay can be gained by a traverse in from the left). From the bay, climb the ice to a small overhang which is taken on the right, then move back left above it. At the top, either follow the steeper centre of the icefall (IV) or a groove on the left (III).

Upper Left Gantry Crag

This crag lies to the left of the gantry above the tunnel portal and usually holds three distinct icefalls, with a crooked lesser fall issuing from below

Honister Crag Icefalls – Upper Left Gantry Crag

(Photo: Colin Downer)

1	Slate Cap	IV
2	Turf at the Top	V
3	Captain Patience	III/IV
4	Lesser Fall	III

Western Crags

the top to their right. The crag is gained by following steep ground above the tunnel portal. Descent is down an easy rake to the left of the crag or by abseil.

Slate Cap   **40m IV ★★ 1987**
The left fall containing an obvious wedged slate chockstone.

Turf at the Top   **40m V (5) ★★★ 1995**
The central fall is the steepest and may form a free-standing icicle.

Captain Patience   **40m III/IV ★★ 1995**
The easiest of the trio, though harder if the top section is not fully formed.

Lesser Fall   **45m III 1997**
The fall furthest to the right comprises easier ice with a steeper lower section.

Gantry Crag

This, the most significant buttress on Honister, presents four major lines and numerous variations. When in condition a large curtain of ice forms right of *Cable Gully*, and further right, on the front face of the crag, a striking and independent icefall forms which sometimes has two parallel lines.

Directly below the crag, extensive slate scree drops to the valley floor. The shortest approach is directly up this from the road in about 20 minutes. This is straightforward if snow covered, but purgatorial otherwise. A longer alternative (which, admittedly, is not much better) is to take the quarryman's ramp from the pass, bypass the tunnel and rejoin the incline at the other side of the tunnel. Descend a scree/snow slope before traversing to the base of the crag – this is also the usual **descent** route from the crag.

The climbs are described from left to right.

Cable Gully   **100m III/IV ★ 1970s**
Follow the gully; a heavy rusty cable provides convenient belays. The right side of the dry stone headwall usually contains a good ice finish onto the gantry ledge.

Honister Crag Icefalls – Gantry Crag

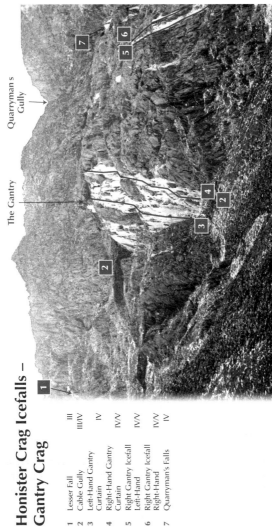

1	Lesser Fall	III
2	Cable Gully	III/IV
3	Left-Hand Gantry Curtain	IV
4	Right-Hand Gantry Curtain	IV/V
5	Right Gantry Icefall Left-Hand	IV/V
6	Right Gantry Icefall Right-Hand	IV/V
7	Quarryman's Falls	IV

(Photo: Phil Young)

Western Crags

Left-Hand Gantry Curtain   100m IV (4) ★★★ 1970s
A direct line can be taken starting just to the right of the base of *Cable Gully*. Two pitches lead to the ledge which runs across the left side of the crag at two-thirds height; belay on the break (70m). Follow the top icefall above the ledge direct (30m).

Right-Hand Gantry Curtain   100m IV/V (4) ★★★ 1970s
The right-hand icefall is generally steeper.
1   35m. Follow steep ice to bare rock and a peg belay.
2   35m. Move left and up to the ledge. A traverse right leads to a belay below the right-hand top icefall.
3   30m. Climb the icefall, or the smaller though steeper icefall to the left, to finish direct onto the gantry ledge.

Right Gantry Icefall
(Left and Right-Hand)   120m IV/V (5) 1970s
The distinctive ice smear on the right front face of the crag. The main pitch may form as two independent icefalls, with the right-hand usually the harder and thinner of the two.
1   30m. Climb easy-angled ice to where it steepens beneath the main fall.
2   30m. Follow the nearly vertical ice direct, before the angle thankfully eases.
3   30m. Scrambling and easier-angled ice leads to the base of a great corner.
4   30m. The ice corner leads to the gantry ledge – a great pitch.

Quarryman's Gully Falls
Follow the incline further right until it crosses *Quarryman's Gully*. Beneath the incline, a 30m curtain of ice can form. Access is by abseil from the small gantry on the incline above.

Quarryman's Falls   30 to 45m IV (4) ★★ 1996
The falls comprise three obvious icefalls, all of a similar nature.

Honister Crag Gully   200m IV (5) 1969
To the right of the large buttress right of *Gantry Crag*, a long distinctive gully rises from the screes not far above the road and soars directly to the top of Fleetwith Pike, splitting the Honister face – this is *Honister Crag Gully* (NY 214 142).

Avoid an impressive overhanging block at the foot of the gully on the right by a traverse before returning to the gully and climbing it direct. Several short but steep ice pitches lead to the top.

WARNSCALE BOTTOM

This low-lying valley at the head of Buttermere, between Fleetwith Pike and Haystacks, contains a number of gullies and streams making for good water-ice climbing following a prolonged frost and cold northerly or easterly winds.

The approach is via a bridlepath from *Gatesgarth Cottage* (NY 196 149). Fleetwith Pike lies to the left (east), with Haystacks across the valley to the south-west.

On the west side of Fleetwith Pike overlooking *Warnscale Bottom* is:

Fleetwith Gully   60m II 1928
The gully, which is situated to the right of *Striddle Crag* (NY 204 139) – the crag high up on the Fleetwith Pike, is best approached by following the *Warnscale Bottom* bridlepath which runs below it, then ploughing straight up to it. The gully contains one 25m pitch.

A number of the water courses draining into *Warnscale Bottom* can give pleasant ice pitches of II/III after a prolonged freeze. The following two, tucked away in the south corner between Haystacks and *Green Crag* to its left, are worthy of description. Both are tributaries of *Black Beck*, which feeds **Warnscale Beck** (I, 1963).

Green Crag Gully   60m II
This deeply cut gully is home to a stream tumbling down from *Blackbeck Tarn*. It contains a waterfall which gives the main pitch.

Toreador Gully   100m III
This steep gully is found on the left side of the Haystacks massif (NY 199 132). Start at a chimney.
1   20m. Climb up the chimney to icy slabs at its top.

2   30m. After easier-angled climbing, the gully steepens to another chimney pitch which leads to a small amphitheatre.
3   50m. Continue steeply up the gully, over mixed snow and ice, past two large chockstones.

Haystacks
(NY 197 131)
Alt. 400m North facing

A large, rambling and broken crag, situated on the fell of the same name. An easy rake, useful in descent, can be seen rising from bottom right to top left across the left half of the crag. The rock is very poor, and the gullies only form in exceptional conditions. The routes are described from **right** to **left**, in the order that they would normally be approached. The first route, *Long Gully*, lies between two large buttresses to the right of the rake. The steep chimneys of *Stack Gill*, *Warn Gill* and *Y Gully* (located beneath the rake) lie on the far left.

Approach as for *Warnscale Bottom*, along the path from *Gatesgarth Cottage* (NY 196 149). Cross the beck and climb directly up steep scree to the crag.

Long Gully
300m III ★

A water-ice gully taking a direct line between the buttresses which make up the right side of the face. A series of easy short pitches with poor belays lead to a steeper 50m pitch and a peg belay. A further steep section (15m) leads to easy ground and the summit.

The next three gullies can be found at the bottom of the far left end of the face.

Stack Gill
150m III 1963

The rightmost of the three gullies. The first cave pitch, climbed from right to left, proves the crux. Further climbing up chimneys and over chockstones leads to a final ice pitch. Said to have given superb water-ice climbing on the first ascent.

Warn Gill
200m IV (4) 2001

The middle of the three obvious gills. The steep initial entry to the gill bed can be avoided (if unfrozen) by climbing a heathery groove to the right for about 20m, before making a delicate traverse across two rock ribs to gain the bed of the gill (40m). Continue up the gill bed passing some jammed blocks then a steep wall (60m). More heathery climbing leads to the top.

Y Gully   100m IV (5) 1963

The leftmost gully and possibly the best of the trio. Climbed in the 'big freeze' of 1963, this gully was said to be a fine climb under such conditions – certainly finer than it is in summer, when it has been described as having 'areas that make Lego look solid'.

BIRKNESS COMBE   (NY 175 145)

Marked on OS maps as Burtness Combe, this north-east-facing combe lies between the summits of High Crag and High Stile. As well as constituting the rock climbing centre of the Buttermere valley, it has some good ice climbing in its gullies and on its cliffs.

From Gatesgarth Farm, cross the valley at the head of the lake. Follow the main Scarth Gap track up the hillside, but branch off right on a much smaller track after 50m or so. Cross the fellside, passing under a steep dank outcrop. Pass this on its right and go straight up, crossing some boggy ground and a stile into the combe (1hr). The buttresses are described in a clockwise direction.

Descent is possible down either side of the buttresses described.

Brant Bield Crags   (NY 175 145)
                                    Alt. 520m North facing

Named on OS maps as *Comb Crags*, this is an area of rocky outcrops at the back of the combe to the left of *Eagle Crag*. There are four distinctive gullies visible from the lip of the combe: all give about 100m of straightforward climbing and a good way to the top of High Crag. In many cases the difficulties can be outflanked using heathery buttresses either side of the gullies. The buttresses do not fulfil the potential they promise from below, being somewhat scrappy with loose rock.

The leftmost gully (II/III) is easy apart from a capping stone approximately one-third of the way up, which is best climbed on the right. About

100m to its right is an easy shallow snow gully (I) with no real difficulty other than finding it frozen. Further right are twin gullies with a common start past a short chockstone. The easier left branch (II) runs up to the left of a steep buttress, while the more interesting right branch (III) runs diagonally rightwards across the steep buttress and has a few short icy steps, many of which can be outflanked on the buttresses to either side.

The next buttress is split by two parallel gullies and is separated from *Brant Bield Crag* by a grassy gully. The gullies (**Parallel Gully Left** and **Right**) both contain short steps (II, 70m, 2001). The gully to the right of the buttress, **Right-Hand Gully** (II, 100m, 2001), contains several pleasant short ice steps.

Eagle Crag (NY 172 145)
Alt. 600m West and north facing

This large centrally situated crag dominates the back of the upper combe. From the base of the combe the following features can be recognised. The easy *West Gully* lies right of the striking main buttress. This buttress is split by the cleft of *Central Chimney*, obvious in its upper portion. Left of this, and hidden by the bulk of the buttress, is *Birkness Chimney*, with the slanting *Birkness Gully* further to its left. *Border Buttress* bounds the far left side of the crag.

The routes are described from left to right.

Border Buttress bounds the left side of the crag and lies high up in the combe. It is situated about 50m along a grassy/snowy terrace running left from *Birkness Gully*, at the point where the gully steepens and its walls close together. It is bounded on the left by the short **Easy Gully** (I).

Border Buttress Gully 50m III/IV 1986
The first gully to the left of *Birkness Gully* and bounding *Border Buttress*. It starts just right of *Easy Gully*, and is hidden from sight until you are underneath it. A steep and strenuous ice pitch leads to a narrow bay with poor potential for rock runners or belays. Above is a short but very steep (sometimes undercut) carapace or column of ice which eases off onto easier ground after about 5m.

Border Buttress (III/IV, 50m, 1984) itself also carries an icefall down its front in a good year. Then it will appear as an obvious ice sheet between

Eagle Crag

1	Border Buttress Gully	III/IV
2	Border Buttress	III/IV
3	Birkness Gully	IV
4	Birkness Gully Wall	V
5	The Eagle's Claw	V
6	Birkness Chimney	IV
7	Central Chimney	V
8	Eagle Front	VI
9	West Gully	I

(Photo: Stephen Reid)

Birkness Gully and *Border Buttress Gully*. Two similar pitches of moderately steep ice can be climbed with a belay at the base of a corner half way up.

Birkness Gully   50m IV (4) ★★★

The rather hidden left-slanting diagonal gully on the left side of the main crag. Short but interesting. Follow easy snow up the gully until it steepens dramatically.

1   25m. Climb to a large jammed boulder and behind it to a peg belay.
2   25m. The meat of the route. Move onto the boulder and traverse the right wall to gain ice which can be climbed to a peg belay in a rock outcrop.

Birkness Gully Wall   50m V (4) 1984 ★★

Forms more readily than the gully. Start 10m below the steep pitch in *Birkness Gully*.

1   20m. Climb diagonally rightwards over mixed ground to a spike belay.
2   30m. Climb up the icy groove and icefall on the left to the top.

The Eagle's Claw   70m V (5) ★ 1985

Between *Birkness Chimney* and *Birkness Gully* an impressive hanging icefall forms high up on the headwall.

1   25m. From the foot of *Birkness Gully*, traverse rightwards and then climb up to a large snow ledge at the foot of the narrow section of *Birkness Chimney*. In a good year the icefall may reach this ledge; if not, another 20m pitch on turf is required (start from the lower left side of the snow ledge and zig-zag up left and then back right).
2   45m. Climb the large icefall on the left wall. It is possible to finish to the left or right depending how the ice has formed.

Birkness Chimney   65m IV (5) ★ 1941

The chimney-line which divides the steeper *Easter Buttress* from the slabbier *Far East Buttress* to its left. It is not an obvious route to spot from below during the approach. In addition, look at the grade and spare a thought for the first ascentionists, Bill Peascod and Bert Beck, tackling the route with no ice axes, crampons or gloves! Then thank Providence for modern gear…

1   15m. The initial chimney pitch can be fun, though is not often iced. It is usually avoided by traversing in from *Birkness Gully*.

Glenn Wilks on Pitch 1 of Birkness Gully Wall *(V), Eagle Crag, Buttermere (Photo: Bryan McGowan)*

2   20m. Follow the next chimney pitch to a ledge (a large icefall, *The Eagle's Claw*, often forms above here on the left). Above is the crux where the chimney narrows. Belay below the wider terminal chimney above.

3   30m. Easier climbing up the final chimney leads to the top.

Central Chimney   150m V (5) 1963

The astute will instantly discern that this is the chimney in the middle of the crag. Start at the lowest point of the crag.

1   50m. Follow the chimney, which is not well defined initially and is escapable by traversing to the left at a number of points.

2   40m. The chimney steepens and the climbing starts in earnest. Although it follows the line of the chimney, the climbing is exposed and requires well-frozen turf. The crux is saved till last: it comprises

difficult and precarious moves over chockstones to gain the deeper sanctuary of the chimney proper.

3   60m. Standing proud from the hillside, the deep cleft does not often contain much ice and is climbed in traditional style, with belays where required. There are some hard moves, but the walls of the chimney take away the feeling of exposure.

The classic VS rock climb of **Eagle Front** was climbed during an exceptionally hard winter in 1963 which allowed neve and ice to build up on the crag: essential for the ascent, particularly for crossing slabby sections. The route follows the summer line (described in the FRCC Buttermere guide), winding its way up the more vegetated lower section of the cliff to a prominent left-facing corner high at the top of the crag. As far as is known the climb is unrepeated, but the grade would presumably be at least VI.

Pigott's Route   100m IV 1963

A slightly more direct line than the summer route. *Pigott's* lies on the west face of the crag and starts 5m above the scree at the corner of the buttress.

1.   30m. Climb a hanging chimney and bulging rock above (crux).
2.   70m. Follow various snow banks and small icefalls steeply rightwards to the top.

West Gully (150m, I) on the right of the buttress is an easy snow climb and makes a useful **descent**.

Above and to the right of *Eagle Crag* is an area of broken buttresses and scree gullies. There is a conspicuous narrow ridge to the left of the second scree gully from *Eagle Crag*. This is **The Barn Door** (45m, II, 1935), an interesting route.

Grey Crag   (NY 172 147)
Alt. 670m East facing

This crag comprises a collection of buttresses on the right-hand side of the combe. Facing south, they tend to catch the sun, and snow strips readily. The climbs described can be combined to produce a good outing – but only if you can catch the fleeting winter conditions.

'Mitre Ridge' is recorded as having been ascended under snow (1925). It is to be assumed that this means **Mitre Buttress Ordinary**, which lies on the left-hand of the two lower buttresses. The grade is unknown but it is M in summer, and the description can be found in the FRCC Buttermere guidebook.

Harrow Buttress   45m III 1960

This is the right-hand and smaller of the two lowest buttresses. A sunny route which can get quite hot.

1   10m. Start up a corner, just left of the toe, to a ledge.
2   35m. Follow the chimney above then move 3m left and up a groove.

Oxford and Cambridge Ordinary Route   42m IV (4) 1986

The uppermost buttress is the *Oxford and Cambridge Buttress*. Start up an arete separating the left and right faces of the buttress. Climb the arete for 15m to a ledge then move leftwards across the face to a right-facing corner. Near the top of the corner step onto an arete on the left.

BLEABERRY COMBE

The next combe to the north, between the summits of Red Pike to the north and High Stile to the south, contains Bleaberry Tarn, and above it the buttresses that make up *Chapel Crags*.

Sourmilk Gill   350m I/II

This gill, situated at the north-west end of Buttermere and overlooking the village, tumbles down from Bleaberry Tarn. It can provide a lengthy outing during an ice age, but its low starting altitude means it is rarely in complete condition (NY 172 163).

Chapel Crags   (NY 167 149)
Alt. 6700m North-east facing

A series of damp vegetated crags ring the back of the combe. The highest and leftmost is *Number One Buttress*, which stands below the summit of

High Stile and is split by a gully (*Little Sod*) on its right-hand side. To the right, across a wide scree chute, is *Number Two Buttress*. The right side of this vegetated buttress is split by a wide gully containing two large chockstones (*Black Chimney*). Down and right of these upper buttresses is the largest buttress, *Central Buttress* (also known as *Number Three Buttress*), which is bounded on its left by the obvious *Curving Gully* and split by the prominent faults of *Bleaberry Chimney*, just right of centre, and *Chapel Crag Gully* towards its right-hand side. It is bounded on the right by the easy *Wide Gully*, which makes a good **descent**. Right of *Wide Gully* lies *Number Four Buttress*, which is split by two lesser faults, the right one being *Sunday Chimney*. Right of this final buttress is the easy *Narrow Gully*. Many of these features are discernible from the valley.

Although many people appear to have climbed here over the years (Don Greenop climbed *Chapel Crag Gully* and *Curving Gully* after being told about them by 1940s and 50s Buttermere pioneer Bill Peascod for example), nothing has previously been recorded. It is therefore probably safe to assume that at least the easier gully lines will have seen earlier ascents than those recorded, but the climbers remain unknown.

From the village of Buttermere, take the path past the Fish Hotel to the foot of *Sourmilk Gill*. Follow the steep but well-made path up leftwards through the woods, then back right across the hillside into the combe. The main track continues onto Red Pike; however, once in the combe, leave it, passing to the south-east of Bleaberry Tarn, and head up to the buttresses above (1hr 30mins).

Descent is down one of the easy gullies or scree chutes bounding the individual buttresses.

Number One Buttress

The highest buttress in the combe. It lies high on the far left side of the crag, below the summit of High Stile. The middle of the buttress has a prominent corner starting about halfway up the crag and a deep chimney (*Deep Cut Chimney*) cutting through the right-hand wall. The right-hand side of the buttress is bounded by the gully of *Little Sod*, and right of this is a pinnacle.

Turf Wars   **45m II ★ 2003**

At the left-hand side of the crag are several lines of turf running to the top of the crag. Climb the left-hand one, stepping right into the right-hand line at about half-height.

Chapel Crag – left-hand section

1 Turf Wars — II
2 Deep Cut Chimney — III
3 Little Sod — II
4 Grass Corner — II
5 Bear Left — IV
6 Right Frog — IV
7 Black Chimney — III
8 Gully Arete — I/II

(Photo: Dave Willis – Copyright FRCC)

To the right, a prominent bay lies about halfway up the crag, with a striking corner above it (as yet unclimbed).

Turf's Up   70m IV (4) ★★ 2003

Start at a turfy ramp below the prominent bay.
1. 30m. Climb up turf into a bay below the prominent corner.
2. 20m. Follow the first line of turf to the right of the corner, with an awkward finishing move onto a large ledge.
3. 20m. Trend leftwards up easy ground to the top.

New Turf   70m IV (4) 2003

A line between *Turf's Up* and the deep cleft of *Deep Cut Chimney*. Start as for *Turf's Up*.
1. 30m. Reach the bay below the corner as above.
2. 20m. Climb the turf runnel immediately left of the deep chimney to the large ledge above. An awkward move at the top provides the crux, but is escapable by stepping right into the chimney.
3. 20m. Trend leftwards up easy ground to the top.

Deep Cut Chimney   70m III 2003

To the right of the turf ramp used by the previous two routes is a short icy and turfy corner.
1. 30m. Use the short corner to reach a bay at the base of the prominent corner.
2. 20m. Enter the deep chimney and squirm up between chockstones to pop out just below the large belay ledge used by *New Turf*.
3. 20m. Easy climbing, trending leftwards, leads to the top.

Turf Walls   70m IV (5) ★ 2003

1. 30m. Follow *Deep Cut Chimney* to the base of the chimney.
2. 20m. Move right, with a tricky step to get established on some large sods which allow progress to be made up the wall right of the chimney to the large belay ledge above.
3. 20m. Trend leftwards up easy climbing to the top.

Little Sod   65m II 2001

Bounding the right side of this short buttress is a gully. Climb it passing a phallic pinnacle. The gully is likely to bank out into a Grade I snow slope given a good build-up.

The pinnacle which forms the right wall of *Little Sod* has two grooves on its right side.

Pinnacle Groove   30m II 2003

Climb the right-hand of the two grooves in the right-hand side of the pinnacle. At the top of the groove, either walk off right or spiral round the top of the pinnacle to the summit.

Number Two Buttress

The next buttress lies to the right of a wide scree gully and has a prominent slab at its top. The left side of the buttress contains a large grassy corner. The first route climbs this feature. On its right-hand side the buttress is split by the deep cleft of *Black Chimney*.

Grass Corner   60m II 2002

At the left side of the buttress, before it runs round into the wide gully, is a grassy corner/recess with a capstone at its start: this is about 20m left of a pinnacle. Passing the capstone on its left gives access to a large meadow and a choice of lines for the upper half. On the first ascent a turfy line on the left leading into a wide open corner was taken.

The next route climbs a turfy recess below and left of the prominent slab. Two further routes take the slab direct.

Turf Time   90m III 2003

Climb easy turf to the left of the deep gully a few metres left of *Bear Left* (40m). Below the prominent overhanging slab move left into a turfy recess and make steep moves to break through the overhang and come up to the left of the slab (25m). Climb corners above to the top (25m).

Bear Left   90m IV (6) ★ 2002

The right side of the crag is split by the deep gully of *Black Chimney*. To its left, high on the crag, is a prominent slab. This climb starts at a turfy depression, or at the rib to its right overlooking the chimney, and follows either to the overhang.

1   50m. Climb the turf to an overhang overlooking the gully to the right.
2   40m. Climb through the overhang at a corner by stepping off a small pedestal. Move up the corner for 5m before a delicate move left allows a left-trending groove/corner to be gained and followed to the top.

Right Frog   90m IV (5) ★★ 2002

1   50m. Start as for the previous route or take a different line up the
     turfed recess to the overhang.
2   40m. Break through the small overhang as before, but follow the
     corner upwards until it peters out at an overhang. Step right onto
     the front of the buttress and follow turf to the top.

Black Chimney   100m III (4) ★ 2003

This deep gully is a fun route. Easy snow leads to the first of two steep
chockstones which is turned on the right wall. The second allows useful
hooks and foot-ledges on the outside, or sometimes a squirmy through-
route. The remainder of the gully is straightforward.

  Between the two chockstones, the gully can be entered or exited at
either side. The access point to the right leads to an easy ramp-line up to
the ridge. That to the left leads to a ledge and the small pinnacle and the
belay of *Right Frog/Bear Left* below the prominent slab. The buttress can
be traversed (II, 2003) at this level using these sections to pass the gully
and turf to move along below the prominent slab.

Right of *Black Chimney* is a pleasant mixed ridge (**Gully Arete** I/II,
2002).

Central (or Number Three) Buttress

The largest, lowest and most prominent of the 'buttresses' actually consists of several discrete individual buttresses.

  Descent is down the easy *Wide Gully* on the right.

Straight Gully   I 130m 1999

This route is situated more or less in the centre of *Chapel Crags*. It starts
further up the hillside than the lowest rocks, up and left of the start of
Curving Gully, and is joined by the *Left-Hand Branch* after about 50m.

Straight Buttress   150m I/II 1999

Climbs the buttress between *Straight Gully* and *Curving Gully*. Several
lines are possible, and it has been climbed on its left and right sides. All
routes culminate at a miniature rocky subsidiary summit, from which a
short section of down-climbing is required before following one of several easy options to the top.

Steve Prior at the first chockstone in Black Chimney *(III),*
Chapel Crags (Photo: Stephen Reid)

Western Crags

Chapel Crag –
right-hand section

1	Straight Gully	I
2	Straight Buttress	I/II
3	Curving Gully	II
4	Curving Gully Direct	III
5	Bleaberry Chimney	III
6	Chapel Crag Gully	II
7	Flying Buttress	IV
8	Wide Gully	I
9	Monday Chimney	II/III
10	Sodomy	III
11	Sunday Chimney	II
12	Narrow Gully	I
13	Turf Accountant	III

(Photo: Dave Willis –
Copyright FRCC)

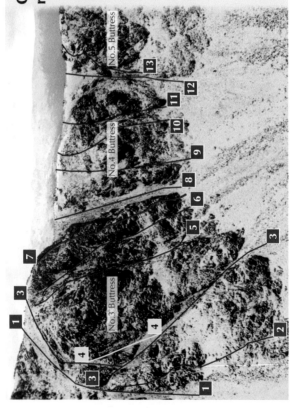

Curving Gully 60m II 1960

The gully bounds the left side of *Central Buttress*. As was their wont it was christened *Central Chimney* by the Victorian pioneers who scrambled up it; this rather misleading name has been changed to something more meaningful to modern climbers. A small chockstone bars the way after the first 20m, after which the left-hand branch of the gully leads to a bay. From here it is straightforward to climb to a col, where a junction is made with *Straight Gully* which is followed easily to the top. Alternatively, from the bay, follow steep snow and turf rightwards to arrive at the top of the steep ice pitch of the *Direct*, and climb more easily to the top.

Curving Gully Direct 160m ★ III (4) 2001

Follow the gully, but take the right branch to an impasse and avoid this by its iced left wall. Easy ground leads to the top.

Central Buttress Variation to Curving Gully 100m II/III 2005

Less of a variation than a separate climb, this route branches out of *Curving Gully Direct* at a point just below where that route steepens and narrows.

1   30m. Climb a rightward-leading ramp up to an obvious block and notch in the right-bounding ridge.
2   30m. From the crest, follow the steep buttress above, via turf grooves and a short wall, moving slightly right to a pinnacle belay.
3   40m. Easier ground leads to the top.

Bleaberry Chimney 170m III ★★★ 1960

The obvious shallow chimney in the grassy buttress to the left of the prominent *Chapel Crag Gully*. An entertaining route on turf and ice smears.

1   30m. Scramble up the gully bed to the foot of the chimney.
2   40m (4). A sustained pitch. Gain the narrow chimney via steep ice and climb it to a belay at an open break and division in the chimney.
3   50m (4). A short, hard, but well-protected section up the left-hand branch soon leads to much easier climbing.
4   50m (2). Follow the easy gully to the top.

Chapel Crag Gully 160m II ★★ 1960

This gully splits the right side of the buttress 10m left of *Wide Gully*. A fine atmospheric route.

1   50m. Bypass the first chockstone by heading up the shallow gully at the start of *Bleaberry Chimney* to the left, then traverse back right above the point of the first chockstone. Alternatively use turf to climb the buttress just to the left of the gully, or climb a turfy groove just right of the gully to a narrow ledge and traverse back left into the gully. All these ways lead to a spike belay on the left.

2   50m (3). Move up to where the gully narrows. 20m below the second chockstone a chimney and/or an icefall on the left leads to a small pinnacle belay.

3   60m. From the pinnacle, traverse right back into the gully above the second chockstone and follow it to the top.

Direct Start   70m V ★ 2003

The direct route tackling both the chockstones requires a reasonable build-up of ice – and it may get banked out in heavy snow.

1   20m (6). Climb a short pitch to the icy chimney. Back and foot to a rest in a small cave below the chockstone before launching out over it to the gully above.

2   50m (4). Follow the gully bed to the second chockstone which is taken direct.

Right-Hand Variation   80m III 1998

2   50m. To the right of the second chockstone is a narrow subsidiary gully. Follow this and either move left back into the gully above the chockstone or onto the buttress on the right.

Flying Buttress   180m IV 1999

The ridge between *Chapel Crag Gully* and *Wide Gully*. Start at the foot of an obvious chimney/groove in the centre of the buttress.

1   45m (5). From the foot of the chimney, follow a line of turf diagonally right to a ledge on the right crest of the ridge (crux), then move up and back left to a turfy corner and go up to a large ledge.

2   135m. Another steepening leads to a second ledge and belay. Follow the turf close to the crest for a further three pitches.

Right-Hand Start   III 1999

An easier start is possible from the gully on the right from which the ledges can be reached.

Wide Gully 130m I

The easy wide gully on the right of the buttress. A good **descent**.

Number Four Buttress

To the right of *Wide Gully* is a buttress containing two merging fault-lines (*Sunday Chimney*) towards its right-hand side.

Monday Chimney 90m II/III 1999

The first gully right of *Wide Gully*. Take the first two chockstone direct, with the larger third stone passed by climbing onto the buttress on the right and back into the gully just above it.

Sodomy 95m III 95m 2001

Immediately left of *Sunday Chimney* is a chimney which merges with that route after its first pitch. Just left of this is a shallow depression. Climb the depression directly, then the continuation cleft, and finish easily leftwards.

Sunday Chimney 95m III ★★★ 1999

The chimney splitting the buttress slightly right of its centre. The lower half contains two faults that merge after about 50m and has a large chockstone near the top.

1   20m. Climb the right-hand of the two initial chimneys to a ledge and a flake belay on the right.
2   45m. Continue up the steep narrow chimney until it widens and the angle eases. Continue up this to just below the large chockstone: a pedestal belay is possible on a ledge on the left.
3   30m. (4) From the top of the pedestal, move up onto ledges, which lead back right into the gully, and climb easily to the top.

Narrow Gully 90m I 1999

The narrow snow gully on the right of *Sunday Chimney*.

Number Five Buttress

The buttress to the right of *Narrow Gully* contains the following climb on its left side.

Turf Accountant 75m III 2001

Go up easy ground to a shallow bay at the foot of the buttress proper. (This point is 10m left of a pinnacle a short way up the crest.)

Climb the left-hand of two faults (the right one looks similar) to a gain a broad depression. Climb this and its narrower continuation. Trend left, then back right, over ledges to the top.

Lying to the north of Bleaberry Combe, the next climb comprises the main fall of the east-facing **Scale Beck** (NY 151 172, alt. 250m). From the village of Buttermere, take the path to Crummock Water, then follow the right-hand branch north along the side of the lake for about 500m until the path moves round into the next gill line. The beck descends down the left flank.

Scale Force   40m V (4)   ★★ 1962

The longest free-falling waterfall in the Lake District. When complete it gives a magnificent and sustained ice pitch, but as it is at a low altitude it takes a prolonged freeze to reach a climbable state.

GRASMOOR   (NY 175 203) Alt. 852m

This bulky mountain, standing on the eastern shore of Crummock Water, has the amenable *Lorton* and *Buttermere Gullies* on its western flank, and the rather more impressive *Dove Crag* hidden away on its north side.

Dove Crag   (NY 177 205) Alt. 700m North-east facing

Dove Crag runs along the right flank of a large combe which lies secreted on the northern flanks of Grasmoor. On its right is *Spiral Gully*, and it is bounded on the left by the deep cleft of *Dove Crag Gully*. Left again, a broad easy descent gully takes the central area of the combe. The left side of the combe holds three shorter, easier-angled buttresses steepening towards the top.

The shortest approach is from Lanthwaite Green. A path contours the north slope of Grasmoor above Gasgale Gill. A small ruined building

Jim Fotheringham overcoming thawing conditions on Scale Force *(V), Buttermere (Photo: Martin Armitage)*

is passed below, near to the stream, before a steep arduous ascent leads directly to the base of *Dove Crag*. The path may also be followed until a second ruined stone building on the north bank of the stream, from which area a natural corridor leads up until easier ground may be traversed rightwards to the base of *Dove Crag*. **Descent** is down the easy gully to the left of the crag, or by descending to Coledale Hause and down into the combe of Gasgale Gill.

The climbs are described as they are usually approached, i.e. from **right** to **left**.

Spiral Gully   135m III/IV 1970

The obvious twisting break about 60m from the right end of the crag.

1   15m. Climb a small wall to gain a rightward-sloping ramp with a peg belay on the right.
2   20m. Follow the gully ahead by a short bulging ice pitch then snow to a peg belay in a cave.
3   30m. A vertical ice pitch is climbed to where the angle eases after 15m, then continue up easy snow.
4   70m. Continue up easier snow slopes with the odd short ice step. Snow belays and deadmen may be useful due to the poor nature of the rock.

Robinson's Gully   190m V (5) ★★★ 1978

A superb steep and technically demanding climb. The ice build-up is usually slight and protection is sparse: it is graded accordingly! Located to the right of *Dove Crag Gully*, this undercut line starts high up the cliff, with entrance gained from a rightward-sloping ramp.

1   30m. Follow icy slabs to gain the ramp and follow it with increasing difficulty rightwards to move round to a sloping stance but no belay at the foot of the gully proper: do not despair, a further 5m above, below a bulge, is a good peg crack on the left.
2   20m. A poorly protected pitch. Climb the gully to an awkward stance and poor anchors below a bulge.
3   50m. Step right, and up and round the bulge with difficulty, and continue to a small cave. A narrow overhanging chimney above gives the crux (Friend), which leads to a small bay and possible poor belay. Better to continue, passing a bulge above then a chock-stone, to pull out left to a ledge and belay.
4   90m. Move back right, and follow the easier-angled gully above, with one further steep section, leading to a snow finish.

Dove Crag, Grasmoor

1 The Chicken Variation   III
2 Dove Crag Gully   IV/V
3 Chicken Out   V
4 Robinson's Gully   V
5 Spiral Gully   III/IV

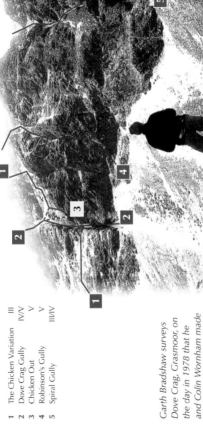

Garth Bradshaw surveys Dove Crag, Grasmoor, on the day in 1978 that he and Colin Wornham made the first winter ascent of Robinson's Gully (V). (Photo: Colin Wornham)

Dove Crag Gully   165m IV/V ★★★ 1966

An excellent climb with two contrasting steep ice pitches. The first pitch is slow to form, but the buttress to its left provides a worthy alternative start. The second icefall may also be gained by traversing in above the buttress to the left of the gully.

1   15m (4). An unusual pitch. Climb the wide but narrowing chimney via steep ice on its left wall, then back and footing, to exit up left-wards at the chockstone. It is also possible to climb the buttress to the left.

2   50m. Continue up snow to a stance and belay on the left under the steep icefall.

3   50m (5). The steep icefall directly above gives access to an easy snow slope. Look for a peg belay up to the right. If unformed – or too scary! – an easier alternative is afforded by the *Chicken Variation*.

4   50m. Finish direct or by variations to the right or left.

The Chicken Variation   165m III ★★

An atmospheric traverse through impressive ice formations (often climbed due to the main icefall pitch of *Dove Crag Gully* not being formed).

1   15m (3). Climb the buttress well left of the initial chimney of *Dove Crag Gully*.

2   50m (2). Make a diagonal traverse rightwards round into the gully, under its main icefall, and up a wide easy-angled snow ramp on the right to belay where the snow steepens beneath an extensive shield of icicles.

3   50m (3). Up a short steepening, then follow a series of exposed ice ramps back left across the top of the steep lower section of *Chicken Out*.

4   50m. Either continue into the easier upper part of *Dove Crag Gully* or take an alternative snow ramp out to the right.

Chicken Out   115m V ★★ 1990s

A worthy companion route to *Dove Crag Gully* and more likely to be in condition. Start from the top of pitch 2 of *The Chicken Variation*.

3   20m (4/5). Pick a line up the steep icicled wall to a large belay ledge (harder variations have been climbed/top-roped on the hanging icicles to the left).

Stuart Holmes tackling a difficult variation on Chicken Out *(V), Grasmoor (Photo: Peter Bailey)*

4   30m (5). Continue up the steep icicled wall above – it gradually eases.
5   65m. Easy ground leads to the top of the crag.

Dove Crag Left-Hand consists of three short buttresses to the left of the combe: all have been climbed (II/III). The gullies in between are easier (I), but may be corniced and can be prone to avalanche.

Returning to Buttermere, the **West Face of Grasmoor** has two easier gullies (NY 164 204) described below. It is sometimes possible to park on the road nearer the routes, but more parking is available a short distance to the north at Lanthwaite Green.

Lorton Gully   275m II 1963

This large forked gully consists of straightforward snow interspersed by steeper ice. The exit may be awkward and should be treated with care after heavy snow.

Buttermere Gully   250m II 1963

Situated to the south (right) of the Y-shaped *Lorton Gully*. It involves mainly easy scrambling in its lower section, with one 10m steeper ice pitch before easy ground leads to the steeper upper section.

Further up Buttermere, east of the village, the broken south-west facing **Goat Crag** (NY 190 163) sits at an altitude of 300m and is obvious on the hillside above Hassness, the large white house near the lake shore.

Goat Gill   150m IV ★★ 1954

The bed of the gill is followed pleasantly to a steep vertical pitch near the top. This can be avoided, reducing the route to a Grade III.

NEWLANDS

The Newlands Valley lies between Buttermere and Borrowdale and is accessible from the village of Braithwaite in the north (4km to the west of Keswick on the A66) or from Buttermere village via Newlands Hawse.

Newlands Hause Waterfall   110m III ★

Situated only five minutes from the road at the top of the *Newlands Hause* (NY 193 175, alt. 330m) the frozen waterfall, more correctly known as *Moss Force*, gives an excellent and accessible introduction to water-ice climbing. If it's 'in', follow the queue of climbers up the path from the car park.

1   15m. The shortest and easiest pitch up ice.

2   25m. More of the same water ice but slightly longer.

3   50m. The longest and steepest pitch, the crux is passing a protruding block just below halfway up. Either side of the block may be climbed.

4   20m. Easier ice to easy ground.

COLEDALE

This small valley contains the remnants of old mine workings at its head. It lies parallel to, but north-west of, the Newlands Valley and runs in a north-east to south-west direction. From Braithwaite, head west on the B5292 towards Whinlatter Pass. Just after leaving the village, the road zigzags at the start of the climb up to the pass. There is limited parking on the left at the start of a private track which leads to mine workings at the head of the valley. All the climbs are accessible from here and are clearly visible.

Force Crag   (NY 197 215)
                                          Alt. 300m North-east facing

Force Crag lies at the head of the Coledale Valley and can hold an excellent ice climb on the waterfall which gives the crag its name.

Force Crag Waterfall   250m IV (4) ★★★ 1966

A prolonged freeze and/or strong north-easterly is necessary for this magnificent climb to be complete. A series of short pitches lead to an interesting 25m pitch. Above, the stream widens and leads to a vertical curtain of ice offering some tremendous climbing with harder direct variations possible (IV/V). Beyond, the ice eases slightly and is then followed by a further 30m of ice.

Martin Armitage on the steep icefall of Force Crag Direct *(IV/V), Coldale*

The Enforcer
70m V c.1991

A mixed route which can rescue the day if the main fall is incomplete. Start at the foot of the main fall.

1   35m. Traverse up a gully on the left to a tree belay.
2   35m (5). Climb up to the right and traverse right above the overhangs on ice smears and torquing to a shallow gully leading to the top.

Pudding Beck
150m III 1982

This is essentially a continuation of *Force Crag Waterfall* and provides a good way onto the tops.

Eel Crag
(NY 192 209)
Alt. 600m   North facing

Western Crags

The crag overlooking *Force Crag*. Continue past the mine workings; the path passes under the crag which is on the left.

Eel Crag Gully
I 1994

The easy gully at the left end of the crag (NY 192 207), often full of snow.

Eel Crag Main Ridge
I 1994

The ridge to the right of the *Eel Crag Gully* gives a pleasant winter scramble to the minor summit above the crag (NY 195 208 to NY 191 206).

Scott Crag
(NY 195 204)
Alt. 630m   North-east facing

Scott Crag stands prominently on the north-east face of Crag Hill. The impressive central icefall is *Arctic Spring*, with *Scott Gully* to its left.

Scott Gully
70m III 1994

Follow the left-hand gully. This steepens and narrows into a chimney before exiting onto a faint ridge and steep vegetation.

Arctic Spring
70m III (4) 1996

The prominent central icefall.

1 30m. Climb the right side of the central fall.
2 40m. Further ice trends rightwards into a wide gully. Vegetation and broken rocks lead to the top.

WHINLATTER

Hobcarton Crag

(NY 187 221)
Alt. 600m North facing

This is a large crag on Hopegill Head which forms the head of Hobcarton Combe. It sees few visitors, although the approach from the Whinlatter Pass road requires little altitude gain. A forestry track leaves the main road at (NY 192 246) – either branch will get you there but the right-hand one is the shortest and runs up into the valley below the crag. The crag is a reasonable middle-grade venue when well frozen.

However, please note that *Hobcarton Crag* is the only English site for an exceedingly rare plant, the alpine catchfly, and that the gullies on this crag are very prone to erosion – please climb here only in truly frozen conditions or, better still, climb somewhere else! Please also read the chapter 'Winter Climbing and Nature Conservation'.

Two easy-to-recognise routes are located at the back of the combe: *Thompson's Chimney* is an obvious right-to-left diagonal line, while *Cave Route* is a gully about 20m to its right. On the right-hand side of the combe is another buttress containing three gullies. The routes are described from **left to right.**

A Carton of Hobnobs

100m III 2001

The route takes a shallow depression in the buttress left of *Thompson's Chimney*.

From the foot of *Thompson's Chimney*, walk up leftwards on an easy terrace to a ridge in the ground at the crag's foot, below a tiny rock tower. Climb diagonally right to gain the depression and climb it, passing to the right of a bigger tower, to the top.

Hobcarton Crag

1	A Carton of Hobnobs	III
2	Thompson's Chimney	II/III
3	Cave Route	II/III
4	Slab and Groove	II
5	Left-Hand Gully	II
6	Middle Gully	II/III
7	Sheep Buttress	I/II
8	Right-Hand Gully	I/II

(Photo: Dave Willis –
Copyright FRCC)

Thompson's Chimney   100m II/III

The clearly defined right-to-left chimney contains a 15m ice pitch halfway up.

Cave Route   100m II/III 1983

To the right of *Thompson's Chimney* is an easy runnel.

1   60m. Follow the runnel and the steep continuation chimney to a gully which leads to a cave.
2   40m. Exit from the cave, using ice on the right, and climb to the top.

Slab and Groove   130m II 1998

About 50m right of *Cave Route* is an obvious shallow corner starting about 50m up and running to the top of the crag. Start up an ice runnel and climb over slabby rock to reach the corner, then follow this to the top.

The right-hand side of the combe has three obvious gully lines all climbed in 1998. **Left-Hand Gully** (170m, II) is the most continuous, but nowhere as steep as the ice pitch of the *Middle Gully*. **Middle Gully** gives a 15m ice pitch before easing off to a pleasant ice line passing through some impressive pinnacles (II/III). **Sheep Buttress** (200m, I/II, 2001) starts between *Middle* and *Right-Hand Gullies* and climbs the buttress between them, close to the crest. The only problem encountered by the first ascentionists was crampons balling up with frozen sheep turds! **Right-Hand Gully** is an easy ramble up rock and turf (I/II). All allow a satisfying climb to the summit of Hopegill Head.

BORROWDALE

This popular valley to the south of Keswick, famed for its rock climbing, has many low-level gills that require extreme cold spells to form, but also boasts several more reliable venues. In fact *Great End,* at the head of the valley, gives some of the most consistent winter climbing in the Lake District, thanks to its northerly aspect and high altitude.

The crags and climbs are described from left to right anti-clockwise around the valley, starting on the east side and heading south from Keswick before returning back northwards along the west side.

BORROWDALE EAST

This section describes all the climbs on the east of the valley, as far as *Great End.*

Walla Crag Gully   50m III 1978

Located on the east side of the valley, **Walla Crag** (NY 274 212) is the first cliff on the left of the road going south from Keswick. *Walla Crag Gully* is in the centre of the crag. Situated at an altitude of only about 250m, an exceptional winter is required to find reasonable conditions in this gully. Fifty metres of climbing concludes at a tree which marks the end of the major difficulties, and from which an abseil may be made. Alternatively, the less well-defined continuation gully can be followed to the summit.

Ashness Gill   II/III

From Ashness Bridge on the Watendlath road, go upstream until this waterfall (NY 283 193) is reached at about 500m after about 20 minutes. The left fork in the gully is best: a 12m vertical ice pitch (III). The right fork is easier (II).

The popular summer rock climb **Little Chamonix** (1961) on **Shepherd's Crag** (NY 263 185) received a number of ascents under thick snow and

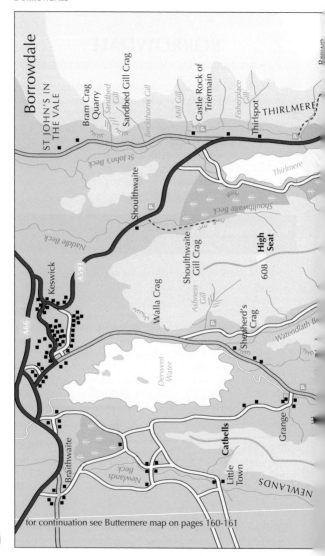

Borrowdale

ST JOHN'S IN THE VALE

Bram Crag Quarry

Sandbed Gill

Sandbed Gill Crag

Beckthorns Gill

Mill Gill

Castle Rock of Triermain

Fisherplace Gill

Thirlspot

THIRLMERE

St John's Beck

Thirlmere

Shoulthwaite

Shoulthwaite Beck

Shoulthwaite

High Seat

Naddle Beck

Keswick

A591

Shoulthwaite Gill Crag

608

Walla Crag

Ashness Gill

Shepherd's Crag

Watendlath Beck

A66

Derwent Water

Grange

Braithwaite

Catbells

Newlands Beck

Little Town

NEWLANDS

for continuation see Buttermere map on pages 160-161

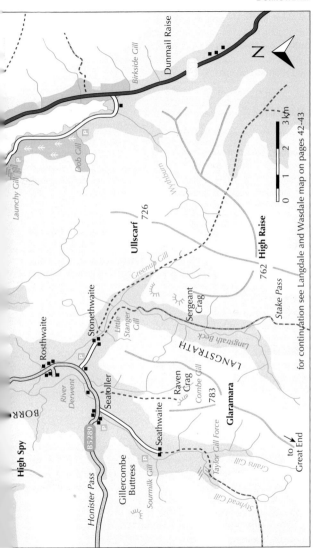

Dunmail Raise

Birkside Gill

N

Dob Gill

P
P

Launchy Gill

0 1 2 3 km

Ullscarf 726

Wythburn

Greenup Gill

762 **High Raise**

for continuation see Langdale and Wasdale map on pages 42-43

Stake Pass

Sergeant Crag

Rosthwaite

Stonethwaite

Little Stangen Gill

Seatoller

River Derwent

P

BORR

P

B5289

Seathwaite

High Spy

Honister Pass

Gillercombe Buttress

Sourmilk Gill

LANGSTRATH

Langstrath Beck

Raven Crag

Combe Gill 783

Glaramara

to Great End

Taylor Gill Force

Grains Gill

Styhead Gill

ice during the 1960s. However, recent milder winters have not provided the conditions to climb on low-lying valley crags without causing severe damage and scarring to the rock of such classic routes. In the event of climatic miracles, however, the route description can be found in the FRCC Borrowdale guide.

Black Crag

(NY 263 172)
Alt. 300m West facing

Troutdale Pinnacle had several winter ascents during the 1960s, which closely followed the summer route throughout. It would be hard to imagine it having been less than Grade V (and even harder to imagine it with sufficient snow on it nowadays). The route description can, again, be found in the FRCC Borrowdale guide.

Troutdale Gully   60m III

This partially hidden gully is found to the right of the crag, just right of the descent path where it crosses the stile. Descend down grassy/snowy slopes to the start. The gully gives two reasonable ice pitches of 15m and 25m with a belay in between.

Moving south up the valley, the next climbs are accessible from the village of Stonethwaite.

Little Stanger Gill   150m IV (4) ★★★ 1980

This is the obvious gill (NY 264 131) clearly visible in the woods to the right (west) of the farm track south of the Langstrath Hotel, Stonethwaite. There are usually four ice pitches with tree and spike belays.

Sergeant Crag Gully   170m II/III ★ 1960

Situated high up on the east side of Langstrath at an altitude of 450m, this gully forms a dark cleft splitting **Sergeant Crag** (NY 274 116). The gully does not take a great deal of drainage and, combined with a relatively low altitude, may not often be found in condition. From Stonethwaite, take the Langstrath valley path, crossing the stream via a footbridge, and then go straight up the fellside.

1   50m. Ledges lead into the gully proper. Two short steps lead up to a belay below a chockstone.

2   50m. Climb the left wall to the snow slope above. Follow this past another small step.

3   70m. Continue upwards to the top of the gully passing two further steps and a belay on easy slopes.

Combe Gill, the small but picturesque valley to the west of Langstrath, is home to the classic *Raven Crag Gully*. Where the Rosthwaite to Seatoller road crosses the humpback bridge over the River Derwent, a side lane runs off left opposite some houses (NY 251 137). There is limited parking about 200m up this road on the right next to the river. Return a short way back down the lane and over a stile to follow a footpath that curves up through trees and into the combe.

Raven Crag   (NY 248 115)
Alt. 460m North-east facing

Raven Crag, on the west (right) of the combe, is reached in about 45 minutes. The routes are described from **right** to **left** (as approached).

Crowdless Raven   180m V (6) 1995
This winter version of *Summit Route* may help avoid the crowds in the gully. The summer route was followed throughout; three pitches up broken walls and corners lead to a steep corner with a tricky exit. The crux is the final crack over an overlap, overlooking *Raven Crag Gully*.

1, 2 and 3 135m. Follow the line of least resistance up short steep walls and corners on the right-hand side of *Raven Crag Gully*.

4   20m. From the bay, climb the steep corner/scoop (crux) to an awkward exit onto a sloping ledge on the left, and go round the corner leftwards to the foot of a steep crack

5   25m. Climb the steep tricky crack to the top.

Raven Crag Gully   145m III/IV ★★★
The obvious deep gully towards the right side of the crag. A popular and classic route, with unusually varied climbing and an atmospheric finale, although its low position makes it less reliable as a winter climb, and it is much harder in anything less than perfect conditions. The ice climbing, though technically interesting, is not too serious in banked out conditions, with large stances between pitches. In a prolonged freeze with little snow, however (the condition it has been found in most often

in recent years), it may form an exciting challenge on steep chande-
liered water ice and is then technically around Grade 5, with potentially
poor protection between stances.

1   15m. A small preliminary pitch on the left leads to a good stance
    and belay.
2   15m. Bulging ice on the right leads to another good stance beneath
    a chimney. In lean conditions, however, this pitch may be trans-
    formed into a much longer and more serious pitch which consti-
    tutes the crux of the climb. Steep and strenuous climbing up brittle
    'organ pipe' chandelier ice and umbrellas may be necessary. An
    alternative up a verglassed ramp on the right is less steep but can be
    precarious with scant protection.
3   20m. Scale the wide crack on the right, then the chimney. Step left
    across the chimney and up to yet another large stance. If the chim-
    ney is insufficiently iced, a good mixed alternative can be taken up
    the rib on the left.

4   20m. Wander easily up the gully to the waterfall pitch. Climb to the chockstone; this is usually easier on the right wall.

5   50m. A steepening snow slope leads to the foot of the final pitch.

6   25m. The magnificent broad ice flow above is regarded by many as the most beautiful pitch in the Lakes. Climb bulging ice into a corner on the left (rock protection possible) and continue right and up to an often tricky and exposed finish over a lip, thence up easy snow to a tree belay.

Tyro's Gully   110m I/II

The left of two shallow gullies to the left of *Raven Crag Gully*. This gully normally presents an easy snow slope from top to bottom.

Colin Wells on the main pitch of the classic Raven Crag Gully *(III/IV), Combe Ghyll, high up at the head of Borrowdale (Photo: Alastair Lee)*

Corvus   150m IV (6) ★ 1960s

This classic and very popular summer route has been climbed under good winter conditions. Start as for *Tyro's Gully*.

1   30m. Avoid the well-marked slabs of the summer route by climbing up *Tyro's Gully* to a V-shaped cleft in the left wall.
2   30m. Climb the cleft, then traverse ledges leftwards to an ice-filled corner.
3   30m. Climb the corner and an ice-filled chimney above to a large belay ledge below a rib on the right.
4   30m. Climb the rib to belay below the *Hand Traverse* pitch of the summer route.
5   30m. Take the icefall that forms on the right of the *Hand Traverse*, then another rib to follow. Continue to top of crag. The *Hand Traverse* can be followed at the same grade if the icefall hasn't formed.

Raven Crag Grooves   130m VI (6) 1995

This starts up cracked slabs in a recess to the left of *Corvus*.

1   20m. Follow the right-hand crack in the centre of the slab moving left and then back right (crux) to belay at a large ledge below a groove.
2   20m. Follow the grooves to a belay ledge below a chimney crack.
3   45m. Climb the chimney crack and the groove above to a belay.
4   45m. Trend up left over broken ground to the top.

Nexus   90m IV (4) ★ 1980

This follows the iced wall at the left side of the crag, 30m left of *Corvus*, in the area of the summer line of *Slab Route* – the exact line taken can depend on the ice build-up.

1   50m. Climb the iced slab to a tree belay.
2   40m. Move left and climb steep mixed ground to a belay near a dry stone wall.

On the open hillside to the left of the crag a series of icy steps form. Linking them up gives three or four pitches of good ice (III) and can be a useful way of salvaging a visit if *Raven Crag Gully* is full of people or too thin to climb.

Combe Head   (NY 249 110) Alt. 640m North facing

This vegetated and dank crag lies at the head Combe Gill. When frozen it is possible to climb almost anywhere at Grade III, with the harder sections generally near the top and bottom of the crag, but they can often be out-manoeuvred. A line has been climbed up the centre starting from the lowest point of the crag (80m, III, 1996). It is a worthwhile alternative to an unfrozen *Raven Crag Gully*. Other routes have been claimed, but are not worth recording: follow your nose!

The upper ravine of **Combe Gill** is also entertaining (III ★, 1963).

The broken crag on the other side of the valley, to the north (left) of *Doves' Nest* and directly opposite *Raven Crag*, is split by the well-defined but short *Columba's Gully*.

Columba's Gully   30m IV (5) 1960
Rarely in condition. However, if you do find it in nick, climb into the back of the gully, then up the iced wall to the chockstone. Climb out around the chockstone to easy snow above.

In **Seathwaite**, on the north-west side of Glaramara, **Hind Gill** (II, 1963, NY 240 116) has some interesting icy steps when frozen.

GREAT END AREA

The area to the south of Styhead Tarn is dominated by *Great End*, the large crag that forms the north-eastern end of the Scafell group.

Being centrally located, *Great End* is very accessible from a number of points. The approach from Seathwaite in **Borrowdale**, passing through the farmyard at the end of the valley road and following the path alongside *Grains Gill*, is probably the best and shortest (1hr). **Grains Gill** itself, and **Ruddy Gill** which flows down from *Great End* into *Grains Gill* (NY 234 098), can be climbed as an alternative to walking if conditions are good (II, 1963). NB. *Ruddy Gill* is important for its rare flora – please do not climb here unless it is fully frozen – see the section 'Winter Climbing and Nature Conservation'.

Borrowdale

Alternative approaches can be made from **Wasdale Head** via Styhead Pass and Sprinkling Tarn, and from **Langdale** – by struggling up Rossett Gill and over Esk Hause. The routes are described from **right** to **left**.

Skew Gill   180m I 1887

Actually situated in Wasdale, but included here because of its proximity to the crag, the gill forms an interesting but easy chasm in the upper reaches of the Wasdale Valley. It makes a good approach to *Great End*. Starting just above the old packhorse route from Wasdale Head to Styhead (NY 219 092), at an altitude of about 420m, it is crossed at the bottom by the path of the Corridor Route. Scramble up the bed of the ravine for 150m to the exit wall, which is best climbed starting on the left. Finish up a small gully on the left onto easy snow.

Skew Gill Left-Hand Branch   200m II and III 1996

Approximately 150m up *Skew Gill*, the left-hand walls recede and the gill opens out. A rock tower stands at the foot of the left-hand branch. To the right of this, a short icefall runs into the bed of the main gill. Starting here, climb the little icefall and easy snow to a large table block resting on the left-hand wall. The steeper gully above is defined by rock walls on its left and a large rib on the right overlooking *Skew Gill*. Climb either on the left to an icicle in a corner before stepping right to finish up steep ground (II, 1996) or the harder offwidth crack on the right to the same point (III, 1997).

Skew Gill Direct Finish   20m III 1987

This is right of the normal finish to the gill.

Spout Head (NY 223 092) is the west-facing outcrop (alt. 530m) just to the left of *Skew Gill*. **Central Icefall** (90m, III/IV, 1985) is, as might be expected, the icefall down the centre of the crag, just right of a snow gully. Follow a narrow snow gully to gain the icefall.

From *Spout Head*, a walk up the snow slope to a small col on the ridge brings one to the right end of *Great End*. Immediately to the left is *Cust's Gully*, which is easily recognised by its large bridged chockstone halfway up.

Colin Wells sauntering up the finishing snow slope of Cust's Gully *(I), Great End (Photo: Stephen Reid)*

Great End

(Photo: Colin Wells)

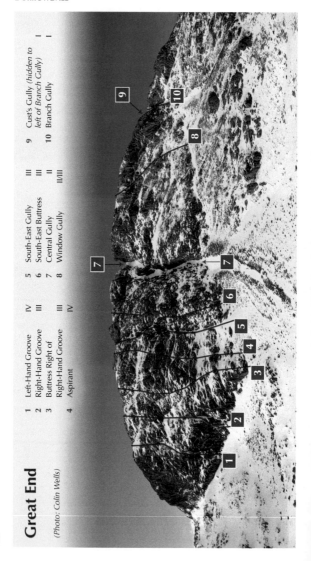

1	Left-Hand Groove	IV
2	Right-Hand Groove	III
3	Buttress Right of Right-Hand Groove	III
4	Aspirant	IV
5	South-East Gully	III
6	South-East Buttress	III
7	Central Gully	II
8	Window Gully	II/III
9	Cust's Gully (*hidden to left of Branch Gully*)	I
10	Branch Gully	I

Great End

(NY 228 086)
Alt. 720m North-east facing

This large crag forms the north-eastern end of the Scafell group. Its northerly aspect and high altitude mean it is in winter climbing condition more often than any other crag in the Lake District save the Helvellyn coves. Needless to say, such reliable conditions make it a popular climbing ground in winter and queues are to be expected; if it is too busy, it is worth considering some of the other venues close by such as *Gable* and *Green Gable Crags*. Although the crag itself is not steep, its gullies cut deeply into it, giving some great pitches.

The buttresses of *Great End*, particularly on the ground between *Central* and *Cust's Gully*, offer many possibilities for mixed climbs at about grade II/III – only the most compelling lines have been recorded.

Branch Gully
200m I ★ 1886

The open gully branching out rightwards from the start of *Cust's Gully*.

Cust's Gully
310m I ★ 1880

Commonly confused with *Window Gully* because of its large chockstone arch which appears to form a big 'window', this gully is generally a straightforward snow slope, but early in the season it can offer two or three short steps (2). Often used as a means of **descent**. Combined with *Skew Gill* it gives a classic winter mountaineering excursion to the summit of *Great End*.

The First Cut is the Deepest
40m V (7) ★★ 2004

Start 30m up *Cust's Gully*. The most obvious fault-line in the left wall of the gully is climbed on hoared-up rock and turf.

Evolution
70m IX ☆☆ 2005

Starting higher up *Cust's Gully*, this hard route climbs the left wall of the gully up underneath the big chockstone before heading up and over it. The nature of *Cust's Gully* means that you can have a reasonable look at the crux section from below before embarking!

On the first ascent an axe was dropped, and after its retrieval the highpoint regained by climbing straight to the end of the traverse on pitch two. This is a safer option for a second, but misses out some of the best climbing.

1   30m (6). From the first step in *Cust's Gully*, climb big flakes leaning against the left wall to a belay.

2   40m (10). From the belay, step up to place gear under the roof, then return to the belay. Traverse right across the wall level with the belay (on the first ascent ice was needed to make a crucial move pulling off the traverse). NB. A fall from the end of the traverse could result in hitting the gully bed. From the end of the traverse, head straight up for the chockstone. Move up to a crucial Friend 5 placement. Pulling into the overhanging niche above provides the crux of the climb. A couple of committing moves on poor hooks allow you to hook the gap between the chockstone and the gully wall and head for turf over the top. From the top of the chockstone head up and right for 10m to a good belay.

One Pitch Gully   120m II

This runs up left of the left-bounding buttress of *Cust's Gully*. Easy snow steepens with height to where the gully splits into two small chimneys. Climb the right one, which offers a short pitch on the left wall to the top.

Duncan's Groove   30m IV (5) 1986

Takes a prominent groove through the steep rocky band high on the buttress right of *Window Gully*.

Window Gully   110m II/III ★★

An interesting climb made better by taking the *Icefall* to finish. The climb takes its name from a peculiar rock formation on the left below the final pitch. The climb forms quite quickly early in the season as a runnel of water ice, and is often one of the only routes in condition on the crag. Start above a shallow snow bay midway between *Central* and *Cust's Gully*, where an ill-defined gully leads to a line of weakness through the upper buttress.

1   35m. A variety of lines can be taken up snow to belay at the foot of a chimney.

2   30m. Follow steepening ice for about 10m onto further snow. Step left and climb up an ice bulge and out onto an easy snow slope.

3   30m. Cross the snow slope to another ice pitch below a defined gully section. Climb this and the slope above to belay below the final pitch.

4   15m. The final pitch to the top.

Stuart Holmes on the superb Window Gully Icefall *(III), Great End
(Photo: Jenny Griffith)*

Window Gully Icefall   30m III ★★ 1974

Also known as the **Wall and Groove Finish**: an interesting icefall is frequently present to the right of the gully just above ice leading to the upper defined section of the gully on pitch 3. Step up and right onto the ice bulge from the gully bed. Continue up into a leftward-slanting groove and follow this to the summit of the crag. Several other variations of this climb are possible depending on conditions.

Upper Icefall Finish   II/III

A good alternative ice pitch usually forms on the right of the snow bay just below the final pitch and opposite the *Window*. This is further up the gully than *Window Gully Icefall*.

The buttress between *Window* and *Central Gullies* can be climbed almost anywhere (II/III).

Central Gully Right Arete   170m II

A useful alternative to *Central Gully* if it is knee-deep in powder snow and/or climbers.

From the base of the *Central Gully*, it takes the right-hand arete. Follow easy-angled snow for 60m, then a series of small grooves through a stepped rocky section. For the final 30m trend right or join the final slopes of the *Right Branch* to finish. This arete can also be gained via a ramp from further up the gully if the queues become too much.

Central Gully   1887

This, the best-known winter climb in the district, is invariably busy. It follows the long rightward-slanting gully which starts to the right of the centre of the crag and passes through some fine rock scenery to the *Amphitheatre*, where there is a choice of numerous variation finishes if the press of flesh becomes too much. **WARNING:** The broad upper slope of the *Right Branch* collects blown snow from the plateau above and is very **AVALANCHE PRONE** during fresh snow conditions – any avalanche will (and frequently does) sweep down the lower gully. There have been fatalities here, and this is definitely a gully to avoid after heavy snowfall. Also, there has been considerable rockfall in the gully over the last few years – so a place to avoid, too, if it is not fully frozen.

The **variations** are described from right to left:

Great End, Central Gully

1	South-East Gully	III	**6**	Central Gully Arete		
2	The O.G.J. Way	III		and Grande Finale	VI	
3	Far Left Branch	III	**7**	Chimney Finish	IV	
4	Left Branch	III	**8**	Central Gully Right Branch	II	
5	Left Branch Middle Way	III/V	**9**	Central Gully Right Arete	II	
			10	Window Gully	II/III	
			11	Upper Icefall Finish	II/III	
			12	Window Gully Icefall	III	

The Amphitheatre

Central Gully

*(Photo: Dave Willis –
Copyright FRCC)*

Borrowdale

Central Gully Right Branch **200m II ★★ 1890**

The classic route, and frequently done, but very variable in condition. An ascent in lean conditions can give a difficult crux (3) on the pitch above the *Amphitheatre*, whilst a snowy year may only offer a snow plod (1) and leave you wondering what the grade is all about!

1   35m. Start at a small chockstone pitch followed by easy snow or ice pitches.

2   45m. The cave which follows can be turned on the left and leads to the small *Amphitheatre*, where the gully branches.

3   30m. A short stretch of steeper snow leads to a short pitch of vertical ice on the right (if it is not banked out). This may be turned on the left by some rock moves or via the chimney groove formed between the rock and ice on the right, stepping left at the top. Climbing the ice direct is harder. Continue past a chockstone to the upper snow slopes.

4, 5 90m. Continue up a straightforward snow slope to the top.

Chimney Finish **30m IV (5) 1972**

This takes the prominent corner high up on the left from the final snow slope of the *Right Branch*. It was first climbed with ice, but is all right as a mixed pitch and is usually in condition if *Central Gully* is climbable. Climb the corner to where it steepens. Traverse out right, then up a line formed by a crack and a flake to further iced cracks and the top.

Left Branch Middle Way **90m III/V ★★ 2006**

The obvious continuation up the cleft in the headwall directly above the line of the V-corner makes an excellent finish.

1   45m (3). Just to the right of the main ice pitch in the *Left Branch* is a small pitch up a V-corner leading to the final snow slopes of the *Left Branch*. You can exit via the *Left Branch* at Grade III or continue up the cleft in headwall.

2   45m (6). Climb into the cleft, the continuation line directly above the previous pitch and about 5m left of the *Grande Finale* finish. It is steep at first until a large turfy niche is reached. Continue up easier snow slopes to another recess whence hard poorly protected moves lead to the top.

Central Gully Arete and Grande Finale **60m VI ☆ 2001/2006**

From the *Amphitheatre* the narrow arete splitting the *Left* and *Right Branches* gives delicate climbing in an exposed position and is a bit thin

*Tony Halliwell on the excellent Left Branch of Central Gully (III), Great End
(Photo: Tim Hogan)*

on gear. The parallel cracks in the headwall above provide a more muscular finish.

1   20m (3). Climb up to belay below a prominent parallel crack sys-
     tem on the crest of the buttress in the headwall above the
     Amphitheatre.
2   40m (7). Climb the easy groove to a ledge below the cracked wall.
     Climb the wall using both cracks to an overhung niche, swing left
     and follow the groove above, stepping right to finish up easy steps.

Left Branch   110m III ★★ 1887

Keep to the left of the buttress dividing the amphitheatre. A good climb
which benefits from an early start before the good ice pitch is hacked to
pieces

1   20m (3). A good pitch on ice.
2   90m. Ascend the pleasantly open snowfield. A further small ice
     pitch is sometimes present near the top.

Far Left Branch 90m III

Left of, and opposite the start of the dividing buttress in the gully amphitheatre, a further branch runs out left.

1   60m. Climb out of the main gully on ice and follow snow to the headwall of a small couloir.
2   30m. Climb a chockstone pitch on the right to a final snow slope. The chockstone can be awkward in lean conditions with a poor landing above.

The O.G.J. Way 130m III ★

This next variation follows a well-defined chimney line to the left of the amphitheatre of *Central Gully*, but invisible from that route. Start just above the big chockstone at the bottom of the amphitheatre. An ill-defined groove goes up the left wall, opposite a pinnacle belay.

1   20m. Climb the groove on ice for 10m and then easier snow above to belay at the wall.
2   15m. Climb up into the chimney and belay before the steep section.
3   20m. Continue up the steepening chimney moving right at the top. An awkward move left leads into a short steep groove and easier ground.
4   25m. Traverse easy snow above the couloir to the base of a steep corner.
5   30m. The final pitch of *Far Left Branch*. Turn the chockstone on the right to an awkward landing and go up snow above to belay on the right.
6   20m. Continue to the summit.

South-East Buttress 180m III 1891

No detailed description of this route is available, but it climbs the buttress between the two major gullies of *Central* and *South-East*.

South-East Gully 190m III ★★★ 1890

If *Central Gully* is crowded, try this other classic to the left, starting just right of the lowest point of the crag. (NB. *South-East Gully* is the only Cumbrian location for a plant called dwarf cornel – please climb here only in truly frozen conditions – see the chapter 'Winter Climbing and Nature Conservation').

1   60m (2). An often icy snow slope leads to a chockstone, which is turned on the right.

Carmen Elphick in South-East Gully *(III), Great End (Photo: Simon Caldwell)*

2   40m (3). Follow the right fork up steep snow to an icy chimney. Climb this direct or turn it on the right wall.

3   90m (3). The gully curves gently to the right with one or two small pitches leading to the summit.

Left Fork

On pitch 2 follow the left fork to an open snow slope. Not as good as the original.

South-East Gully Left-Hand Buttress   200m III 1996

Quite a worthwhile variation if there is a traffic jam in the gully.

Follow *South-East Gully* to just below the first step (the chockstone). Exit the bed of the gully by a shallow V-groove which leads onto the buttress on the left. Ascend the buttress direct, breaking through steeper sections at their weakest points to gain easier slopes above.

Aspirant   210m IV (4) ★ 1987

To the left of *South-East Gully*, before the lowest point of the crag, a leftward-facing corner starts at mid-height up the cliff: the highlight of this route. This is part of a fault-line running up the full height of the crag.

Follow the fault. Easy climbing leads to the corner. This gives a good full-length pitch (45m) before further easier ground leads to the top.

To the left, 20m past the lowest point of the crag, are two prominent groove systems separated by a steep grooved wall. Both, particularly the left one, require heavy snow and ice conditions for an ascent. The buttresses to either side also give interesting climbing, with much scope for variation.

Buttress Right of Right-Hand Groove   200m III (3) 1995

Follow the obvious way up the buttress. The best finish is by a direct line, though an easier finish is possible to the right.

Right-Hand Groove   150m III ★ 1978

The right-hand groove system, 20m left of the toe of the buttress. A good build-up of snow is needed.

1   35m. Climb the snowed groove for 15m, then move to a second groove above on the right. This leads in 20m to a snowfield.

2   50m. Cross the snow slope up rightwards towards a recess in the upper rock band. Climb ice to the recess with a crack in the back.

3   20m. Follow a small iced groove on the right, then traverse right and climb the wall at a weakness. Continue up leftwards, then rightwards, to easier ground.

4   45m. Continue up easier snow and ice, bearing leftwards to the top.

Left-Hand Groove   150m IV ★★ 1978

This large left-facing corner-groove lies further to the left, about 10m from *Right-Hand Groove*. It has four excellent pitches, and in lean conditions can prove quite a battle!

1   20m (4). Climb bulging ice onto snow, followed by a short, but overhanging, ice section. Zigzag up leftwards over easier ground, then back right, to belay in small bay at the bottom of a groove. Sometimes it is possible to climb the initial groove direct.

2   30m (4). A steep pitch. Ascend the groove to an icicle and bear left over steep mixed ground, with a final 5m ice groove to pull out right onto easier snow.

3   45m. Ascend the snowfield directly to a stance below a steep icy crack.

4   15m (3). Climb the crack or, if it is not in good condition, a left-facing shallow turfy corner just to the left to a small snow ledge.

5   40m (3). Continue up a turfy groove to a steep snow slope and bear leftwards to the top.

Original Finish
The climb originally moved diagonally right on easy ground from the top of pitch 2 and finished as for *Right-Hand Groove*.

A winter ascent of the summer line of **Born Free** (IV, 1983) has been recorded. It reputedly gave two big ice pitches, but unfortunately has not been possible to locate, in summer or in winter.

Buttress Left of Left-Hand Groove   110m III (4) 1995
Follow the easiest turfy line 20–30m left of *Left-Hand Groove*. A slanting ramp near the top provides the crux.

Towards its left end the crag becomes distinctly more rocky, and towards the right-hand side of this area is a large open corner, the most prominent feature in this area.

Arlecdon Aquarian   65m V 1991
A good line but seldom in good winter condition. Start under the corner.
1 20m. Easy scrambling leads to a large block at the base of the corner.
2 45m (5). Climb the corner, and at its top follow a short groove which is set slightly back from the steep left wall.

Further left, the crag turns another corner, and just round this corner is a huge cave (the summer line of *Briggs's Climb*). Roughly halfway between the far left end of the now broken crag and *Briggs's Climb*, a 25m grade icefall (II) sometimes forms in a break to the left of a roughly triangular area of rock.

Girdle Traverse   340m IV ★ 1978
A left-to-right traverse starting up either the *Left* or *Right-Hand Groove*, crossing the two main gullies and finishing up *Window Gully*. The start up *Left-Hand Groove* and the descent into *Central Gully* across slabs provide the cruxes. Originally climbed in very good snow/ice conditions, the crux sections would prove much harder if lean.
1 50m. Climb *Left-* or *Right-Hand Groove*.
2 45m. Traverse the large snowfield right and slightly upwards.
3 60m. Continue the traverse right, then follow a line slightly downwards, descending into *South-East Gully* at the fork.
4 30m. Go up rightwards to below a steep chimney, then up the small ramp to a ledge above.

Borrowdale

5   60m. Descend diagonally rightwards for 10m, then continue traversing, taking the easiest line over snow and slabs, to descend slabs into *Central Gully*.

6   50m. Follow *Central Gully* for about 20m, to where a small right-sloping ramp leaves the gully bed. Follow this, then continue the traverse under a rock band and some icefalls, to below the second main pitch of *Window Gully*.

7   45m. Finish up *Window Gully*.

Grossbuttock   270m III 1973

Another, shorter, left-to-right girdle starting up *Right-Hand Groove* and finishing up *South-East Gully*.

BORROWDALE WEST

The climbs on the west side of Borrowdale are now described. The first three routes are approached from Seathwaite.

Taylor Gill Force   50m III ★ 1962

Draining from Styhead Tarn, Taylor Gill leaves the hanging valley (NY 229 109) just above Stockley Bridge, where it results in a spectacular waterfall. At an altitude of only 300m, like most Borrowdale winter climbs it seldom freezes fully, but when it does it gives a fine 30m ice pitch.

Base Brown   250m II 1995

On the south side of Base Brown at the top of *Taylor Gill Force* (NY 229 112) is a crag which is split by three clefts. The central one makes a good **descent**, being the broadest and easiest. The left gully gives several short steps and one longer 10m pitch, taken on turf on the left or mixed ground on the right. At the top the gully splits to give a left and right finish. The right finish has a short ice pitch to exit.

Sourmilk Gill   245m II/III ★★★

On the west side of the upper Borrowdale valley, this gill cascades from the hanging valley of Gillercombe (NY 233 122). At an altitude of 120m, a long period of frost is required for a complete freeze, though the higher reaches may be in condition more often. Take the path due west from the farm at Seathwaite, and follow the path towards the hanging valley of Gillercombe. This follows the left bank of the stream, and gives a convenient way of joining or leaving the climb at any point. The bed of the stream is followed in its entirety. Halfway up, a long pitch gives some interest, but the top icefall is the crux, and may contain 15m of steep ice.

Gillercombe Crag
(NY 222 124)
Alt. 460m South-east facing

Marked on the OS map as *Raven Crag*. Although not noted for its winter climbing, in exceptional conditions this south-easterly-facing crag can provide a continuation to *Sour Milk Gill*.

Approach via the path on the left of *Sour Milk Gill* or climb the gill (if frozen). The crag is directly opposite the top of the gill. It can also be approached from the summit of Honister Pass (quicker).

Gillercombe Gully
670m II

The obvious gully to the left of the main section of buttress and just left of *Gillercombe Buttress*. This provides a worthwhile way up the crag, and is a better winter climb than a summer one. The main pitch is near the top. The difficulties can vary quite considerably with conditions.

Gillercombe Buttress
110m IV (5) 1960 ★★

This classic summer climb starts at the foot of the buttress right of *Gillercombe Gully* and just left of a rocky ramp in the path. Take a line diagonally left towards the gully, then back right and up the centre of the buttress – a copy of the summer description would probably be useful (see the FRCC Borrowdale guide). The climb can be very good, but the snow conditions necessary for an ascent are an infrequent occurrence.

On the north side of the *Honister Pass* road are the east-facing gills of **Scaleclose Gill** (NY 244 146) and **High Scawdell Gill** (NY 244 150) on High Scawdell Fell. When frozen these low-lying gills give some enjoyable pitches (II, 1963).

On the west side of Borrowdale, 2km south of Grange, is Tongue Gill. A track runs up the south side of the gill and leads to the York

Mountaineering Club Hut, and also on to north-east-facing **Rigghead Quarry**, 400m, the highest of the old slate quarries (NY 238 153). Seepage from the upper cave may produce a thick continuous wall of ice. However four distinct 25m ice lines (Grade III–IV) leading to the cave are more likely; all were climbed in 1991.

During hard winters an icefall forms in Goat Crag Gill above and right (just north) of **Goat Crag** (NY 245 165). This is **Goat Crag Icefall** (IV, 1963).

Heading north on the minor road from Grange, a signpost marked 'Place Howe' is reached before the hamlet of Manesty. The broken, heathery **Blea Crag** (NY 238 172) on the east flank of the High Spy/Maiden Moor hillside contains three gullies. The left one is **Mouse Gill** (II, 40m); **Bridge Gully** (II, 45m) is the central one; and the short gully on the right is nameless.

Looking down Sharp Edge, Blencathra (photo: Nick Wharton)

NORTHERN FELLS

This section covers the northern fells of Blencathra, Skiddaw and Carrock Fell. The climbing here, although on mountain crags, is still generally at low altitudes and so requires a prolonged freeze to come into condition.

SKIDDAW

The great bulk of Skiddaw dominates the view north from Keswick, but although one of the highest of the Lakeland Fells it provides little winter climbing. On the north side of Skiddaw can be found the waterfall of *Dash Beck*, and to its west *Dead Crag*. Lonscale Fell to the south of Skiddaw has one route. All of these climbs start at a low altitude and do not come into condition often.

Whitewater Dash Waterfall   50m II ★

The waterfall on **Dash Beck** (NY 273 313) gives a pleasant outing on ice which looks steeper than it actually is, but its situation at a lowly altitude of 400m ensures that sustained cold temperatures are required. Approach easily from Bassenthwaite on the north side of Skiddaw.

Dead Crag   (NY 267 311)
Alt. 550m   North-east facing

Dead Crag lies to the right of the path when approaching *Whitewater Dash Waterfall* from the north.

Central Icefall   160m III/IV 1991
The obvious central icefall.
1   50m. Climb the steep ice in the centre of the crag, then follow ice bulges trending left to a small tree belay.
2   40m. Traverse the snow bay on the right and round into a narrow gully with a peg belay.

3   50m. Follow the gully past several small steps to just below the top and another peg belay.

4   20m. From the top of the gully exit right to the summit.

Diagonal Gully   150m II 1991

This aptly named gully is not visible from the path. It splits the crag from left to right.

1   60m. Follow steepening ice to the start of the diagonal gully.

2   40m. Continue up the gully passing icicles on the left into a snowy amphitheatre.

3   50m. From the top of gully move left up the amphitheatre headwall to the summit.

Lonscale Crags   (NY 293 270)
Alt. 500m   East facing

These crags are to be found on the east flank of Lonscale Fell, a low hill that lies to the south-east of its larger neighbour Skiddaw.

Kirkby's Folly   230m II 1991

Follow the mine track to the east of Lonscale Fell. Climb an obvious gully to the left of an arete (possible large cornice).

BLENCATHRA (SADDLEBACK)   (NY 323 277)

This bulky and distinctive mountain is immediately recognisable by its saddle shape as one drives west along the A66 from Penrith; it lies just north of that road. Its numerous truncated spurs offer some fine ridge climbs and scrambles which make enjoyable winter outings.

Hallsfell Ridge   300m I ★

While only really worth the grade in icy conditions, this ridge still provides an interesting and scenic route with which to ascend or descend the mountain. From Threlkeld village, follow the footpath that contours round the foot of the spurs to the east. **Doddick Gill** (II) to the east of the ridge may be followed for a while before joining the ridge.

Penny Clay in winter conditions on Hallsfell Ridge *(I), Blencathra
(Photo: Colin Wells)*

North of the A66, a minor road leads east from the White Horse Inn (NY 343 269) to a small parking area whence a path leads up Mousethwaite Comb and then north-west to Scales Tarn (NY 328 281), at which point the ridge of *Sharp Edge* is most easily gained. If this road is blocked by snow or ice, or the car park full, an alternative approach can be taken starting by the A66 at NY 340 268 (300m west of the pub). This gives an easy walk which contours around the east end of Scales Fell to join the track to Scales Tarn.

Several 200m shallow snow gullies run up from Scales Tarn to the summit of Atkinson Pike. They are mainly Grade I, but the one immediately left of *Sharp Edge* gives more worthwhile climbing, with quite an alpine feel (**Sharp Edge Gully** I/II).

Sharp Edge   215m I/II ★★ 1873

This fine ridge (NY 328 284) lies just to the right (north) of Scales Tarn. Initially fairly level, the ridge steepens where it abuts the mountain and becomes steep and slabby (NB. This point has been the scene of numerous accidents.) For the full experience and exposure follow it directly. An easier alternative is to follow the snowy trough on the right.

A good **descent** from this ridge is to continue left across the saddle to the summit, and then follow *Hallsfell Ridge* down to Gate Gill.

On the east end of *Sharp Edge*, at the foot of the main ridge, may be found *Brunt Knott* and, well to its right, the prominent chimney of *Blunt Gully*. **Brunt Knott** itself gives a 50m turf climb (II) which can make an interesting alternative start to *Sharp Edge*.

Blunt Gully   60m II/III ★ 1995

This gully/chimney starts almost at the point where the base of *Sharp Edge* meets the base of *Foule Crag*, just left of *Foule Crag Gully*. The steep start soon eases and leads to the crest of *Sharp Edge*.

Foule Crag   (NY 324 284)
Alt. 750m North facing

To the north of *Sharp Edge* lies the long blocky face of *Foule Crag*. It is generally easy angled, and it is possible to wander almost anywhere here in good winter conditions, making the recorded lines rather difficult to identify. The rock, being Skiddaw Slate, is poor, and there is little reliable rock protection to be found. Being on the side of a ridge means that there is low drainage and therefore little ice build-up, and the climbing is mainly on frozen turf or snow.

Follow the path as for *Sharp Edge*, but where this ascends to Scales Tarn continue traversing beneath *Brunt Knott* and ascend beneath the northern flank of *Sharp Edge* before traversing left and up to the crag.

Foule Crag Gully   80m I

The obvious easy right-slanting gully formed by the junction of *Sharp Edge* and *Foule Crag* ends on *Sharp Edge* at the point where it steepens. It is only easy in good snow cover, though – in lean conditions it is mostly bare rock. There are two branches; the right-hand one can sometimes give a 5m icefall (II).

Seen from *Sharp Edge*, or from below, a faint diagonal rises across the crag from bottom left to top right. This starts about 50m right of *Foule Crag Gully*.

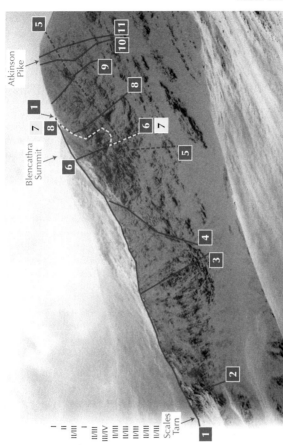

Eastern Crags

Foule Crag

1	Sharp Edge	I
2	Brunt Knott	II
3	Blunt Gully	II/III
4	Foule Crag Gully	I
5	Traverse of the Sods	II/III
6	Pulse Direct	III/IV
7	Pulse	II/III
8	Wowzers	II/III
9	Vegiburger	II/III
10	Smoken	II/III
11	Secondhand	II/III

(Photo: Nick Wharton –
copyright FRCC)

Traverse of the Sods   180m II/III 1995

Follow the diagonal traverse line rightwards, starting up a bay located roughly one-third of the way in from the left side of the crag.

Pulse   60m II/III 1995

Start right of the bay where *Traverse of the Sods* starts. Climb a corner to cross this route, then follow a wide crack until the angle eases and a steep wall is reached. Avoid the chimney-crack directly above, and traverse down and right, avoiding the impending steps, until a crack leads up rightwards to a platform in a corner. Continue directly up the steep wall and ledges above to the top.

Pulse Direct   III/IV 1996

Continue directly up the chimney-crack on frozen turf.

Wowzers   60m II/III 1995

In the centre of the crag a hanging triangular rock corner forms a distinct feature. This route starts up a rib immediately to its right and follows a fairly direct line until near the top, where it pulls out rightwards onto easier ground.

Vegiburger   60m II/III 1995

A blank-looking wall can be seen at mid-height. This route climbs a line left of this. Move up and follow a ramp rightwards to the bottom left corner of the blank wall before moving left and following the line of least resistance to the top.

Smoken   60m II/III 1996

Below and to the right of the blank wall there is a corner, below which some ice can usually be found. Climb the ice and pass ledges to gain a corner. Climb this, exiting left to easy ground. When this steepens, trend right to easier ground.

Secondhand   30m II/III 1995

The line of least resistance up the far right side of the crag.

CARROCK FELL	**(NY 348 336)**
	Alt. 450m East facing

This Lakeland outlier stands north of Blencathra. About 2km west of the Ullswater turning off the A66, a minor road is signposted to the north leading to Mungrisdale. Follow this through the village and past a phone box to park just north of Stone Ends. From here the crag is visible about 150m above the road. The eastern side of the fell contains a number of small outcrops, the northmost of which is separated from the others by a stream and contains a deep gully.

Trough Gully   **70m III ★★ 1950s**
Known locally as *The Trough*, the short gully splitting the buttress gives a good two-pitch route that forms quite readily in a freeze and has a tricky section in the middle. A bit of a minor classic.

Icicle Start   **15m IV 1986**
To the left of the start of the gully, an impressive icicle can form. Climb it if you dare.

Carrock Fell Icefall   **25m II/III 1950s**
At the same height, but about 300m south of *Trough Gully*, a short slab forms an icefall.

Several other short icefalls on this hillside make good practice routes.

THIRLMERE

The Thirlmere valley runs in a north–south direction and is bisected by the A591 Ambleside to Keswick road. Most of its climbs follow water-courses and, as many of theses routes start at low altitude, a sustained period of cold temperatures is required before they come into condition. Please see the map 'Borrowdale' on pages 246–7.

The climbs are described clockwise around the valley starting from the north-eastern corner.

The east side of the valley contains a number of water courses which can offer some good ice pitches during a prolonged cold spell. Bolts have been placed for belays in some of gills, presumably by so-called 'canyoners' abseiling the gills. This practice is not to be encouraged, particularly as enraged celebrity mountaineers have been known to attack the bolts on discovering them, resulting in expensive ice axe breakages. The first climbs are in the subsidiary valley of St John's in the Vale.

Bramcrag Quarry Fall   III/IV ★ 1976
A two-tier icefall sometimes forms in the right-hand lower quarry (NY 319 219) – this is to the south of the quarry with the rock climbs in it.
1   20m (4). The obvious iced corner to a huge ledge. Walk 15m left to an iced slab.
2   20m (3). The slab.

Sandbed Gill   180m II/III
Situated above the east side of St John's in the Vale (NY 320 218), this deep atmospheric rift cuts through the crags. The difficulties are short, but can be quite exciting when thin ice build-up may force a turf expedition onto the left wall. The *Right-Hand Finish* is Grade III.

Descent is possible down Fisher's Wife's Rake to the left (looking up); don't try descending *Beckthorns Gill* to the right as it contains a number of troublesome hidden steps.

Sandbed Gill Crag   40m VI (5) 1985
The crag to the right of the main gill (NY 322 215) can give a steep

technical problem. A thin ice smear runs down from the main over-hang. Climb this and move left onto the rib to gain the top groove.

Beckthorns Gill   200m II/III 1996
The next gill to the south at (NY 321 210). Follow the gill; the right-hand branch gives the best continuation.

Mill Gill   150m III 1995
The gill just north of *Castle Rock of Triemain* (NY 324 198). Follow the gill bed passing two 15m icefalls. Rock and tree belays can be obtained.

The remaining climbs are within the main Thirlmere valley.

Fisherplace Gill   200m III/IV 1991
The gill located at (NY 321 183) about midway between King's Head Hotel at Thirlspot and the junction of the A591 and the St John's in the Vale road contains many interesting small ice pitches and a steep 20m pitch with three bolts at its top.

Birkside Gill   I/II 1986
Easily accessible from Dunmail Raise, this gill runs down from Dollywaggon Pike to the south of a plantation (NY 326 125) and gives several hundred metres of easy and pleasant climbing and an interesting way to the summit.

The west side of the valley contains fewer routes.
    In good conditions **Dob Gill** (NY 315 138), the stream leading up to Harrop Tarn, gives 170m of Grade II climbing with the most difficult part in the lower section (1991/2). The conspicuous **Central Tarn Crag Gully** in the crag above the tarn has also been climbed (1915), but the grade is not known.

Launchy Gill   180m III ★★★
Situated on the west side of Thirlmere. Approach straight from the car park at Fisher Gill (NY 306 171) to the north of the gill. The climb starts at an altitude of around 250m (NY 308 158), and it is well worth waiting for it to freeze. Climb a number of small pitches to an impressive 20m main fall. Continue above, either direct or via the more interesting right fork.

Eastern Crags

Tony Daly on the Thirlmere classic Shoulthwaite Gill *(V) (Photo: Tony Daly)*

There are several short icefalls, both on *Iron Crag* and in its environs.
Mere Gill (NY 295 187) to the south of *Iron Crag* produces a series of icy
steps, for example (1982).

Shoulthwaite Gill 50m V (4) ★★ 1976

Situated on the hillside between *Iron Crag* and *Goat Crag* at an altitude
of around 300m (NY 297 196), this single-drop icefall is very obvious
from the road when frozen and gives an exciting pitch. It may be possible to find some rock protection, though generally it is a serious lead as
the narrow top section can be thin and detached from the rock. It can,
however, easily be top-roped.

HELVELLYN MASSIF

Being the highest mountain outside of the Scafell massif, Helvellyn and its close neighbours hold snow well in their east-facing coves and are comparatively often in condition. The climbing areas extend from *Brown Cove Crags* in the north to Dollywaggon Pike in the south. There are five major coves all told, as well as *Tarn* and *Falcon Crags* at the southern extreme, all containing a variety of climbs including many easy gullies at Grade I/II. Whilst all of these have been climbed numerous times, only the more obvious have been described. These coves offer an excellent place for beginners, though beware: the cove headwalls tend to form steep snow slopes, usually with a cornice along the top, and avalanches are not unknown. More recent mixed routes provide plenty to go at for the more experienced. In contrast to the rugged crags and coves of the eastern flank, the easy-angled western slopes of Helvellyn offer climbing only on frozen gills: these are covered in the Thirlmere section of the guide.

Without question the Helvellyn and Fairfield range is the most important and vulnerable area of the Lake District with regard to rare plants. This north–south ridge possesses a geological structure, altitude and aspect that is conducive to the growth of rich upland vegetation. The east-facing coves, their backwalls and their gullies contain the most important English populations of many alpine plants. In *Red Tarn Cove*, Nethermost Cove, Ruthwaite and Cock Cove, in the gullies at *Tarn* and *Falcon Crags* and, on the Fairfield side, Sleet Cove to Link Cove (including *Scrubby* and *Hutaple Crags*) there are extensive stands of tall herb ledge vegetation together with locations for the rare arctic-alpines and mountain willows. The real rarities grow here – alpine saxifrage, scrubby cinquefoil, holly fern and downy willow. Climbing should only take place in these areas in true fully frozen winter conditions to minimise any potential damage to the flora, and in order to obviate the very real risk of restrictions being imposed on mountaineering (see page 34 for more information).

The coves, and the routes therein, are described from north to south – that is from **right** to **left**.

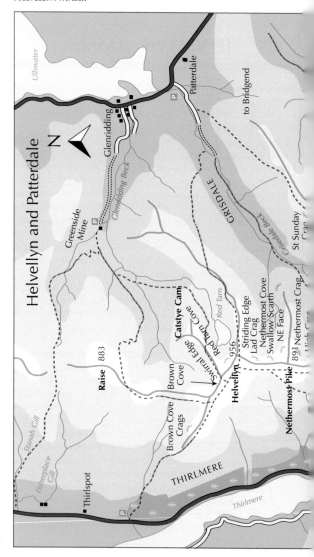

Helvellyn and Patterdale

N

Ullswater

Glenridding

Greenside Mine

Glenridding Beck

GRISDALE

Grisedale Beck

Patterdale

to Bridgend

St Sunday Crag

Raise

883

Catstye Cam

Red Tarn

Red Tarn Cove

Swirral Edge

Brown Cove

Helvellyn

956

Striding Edge

Lad Crag

Nethermost Cove

Swallow Scarth

NE Face

Nethermost Pike

891 Nethermost Crag

High Crag

Brown Cove Crags

THIRLMERE

Stanah Gill

Fisherplace Gill

Thirlspot

Thirlmere

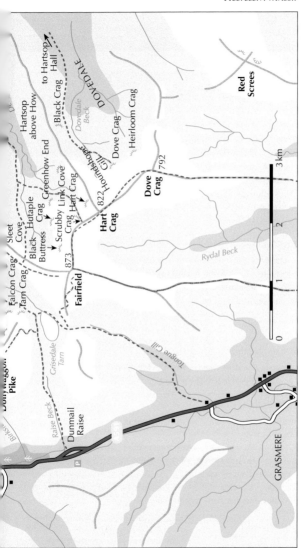

to Hartsop Hall

DOVEDALE

Dovedale Beck

Black Crag

Hartsop above How

Dove Crag

Heirloom Crag

Sleet Cove

Hutaple Crag

Greenhow End

Black Buttress

Scrubby Crag

Link Cove

Hart Crag

822

Houndshope Gill

Falcon Crag

Tarn Crag

873

Fairfield

Hart Crag

Dove Crag 792

Red Screes

Rydal Beck

Dollywaggon Pike

Grisedale Tarn

Tongue Gill

0   1   2   3 km

Raise Beck

Dunmail Raise

P

GRASMERE

HELVELLYN

Brown Cove Crags (NY 330 158)
Alt. 800m North-east facing

The most northerly climbing in the area, and easily accessible, *Brown Cove Crags* (which confusingly are not in *Brown Cove*) are best approached from the Swirl car park on the A591 on the Thirlmere side of the mountain (NY 316 169). From the car park, follow the well-made Helvellyn path north-east up the ridge, but traverse left into *Brown Cove Crags* after about 1km. The crag, which is visible for most of the approach, consists of two main buttresses bounded by easy gullies and separated by *Central Gully*.

Two Grooves 80m IV ★★ 2006

The first route is found on a two-tiered buttress to the right of the main concentration of climbs. A short steep buttress at the top of the combe is split by a prominent V-groove (the top pitch) which can be clearly seen on the approach.

1   40m (3). Below and left of the higher prominent V-groove is a less steep, more vegetated groove. This leads to a sloping ledge below the top groove.
2   40m (6). The prominent V-groove is gained via an easy introductory wall. Go up the groove, tricky in the middle, to an awkward exit up an excellent crack on the right.

Right Buttress Crack 100m III ★ 1994

The slabby right-hand buttress is split down its centre by a wide crack.

1   10m. From the toe of the buttress, follow a groove to a ledge.
2   60m. From the ledge, move right to the wide crack and follow this past several chockstones.
3   30m. A variety of lines are possible at a similar grade through the broken upper portion of the buttress.

Central Gully 100m I

The broad open gully dividing the two distinct buttresses. Initial

Brown Cove Crag

1 Left Buttress — II
2 Stepped Ridge — III
3 Left Branch — II
4 Central Gully — I
5 Right Buttress Crack — III
6 Two Grooves — IV

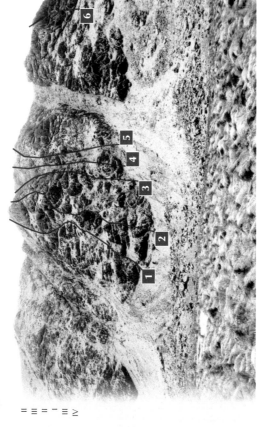

*(Photo: Nick Wharton –
Copyright FRCC)*

steepening snow leads to a small pitch (in lean conditions) at the bottom of the gully. Above, snow is followed to a cornice finish.

Left Branch   120m II

This gully runs up diagonally left of the indistinct buttress immediately left of *Central Gully* and finishes behind the main buttress. It can present a small pitch at the start.

The next two routes are on the larger, more distinct buttress left of *Central Gully*.

Stepped Ridge   100m III ★

This popular summer scramble up the right-hand side of the buttress also makes an excellent winter route. Climb up walls and grooves about 20m left of *Central Gully*. Follow a rock rib halfway up the buttress, and from its top trend right to the foot of a steep wall. Climb under a chockstone forming a window to gain a ledge overlooking *Central Gully* (a groove to the right also leads to the same ledge). Continue up to the centre of the final steep section of the buttress and, following a vague depression from just right of centre, make a rising traverse to the right arete. Continue easily to the top.

Left Buttress   160m II

The left side of the larger of the two buttresses. A shallow gully towards the left of the buttress may be gained by several alternative starts. Follow the gully past several steepenings. In about 100m this leads to the steeper upper buttress, which is turned by short walls and chimneys on the left to finish on the summit ridge.

Variation Finish   30m III

A line of grooves and cracks is taken directly through the upper tower of the buttress.

The twin parallel gullies left of *Left Buttress* are both Grade I, and the stepped ridge in between them is a pleasant Grade II.

All torque! Dom Donnini experiencing mixed conditions on the first ascent of Two Grooves *(IV), Brown Crag Cove (Photo: Nick Wharton)*

Eastern Crags

Brown Cove

(NY 338 154)
Alt. 890m   East facing

Brown Cove is the cove on the north side of *Swirral Edge*. It contains many short possibilities, but nothing worth an individual description.

Red Tarn Cove

(NY 343 152)
Alt. 830m   North-east facing

This north-east facing cove provides some of the most accessible mountain routes in the Lake District and is often in condition early in the season. The cove is bounded on the left by *Striding Edge* and on the right by *Swirral Edge*, the complete traverse of which gives a popular winter day out.

There are two main approaches. From **Thirlmere**, leave the Swirl car park (NY 316 169) on the A591 and follow the obvious Helvellyn path north-east up the summit ridge path of the mountain. A descent of *Swirral* or *Striding Edge* allows access to the climbs around Red Tarn. From **Glenridding**, vehicular access to the old Greenside Mine is permitted from October to Easter. Follow the path on the left side of the beck. About 1km above the mine follow the right branch of the stream – a path leads up into the cove.

Red Tarn Cove (especially the low crags around the base of *Viking Buttress*, and a couple of lines to the left) is home to rare alpine plants – please climb here only in truly frozen conditions (see the introduction to this chapter and the chapter 'Winter Climbing and Nature Conservation').

In the cove itself, the open snow bowl to the right of the summit sees the occasional ski descent and numerous sliding descents (not all voluntary!). The broken buttress right of the snow bowl contains several easy lines, while *Viking Buttress* on the left of the snow bowl is home to numerous mixed routes, including the original classic of that name. Left again, two obvious and prosaically named gullies, 1 and 2, separated by a narrow buttress, lead almost to the summit. The more broken ground between the gullies and *Striding Edge* has a few interesting pitches which may be linked together to provide some entertaining climbing to the summit plateau. The rim of the cove often contains a cornice, and avalanches, especially of the snowbowl, are not infrequent.

Beautiful alpine conditions on Striding Edge *(I), Helvellyn*
(Photo: Eric Shaw)

The hill at the east end of Swirral edge is Catstye Cam. Its north flank contains the pleasant **Catstye Cam Gully** (I/II) which makes a fine way to the summit.

Striding Edge and Swirral Edge
I ★★ 1894

These are the ridges bordering *Red Tarn Cove*. Their passage, up *Striding*, taking in the summit of Helvellyn and descending by the easier *Swirral*, is one of the most popular winter excursions in the Lake District (and one of the most frequently fallen from by those not equipped with ice axe and crampons). From the entrance to the cove, continue along a good path which leads up the slopes on the left of the cove to where the ridge becomes more defined and the arete proper starts.

Either follow the arete, keeping to its highest point, with the occasional rock step, or take the line of the path which runs about 17m below the arete summit on the Red Tarn side. Where the ridge abuts the mountain, a small 6m chimney may be awkward to descend in icy conditions. The snow slope leads up to the summit of Helvellyn and the crossed walls shelter. Continue 300m north along the ridge to another slope (NY 34118 15255), which is descended to *Swirral Edge*. This ridge is shorter and less well defined than *Striding* and soon leads onto a

Red Tarn Cove

1	Gully 3	III
2	Wall and Ramp	III
3	Arete between V-Corner and Wall and Ramp	III
4	V-Corner	III
5	V-Corner Extended Finish	III
6	Gully 2	I
7	Gully 1 Buttress	II/III
8	Blade Runner	IV
9	Gully 1	II
10	Rape and Pillage	IV
11	Viking Buttress	IV
12	Thor's Corner	IV

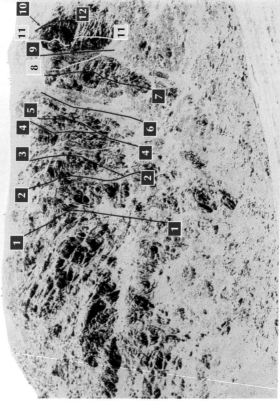

(Photo: Nick Wharton – Copyright FRCC)

broader ridge. Continue over the summit of Catstye Cam or follow the path down to Red Tarn Beck and back to Greenside Mine.

In bad weather locating either ridge from the summit area can prove difficult. If ascending *Striding Edge* and the weather deteriorates, rather than chance finding *Swirral Edge* in a whiteout, it is better to continue north along the main ridge to the summit of White Side. This can then be descended on easy slopes.

Pear Buttress

This is the small buttress right of the snow bowl. It gives several short pitches (III).

Viking Buttress

This is the largest buttress in the cove. It is bounded on the left by *Gully 1*.

Viking Buttress   **190m IV ★ 1986**

This ridge forms the right-hand side of the obvious gully just right of the centre of the crag.

1   60m (4). From the lowest rocks climb directly to arrive at the base of a small high-angled slab.
2   35m (4). Go diagonally rightwards to a recessed belay.
3   15m (5). Move left and up to an obvious groove which, if iced, is followed to the top.
4   80m. Continue up the easy snow ridge to the top.

Left-hand Finish   **25m IV (5)**

3   A better alternative under lean conditions. From the base of the groove on pitch 3, step round left to a large flat platform and climb the wall via a thin crack/block (crux) before traversing rightwards back into the groove and continuing as for the standard route.

Variation Finish: Thor's Corner   **20m IV (4) 2002**

2   20m. From the belay at the top of pitch 1, move right to climb a turfy groove forming the right-hand side of the upper buttress.

The next two routes start up *Gully 1*, the gully which bounds *Viking Buttress* on its left.

Rape and Pillage   80m V 2001

Starting 10m up *Gully 1*, this route starts up the gully wall of *Viking Buttress*.

1   40m (7). Climb the obvious corner on the right wall to the roof. Pull through the roof and step right to easier ground and a belay.

2   20m (5). Climb the steep groove to the right of *Viking Buttress*, negotiating a small roof at half-height. Continue up the groove left of *Thor's Corner* to a good ledge.

3   20m (4). Continue up the groove above until it is possible to step right around the arete. Follow turf to the summit ridge.

Variation Finish   IV (6) 2002

3   25m. Step left where the groove finishes, and continue straight up cracks to the left of the arete.

Loki   80m IV 2004

A series of variations on *Viking Buttress*. Start 15m up *Gully 1*.

1   40m (3). A few metres up from the capped corner of *Rape and Pillage* is an open groove in the right wall of the gully. Climb this to the *Viking Buttress* belay.

2   40m (5). Climb a few metres of *Viking Buttress*, pitch 2, but where *Viking Buttress* moves right, continue up the obvious corner to join *Viking Buttress* at the top groove and finish up *Viking Buttress*.

Gully 1   90m II

The narrow gully to the left of *Viking Buttress* gives about 50m of climbing to a snow slope which leads to the summit. Harder in water-ice conditions.

Blade Runner   100m IV 2002

Start about 10m up *Gully 1*, opposite the obvious short corner of *Rape and Pillage*.

1   50m (4). Climb the turfy chimney-groove, then continue in the same line to a short, wide, steep turfy groove. Pull up left out of this to a belay.

2   50m. Easier ground, trending left at first, leads to the top.

Gully 1 Buttress   100m II/III

Start to the right of the toe of the buttress and climb out left onto the buttress. Continue to easier ground, cross a snow basin, and finish up another steepening buttress.

Gully 2   90m I

The broad gully to the left of the narrow buttress gives straightforward climbing to the summit.

V-Corner   80m III ★★ 1987

A distinct V-corner lies about 70m left of *Gully 2*. It can be banked out or give plenty of ice.

1   10m. A stepped icefall leads to a good ledge and block belay.
2   10m. Climb the short slabby groove to the final V-corner.
3   20m. The V-corner.
4   40m. Easier snow leads to the plateau.

Extended Finish   20m III Pre-1995

3   From the base of the V-corner pitch, traverse easily right, and cross the rib bounding the corner, to the bottom of a large turfy slab with an overhanging left wall. Belay at the base of the slab. Climb the slab (peg) and exit directly up the corner (crux). The final tricky corner can be escaped on the right. Follow easy broken ground to the top.

The arete between *V-Corner* and *Wall and Ramp* has been climbed (III).

Wall and Ramp   70m III

About 30m up and left of *V-Corner* is a distinctive wall with a left-facing groove to its right.

1   30m. Climb the groove, then a leftward-trending ramp over blocks, to a continuation groove.
2   40m. Easier snow leads to the plateau.

Gully 3   165m III

This gully starts about 20m left of *Wall and Ramp*. Follow the gully on snow with some steep ice near the top and rock belays where required (65m). A further 100m of snow leads to the summit.

Eastern Crags

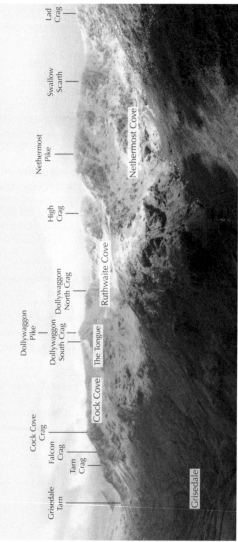

Helvellyn Range
(Photo: Nick Wharton – Copyright FRCC)

The Nethermost/Dollywaggon escarpment to the south of Helvellyn's Red Tarn Cove showing the location of the coves, major crags and features

Grisedale Tarn

Cock Cove Crag

Falcon Crag

Tarn Crag

Cock Cove

The Tongue

Dollywaggon South Crag

Dollywaggon North Crag

Dollywaggon Pike

Ruthwaite Cove

High Crag

Nethermost Pike

Nethermost Cove

Swallow Scarth

Lad Crag

Grisedale

NETHERMOST COVE (NY 347 145)
Alt. 650m East to south facing

This high cove is bounded by *Striding Edge* to the north, and broken buttresses and outcrops below Nethermost Pike to the south.

Nethermost Cove is most easily accessible from Patterdale, via the road into Grisedale.

Nethermost Cove, and in particular *Nethermost Gully*, is home to rare alpine plants – please climb here only in truly frozen conditions (see the introduction to this chapter, and the chapter 'Winter Climbing and Nature Conservation').

The back of the cove contains two crags, *Lad Crag* (containing the classic *Nethermost Gully*) on the right, and *Swallow Scarth Crag* on the left.

Lad Crag (NY 345 147)
Alt 700m East facing

Nethermost Gully is the only one of the four gullies on this crag that really warrants a description.

Nethermost Gully 200m I/II ★

An excellent climb of its sort, this popular gully can be found running up just left from where *Striding Edge* joins the main mountain ridge. There is often a large cornice.

From the floor of the cove, ascend a long snow slope to where the gully divides after about 100m. The right branch may have a small pitch leading out onto steeper snow (70m). This is followed through to the summit ridge (130m). The left branch contains a small pitch in early season or lean conditions.

Chimney Variation 65m II H

The buttress between the two branches of *Nethermost Gully* is split by a chimney which gives an interesting variation finish to the gully.

To the left, the rest of the crag contains three more distinct gullies about 200m long. All are Grade II. The first two are continuous from the bottom of the crag, but the farthest left line starts only about halfway up the crag.

Eastern Crags

HELVELLYN MASSIF

Nethermost Cove

1 Swallow Gully	I
2 Swallow's Rake	II
3 Nethermost Gully	I/II
4 Striding Edge	I

Helvellyn →

Striding Edge

4

Lad Crag

3

Swallow Scarth

2

1

(Photo: Nick Wharton – Copyright FRCC)

296

Swallow Scarth

(NY 345 143)
Alt. 700m East facing

This small east-facing crag in the back of *Nethermost Cove*, between *Lad Crag* and Nethermost Pike, contains some interesting lines and short icefalls that can be linked to provide worthwhile climbing. Although climbed on for many years, no routes were described in previous guides; the two described here give a feel of what's on offer.

Swallow's Rake
150m II 2003

The highest of the obvious diagonal rakes running from left to right from a snow basin at the base of the crag.

1 45m. Climb the easy gully between the buttress on the left and the slope on the right. Belay in a corner on the left.
2 45m. Follow the wide rightwards-sloping ledge to its top left-hand corner. Traverse right 5m around a block on a narrow ledge, follow easier ground for 5m to a wide sloping ledge, and belay at a small rock spike.
3 50m. Climb the narrow rightwards-slanting groove, bounded on its left by steep rock (in lean conditions this can be bypassed via a steep turf rake 5m to the right). Follow the gully above to belay on the right side of a large block as the gully ends.
4 10m. Follow easy ground over a possible corniced finish.

Swallow Gully
150m I 2003

The shallow gully to the left, at the back of the snow basin. For added interest, the lower section may be climbed via easy lines through rocks below and to the left of gully, before traversing right over easy ground to the open snow gully. Follow the narrowest groove up the centre of gully: this may contain water ice. Turf and snow lead to the top.

Nethermost Pike North-East Face

(NY 346 142)
Alt. 760m

The north-east face of Nethermost Pike is made up of numerous small buttresses and ridges interspersed with many gully lines, making it possible to ascend the face almost anywhere at about Grade III. Below are two suggested lines.

Eastern Crags

Pike Gully   120m I/II

The following route goes up through the centre of this face.

1   30m. Climb up steepening snow between two small buttresses.
2   40m. A steeper section mainly on snow ice follows.
3   50m. The snow slope to the cornice, which may be quite large and has been known to require tunnelling.

Huckleberry Grooves   100m III/IV 1986

Start about 15m right of *Pike Gully*, below the highest point in the crag, and traverse left along a shelf. Climb grooves just left of the steepest part of the crag. Exit rightwards along ramps to finish near the highest point of the crag.

RUTHWAITE COVE
(NY 346 136)
Alt. 700m South-east facing

This large cove sits between Nethermost and Dollywaggon Pikes. Prominent at the back of the cove is the buttress of *High Crag*. A small subsidiary cove containing Hard Tarn sits between *High Crag* and Nethermost Pike and contains the classic and relatively reliable *Jogebar Gully*.

For *Tarn and Falcon Crags*, and climbing at the southern end of the mountain, park at Dunmail Raise on the A591 and take the path up Raise Beck to Grisedale Tarn. For *Tarn* and *Falcon Crags* and Cock Cove, contour round beneath these crags. Ruthwaite Cove is best approached by following the path from the tarn over Dollywaggon Pike and then down to the col to the north. The steep slopes into the cove require care.

Ruthwaite Cove, *Striding Edge* and particularly Nethermost Cove are also easily accessible from Patterdale by following the road into Grisedale and continuing up to the respective cove.

Ruthwaite Cove is home to rare alpine plants – please climb here only in truly frozen conditions (see the introduction to this chapter and the chapter 'Winter Climbing and Nature Conservation').

Andy Lunn sandwiched in the groove of the classic Jogebar Gully *(III)*,
Nethermost Pike (Photo: Colin Wells)

Nethermost Pike South Face (NY 346 139)
Alt. 750m

(Also known as **Nethermost Crag**). This contains one of the best gully lines on Helvellyn: it is prone to sun-rot in clear conditions, but is well worth getting up early to catch it frozen.

Jogebar Gully 100m III ★★
The most prominent gully splitting the crags on the south-east side of Nethermost Pike. Start below the line of the gully.

1 30m. Steepening snow slopes lead to where the gully becomes better defined. Follow the gully to a large snow terrace.
2 35m. Continue up steepening snow, then an icy chimney above, to a snow ledge on the right.
3 35m. The iced slab above leads to a sometimes corniced finish. Beware of potential windslab on the exit slopes above.

Below and left of *Jogebar Gully* there are several areas of rock split by terraces. Many good icefalls form here, and various lines (up to Grade IV) have been climbed. Once again it is worth remembering that the south-easterly aspect of the face means an early start can pay dividends.

Terrace Ice 60m III ★★ 1970s
The following line takes in the best of the ice mentioned above.

1 15m. From the lowest rocks, follow a shallow gully.
2 25m. A steeper ice pitch on the left leads to a terrace.
3 20m. The final splendid icefall to the next terrace.

High Crag (NY 345 137)
Alt. 750m

Immediately below the summit cairn of the subsidiary summit south of Nethermost Pike, two short gullies are situated in the side of the crag facing *Jogebar Gully*.

Gully A 110m II
The obvious left-hand groove in the buttress leads to a diagonal traverse right over ice-covered slabs; then go directly to the top.

AB Buttress   105m III ★★ 1980

The buttress between the two gullies.

1 40m. Climb *Gully A* for 10m, and then follow a steep turfy ramp
   going to the right for 15m (crux). Keep towards the left side of the
   buttress to reach a rocky step and a belay crack.
2 45m. Move up 25m to a step left towards the gully. A spike belay is
   reached in a further 20m.
3 20m. Continue to the top of the buttress.

Gully B   75m I

The right-hand and larger of the two grooves leads over bulges to a right-
hand finish.

Left Branch   35m II

Where *Gully B* branches, take the left fork directly up to an icy chimney
which leads to an easy snow finish.

A subsidiary buttress stands to the left, south of *High Crag*. The gully
running up between the two buttresses is Grade I.

Dollywaggon North Crag   NY 344 132
                          Alt. 780m North facing

This elevated crag is situated just north of a saddle between the true
summit of Dollywaggon Pike (NY 346 131) and the northern subsidiary
summit (NY 344 132), and is often in condition. The distinctive ramp-
line of *Ramp It Up* is a good landmark. The routes are described from
right to **left**.

Dolly Daydream   50m III ☆ 2006

Right of *Ramp It Up,* the crag turns around a prow with a steep clean
wall on the right. Immediately right of this wall there is a groove which
becomes larger higher up the crag. At its base there is normally a small
ice weep. Start up this, and follow the ramp above rightwards to a steep
corner. Climb this with difficulty to a ledge, move left, and climb the icy
corner. Follow the obvious line above trending left to finish above the
steep wall.

Eastern Crags

Dollywaggon North Crag

1	South Gully	II
2	Solo Symphony	III
3	Dolly Mixture	IV
4	Rescue Groove	IV
5	Mono Culture	III
6	Terminal Velocity	IV
7	Thrash Corner	II
8	Ramp It Up	II
9	Acceleration due to Gravity	IV
10	Dolly Daydream	III

(Photo: Harry Worsnop)

Acceleration due to Gravity · 50m IV 2003

Takes turfy grooves in the face right of *Thrash Corner*. Start just left of the toe of the buttress.

1 35m (5). Climb a shallow corner with a wide crack in the back to easy turf. Go up another short corner to emerge at the narrow section on *Ramp It Up*. Pull left onto the face, and up the left-hand of two short corners, before stepping back right to pull though the bulge and belay on the crest.

2 15m. Easy ground the top.

Ramp It Up · 50m II 2003

This follows the left-to-right ramp-line slanting through the main buttress, just right of centre, to emerge on the crest of the buttress, from where the top is soon reached.

Thrash Corner · 50m IV ★★ 2003

Start in the centre of the crag a few metres left of the ramp-line of *Ramp It Up*.

1 25m (3). Climb the open groove-line leading to a block belay.
2 25m (5). Climb the corner above with difficulty and then more easily to the top.

Variation · III

2 25m (3). The crux corner (described above) can be avoided in lean conditions by moves on the right.

Terminal Velocity · 50m III (3) 2003

Start from a block at the top left of the snow bay, also used by *Mono Culture*. Climb a ramp diagonally up right to below a large roof – this is just left of the block belay on *Thrash Corner*. Traverse left onto the arete and finish directly as for *Mono Culture*.

Mono Culture · 50m III (4) 2003

Start from the block at the top left of the snow bay and climb the first few metres of *Rescue Groove* before moving onto the arete on the right. An awkward section with a balancy crux leads to turf and the top.

Rescue Groove · 50m IV (4) ★★ 2003

This climbs the obvious large groove-line. From the block mentioned in *Mono Culture* climb the groove to where it steepens. A nut placement low on the left wall offers protection before hard moves round the bulge to a ledge. Further awkward moves lead past a poised flake and the top.

The next routes start in the left side of a bay to the right of *South Gully*.

Dolly Mixture   50m IV (4) ★ 2003

At the bottom left of the bay, below and left of the block start of *Rescue Groove*, is a blocky arete. Climb this to a turf ramp, cross the ramp, and climb through the overlap to a groove which is followed to the top.

Solo Symphony   50m III 2006

Start 10m right of *South Gully* and climb the rightwards-trending ramp for 10m. After passing a prominent fault, climb the wall on the left to gain a ledge, then make an awkward step left (crux) onto another ramp. Follow this briefly then step left again over a block (possible belay). Contour round to the right and up to gain a short icy corner, then follow easy ground to the top, bearing right (away from *South Gully*).

South Gully   50m II 2003

The left end of the crag is defined by a shallow runnel which gets more difficult with height.

The Tongue is the long ridge running north-east from Dollywaggon Pike. Midway along its north side the flank of the ridge is split by **Tongue Gully** (100m, I *).

COCK COVE   (NY 349 131)
                                                   North-east facing

The compact Cock Cove nestles between Dollywaggon Pike and *Falcon Crag*, and contains two crags of interest, *Dollywaggon South Crag* and *Cock Cove Crag*. Both are easily accessible from *Dunmail Raise* and the path leading to Dollywaggon Pike. For *Cock Cove Crag* leave the path at the top of the zigzags and head to a small col between Dollywaggon Pike and *Falcon Crag*, where an easy gully just north of the crag gives access to the bottom of the cove. For *Dollywaggon South Crag*, continue until nearly at the summit before heading into the cove.

Cock Cove is home to rare alpine plants – please climb here only in truly frozen conditions (see the introduction to this chapter and the chapter 'Winter Climbing and Nature Conservation').

Dollywaggon South Crag
(NY 346 130)
Alt. 820m South-east facing

This small crag on the north side of Cock Cove is situated just below the summit of Dollywaggon Pike, on the south side of *The Tongue*. The central groove is the line of *Turf-tastic*.

Dollymixture   40m III 2003

This climb, not to be confused with its similarly named neighbour on the *North Crag* (although it probably will be), follows an obvious line a few metres left of *Turf-tastic*. Start below two large flakes.

Climb up to the flakes and continue up to a ledge, using turf and cracks. Traverse a few metres left, then climb a mossy block and small rock steps to the top.

Turf-tastic   60m III 2003

The prominent cleft in the centre of the crag.
1   30m. Climb the obvious steep pitch, passing a bulging chimney section on ice and turf.
2   30m. Continue more easily up the gully-line to the top.

Cock Cove Crag
(NY 349 129)
Alt. 750m North facing

This crag lies up and right of *Falcon Crag* and is ideal for a short day, or when its bigger neighbours of *Falcon* and *Tarn Crags* are not in condition. Various people have climbed in this area over the years, and it seems likely that many of the climbs on this crag have been done in the past but were not recorded due to their brevity. The routes are described from left to right.

Easy Gully   70m I

The gully on the left of the crag separates *Cock Cove Crag* from the upper portion of *Falcon Crag* and finishes next to *Chock Gully* on that crag.

Eastern Crags

(Photo: Adrian Clifford)

Cock Cove Crag

1	Bobbins Groove	V
2	Ramp Route	V
3	Central Route	III
4	Thanks for the Tip	II
5	Coco-Tara Direct	IV
6	Turf Corner	II

Bobbins Groove   30m V (7) ★ 2002

Climb the steep groove just right of *Easy Gully*. After a few metres, turf on the right eventually leads steeply to an overhanging wide crack/chimney. Climb this, with a chockstone for comfort.

For the next 20m the crag presents a steep bulging wall.

Ramp Route   40m V (6) ★★ 2002

The ramp to the right of the bulging wall. Climb the corner for a few metres before making tricky moves to cross the ramp to turf on the arete. Follow the turf right before a stepping back left into a shallow gully. Follow this to the top.

Direct Start   40m V (6) 2006

Climb the first turfy groove to the right of the start of *Ramp Route*. This gives a more direct line up the crag to join *Ramp Route* at the upper groove.

Central Route   50m III (3) ★ 1994

About 20m right of *Ramp Route*, in the centre of the crag, is a shallow chimney. The steep section at mid-height provides the crux.

Coco-Tara Direct   50m IV (4) 2003

1   20m. Start about 5m right of *Central Route* at easy snow below a short chimney. Climb easily to the short chimney at 10m. Climb this to easy ground and belay at the base of a corner with an overhanging start.
2   30m. Climb the corner (crux), then easy ground to the top.

Thanks for the Tip   50m II 2002

Start as for *Coco-Tara Direct*. At the base of the chimney, traverse 20m right into the corner-line of *Turf Corner* and follow this to the top.

To the right of *Thanks for the Tip*, the base of the crag overhangs for the next 15m. *Turf Corner* climbs the corner bounding this area on the right.

Equinox   45m V (7) 2006

Start under the big roof 5m left of *Turf Corner*. Climb the corner in the back of the recess under the roof, and traverse right from the back using overhead torques in the roof crack. Pull out around the roof on hooks and using turf (care is required with a dangerous flake on the left as you exit the roof). Continue up right on a turfy ledge to join *Turf Corner* and follow this to the top.

Turf Corner   40m II 2003

Climb the corner to the right of the overhanging section, with the difficulties in the lower half.

DOLLYWAGGON

Tarn Crag and Falcon Crag   (NY 352 127)
                                                    Alt. 620m East facing

The southern end of the Helvellyn ridge is marked by the east-facing buttresses of *Tarn* and *Falcon Crags*. They can be quickly reached from *Dunmail Raise* by traversing the north side of *Grisedale Tarn* and continuing round to *Tarn Crag,* then *Falcon Crag*. These often give excellent winter climbing, but the harder routes can be disappointing in all but the best of years, the 'Cold Climbs' classic of *Chock Gully* being a case in point.

   Tarn and *Falcon Crags* are home to rare alpine plants, mostly in the obvious and well-climbed gully-lines, but also at the bases of most climbs and on the buttresses too. This area has recently been surveyed and the results are described as 'impressive' – please help keep it that way by climbing here only in truly frozen conditions (see the introduction to this chapter and 'Winter Climbing and Nature Conservation').

   The crag becomes bigger towards the right-hand end. The routes are described from left to right, the first three gullies starting from a small amphitheatre on the left side of the crag.

Tarn Crag Gully I   120m I/II ★

The first gully on the left of the amphitheatre. This narrow gully curves gently to the right, with one small pitch after about 80m.

Tarn Crag Buttress I   II ★ 1995

This takes the buttress to the right of *Tarn Crag Gully I*. Start up the initial

Tarn and Falcon Crags

1	Tarn Crag Gully I	I/II
2	Tarn Crag Gully II	I
3	Tarn Crag Gully III	I
4	Dollywaggon Gully	III
5	Dollywaggon Chimney	III
6	Falcon Crag Gully	II
7	Chock Gully	IV
8	Dollywaggon Great Chimney	V

(Photo: Nick Wharton – Copyright FRCC)

Eastern Crags

309

The end of a beautiful day, Dollywaggon Pike (Photo: Ron Kenyon)

short wall of *Tarn Crag Gully I* and, before the gully proper starts, move right and climb the buttress, keeping to the left side, overlooking the gully.

Tarn Crag Gullies II and III 100m I

Both of these short gullies start from the top of the amphitheatre and give straightforward snow slopes either side of the dividing buttress.

Dollywaggon Gully 130m III ★★ 1936/7

The larger gully to the right of the amphitheatre.

1 15m. The chockstone is passed by a crack on its left side to gain a snow slope.

2 40m. Continue up the snow slope to a steep groove.

3 30m. In 10m the groove leads to another snow slope, which is followed to the final pitch.

4 45m. The ice wall on the right leads to further snow and the top.

Dollywaggon Chimney 130m III

This is the narrow chimney immediately right of the start of *Dollywaggon Gully*.

1   50m. Follow snow to a narrowing chimney pitch.
2   50m. Follow the broader chimney to a headwall.
3   30m. Follow a narrow chimney through the headwall and onto mixed ground to finish.

Right-Hand Finish   80m IV (4) 1991
Start 50m up the chimney, where it narrows to a crack.
1   30m. Climb the steepening groove on the right on frozen turf.
2   50m. Finish up mixed ground.

The crag is split by an indefinite gully line round towards the right of the bigger section.

Falcon Crag Gully   135m II ★
1   40m. Several short ice bulges lead to a snow bay.
2   40m. From the bay follow the gully to another smaller snow bay.
3   55m. Climb the gully to finish.

Tic Tac Man   140m IV (4) 1987
A meandering route up the steep buttress left of *Chock Gully* passing through some impressive situations. Start on the left, at the base of *Chock Gully*.
1   40m. Trend left to a steep wall past a small sapling to easier ground. Move left along an easy gangway, then up and back right to the base of a steep corner.
2   30m. A traverse right leads into *Chock Gully*. Climb diagonally left up the wall of the gully to gain a ledge above the steep corner. Traverse left to a detached pinnacle. With sufficient snow build-up, it is possible to reach the pinnacle directly from the steep corner.
3   50m. Climb the pinnacle and gain a gangway leading rightwards. Follow this for a few metres to a shallow corner and continue steeply to a second rightward-slanting gangway. This ends in a steep wall above *Chock Gully* and an escape up a shallow weakness to easier ground.
4   20m. More easy ground leads to the top.

Chock Gully   135m IV (4) ★★ 1936/7
The deeply cut gully at the right side of the crag overlooking Grisedale. A classic in the right conditions, but with a lean ice coating it becomes very much harder than the grade indicated. It is usually lean!

Eastern Crags

1   25m. The crack on the right of the chockstone leads to easy snow.
2   20m. A steep but short ice bulge leads to a belay on left.
3   25m. Climb to the capstone (crux) and pull out leftwards over the top.
4   55m. Easier ice or snow leads to the top.

Dollywaggon Great Chimney   100m V ★★ 1986

Round the corner to right of *Chock Gully*, the buttress is split by a shallow chimney-line.

1   30m (4). Climb the vegetated narrow gully, just above a ledge. Belay beneath a steep corner crack on the left.
2   20m (3). Follow the crack, using a jammed flake, to the *Birdcage*. Move right below the roof and climb through the *Skylight*. Continue up the easy gully above through a second archway to belay.
3   50m (2). Continue up the gully and buttress above to finish just right of the top of *Chock Gully*.

Pinnacle Climb   80m IV (4) 2004

Start halfway between *Dollywaggon Great Chimney* on *Falcon Crag* and *Easy Gully* on *Cock Cove Crag*.

1   40m (4). Follow turfy ledges and grooves up rightwards until nearly looking over *Easy Gully*, next to a rock pinnacle/spike. Climb the wall behind the pinnacle, and ledges above, to a belay.
2   40m (2). Finish easily up the wall.

Grizedale Tarn (photo: Nick Wharton)

PATTERDALE AND ADJACENT VALLEYS

Patterdale itself is a poor winter venue, but many of its subsidiary valleys give excellent climbing. Sleet Cove and Link Cove in Deepdale come into condition relatively frequently and offer several fine climbs on a number of crags. As well as more traditional routes such as *Inaccessible Gully* and *Black Crag Icefall* in Dovedale, there are many modern mixed climbs to be found, particularly on the crags of *Scrubby* and *Hutaple*. Please see the maps 'Helvellyn and Patterdale' on pages 282–3 and 'Far Eastern Fells' on pages 352–3.

PATTERDALE – EAST

The routes on the east side of the main valley of Patterdale are described first. Starting in the north, there are two low-lying watercourses which offer good ice climbing in a sustained freeze.

Swarthbeck Gill   120m II

On the east side of Ullswater, this west-facing gill on the western slopes of Arthur's Pike overlooks the lake (NY 453 208). Starting at the low altitude of about 250m, it needs a prolonged frost, so it's worth checking it out from the across the lake before making the long drive round.

To the east of Ullswater, the secluded valley of Bannerdale is accessible from Pooley Bridge. The western slopes of the head of the valley contain a line of crags marked on the map as **Heck Crag** and **Buck Crag** (NY 420 151). North-east-facing *Buck Crag* is split by the obvious **Bannerdale Gully** (130m, II), which gives a pleasant climb passing a couple of chockstones.

Rampsgill Head Crag

(NY 443 129)
Alt. 670m North-west facing

Rampsgill Head, on the old Roman road of High Street, has a broken crag below its north-west face, overlooking the valley of Ramps Gill. Isolated buttress are scattered across the hillside just north of the main summit. The most significant of these is visible from the approach path as it rounds the Knott. From this point the buttress looks like an isolated top connected to the main mass of the mountain by a col; this is 200m past the summit of the mountain. Closer inspection reveals that it is in fact made up of three pinnacles with impressive gullies between them that provide some excellent traditional mountaineering routes about 100m long. Beware of loose blocks and flakes.

From the car park in the village of Hartsop, follow the bridleway to Hayeswater and continue along it, up the hillside to the north of the reservoir, to where the path curves south round the Knott. At this point the buttresses can be clearly seen. Strike east to the summit of Rampsgill Head. The main *Pinnacle Buttress* is 200m to the north, and is reached after a scramble down to the col between it and the main mountain (1hr 30mins). Take care on the final **descent** by keeping on the right side (facing out) to avoid steep rocks to the left.

The first route is separate from the others on the most southerly buttress immediately below the summit. The top of the buttress is marked by a large cairn located about 20m north of the smaller summit cairn and at a slightly lower elevation on the Ramps Gill side of the hill.

Southern Buttress

The most southerly buttress has a steep wall at its base and is split by a large rambling ledge system, above which are easy turfy rocks that can be climbed anywhere at Grade II.

Original Route   90m II 2005

You've guessed it – the first route on the crag.

1   50m. Climb an easy turfy groove to the right of the steep lower section of buttress. Belay at the back of the rambling ledge.
2   40m. Continue up the middle of the back wall in the same line.

Rampsgill Head Crag

1	Easy Buttress	I/II
2	Umbrella Gully	II/III
3	Gendarmerie	III
4	Left Gully	III
5	Blow Out (approx. line)	IV
6	Buttress Groove	II
7	Right Gully	II
8	Wind Up	I/II
9	North Gully	IV
10	Central Gully	III
10a	Central Gully North	
	Pinnacle Exit	IV
10b	Escape Exit	II
11	Central Ridge	IV
12	South Gully	III
13	Friends Above	V
14	South Pinnacle Ridge	IV
15	South South Gully	II
16	Windy Buttress	III
17	Original Route	II

(Photo: Nick Wharton – Copyright FRCC)

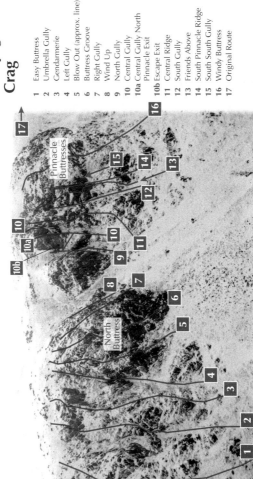

Windy Buttress   95m III 2005

The narrow buttress some 200m left of *Original Route* and immediately right of *South South Gully*.

1   45m. Climb a shallow left-trending groove to a rock wall.
2   25m (3). Climb the wall by a groove (the right-hand of two), then another short wall.
3   25m. Finish easily.

Pinnacle Buttresses

The three pinnacles are named *South*, *Central* and *North*. The col behind *Central Pinnacle* is a convenient place to leave sacks, as many routes end back at this point. The best **descent** from here is to the north, past *North Pinnacle* and a gully to its north, and past another smaller buttress to a broad gully of snow/very loose scree. Descend this and contour back under the crag.

South South Gully   90m II 2005

The gully at the right-hand side of *South Pinnacle* contains a couple of small steps which may bank out. With care it makes a descent from the col behind the pinnacles.

South Pinnacle Ridge   90m IV ★★ 2005

A climb up *South Pinnacle* via its right side, passing a large shaped rock – the *Diving Board*.

1   40m (3). Climb a prominent groove in the middle of the base of the pinnacle and follow easy ground to belay where the buttress steepens.
2   50m (6). Climb a groove on the right of the buttress, formed by the right wall and the *Diving Board*. At the top of the groove climb up the right wall of the pinnacle on cracks and turf with some awkward bridging moves to gain the crest of the ridge. The obvious shorter deep groove just to the left may look inviting but isn't. Once on the ridge follow it to the top of the *Pinnacle*.

It's not all over yet: a short abseil into the gully between the two pinnacles will allow the *Central Pinnacle* to be traversed and downclimbed back to the col. If you're careful you can flick off your abseil sling!

Friends Above   100m V ★ 2005

This takes the prominent corner-line on the left side of the buttress, halfway up *South Pinnacle*.

1   30m (2). From the foot of *South Gully*, climb up onto the turfy crest
    of the lower portion of the pinnacle, and continue to belay at the
    base of the groove formed by the *Diving Board*.
2   20m (7). Climb up and traverse left along the quartz ledge at the
    base of the steep buttress. Hard committing moves gain the base of
    the corner on the left side of the buttress. Move further left to a shel-
    tered belay ledge.
3   50m (7). Move back right into the corner, and follow it with difficult
    climbing and awkward protection to good turf at the top, if you can
    reach it. Continue up the pinnacle, keeping to its left side, to a short
    5m corner near the top which provides an avoidable sting in the
    tail.

South Gully   100m III 2005

The obvious gully to the left of *South Pinnacle*. A tree at half height
makes a good belay at the start of the difficulties.
1   40m (2). Follow the obvious gully easily to where it steepens just
    below the tree.
2   50m (3). Surmount the steep wall, past the tree, into a narrower
    cleft. Climb out across the left wall on turf to where the gully
    widens. There are two possible exits from here. The steeper right-
    hand one is the one you want. Climb a vague open corner to the
    narrow gap between *South* and *Central Pinnacles*. Either climb
    through the chockstones at the top and down the other side into the
    top of *South South Gully* or, more aesthetically, climb onto *Central
    Pinnacle* on the left and belay.
3   10m (3). Climb over the top of the *Central Pinnacle* and down the
    back to the col.

South Gully Left-Hand   60m III 2005

Follow the first pitch of *South Gully* to the tree belay.
2   30m (3). Climb past the tree, then either to the back of the narrow
    gully and up past jammed blocks or up the turfy left wall of the
    gully from just after the tree. Where the gully widens above climb
    the left exit to a wall/buttress about 10m below the narrow chimney
    on *Central Ridge*.
3   30m (4). From the belay several exits are possible (mentioned in the
    Central Pinnacle Gully description). On the first ascent, the centre
    of the buttress to the right of the belay was climbed to the top of the
    pinnacle.

Eastern Crags

Central Pinnacle Gully 90m III (4) 2005

From the base of *South Gully*, a shallow gully line runs leftwards up the side of *Central Pinnacle*. Follow this without difficulty until it ends at a ledge which is the junction with *Central Ridge*. Traverse awkwardly 2m right below a rock wall and continue up the side of the wall to join the upper portion of *South Gully Left-Hand*, about 10m below the narrow chimney on *Central Ridge*. From here a variety of finishes are possible. Either finish up the chimney as for *Central Ridge* (climb the centre of the buttress above) or climb up chockstones to the right of the buttress and then continue up to the summit.

Central Ridge 90m IV ★★ 2005

An entertaining route. The upper section overlooks *Central Gully*.

1 20m (2). From the foot of *Central Gully/North Gully*, climb diagonally rightwards onto the turfy ridge and up to a small rocky wall.

2 40m (5). Climb up a groove to the top of a flake (5m), then make moves over a sloping rock ledge to turf. Climb a wide groove to another ledge with a spike runner and make delicate moves up a shallow corner to a large ledge with a large block on its right-hand side and a spike protruding out from the face at right angles. Chimney up behind the block and move up onto a ridge that is followed to the base of a narrow chimney on the left side of the pinnacle.

3 30m (4). Climb the chimney and a turfy groove overlooking *Central Gully*. Easy ground then leads to the top of the pinnacle.

Central Gully 90m III ★ 2005

The obvious gully to the left of *Central Pinnacle* finishes at the col.

1 50m (3). Start up a shallow turfy groove/depression on the left of *Central Pinnacle*. After about 30m, a steeper step gains access to the well-defined gully which has some impressive walls. Pass another steep step and belay about 10m above this, below the prominent large chockstone blocking the gully.

2 40m (4). Climb up a groove on the left of the chockstone and step across rightwards back into the base of the gully, below some more jammed chockstones. Continue up the main gully-line, which curves to the right to finish on the col.

Escape Exit 20m II ★★ 2005

Just below the second steep step (10m below the chockstone), climb the turfy left wall of the gully to easy ground and traverse left into the easy top section of *North Gully*.

Central Gully North Pinnacle Exit   40m IV (5) 2005

From the top of pitch one of *Central Gully*, pass the chockstone and, where the main gully goes up the right exit, take the corner-line on the left to finish on *North Pinnacle*. There are some loose flakes on the walls, and the lower half is poorly protected.

North Gully   90m IV ★★★ 2005

The obvious gully to the left of *North Pinnacle*. The top pitch is an impressive narrow leaning cleft.

1   60m (2). Climb the easy turfy gully to the left of *North Pinnacle*, passing one steeper section, to belay at the base of the slanting cleft at the top.

2   30m (5). Thrutch up the cleft, with an excursion onto the left wall at an obvious ledge where it narrows (several chockstones for protection – take at least five large slings). Belay at the buttress on the right at the top of the gully.

North Buttress

To the left of the wide **descent** gully (facing in) is a vegetated buttress. From the bottom of the descent gully, a gully containing a chockstone near its top is clearly visible on the right-hand side of the buttress (*Right Gully*). A traverse around the base of the buttress reveals another gully (*Left Gully*) with a short pitch up a series of chockstones about 40m up the easy gully.

Wind Up   60m I/II 2005

The shallow right-trending gully to the right of *Right Gully*, and just left of the descent gully.

Right Gully   50m II 2005

From the base of the descent gully, climb the obvious gully on the right of the buttress to a chockstone. Surmount this and continue easily to the top.

Buttress Groove   50m II 2005

To the left of *Right Gully* is a faint vegetated groove running up the front of the buttress. Climb this to easy ground and pass a series of small walls to belay just left of the finish of *Right Gully*.

Eastern Crags

Blow Out
90m IV (3) 2005

On the *North Buttress* between *Buttress Groove* and *Left Gully* is a large vegetated depression.

1   45m. Climb the depression to a big shattered spike (hard to see from below), then slant leftwards to belays.

2   45m. Continue in the same line, passing left of a protruding buttress, and finish up a vague ridge.

Left Gully
80m III ★ 2005

The most prominent gully on the left side of the buttress.

1   30m. Climb the easy turfy lower gully to belay at the base of the steep rock pitch where the gully walls narrow.

2   50m (4). Climb the chockstones on the right side of the gully (crux), then continue easily, passing two short steeper sections, and belay at the top, just after a narrowing of the gully walls.

Gendarmerie
90m III 2005

Between *Left Gully* and *Umbrella Gully* is a shallow buttress with a prominent gendarme near its top.

1   35m. Climb the buttress just right of its crest to a spike belay.

2   45m. Continue just left of the crest. Pass immediately left of the gendarme and belay at the col.

3   10m. Finish leftwards.

Umbrella Gully
95m II/III 2005

The next shallow gully left of *Left Gully*.

1   35m. Follow the left-trending gully to a chockstone.

2   45m. Pass the chockstone on its left and follow the gully as it bends rightwards. Shortly before it peters out, climb straight up to a belay.

3   15m. Finish by a slim groove 7m left of the gendarme of the last route.

Easy Buttress
125m I/II 2005

Left of *Umbrella Gully*, start at a lower level and climb the easy grassy buttress in three pitches, taking the easiest line.

Col Gully lies immediately left of *Easy Buttress*, and gives a very easy **descent** from the col between Rampsgill Head and High Raise.

Threshwaite Cove

(NY 424 102)
Alt. 770m North facing

This cove on the east side of the valley is more famous for its rock climbing, but its pleasant isolated gully gives an enjoyable mountain day if combined with a return along the ridge over Hartsop Dodd.

Threshwaite Gully   170m III ★ 1995

From the village of Hartsop, make the long trek to the head of the cove. The buttress to the west of the col can be clearly seen on the approach and is split by a deep gully. A chockstone guards the entrance, after which easier climbing leads to a steep 15m ice pitch about halfway up. Above this, 30m of easier-angled ice, and then scrambling, lead to the ridge between Beacon and Stony Cove Pike.

PATTERDALE – WEST

The routes on the west side of the main valley are now described. In the north is *Aira Force*, just above the western shore of the lake. This is the only climb on the west side of the main valley, but that is more than made up for by what can be found in the side valleys.

Aira Force   25m III Pre-1962

On the west shore of the lake, Aira Beck flows into Ullswater just north of the junction of the A592 Penrith road and the A5091 Keswick road. About 500m upstream from the lake is the famous waterfall at (NY 399 205). There is parking at the road's closest point to the fall. When frozen, the fall is approached by a narrow short gorge. However, being south-facing and at an altitude of only 200m, the force seldom freezes. When it does the main difficulty usually depends on the amount of water still coming down it.

GRISEDALE

The valley of Grisedale, leading off Patterdale to its west, gives access to the crags and coves on Dollywaggon Pike and Nethermost Pike, though they are more easily and more regularly accessed from Dunmail Raise or Swirls car park on the side of Thirlmere to the west: they are all covered in the Helvellyn section. However, St Sunday Crag (found on the southern flank of Grisedale) is best approached from Patterdale.

St Sunday Crag	(NY 368 139)
	Alt. 600m North-west facing

This crag high up on the southern side of Grisedale offers panoramic views into the Helvellyn coves. The crag has four main gullies and several minor ones not worth detailed descriptions. Many of these routes were done during snowy winters in the 1960s, and the gullies particularly do not usually receive the build-up of snow necessary to give them complete cover. This has lead to a decline in the crag's winter popularity, though the ridges can still offer interesting sport.

Just north of Patterdale village, a side road leads into Grisedale. This becomes a private road with restricted access, so parking is limited and confined to the lower part of the road. Follow the path up the Grisedale valley until a wooden bridge is reached. A good view of the crag and its gullies is available from here. Ascend the hillside from here to the crag. Alternatively, if you know the lay-out of the crag, follow the zigzag path up from the end of the Elmhow plantation and traverse right to the crag.

Directly above the bridge is *West Chockstone Gully*, with *Y Gully* 100m to the left, in the centre of the crag. The left branch of *Y Gully* joins *Pillar Gully* at half-height. A further 50m left of *Y Gully* is *Pillar Gully*, separated from the former by the almost detached pillar. About 170m left again is *East Chockstone Gully*, the most interesting of the gullies.

West Chockstone Gully   70m I/II
When in condition this is a steep snow gully with a small rock step at

Kate Harper enjoying fine alpine conditions on Pinnacle Ridge *(II), St Sunday Crag (Photo: Stuart Miller)*

half-height. Near the top of the gully it is possibly to move left over the rib into *Y Gully*. The ridge to the left can give an interesting winter climb in its own right.

Y Gully (Right Fork) 65m I

When containing enough snow this is the useful as a means of descent, providing the cornice at the top can be passed. The left fork of the gully leads into *Pillar Gully*.

Boneyard Wall 42m III ★ 1963

A good climb. About 35m up the right branch of *Y Gully* is a big right-angled corner above a triangle of ribs and snow-covered grass. Follow the grassy snow ledge down left for 10m and belay where the ledge ends beneath an exposed wall.

1   20m (4). Climb diagonally left across the wall to reach a flat ledge at the base of a clean-cut corner. Climb the iced slab on the right and belay at the top of the corner.

2   22m (3). Move back right and climb the overhang. Turn a second overhang on the left and move up over a nose to easier ground.

Pillar Gully 75m I

The straightforward snow gully to the left of the pillar.

East Chockstone Gully 70m I/II

The most interesting of the gullies. There are often two rock steps low down; their difficulty varies with the snow build-up.

Pinnacle Ridge 180m II ★ 1977

About 180m left of *East Chockstone Gully*. Follow the line of the serrated arete to the summit. An interesting and enjoyable climb, though all difficulties can be turned.

Girdle Traverse 700m III 1978

The Lake District's answer to Scotland's Creag Meagaidh Crab Crawl?! A right-to-left girdle of the complete crag. Starting up *West Chockstone Gully*, and at approximately half-height, it follows an obvious line past *East Chockstone Gully*. Here mixed ground is followed to the area of the summer routes *Chockstone Gully Rib* and *Slab Route*. Under suitable conditions it is possible to climb almost anywhere on the crag at Grade III.

DEEPDALE

Many of the routes in Deepdale come into condition quickly after the onset of a cold spell and this makes it an excellent centre for winter climbing. The grassy truncated spur of *Greenhow End* divides the head of the valley, with the high hanging valley of Link Cove on its left. Link Cove contains the broken *Hart Crag* on its left and the more impressive *Scrubby Crag* on its right. The more major branch of Deepdale, to the right of *Greenhow End*, is Sleet Cove, and this contains the extensive *Hutaple Crag* and the smaller *Black Buttress*.

There is parking by the telephone kiosk at *Bridgend* (NY 399 144) on the main Ullswater road, A592. If this is full, a larger car park lies 1km to the south near a sharp bend in the road. A good path leads initially past farms, then over the valley bottom, to below *Greenhow End*. For *Hutaple Crag* (about 750m further up on the right), cross the stream and, keeping it on your right, climb the hillside, past the slabs of *Mart Crag*. Link Cove, and the climbs on *Greenhow End*, can be approached by a choice of frozen gills that give good climbs in their own right.

Sleet Cove and Link Cove (including *Scrubby* and *Hutaple Crags*) are home to rare alpine plants. The bits away from the crags are even better, some of the crumbly easier gullies being rich with rare plants – please climb here only in truly frozen conditions (see the chapter 'Winter Climbing and Nature Conservation').

The first climbs are two gills on the left (NY 374 122, alt. 400m), just before *Greenhow End*, which make a more interesting way of reaching Link Cove or the climbs on *Greenhow End*.

Link Cove Gill (Left Branch)   70m III

Less often in climbable condition than its neighbour due to its enclosed position, this popular scramble is nevertheless worthwhile when ice does form.

Link Cove Gill (Right Branch)   60m II

The more open of the two streams. An initial short steep ice pitch is followed by further easy-angled ice that peters out almost level with the start of the climbs on *Greenhow End*. There is another fall of a similar standard further up the stream. Often in condition.

Eastern Crags

Deepdale Overview
(Photo: Nick Wharton – Copyright FRCC)

1	Step Gully	II/III
2	Greenhow Gully	III
3	Link Cove Gills	II and III

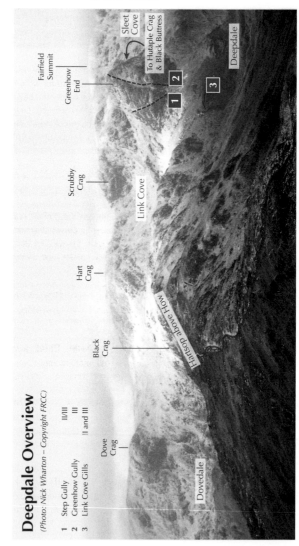

Link Cove
Alt. 700m East facing

The following climbs and crags are all in *Link Cove*, the prominent hanging valley to the left of *Greenhow End* when approaching up Deepdale. On entering the cove, a series of short but interesting icefalls form over a rock band on the right. *Scrubby Crag* is the obvious crag high up on the right of the cove, to the right of *Link Hause*, while to the left are the broken and scattered buttresses of *Hart Crag*.

Hart Crag
(NY 370 114)
Alt. 700m North facing

This is the rambling collection of broken buttresses to the left of the col of Link Hause. High elevation and a northerly aspect make for the most reliable and quick-forming ice on the Fairfield massif. Several good ice pitches form which may be linked together as you please – the routes described make the best of them.

Left Runnel
80m III (3)

The first shallow gully-line on the left is usually water ice with two steep sections.

Hart Crag Ice Falls
110m III (4) ★★

The series of icefalls to the right is linked by mixed turf climbing.
1 30m. Climb a short icefall to easier ground and continue to a steep wall.
2 30m. More ice leads to mixed ground. Belay left of the next icefall (pegs useful).
3 30m. Climb the icefall, trending right.
4 20m. Step left, and climb a groove and another steep icefall to the top.

Cold Lazarus
170m III (3) ★★

Located on the central and highest buttresses, a series of stepped ice pitches form with good ledges and belays between each pitch. The difficulties increase with height. Start below a broad ice groove 100m to the right of the previous routes.

Eastern Crags

1   60m. Climb the groove to a broad ledge.
2   30m. Traverse right and climb a shallow chimney to ledges, then go
    up right to belay below an ice runnel.
3   30m. Climb the runnel to belay on a block on the right.
4   50m. Easier climbing to the top.

Variation   IV (4)

A steep icefall often forms to the left of pitch 2 and is reach by traversing
left from the top of the shallow chimney.

Short Chute   50m III (3) ★★

Right again is a prominent steep buttress. An excellent icefall often
forms on the right of this. Climb the fall which narrows into a chimney
at the top.

Six metres to the right again, an ice smear forms (IV 5).

Scrubby Crag   (NY 367 115)
                                       Alt. 710m South-east facing

A good concentration of interesting technical routes are found on this
crag, plus the more traditional *Pendulum Gully* on its right edge. Its elevated position means the latter is often 'in', and the mixed climbs are
soon do-able in a cold snap. A more prolonged freeze allows ice smears
to form on the main crag, which, when complete, give some fine hard
routes.

The routes are described from left to right. The prominent corner-
line at the left end of the crag is *Juniper Crack*. The first climb takes the
buttress to the left of this but starts from the base of the corner. The
safest **descent** is from Link Hause (to the left of the crag when facing
it).

Wall Climb   75m IV 1987

A steep route up the buttress to the left of the prominent corner of
Juniper Crack.
1   25m (4). From the base of the corner of *Juniper Crack*, climb
    grooves on the left to a ledge and climb the wall above to a juniper-
    covered ledge and large flake runner. Follow the leftwards-rising
    crack awkwardly to a small stance where the crack straightens.

Scrubby Crag

1	Wall Climb	IV
2	Juniper Crack	V
3	Long Ledge Entry and Exit	V
4	Heorot	VI
5	Midnight Special	V
6	Ringway Finish	V
7	Grendel	VI
8	Firedragon Finish	IV
9	Ginny Clegg	V
10	Pendulum Ridge	III
11	Pendulum Gully	II/III

(Photo: Nick Wharton –
Copyright FRCC)

Eastern Crags

329

2   20m (4). Ascend the wall above for 3m until it is possible to traverse right and round a corner into a bay. From the back of the bay climb the corner to a stance beneath a corner crack.

3   30m (3). Follow the obvious right-trending ramp-line at first, then go straight up.

Juniper Crack   70m V ☆☆ 2003

The obvious corner at the left end of the crag is a mossy and damp Hard Severe in summer: it makes a far better winter route.

1   25m (6). Climb the obvious corner to a stance below where the upper wall steepens.

2   45m (5). Move up the corner a few metres until it steepens, then move left onto the wall and traverse left over blocks to a pinnacle on the arete and a ledge. It is possible to split the pitch here; otherwise continue up a crack then move to a ledge round the rib and finish up the corner crack.

Long Ledge Entry and Exit   80m V (6) ★★ 1972

The first of the mixed routes on the crag. Start as for *Juniper Crack*.

1   20m. Climb most of the first pitch of *Juniper Crack*, up the corner to a block belay.

2   30m. From the belay, traverse the wall on the right and move up to an overhang and peg runner. Move back down, teeter right to an icicle, and continue moving right to the welcoming *Long Ledge*.

3   30m. Finish up the steep dirty corner above, the top pitch of *Heorot*. This corner pitch can be thickly iced and offer easy climbing protected by ice screws, or can be a thin smear of ice on one wall which is hard and poorly protected in its lower half. Either way the climbing is brilliant.

Heorot   70m VI (7) ★★★ 1987

This is the prominent right-facing corner-line high on the crag, above and right of *Juniper Crack*. The first pitch is thin and sustained; the second is brilliant. One of the best routes in the cove.

1   40m. This pitch follows a very shallow groove-line, which is not obvious, but is directly below the corner-line of the top pitch. From the left end of the ledge below the corner, below a flake, climb the right-hand of the two grooves to the obvious top corner.

2   30m. The obvious corner above as for *Long Ledge and Exit*. Superb!

Between the prominent corner of *Heorot*, and the deep groove-line of *Grendel* to its right, the wall is crossed by a leftward-slanting ramp-line leading to the top pitch of *Heorot*. This is *Midnight Special*.

Midnight Special   70m V (5) ★ 1986

A good mixed route that is often in condition. Start about 20m right of *Heorot*.

1   40m. The left-slanting ramp-line is gained from well to the right. Climb the ramp-line to a ledge and traverse this leftwards to the corner of *Heorot*.
2   30m. If you haven't done it yet, finish up the top corner of *Heorot*.

Ringway Finish   40m V (5) 1995

For those who've already climbed the top corner of *Heorot*: from the ledge move right for 8m to follow a steep arete to the top.

Grendel   90m VI ★★★ 1991

The fine groove right of the centre of the crag ices up in winter to give a superb route. The winter route climbs the main groove to *Long Ledge* before traversing left to exit up the top groove of the summer route *Sennapod*, which ices up more readily than the summer finish.

Al Phizacklea on Grendel *(VI), Scrubby Crag (Photo: Paul Cornforth)*

Eastern Crags

1   45m (7). Gain the pedestal at the foot of the corner-groove. Move
     left to easier ground to enter the main groove. Follow this until it is
     blocked by an overhang at the top that forces moves right to the
     arete. Follow this to *Long Ledge*.
2   45m (5). Move leftwards up a step to the upper ledge. Climb the
     wall for a few metres to a ramp-line running left to an iced corner
     and follow this to the top. A poorly protected pitch. The cornerline
     top pitch of *Firedragon*, the last corner on *Long Ledge* approxi-
     mately 10m to the right, has been used as a useful alternative finish
     and comes into condition readily.

Ginny Clegg   105m V 1987

About 20m right of *Grendel* is a vegetated bay leading to a steep wall
below the *Long Ledge*. This climb takes a meandering but central line up
the large bay starting just left of the crag's lowest point and winds its way
up to the higher rock buttress – really a winter version of the summer
route *Firedragon* which goes up the back of the bay.
1   30m (3). Take as direct a line as possible up icefalls and turf ledges.
2   15m (4). Head leftwards to an ice pillar with runners in a bay on the
     right. Climb the pillar and belay to the right.
3   30m (5). A poorly protected pitch, made more serious by its tra-
     verse. Traverse left for 15m and precariously around a corner onto a
     ramp. Follow the ramp to belay on the obvious large flake above.
4   30m (3). Move left and up, with a difficult move onto *Long Ledge*.
     Follow this to easy ground.

Firedragon Finish   20m IV (4) 1995

From *Long Ledge*, follow a line of turf to the right of the last corner at the
right end of the *Ledge*. The summer line goes up the corner.

Pendulum Ridge   120m III (4) ★★★ 1985

This takes the right-hand turfy arete of the main crag, overlooking
Pendulum Gully to its right. Start to the left of a prominent overhang low
down. The initial moves up the short wall are difficult, after which things
tend to get easier as progress is made up the ridge.

Pendulum Gully   180m II/III ★

The obvious gully defining the right end of the crag. A short ice pitch near
the start of the gully leads to easy snow. The gully gradually steepens and
splits. Follow the right fork to another ice pitch which leads to the top.

Dave Kay on the first winter ascent of Pendulum Ridge *(III), Scrubby Crag
(Photo: Stuart Miller)*

Halcyon **80m III 1991**
Where the gully forks take the left-branch, running back behind the main crag.

Above and right of *Pendulum Gully*, set back at a higher level than the main crag, is a series of broken buttresses mainly separated from each other by easy-angled snow gullies. Generally the buttresses do not give many continuous lines, and they can be climbed just about anywhere at Grade III. The following route has been recorded as a sample.

Tongue and Groove **170m II/III 2003**
This takes the shallow gully-line up the buttress to the right of *Pendulum Gully*. About 20m right of *Pendulum Gully* is a buttress with an easy open gully to its right.

1   20m. Climb the buttress easily for about 20m, and then veer left towards *Pendulum Gully* into another shallow gully line.
2   50m. Follow this gully, which takes a straight line running parallel with *Pendulum Gully* but about 10m to the right. Run the rope out of the gully across some easy ground, keeping left to maintain a parallel course with *Pendulum Gully*, to a spike belay in a small ampitheatre.
3   50m. Continue straight up the gully to a poor belay in a second small ampitheatre. From here it is possible to traverse right for 10m back onto the buttress.
4   50m. Either climb straight up the corner or a make a small zigzag back into the gully (crux), where several large flat rocks block the gully. Pass these (may bank over in heavy snow) to finish.

SLEET COVE

Greenhow End (NY 370 120)
Alt. 600m North-east facing

This large vegetated cliff is rather broken but does possess two interesting gullies. *Step Gully* is a line slanting left from broken ground below the centre of the buttress, and provides a pleasant way into *Link Cove*

Greenhow End

1 Greenhow Gully — III
2 Deepdale Gully — III
3 Central Gully — III
4 East Hutaple Gully — II
5 The Memo — II
6 East Hutaple Groove — II/III
7 Scorpion — IV

(Photo: Nick Wharton – Copyright FRCC)

and the crags there, whilst *Greenhow Gully* takes a rake-line running diagonally rightwards. The routes are described from left to right.

Step Gully   65m II/III ★

Follow a leftward-slanting gully from the centre of the crag. Climb to the gully and follow it over several short ice pitches until easier snow is reached. Belay as required.

Right Wall   35m IV

From about halfway up the gully, icefalls form on the right wall in a good season. Follow these to broken easier ground above or traverse off left when the angle eases.

Greenhow Gully   100m III ★ 1960

Starting right of centre this follows a rightward-slanting diagonal line.
1   30m (4). Gain and follow the narrow chimney/gully, passing a small ice bulge.
2   25m. Easier ground leads to a chockstone.
3   15m (2). Pass the chockstone by bridging moves to an awkward landing above (hopefully!).
4   30m. Either pass the next small chockstone on the left or take the slab on the right and continue to the top.

Variation Finish   III 2003

4   40m (4). Avoid the easy finish by entertaining mixed climbing up the tiered left wall of the upper gully.

Sleet Cove lies to the right of *Greenhow End*. About 100m from the lowest point of the *Greenhow End* is the first of two gullies.

Deepdale Gully   100m III

This contains several ice pitches.
1   20m. Follow the gully up to a chockstone which is passed on the right.
2   30m. Easy ground leads to a steepening in the gully.
3   25m. The steep chimney leads to a belay ledge.
4   25m. Easier snow leads to the top.

Central Gully   80m III

Another worthwhile gully: it lies 30m right of *Deepdale Gully*.

1 25m. A small ice pitch leads to steep snow and turf which is followed to a fork in the gully.
2 20m. Follow the left branch, passing slabby ground, to belay below a large chockstone.
3 35m. Take the chockstone on the left and follow the gully bed, passing further small chockstone and chimney pitches to the top.

The buttresses to either side of *Central Gully* can be climbed at Grade II/III and provide a useful escape if the gully is not in condition.

Hutaple Crag   (NY 367 120)
Alt. 640m North-west facing

This large rambling crag is over 150m high and sits in a prime position in the cove. The crag is bounded by *East Hutaple Gully* on its left and *West Gully* to its right, and is split by the prominent line of *Curving Gully*. To the left of *Curving Gully*, *The Amphitheatre* is a steep open corner above vegetated slabs. A series of ledges run across the top of the crag and must be climbed/scrambled over before making a descent. The best **descent** is on the right of the crag.

The routes are described from left to right.

East Hutaple Gully   100m II
This is really two parallel gullies very close together giving only small ice pitches; climb where it looks best. The turfy buttress dividing the two gullies also gives good climbing (II).

Devious Exit   25m IV 2003
From the bay below the twin ice pitches in *East Hutaple Gully*, climb out left on a snow and turf ramp-line to a horizontal traverse which leads to a belay on the edge of another gully (the right branch of *Central Gully*). Finish easily up this.

The Memo   100m II 2006
A line up the turfy easy angled wall on the right-hand side of *East Huptable Gully*, between the *Gully* and the *Groove*.

Follow the wall on the right-hand side of *Fast Hutaple Gully*. The route steepens at mid-height and can be easily joined there from the gully. From this point, 60m of steep heather and turf lead to a short rock corner. Interest is maintained and warthogs are recommended. Easier ground above leads to the top.

East Hutaple Groove   140m II/III ★★ 1986

A good climb when in condition. Start just right of *East Hutaple Gully* at a clean steep buttress.

1   50m. Take the easiest line up the iced slabs to a steep terrace below the left-hand side of the buttress proper.

2   50m. Wide iced slabs to left of the steep buttress gradually steepen towards the headwall. Traverse right to a block belay on the terrace.

3   40m. Either return back left into the gully and finish up this or climb steep mixed ground on the right of the belay.

Scorpion   120m IV ★★ 1997

The left-facing corner-cleft high on the left side of the buttress.

1   40m (3). Climb the iced slabs of *East Hutaple Groove* pitch 1 to belay where *East Hutaple Groove* goes up the left side of the crag.

2   40m (3). Traverse rightwards 10m to the end of the large ledge and climb the obvious chimney, passing several ledges, to belay below a steep headwall.

3   40m (5). The crux, where it should be. Powerful but well-protected climbing in an impressive position. Climb the steep wall, past the chockstone, to a thread belay and easier ground. Belay well back on the right.

Easier ground leads to the top of the cliff.

East Wall Route   120m IV ★ 1966

A good route venturing up the left edge of the main face.

1   50m (3). Follow *Scorpion* to the base of the chimney on its pitch 2.

2   20m (5). Climb a corner/groove above for 5m until it is possible to step right round the arete and move up to a ledge and belay

3   20m (4). Move diagonally right over slabby ground to belay at a large bollard.

4   30m (3). Climb a small corner near the belay and continue up over broken ground and steep short steps to a rightwards-sloping ledge system at the top.

Migraine   94m III/IV Early 1960s

This climb is not known to have been repeated, and this description is from the FRCC Eastern Crags guidebook. Very much a variant on *East*

Wall, and stances are frequently shared. Start midway between *East Wall* and *Sleet Wall*.

1   40m. Climb slightly rightwards up steep grassy snowed-up rock to the lowest point of a narrow grass/snow ledge. Follow the ledge leftwards and then climb up grooves to the terrace. Walk up right to a scarred area and climb up to the belay at the foot of the wall (as for *East Wall*).

2   15m. Step right and climb a groove to a grass/snow ledge. Move up to a higher ledge beneath a slanting groove.

3   21m. Climb the groove to a ledge, move right and climb slabs to a recess and bollards.

4   18m. Climb the rib on the right of the recess and traverse to the right to a block at the foot of a rib. Climb the rib and ascend the overhang. Scramble up to the traverse ledges.

Sleet Wall   110m VII ★ Early 1960s

A demanding climb with difficult route finding. As the description is recent, the route is graded accordingly. However the first ascentionist maintains it was standard Grade IV. Either he was climbing much better than he realised, or the route was in exceptional condition! About 10m to the left of the open corner of *The Amphitheatre* is a steep shallow corner above broken ground.

1   20m (7). Follow the shallow corner for 7m before moving left across the wall to a ledge, then back right along a terrace to belay on a perched block below an overhang.

2   50m (6). Move right along the terrace to a leftward-slanting weakness through the overhang. Follow this to a snow bay. Use a wide steep crack at the top right of the bay to climb out (it may be easier and better to move right to a large block and go up from there). Follow the crack for about 7m, then make a difficult and precarious mantelshelf onto a ledge on the right. Follow vegetated slabs for about 20m to a ledge and continue to a spike belay on rope stretch.

3   40m (5). Move up and left to a short groove. Follow this to a small grassy ledge, then a large snow bay.

Easy snow plodding leads to the top.

Variation Start   V 1999

Start to the right below the open book corner of *The Amphitheatre*.

1   25m (5). Climb up to the base of the slabby corner, then cross its left wall and pull out onto a grass ledge. Continue up and left to join *Sleet Wall* below pitch 2.

Eastern Crags

339

Accidental Discharge   175m IV (4) ★ 1986

Start below and right of *The Amphitheatre*.

1   35m. Climb easily up, trending slightly left to belay at a ledge in a snow bay.

2   35m. At the left end of the ledge is an obvious ramp. Make some awkward moves to gain this and follow it to another large snow bay and block belay.

3   40m. A zigzagging pitch. From the back of the bay, follow a series of vague grooves and ledges, first leftwards, then back rightwards, to belay at the foot of a snowy corner.

4   65m. Follow the corner on the right of the belay for 10m until a step left onto the arete is possible. Continue, trending left, to easy ground and the top. The pitch may be split at several places.

Curving Gully   160m IV (5) ★ 1960s

The prominent gully in the centre of the crag. A snow ramp rises from the right to cut through the route. Unfortunately the lower pitches below the ramp are rarely iced.

1   25m. Follow a snowy gully to a narrower chimney section.

2   30m. Climb the steep series of chimneys to the snow ramp and a belay.

3   45m. Follow a second chimney system above to a stance beneath chockstones.

4   25m. Climb past two chockstones to a ledge, and follow the line of the gully into a groove.

5   35m. Easier snow leads to the top of the crag.

West Hutaple Variations   180m III/IV 2001

An unsatisfactory meandering line starting at the summer route *Terrace Wall Variant*. Start about 20m left of *West Hutaple Gully*.

1   60m. Follow a corner and easier ground to a spacious ledge below a steep blank wall.

2   40m. From the left end of the ledge, follow *Curving Gully* for 3m to a tree and traverse under this to a delicate traverse right to a second large ledge above the blank wall. It is possible to escape right and up to easier ground from here, or continue up pitch 3.

3   20m. Climb a turfy right-facing corner in the middle of the wall (probably the summer route *Interrupted Grooves*) to another spacious ledge.

4   60m. Move left, and climb a series of turf-ridden corners and grooves.

West Hutaple Edge   150m IV (4) 2000

From the foot of *West Hutaple Gully*, climb the turfy buttress on the left. This route is probably based on the summer route of *Broken Ridge* in its lower parts.

1   30m. Climb past a small tree to a large block belay.
2   40m. Follow the turfy ramp for 20m until a short groove can be climbed steeply to the foot of an overhang. Break out left and belay above in a shallow cave.
3   40m. Move left and wind up through steep sections to a bay.
4   40m. Up and left on a horizontal ledge to below the final steep wall, which is climbed via some cracks to the top.

West Hutaple Gully   75m II/II

The next prominent gully to the right. In summer this is a dangerously loose rock climb. Make sure it's well frozen and iced up before trying it in winter.

Far West Rib   70m III 1995

The rib to the right of *West Hutaple Gully*.

1   20m. Start 10m right of the gully and climb the rib to a ledge.
2   50m. Move left and continue up the rib to the top.

Western Avenue   50m III 1995

This climb takes the buttress starting from a ledge above and right of *Far West Rib* and makes a good continuation to that route. Follow the buttress and rib on frozen turf.

West Gully   85m I

This prominent gully gives straightforward snow climbing and can be useful as a means of **descent**.

The broken ground either side of *Hutaple Crag* offers several other gullies and much for those of an exploratory bent.

Eastern Crags

Black Buttress (NY 365 118)
Alt 650m North facing

To the right of *Hutaple Crag* is a wide open gully of scree and snow, and to its right is a prominent pillar of rock, *Black Buttress*. The summer rock climb of *Portcullis Ridge* (VD) takes the right-hand edge of this triangular shaped buttress. It also makes an enjoyable winter outing. The left side of the ridge is bounded by a pleasant snow gully, *Black Gully*, containing a few short steps.

Black Gully 100m II ☆ 2006
The obvious gully bounding the left side of the steep left walls of *Portcullis Ridge*. The gully may have a short step at its start, which can bank out. Above there are another couple of steep steps before the gully narrows where the walls close in. Above this, the gully widens and eventually joins the top of the ridge.

Black Groove 100m IV (5) ☆ 2006
Approximately 50m right of *Black Gully* a shallow wide fault/groove runs up the steepest part of the buttress. Climb easy turfy ledges to the start of the fault and continue up this 20m to easier ground. From here it is possible to move right over easy ground to *Black Chimney* or take a traverse line leftwards at a higher level to join the top of *Black Gully*.

Black Chimney 100m V (5) ☆☆ 2006
Approximately 30m right of the groove of *Black Groove* is a deeper cleft about 30m up the crag. Climb to the base of it and struggle up this to easier ground. Follow this to join *Portcullis Ridge* just below the top.

Portcullis Ridge 100m IV ★★ 1963
A mountaineering route with the crux in the lower section of the buttress.
1   20m (4). From the lowest point of the ridge either climb a corner on the left-hand side of the buttress/ridge or, more usually, start up the chimney on the right-hand side of the ridge: either way lands you on a ledge on top of the buttress.
2   30m (4). From the ledge, climb the steep wall, with a difficult but well-protected wall near the top. This leads to the easier ground on the ridge proper.
3   50m (2). The ridge is followed more easily.

Cofa Wall   100m IV (5) ★ 1988

This vague line on the right side of the ridge starts about 10m right of the chimney at the start of *Portcullis Ridge*.

1   30m. About 20m right of *Portcullis Ridge* follow an ill-defined groove on steep turf for 25m, until about 5m below a roof, then traverse 5m right to a stance.
2   30m. Continue up the more obvious groove above.
3   40m. Easier climbing leads to the top.

Ramparts Chimney   60m II (3) 2004

About 30m right of the start to *Portcullis Ridge* is an obvious gully/chimney bounding the right side of the crag. The crux is a chockstone at half height.

DOVEDALE

Dovedale contains fewer climbs than its neighbouring valley, but *Inaccessible Gully* and *Black Crag Icefall* are two of the best routes in the Eastern Fells.

All the crags share the same approach. Start from the Brotherswater Inn on the northern side of Kirkstone Pass. From the car park behind the inn, take the path which keeps to the north side of Dovedale. *Black Crag* is passed on the right after about 30 minutes, whilst *Dove Crag* is the obvious crag at the head of the valley, a further 20 minutes away.

Black Crag   (NY 378 116)
                          Alt. 550m South-east facing

Its south-easterly aspect ensures the crag soon catches any sun, so an early start is necessary, particularly on clear day. The icefall down the centre of the crag is obvious when approaching the crag from the path directly below.

Black Crag Icefall   60m IV ★★★ Early 1960s

The waterfall of the summer Severe *Crepuscule* makes a fantastic route when frozen. Start from trees at the bottom of the fall.

Eastern Crags

343

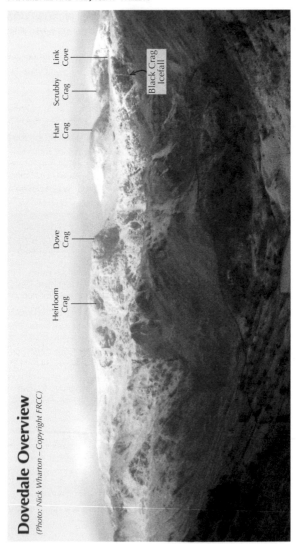

Dovedale Overview
(Photo: Nick Wharton – Copyright FRCC)

Link Cove

Scrubby Crag

Black Crag Icefall

Hart Crag

Dove Crag

Heirloom Crag

1. 30m (4). Follow the fall direct, passing the first steep bulge at 10m and subsequent others, before the sanctuary of a small belay corner is reached.
2. 30m (3/4). Continue up the iced slab on the right to overhanging ice at the top. Either pass this by the chimney on the left (3) or via the **Right-Hand Finish**, gained by an exposed traverse (4).

To the left of the main fall, a line of iced slabs and short walls finishing up a rightward-slanting ramp has been known to form occasionally (**Left-Hand Climb** 50m, III, 1986).

Between *Black Crag* and *Dove Crag*, the path crosses **Houndshope Cove Gill** (NY 379 114, alt. 410m) which can be use to approach *Hart Crag* in Link Cove. Follow the stream up and take the right fork, which gets quite interesting after 100m (II).

Dove Crag

(NY 376 109)
Alt. 600m North-east facing

The main path almost passes by the right edge of this, the major crag of the valley. A broad open gully, possibly filled with snow (if you are lucky), leads to steep slopes reaching to the base of the crag. The routes are described from left to right.

South Gully   100m I/II

This gully (surprisingly enough) bounds the south (left) side of the crag and leads to the summit. It is home to rare alpine plants and should be climbed only in truly frozen conditions. From where the path reaches the base of the crag, traverse left below the lowest point of the crag and into the start of the gully.

1. 70m. A snow slope leads to below a small chimney pitch.
2. 30m. Climb the chimney to easy snow, then a final icy steepening. A further steep snow slope leads to the summit.

Inaccessible Gully   110m IV ★★★ c.1940

The ice pitch up into this hanging gully makes this one of the best climbs in the Lakes, but it needs a good freeze. It takes the obvious gully splitting the south-east aspect of the crag, starting 40m up *South Gully*.

1. 55m (5). From the base of a small ramp, go up right and over an ice

bulge. Pass another bulge to reach a narrow ledge (peg runner and possible belay). Above, 15m of steep ice on the left leads into the gully. A further small ice step gives access to a peg belay on the right.

2   45m (5). Some think this the crux! Steepening snow leads to a chockstone. Bridge up until it is possible to pull out right onto steep snow – this can be very thin. A second chockstone above is turned on the right to gain a belay in cave.

3   10m. Escape left onto easy snow to finish.

Westmorland's Route　　　　**160m IV ★★★ 1970/1971**

Based on the summer classic rock route but with turfy winter variations. The route is not often in good condition as it doesn't readily hold snow. It takes the ridge at the left-hand side of the crag just right of the entrance to *South Gully*. Start to the right of the rock ridge in a turfy bay.

1　40m (3). Follow steepening turf to a rock belay.

2　40m (4). Continue leftwards to two left-slanting vegetated grooves which lead to the ridge. Climb the lower of these over bulges to a corner. Bridge up until a pull over right gains a small platform.

3　40m (5). Above, step right at the top of a short steep section of rock to the base of a broad left-slanting slab in 10m. Ascend the slab for 10m to a short wall on the right which gives access to a narrow left-slanting ramp. Precariously shuffle along this to an exposed position at its end and a rounded spike (crux). Delicately step leftwards onto what ice is available and follow this to good turf if your luck holds. This zigzags left, then right, up to a large ledge.

4　40m (2). A rightwards traverse with some exposed moves leads to a turfy gully. Follow this over a few bulges to easier broken ground and the top.

Right-Hand Gully　　　　　　　　　　**80m IV**

The gully high up on the right side of the crag, right of the cave. Generally easy climbing with one 20m ice pitch.

Heirloom Crag　　　　　　　　(NY 377 107)
Alt. 700m　North-east facing

The crag is found about 500m to the south (left) of *Dove Crag*, and about 100m higher up the hillside. It is best approached as for *Dove Crag*, and then by contouring round leftwards and upwards. The crag has a terrace running along its base; the rocks below this are generally loose. The terrace may be reached from the right or, as on the first and only ascent, up a groove directly below *Heirloom*, the prominent groove in the centre of the crag. This lower tier contains much loose debris and should be treated with care.

Tony Daly and Greg Denwood on the much sought after classic,
Inaccessible Gully *(IV), Dove Crag (Photo: Martin Armitage)*

Heirloom   **56m V 2004**

The attractive central groove-line on this obscure crag is HVS in summer.

1   20m (2). At the base of the crag is a lower tier of broken ground. Scramble easily up this via an obvious groove, directly below the groove of *Heirloom*.

2   18m (6). Climb up the obvious central groove which gives good technical mixed climbing, stepping right onto a good ledge to belay.

3   18m (4). Continue to the top more easily, via a turfy corner with an awkward bulge near its top.

KIRKSTONE PASS

Red Screes East Cove   (NY 396 084)
                                           Alt. 600m East facing

Just to the north of the summit of Kirkstone Pass, on the west side of the road, is the eastern cove of *Red Screes*. This area is very accessible from the road and provides a good practice area that forms ice quite often. There is parking near the summit of the pass. The climbing is reached by a short walk north along the road, before heading up the hillside to the cove.

Raven Crag Left-Hand Gully   **100m II 1983**

This is the obvious gully high up on left side of *Red Screes East Cove* at (NY 395 083). An ice pillar is avoided on the right via a ramp.

Direct Variation   **IV**

Climb the ice pillar direct.

Raven Crag itself (towards the left-hand side of the cove) produces quite a good icefall (III).

The back of the cove contains several easy gullies (I).

Directly above the road, the right-hand side of the cove forms a buttress split by the distinctive **Kilnshaw Chimney** (NY 398 085). The difficulties extend for 80m but are no more than I/II. It can be reached in 15 minutes.

Just north of the pass, on the west side of the road and directly above a small car park, **Kirkstone Curtain**, a 20m pitch of steep ice (IV 4, 1983), occasionally forms on the tiny **Kirkstone Crag** (NY 401 086, where it says 'Kirk Stone' on the 1:25,000 SE map). Beware of loose rocks at the top.

Red Screes North Cove

(NY 398 089)
Alt. 600m North-east facing

On the north by north-east side of Red Screes, above and north of Kirkstone Pass, is a small cove with a crag just below a spur to the east of the summit.

The crag is split by a wide easy gully, a useful **descent**. Facing the crag to the right of the descent gully are four obvious icefalls about 70m long. The left-hand one, **Rob's Icefall** (1995), is the best of the routes, a slightly more pronounced gully with two possible starts at III on the left and II on the right. The other three falls are all about II, with steep starts, and give excellent introductory water ice only 30 minutes from the road. To the left of the descent the buttress is higher, with the obvious gully **Buttress Gully** (II, 70m, 2005) on the right side of the buttress, just 5m left of the descent gully. **Gully Arete** (II/III, 40m, 2006), the arete between this and the descent gully, has also been climbed: it has some pleasant steep moves in its lower section, though there is some loose rock. The centre of the buttress has been climbed from its lowest point, **Buttress Route** (II, 70m, 2006), though it is possible to climb this heathery buttress at any point and a detailed description is not necessary.

Several hundred metres lower down in the centre of the cove a short 15m section of steep water ice often forms (**Lower Icefall** III/IV, 1995) and can be combined with shorter icefalls in the main stream.

Eastern Crags

FAR EASTERN FELLS

The Far Eastern Fells lie to the east of the main mass of the hills around Patterdale and Ullswater, and are generally approached via Shap or Kendal depending on which valley one is aiming for.

MARDALE

Although isolated from the rest of the Lake District, easy access from the M6 though the village of Shap to the head of Haweswater (NY 268 108) makes this valley an attractive proposition, particularly for a short day. During periods of dry easterly winds, ice often forms quickly in Mardale, and the fells round about may collect snow while the rest of the Lake District is bare.

From the north end of Shap village, take the minor road to Bampton. In the centre of the village, turn left and follow the road along the east shore of Haweswater to a car park at the southern end of the reservoir.

The crags are described from south to north.

Harter Fell Crag
(NY 468 098)
Alt. 550m North-east facing

From the car park at the head of the valley, Harter Fell (NY 460 093) can be clearly seen to the south-west, and its gullies reached in about 30 minutes.

As viewed from car park, the fellside is split by a Y-shaped gully. *Arrowhead Buttress* rises up from the confluence of the two branches. *Little Harter Gully* can be seen about 100m to the left of the main *Y-Gully*. *Harter Fell Gully*, which is marked on the 1:25,000 map, can be found by following the Gatescarth Pass path south for about 1km then striking up the hillside to the obvious deep cleft. Approximately 300m to the left of *Harter Fell Gully*, ice forms down the easy-angled terraced face. Connecting the ice together with traverses along ledges gives approximately 150m of Grade II/III climbing. Further left along the face is a gully (I) which makes a useful **descent** when snow filled. The ridge to its left-hand side is pleasant (II) with a tricky 10m start.

Harter Fell Gully   200m II

This gully splits the north-east face of the mountain at an altitude of 500m (NY 467 098). Sadly it only gives about 30m of actual Grade II climbing.

Right-Hand Finish   40m III

A 40m pitch can be found on the upper right wall of the gully.

Little Harter Gully   90m II 2003

About 100m left of *Y Gully* is a parallel-sided gully, clearly seen when walking up to *Harter Fell Gully*. This gully ends on a turfy ridge overlooking *Y Gully*. Once on the ridge, either climb the ridge itself or descend into *Y Gully* and finish up that.

Y Gully, Left and Right Branches   200m II 1997/2003

The Y-shaped gully clearly seen from the car park. There are few difficulties in either branch other than finding them frozen.

Arrowhead Buttress   120m II 2003

Between the two branches of *Y Gully* is a turfy buttress shaped like an arrowhead when viewed from below. Start from the confluence of the Y and keep in the middle. A couple of small rock steps provide some interest but can be outflanked on either side.

BLEA WATER

Situated below the summits of High Street and Mardale Bell, the combe containing Blea Water (NY 448 107) is often referred to by climbers as **Mardale**.

Blea Water is due west of the car park at the head of the valley, and is reached by taking the path round the head of the lake before branching off to the left and ascending into the combe (1hr).

Eastern Crags

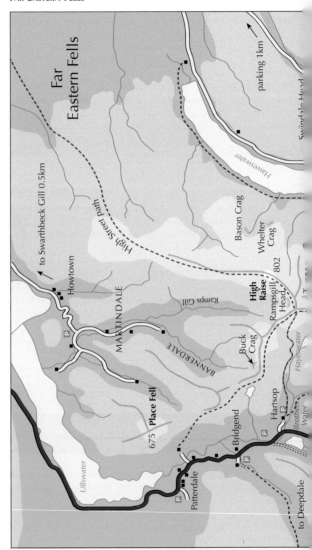

Far
Eastern Fells

to Swarthbeck Gill 0.5km

parking 1km

Swindale Head

Haweswater

High Street path

Bason Crag

Whelter Crag

Howtown

MARTINDALE

Ramps Gill

High Raise

Rampsgill Head

802

P

BANNERDALE

Buck Crag

Haweswater

Place Fell

675

Hartsop

Brothers Water

Bridgend

P

Ullswater

Patterdale

P

to Deepdale

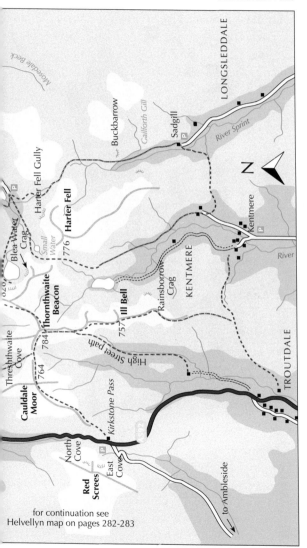

LONGSLEDDALE

Mosedale beck

Buckbarrow

Gallforth Gill

Sadgill

River Sprint

Harter Fell Gully

P

Harter Fell

Small Water

776

Blea Water Crag

N

Kentmere

P

Kentmere River

KENTMERE

Thornthwaite Beacon

Rainsborrow Crag

757 Ill Bell

Threshthwaite Cove

784

High Street Path

TROUTDALE

Cauldale Moor

764

Kirkstone Pass

North Cove

P

East Cove

Red Screes

to Ambleside

for continuation see
Helvellyn map on pages 282-283

Eastern Crags

353

Blea Water Crag

1	Blea Water Cleft	IV
2	Far Left Fall	II/III
3	Blea Water Icefall	III
4	Blea Water Gill	III
5	Blea Water Buttress	III
6	Birkett's Gully	II/III
7	Racecourse Gully	II
8	Racecourse Hill Recourse	IV
9	Grade III Icetalls	III

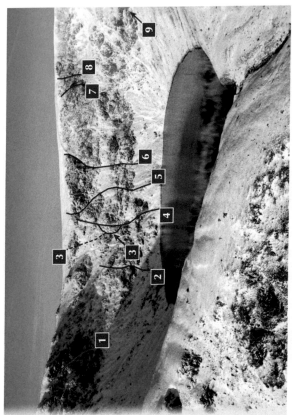

(Photo: Nick Wharton – Copyright FRCC)

Blea Water Crag

(NY 445 106)
Alt 570m East facing

This broken crag, situated at the back of the combe above Blea Water, contains some of the fastest-forming ice in the Lake District. High up is the very obvious cleft of *Birkett's Gully*.

Blea Water Crag is important for rare alpine plants (particularly *Birkett's Gully* and the buttresses to its right) – please climb here only in truly frozen conditions (see the chapter 'Winter Climbing and Nature Conservation').

There are a series of short icefalls at Grade III on the right-hand side of the combe which catch the early sun. Above, and about 300m right of *Birkett's Gully*, is a small hanging valley (NY 443 111) with a short gully on its left side (**Racecourse Gully** II, 2005).

Racecourse Hill Recourse
50m IV 2005

The steep grassy headwall at the back of the small hanging valley leads directly to the summit plateau.

Birkett's Gully
130m II/III ★★ 1973

This well-defined gully is seen as a deep cleft high on the crag, above and right of *Blea Water Gill*. Below the cleft is an icefall, a good long cascade with an initial pitch and then steps. The deeply cut upper cleft can give three short pitches of increasing difficulty, although it may be banked out.

The next routes start down and left of *Birkett's Gully* and not far above Blea Water.

Blea Water Buttress
129m III ★ 1991

In good winter conditions a narrow but substantial cascade of snow ice forms to the right of *Blea Water Gill*, roughly in the middle of the buttress down from, and left of, the well-defined cleft of the upper section of *Birkett's Gully*. It gives an enjoyable outing comprising 40–50m of snow ice followed by mixed ground.

Blea Water Gill
130m III ★★ 1985

An excellent route. Start at a narrow chimney just left of the lowest point of the crag and down and left of *Birkett's Gully*. The chimney leads to a

The pleasant approach to the Blea Water Icefalls, Mardale, Haweswater
(Photo: John Holden)

short but steep ice wall, then a shallow gully which is followed to easy ice and the top.

Blea Water Icefall   30m III ★★ 1985

Follow *Blea Water Gill* to the shallow gully and then move left to climb the fine icefall pitch. Sometimes more short falls above (II and then III/IV) can be linked to make a good outing; or traverse back right and finish up the *Gill*.

Far Left Fall   50m II/III

The most obvious fall left of *Blea Water Gill* peters out halfway up the crag, but a traverse can be made rightwards into the *Gill*.

There are many other short icefalls on the crag, but nothing warranting description.

Blea Water Cleft   130m IV (4) 1996

Well to the left of the other climbs on the crag, on a separate rocky section of the combe and 400m left (south-east) of *Birkett's Gully*, are gullies leading up from right to left and an obvious chimney/cleft. Climb to and then up the chimney, exiting after 15m with difficulty. Continue up easier ground following ice and snow gullies above to finish below a cairn on Mardale Bell.

RIGGINDALE

Eastern Crags

This is the next valley to the north of Upper Mardale.

Warning: Riggindale is part of the core territory of one of England's few resident golden eagles and you are requested not to climb there at all, at any time of year, as disturbance could be critical to the eagle's survival. These descriptions are given only to provide a historical record – please do not climb in Riggindale.

Twopenny Crag

(NY 441 123)
Alt. 650m South-east facing

Situated at the head of the valley, this crag contains two easy gullies left of the crag and to the right of the col, and a shorter deeper cleft through the crag. None is really worth the walk.

Hollyway
80m I 2002

The shallow open left-hand gully is a straightforward snow plod.

Penny Lane
80m I 2002

The right-hand gully has a slight kink at mid-height.

Threepenny Bit
80m III 2004

To the right of the start of *Penny Lane* is a narrow cleft cutting through the steep rock wall. It contains a couple of steps low down and a steeper final 10m. Finish up over the top tier or traverse off.

WHELTER BOTTOM

Warning: Whelter Bottom is part of the core territory of one of England's few resident golden eagles and you are requested not to climb there at all, at any time of year, as disturbance could be critical to the eagle's survival. These descriptions are given only to provide a historical record – please do not climb in Whelter Bottom.

This east-facing low-lying combe lies north-west of Riggindale, along the western shore of Haweswater. Follow the path around the head of the lake and keep going along the rough track near the lake shore. After rounding the ridge containing *Birks* and *Castle Crags* the combe is entered, and *Whelter Crag* and *Bason Crag* (higher and to its north) are visible. Strike up to them by via the left bank of Whelter Beck (1hr 30mins).

Whelter Crag
(NY 462 137)
Alt. 490m East-north-east facing

First Cut
20m III 2003

On the approach to the crag, a short two-tiered wall holds ice well. Several variations are possible.

White Russian
45m IV (4) 2003

The left corner of the crag is a wet stream in summer and ices well.

Bason Crag
(NY 463 143)
Alt. 570m South facing

In summer this black wet crag situated at the back of the combe is obvious. In winter conditions it can be transformed into two tiers 50m high. Rock slabs and turf comprise the bottom half and hold impressive swathes of steep ice. Routes are described from left to right.

Fibre Tube
50m IV (4) 2003

The compelling right-angled corner to the left of the main icefall.
1   25m. Climb up ledges, ice walls and turf to a stance 10m left of the corner.
2   10m. Traverse right on thin turf to reach the corner.
3   15m. Climb the steep thinly iced corner, with no protection.

Flypaper
45m IV 2003

Start 10m to the right of *Fibre Tube*.
1   25m. Climb up turf, ledges and icefalls to the base of the prominent central ice smear.
2   20m. Climb the ice smear: a peg can be placed after 5m.

That 'ard
45m III (4) 2003

In the centre of the crag is a tree. This route takes an ice gully, finishing just left of the tree and 10m right of *Flypaper*.
1   25m. Follow easy-angled ice to the base of steeper terrain which leads left to an obvious stepped corner.
2   20m. Climb an iced wall and corner to finish left of the tree.

Wimp's Route   50m III 2003

The next prominent steep icefall to the right.

1   25m. Climb ledges and intermittent ice to belay by a steep icefall.
2   25m. Climb a turfy wall on the right, then steep turf and ice, to finish right of the main icefall.

SWINDALE

Better known for its rock climbing, Swindale holds little of interest for the winter climber. However, following a prolonged cold spell with temperatures in the minus teens, **Hobgrumble Gill** (IV 4, 1996), which faces north at the head of the valley (NY 501 112), has been known to freeze. It then gives several pitches up a narrow slot with occasional rock protection.

LONGSLEDDALE

The valley is approached from the A6 at Garnet Bridge 7km north of Kendal. This can feel a rather long and, particularly in the kind of frozen icy conditions required to bring these low-lying climbs into condition, rather trying expedition. From the end of the metalled road, the climbing is found about 2km further up a drove road. *Galeforth Gill* and *Buckbarrow Crag* are clearly visible on the right while, opposite these, scree slopes lead to *Goat Crag* and the gully to its north.

Galeforth Gill Fall   45m III (3) 1982

From the end of the metalled road, *Galeforth Gill* is visible on the eastern slopes to the right, about 1km up the continuation track (NY 486 066). The gill forms a fall where it goes over a rock band. A series of short pitches (I/II) lead to the main pitch. After 20m this is split by a small bay that leads to steeper ice and a choice of finishes, the left-hand one being the steepest.

Buckbarrow Crag

(NY 483 073)
Alt. 380m South-west facing

About 2km up the track, at the head of the valley, *Buckbarrow Crag* is the broken crag on the right. The vegetated central buttress is known as *The Dandle*. The chimney-line high on the left side of the face defines the route of *Dandle Face Direct*, starting at a rib at the bottom left corner. The best and safest **descent** is to the right of the buttress.

Dandle Face Direct   100m IV 1996

The obvious groove and chimney at the left side of the face.
1 50m (3). Climb turf to the right of a rock rib to belay at the tree at the base of the short chimney.
2 30m (5). Ascend the chimney and grass ramp above to the edge of the buttress. Move diagonally right along a narrow ramp to a large ledge and belay overlooking the gully.
3 20m (3). Continue up and right along ledges to finish up a chimney-groove.

Dandle Buttress   50m III 1969

This route follows the left edge of the *Dandle Buttress* overlooking the *Cleft*.
1 30m. About 5m below a large chockstone is a corner on the right wall of *Cleft Gill*. Climb the corner to gain the edge of the buttress and follow this up a chimney.
2 20m. Keep to the left edge and continue to the top.

Cleft Gill   80m II 1982

The deep cleft bounding the left end of the buttress. The chockstone may prove tricky and is best taken on its left.

Goat Scar is clearly visible on the left of the track at (NY 477 070). The obvious **Goat Scar Gully** (100m, I, 1986) is the snow gully on its right side and provides a good route to the summit of Kentmere Pike.

KENTMERE

This valley, easily accessible from the south of the district, has a pleasant horseshoe walk round its ridges but not much for the winter climber.

Rainsborrow Crag (NY 444 067, alt. 500m) has a climb following obvious weaknesses and rakes to zigzag up the face of the cliff (II). North-east-facing **Rainsborrow Cove**, to the north of the crag, contains several obvious short gullies (I/II).

Dom Donnini on the easily accessible Blea Water Gill *(III), Mardale, Haweswater (Photo: Nick Wharton)*

OUTLYING AREAS

A few other routes, in Cumbria but not in the Lake District, are covered in this section.

THE HOWGILLS

These rounded fells to the west of the Lake District and the M6 lie between Tebay and Sedbergh. The scenic waterfall of *Cautley Spout* has long been a winter classic, while the summits provide secluded winter walking.

Cautley Spout   250m III ★★ 1967

Visible from the A683 Sedbergh to Kirkby Stephen road at (SD 683 975) this accessible east-facing fall on Calf Fell is low lying at 350m, so requires a sustained period of cold temperatures to form.

Where the track to Calf Fell ascends steeply, contour leftwards into the gorge and climb easily to the main pitch. This can be 30m high, and is usually best taken starting on the left and moving to the centre. Above are several shorter but easier pitches.

Brussels Spout Variation   IV ★ 1995

When the main fall is not fully formed, or is full of climbers, a variation following turf and ice on the left wall may be climbed before returning to the main watercourse. It is actually quite good, being steeper and more strenuous than the main fall, but purists will no doubt feel it rather misses the point!

Black Force   60m II

The impressive little gorge starting at about 400m on the north side of Fell Head at (SD 644 992). Follow the ice.

Jeffrey's Mount Escarpment

(NY 609 024)
Alt. 250m East facing

Just south of Junction 38 on the M6, the cutting at the side of the A685 forms a 100m-wide continuous horizontal icefall. This is visible from the motorway and gives numerous Grade III/IV pitches of 15–30m height (1995). Truly roadside cragging!

NORTHERN PENNINES

South of Kirkby Stephen can be found **Upper** and **Lower Ais Gill** (SD 775 965) and **Hell Gill** (SD 795 975), located to the west and east respectively of the B6259 Kirkby Stephen to Garsdale Head road in the Mallerstang valley. These unusual narrow roofless cave passages offer a

unique combination of Grade II ice and pot-holing: use of a wet suit is optional.

Hope Head Icefall   35m IV ★ 1986

At an altitude of about 400m, the scenic waterfall of High Ashgill near Alston (NY 758 404) can form a short free-standing pillar of ice in a severe winter.

High Cup Nick   (NY 745 262)
Alt. 370m West facing

High Cup Nick and its waterfall have been viewed by many happy Pennine Way walkers but few ever venture there to climb: be warned, the area is known for its poor rock quality. The watercourse cuts an

Simon Caldwell on the popular Blea Water Icefall *(III), Mardale, Haweswater (Photo: Carmen Elphick/Simon Caldwell Collection)*

impressive cleft through a horseshoe of crags on the hillside above the village of Dufton, just off the A66.

Two routes have been recorded on the south side of the Nick and so face north. Approach from the back of *High Cup*, from where the stream runs down into the scree slope. Traverse under the crags to the first obvious deep twin gullies, separated by a prow.

Unsullied Gully   35m I 2006

A mixed climb up the left-hand gully to fan-shaped exit slopes (and possible cornice). A perched block at about half-height needs treating with care.

Grotty Gully   35m III 2006

The right-hand gully is easily identified, as it is bounded on the right by a striking three-tiered rock pillar. The gully is a natural drainage line that ices up readily if conditions are cold enough. Climb the ice trickle (or patches of scree and a beck) to carefully pass a huge Damoclean wedged block right across the gully. Beyond a steeper section of ice there is a choice of finish, either straight up the main gully via another ice step (II, but may be unclimbed) or up a short icy groove on the left wall leading to the prow separating the two gullies, which is followed to the top.

USEFUL CONTACTS

The telephone numbers and websites listed below were correct at time of going to press.

Climbing
British Mountaineering Council.
Tel: 0870 0104878. Web: www.thebmc.co.uk
Fell & Rock Climbing Club. Web: www.frcc.co.uk
National Mountaineering Exhibition, Rheged, Penrith.
Tel: 01768 868000. Web: www.rheged.com

Lake District Weather
Fell Top Weather Forecast. Tel: 0870 0550575 Web: www.lake-district.gov.uk/weatherline/home/index.php

Lake District National Park Authority
Head Office. Tel: 01539 724555. Web: www.lake-district.gov.uk
Bird Restrictions.
Tel: 017687 79633 Web: http://www.frcc.co.uk/rock/birds.htm

Tourist Information

Cumbria Tourist Board	www.golakes.co.uk
Ambleside	015394 32582
Bowness	015394 42895
Broughton in Furness	01229 716115
Coniston	015394 41533
Glenridding	017684 82414
Egremont	01946 820693
Keswick	017687 72645
Kendal	01539 725758
Penrith	01768 867466
Camping Barns	01946 758198
	www.lakelandcampingbarns.co.uk

Other Information
Cumbria County Council Journey Planner. Tel: 01228 606705.
Web: www.cumbria.gov.uk

ACCOMMODATION:
CAMPSITES AND CAMPING BARNS

The campsites and camping barns in the Lake District listed below are only those known to be open during the winter months. Fuller details will be available from the Tourist Information Offices. This information is current in 2006 but will almost certainly alter, and it is probably best to make telephone contact before going to a particular site or barn.

Southern Lake District

Campsites	Grid Ref	Telephone	Website
Coniston, Coniston Hall	SD 304 962	015394 41223	
Coniston, Hoathwaite	SD 297 949	015394 41349	
Coniston, Park Coppice	SD 297 957	015394 41555	www.caravanclub.co.uk
Hawkshead, Croft	SD 353 982	015394 36374	www.hawkshead-croft.co.uk
Skelwith, Tarn Foot	NY 343 038	015394 32596	
Langdale, National Trust	NY 287 059	015394 37668	www.ntlakescampsites.org.uk
Windermere, Troutbeck, Limefitt Park	NY 414 032	015394 32300	www.southlakeland-caravans.co.uk

Camping Barns

	Grid Ref	Telephone	Website
Broughton in Furness, Fell End Farm	SD 239 881	01946 758198	www.lakelandcampingbarns.co.uk
Langdale, Sticklebarn	NY 295 064	015394 37356	
Grasmere, Broadrayne Farm	NY 337 094	015394 35055	
Grasmere, The Hollens	NY 344 073	015394 63831	www.ntlakescampsites.org.uk

Western Lake District

Campsites

	Grid Ref	Telephone	Website
Buttermere, Sykes Farm	NY 173 171	017687 70222	
Buttermere, Dalegarth	NY 186 159	017687 70233	
Lorton, Wheatsheaf Inn	NY 155 259	01900 85199	
Lorton, Whinfell Hall	NY 150 254	01900 85260	
St Bees, Seacote Park	NX 962 120	01946 822777	www.seacote.co.uk
Holmrook, Seven Acres	NY 073 018	01946 822227	
Wasdale, Santon Bridge	NY 111 017	019467 26286	
Nether Wasdale, Church Stile	NY 126 042	019467 26252	www.churchstile.com
Wasdale Head	NY 185 088	019467 26384	
Wasdale Head – National Trust	NY 185 073	019467 26220	www.ntlakescampsites.org.uk
Eskdale, Hollins Farm	NY 178 010	019467 23253	

Camping Barns

	Grid Ref	Telephone	Website
Buttermere, Cragg	NY 174 172	01946 758198	www.lakelandcampingbarns.co.uk
Loweswater, Waterend Farm, Swallow Barn	NY 116 226	01946 758198	www.holmewoodbothy.org.uk
Loweswater, Holme Wood Bothy	NY 123 216	01946 816940	www.lakelandcampingbarns.co.uk
St Bees, Tarn Flatts Hall Farm	NX 947 146	01946 692162	www.lakelandcampingbarns.co.uk
Ennerdale, High Gillerthwaite	NY 142 141	01946 758198	www.lakelandcampingbarns.co.uk
Gosforth, Mill House Barn	NY 100 044	01946 758198	www.lakelandcampingbarns.co.uk
Wasdale, Murt Barn	NY 131 040	01946 758198	www.lakelandcampingbarns.co.uk

Northern Lake District
Campsites

	Grid Ref	Telephone	Website
Braithwaite, Scotgate	NY 235 236	017687 78343	www.scotgateholidaypark.co.uk
Keswick, Castlerigg Hall	NY 280 225	017687 74499	www.castlerigg.co.uk
Keswick, Castlerigg	NY 283 223	017687 72479	www.castleriggfarm.co.uk
Keswick, Derwentwater	NY 260 232	017687 72392	www.campingandcaravaningclub.co.uk
Borrowdale, Stonethwaite, Langstrath	NY 268 133	017687 77234	
Borrowdale, Stonethwaite, Chapel Farm	NY 257 140	017687 77602	
Borrowdale, Seathwaite Farm	NY 232 122	017687 77394	

Camping Barns

	Grid Ref	Telephone	Website
Caldbeck, Hudscales	NY 332 375	017687 72645	www.lakelandcampingbarns.co.uk
St Johns in the Vale, Low Bridge End	NY 316 205	01946 758198	www.campingbarn.com

	Grid Ref	Telephone	Website
Thirlmere, Causeway Foot	NY 294 218	017687 72290	
Newlands, Catbells Barn	NY 243 208	01946 758198	www.lakelandcampingbarns.co.uk
Rosthwaite, Dinah Hoggas Barn	NY 259 151	01946 758198	www.lakelandcampingbarns.co.uk

Eastern Lake District

Campsites

	Grid Ref	Telephone	Website
Hartsop, Sykeside	NY 401 120	017684 82239	www.sykeside.co.uk
Watermillock, Ullswater	NY 435 229	017684 86666	www.uccmp.co.uk
Pooley Bridge, Waterside	NY 463 231	017684 86332	www.watersidefarm-campsite.co.uk
Pooley Bridge, Roe Head	NY 475 242	017684 86363	
Penrith, Lowther	NY 526 263	01768 863631	
Penruddock, Beckes	NY 417 277	017684 83224	
Berrier, Hopkinson Park	NY 405 288	017684 83456	

Bunkhouses

	Grid Ref	Telephone	Website
Glenridding, Gillside	NY 382 168	017684 82346	www.gillsidecaravanandcampingsite.co.uk
Hartsop, Sykeside	NY 401 120	017684 82239	www.sykeside.co.uk

Camping Barns

	Grid Ref	Telephone	Website
Greenside, Swirral Barn	NY 364 174	01946 758198	www.lakelandcampingbarns.co.uk

CLIMBING WALLS

There is a good range of climbing walls available to those living in or visiting the Lake District, of which the best, or most readily accessible, are described here for use on those occasional rainy days and dank evenings.

Ambleside: St Martin's College (formerly Charlotte Mason's College) Low-cost revamped wall at the college, with good bouldering but no leading. Open 13:30 to 21:30 Monday to Friday; 12:00 to 17:00 on Saturdays, but only during the term time. It may be open for reduced hours in the holidays. Not open on Sundays. Tickets available at the wall.
Access check – tel: 015394 30300, www.ucsm.ac.uk

Barrow: Park Leisure Centre
Good access, low cost but limited climbing – rather compact with a tall narrow wall and a bouldering area. Excellent other facilities. Open all day until 21:45 weekdays; 10:00 to 18:00 weekends.
Access check – tel: 01229 871146, www.barrowbc.gov.uk

Carlisle: The Sands Centre
Reasonable, low-cost climbing facility in a large sports centre. Good bouldering and leading. Very good access and excellent general facilities. Open 09:30 to 22:30 seven days a week.
Access check – tel: 01228 625222, www.thesandscentre.co.uk

Carlisle: St Aidan's County High School
Good freeform featured leading wall open to the public. Bouldering may be possible but you might need your own mat. Open 17:00 to 21:00 Monday to Friday (last admission 20:00); 10:00 to 17:00 Saturday and Sunday (last admission 16:00).
Access check – tel: 01228 607469, www.st-aidans.cumbria.sch.uk

Cockermouth: Sports Centre
Varied bouldering with natural stonework and Bendcrete. Low cost and good access. Other sports facilities available. Open 08:00 to 22:00

Monday to Thursday; 08:00 to 21:30 Friday; 09:00 to 17:00 weekends. Access check – tel: 01900 823596, www.allerdale.gov.uk

Egremont: Wyndham Sports Centre

A good facility located in the centre of Egremont on the west coast, only half an hour from Wasdale Head. There are practice areas, bouldering, leading walls and a huge roof. Unfortunately no longer open to the public except on a club booking basis.
Access check – tel: 01946 820356

Ingleton: Inglesport Climbing Barn

Best of the small walls. In Yorkshire, but only just. Very good use of space with leading and bouldering. Regular innovations. Relaxed friendly atmosphere. Cafe and shop nearby. Open 09:00 to 22:00 Monday to Thursday; 09:00 to 17:30 Friday; 08:30 to 18:00 weekends.
Access check – tel: 015242 41146, www.inglesport.co.uk/wall.html

Kendal: The Lakeland Climbing Centre

A magnificent indoor climbing facility with excellent bouldering and leading. Includes a very impressive 18m main wall (with fixed gear) and a huge roof. Located on the Lake District Business Park, across the A6 from Morrison's supermarket. Changing and shower facilities. Open Winter (September to April): 16:00 to 22:00 Monday; 10:00 to 22:00 Tuesday to Friday; 10:00 to 19:00 weekends and Bank Holidays. Summer (May to August): 10:00 to 22:00 Tuesday to Friday; 10:00 to 17:00 weekends and Bank Holidays.
Access check – tel: 01539 721766, www.kendalwall.co.uk

Keswick: Keswick Climbing Wall and Activity Centre

Located on Southey Hill Industrial Estate, at the western end of the town. There is quite extensive bouldering, with some leading and top-roping walls. Friendly atmosphere. Open 10:00 to 21:00 every day, with an extra hour (ie to 22:00) Tuesday to Thursday from October to March.
Access check – tel: 017687 72000, www.keswickclimbingwall.co.uk

Penrith: Penrith Leisure Centre – Eden Climbing Wall

An excellent wall adjoining the town's swimming pool. Good bouldering and excellent leading walls. Cheap entry. Open 10:00 to 21:30 weekdays; 10:00 to 21:00 weekends.
Access check – tel: 01768 863450, www.leisure-centre.com

Other Info

LAKE DISTRICT WINTER CLIMBS – FIRST ASCENTS

1870 Jan 10 **South Gully, Bowfell** J Stogdon, GH Wollaston, AR Stogdon

The Lake District's first recorded winter route. The group set off from Elterwater on a clear morning with a sharp frost to climb Bowfell by 'the great couloir' and then continue on to Wasdale Head. John Stogdon takes up the story:

> 'The slope got steeper and steeper, steps were always necessary, and at last having come up 350 feet or more, we found ourselves within a few feet of the top on a slope of 63°, with an overhanging cornice of ice above us, and snow nearly up to our waists for a few feet below the top, which I could just reach with my axe. The next few minutes must have been pleasant to my friends below me, as the cornice was gradually tumbling upon their ears in a shower of icy fragments. Then I pulled myself up by my hands on to the level snow field above, and a short run up easy slopes soon bought us to the top.'

John Stogdon, 'The English Lakes in Winter',
Alpine Journal (1870)

1873 Mar **Sharp Edge, Blencathra** G Seatree and party

> 'In March 1873 a party of us ascended when the first part of the steep slope from the edge to the summit was snow and ice covered. In those days there were no ice axes or ropes used, and in fact we came very close to a serious accident by reason of the conditions.'

George Seatree, 'Reminiscences of Early Lakeland
Mountaineering', *FRCC Journal* (1910)

1880 Apr 4 **Cust's Gully, Great End** Cust and party

Arthur Cust and over twenty members of the Alpine Club (who said crowds on Great End were anything new?). Almost certainly ascended prior to this by Cust.

> 'On Sunday the party...leaving the carriages at the farmhouse

above Seatoller, climbed Scafell Pike by a very interesting chimney or couloir, which, being filled with snow and ice, gave unexpected satisfaction. There is a very remarkable natural arch in the couloir, which Mr Cust claims to have been the first to discover, and he was therefore entrusted with the guidance of the party.'

DW Freshfield, 'Alpine Meeting at the Lakes',
Alpine Journal (1882)

AL Mumm and JE King glissaded down Cust's Gully in 1882.

1885 Mar 1 Unknown gullies in the Pillar Rock Area WC Slingsby, JA Slingsby, W Ecroyd, G Hastings, C Hastings
'Found the snow in most splendid order, were five hours climbing gullies and couloirs around the Pillar Rock.'

Visitors' Book of the Tysons of Row Farm,
Wasdale Head, 1876–1886

A similar entry appears the following year from G Hastings, J Mason and WC Slingsby:
'Had a capital day on the Pillar Fell amongst the snow couloirs, though in thick mist.'

Wasdale Hotel Visitors' Book, 1885–1891

1886 Mar 29 Deep Ghyll, Scafell WC Singsby, G Hastings
It had been descended in deep snow by AL Mumm and JE King, April 1882.

It was also climbed the following year by John Wilson Robinson who implies in his account (which is wrongly dated as 1885 in his article, but is correct in his diary) that he was already familiar with the climb and surprised to find the pitches banked out.

'The winter [of 1887] was remarkable to us in Cumberland by reason of its unusual snowfall… Round a cheerful fire we found three men: a professor, an Alpine man of Arolla fame, and a Cambridge undergrad. They were full of the awful state of the fells; Brown Tongue, they said, was as hard as ice, it had taken them three days to cut their way up Scawfell. The first day to the top of Brown Tongue, the second to the top of the first limb of Lord's Rake, and in the third to the mountain top, via Great Ghyll… "So now if you wish to go the way is open." We looked, I fear, incredulous, and were solemnly assured with "Alright, you'll see!"

Topping out on Deep Ghyll *(I/II), Scafell, c.1900. Note the lady in long dress and hat!*

That night came nine inches more snow, and instead of the promised steps we had a deep snow plodge. Hard work? I should think so! We sank to our waists in the soft fluff in Lord's Rake. Deep Ghyll was full from end to end. The view from the top of the first limb of the Rake was grand in the extreme. The way to Great Ghyll was cut off by huge piles of loose snow, resting at a steep angle against the cliff, and on the least movement by us off it went in avalanches over the edge and down into the rocks far below – and my friend had left the rope, "No use for it," he said. "No!" I said, "I am not going on. If we had brought the rope we might have had a chance but not now, we would soon be down there in an avalanche." "We will try Deep Ghyll then," he said. "Funny, isn't it? Far end of Lord's Rake dangerous, Deep Ghyll safe by comparison, but so it is, the circumstances are unusual." Steadily we plodded up and up over the first pitch, quite hidden by the snow; then in like manner over the second, no sign of it. Here the snow became suddenly hard; and our axes came into play, for as each step was passed the snow got harder, and near the top was quite formidable; great care was needed, for a slip here meant that we would not reach Lord's Rake but probably be carried into the rocks to the right of it. A return was made by a sitting glissade down into the bottom on the Eskdale side and away into the scree that comes from Mickledore on the south.'

John Wilson Robinson, 'A Novice in the Snow',
FRCC Journal (1907)

1886 Mar 29 Branch Gully, Great End H Hastings, J Mason, WC Slingsby
First recorded winter ascent, but may have been climbed earlier.
'The same party made a variation on Mr Cust's Gully on Great End. They made first for the great or central gullies up which one of this party and a friend had climbed on Easter Monday 1884, but as during the previous night about four inches of snow had fallen on the old hard snow, it was deemed to be unwise to attempt such a steep and awkward gill so they turned to the smaller gully. A grand glissade could have been made from the mouth of the gill down almost to the footpath below. The party cut their way with axes steadily forward and instead of going up through the natural arch of rock, which looked most weird through the mist, they turned up the right hand branch, and after one short awkward climb over a fallen block of rock, and a fairly steep snow slope they found themselves on the top in a furious snow storm. A few good glissades and a scramble down the side of Grain's Gill ended a most enjoyable morning's adventure.'

WC Slingsby, Wasdale Hotel Visitors' Book, 1885–1891

1887 Jan 4 Great Doup Gully, Pillar JW Robinson, TG Creak
First recorded winter ascent, but probably climbed earlier (see Slingsby on Pillar, March 1885 above).
'Mountains covered with ice and snow. Ascent of Pillar via Great Doupe, very tough near the top owing to frozen snow and the cornice.'

Wasdale Hotel Visitors' Book, 1885–1891

'We now decided to try our luck up the Great Doupe, for the moon was beginning to show and the light increasing. Formidable indeed, as we looked up, was the steep snow slope at the head of the hollow, surmounted by an immense cornice. "Shall we want the rope?" I asked. "Oh no, it's in the sack and it won't help us!" I did not feel at all sure about this, as, unable for the moment to get any further, I crouched under the great protruding lip of the cornice, and looked into the black and uncertain depth below. "Can we get out," I said. "We must, so here goes, hold my feet on this big step whilst I try to cut down the overhanging edge." Ten minutes more, a struggle, a gasp, and breathless we emerged into the moonlight of the Pillar – 6.30 p.m. We scurried away to Wasdale, and never were climbers more thankful for their suppers.'

JW Robinson, 'A Novice in Snow', *FRCC Journal* (1907)

1887 Feb 5th **Central Gully, Great End (via the Left Branch)** G Hastings and party (including some or all of the following C Hastings, J Mason, JA Slingsby, CH Slingsby, AE Preston, HA Beeching)

First recorded winter ascent, but may have been climbed earlier (an entry in the Visitors' Book in 1886 March 29th, for example, mentions that Central Gully had been climbed at Easter 1884 by Slingsby or Hastings – however, without a record of the conditions we have no way of knowing if this was a winter ascent).

'Climbed up Great End by the Central Chimney which starts at the head of the long scree close to Grains Gill. The snow came well down onto the scree, and was in good order; we took the left-hand branch and had to take to the rocks to overcome the "block". We then crossed over the Pikes to Mickledore, the rocks of which were very wet. The early part of day was very wet, snowed hard while we were in the "Central Chimney" and did not cease until we got on to Scafell, when it cleared up, and we had a glorious view of the mists rolling up out of the valleys, and disappearing leaving all the hills quite distinct.'

Wasdale Hotel Visitors' Book, 1885–1891

Second recorded winter ascent, probably by the **Right Branch**, JW Robinson, E Carr, G Hastings, E Peile, WA Wilson, 1890 Dec 26th or 27th

'The central gully in Great End took about 2 hours with the help of the steps cut by Mr Robinson's party a day or two before in the magnificent upper ice-fall. Without their assistance it would perhaps have been barely possible within the limits of a winter day.'

RC Gilson, 28th Dec 1890,
Wasdale Hotel Climbing Book, 1890–1919

The final pitch of Central Gully *(II), Great End, prior to 1897
(Copyright: The Abraham Family)*

Chimney Finish, R Bennett, R Lavender, 1972. The **Arete Direct** was added by S Ashworth and P Rowlands, 20th Jan 2001, and **Grande Finale** by S Ashworth and J Kelly, 20th Feb 2006. **Left Branch Middle Way** was the work of B Davison and S Ashworth, 18th March 2006. It was their fourth new route of the day and the third valley visited.

1887 Mar 7 **Skew Gill, Great End** G Hastings and party (including some or all of the following ELW Haskett Smith, C Hopkinson, WC Slingsby) First recorded winter ascent, but may have been climbed earlier.

'Ascended by Skew Gill, a very interesting and neat cut to the north face of Great End. We climbed, duly roped together the western gully on the north face by the snow, and turned up the left of the two forks (Cust's Gully) and after many hundred steps had been cut in the hard snow by our axes, we went through the well known arch of rock and, after one hour forty minutes step cutting we stood in the sunshine on the top of Great End. After a short walk along the top we looked down the fine Central Gully, and Hastings pointed out to us the steps he had cut on the ascent of this gully on February 5th. After a capital glissade, we made our way over the moors to Stickle Tarn to attempt the ascent of Pavey Ark by the Central Gully.'

Wasdale Hotel Visitors' Book, 1885–1891

'To go by Grainy Gill and this one [Skew Gill], and so up Cust's Gully, has for many years been the regulation expedition for the first day of a winter sojourn at Wastdale Head.'

WP Haskett Smith, *Climbing in the British Isles* (Longmans, 1894)

The **Direct Finish** was added by M Green and J Bradley in 1987, and the **Left-hand Branch** by P Kennet and party in February 1996, while the **Grade III Variation** appeared in January 1997.

1890 Jan 3 **South-East Gully, Great End** RC Gilson and party
First recorded winter ascent.
'At the point where the gully forks, less than half way up, we chose the steeper left-hand branch, but finding it very full of hard ice took to the arête between the two branches and crossing this with some trouble followed up the right-hand side to the point where the branches reunite, hence over easy rocks to the top. Time 3 hours 20 mins: every ledge being choked with ice or glazed snow.'

Wasdale Hotel Climbing Book, 1890–1919

The entry in the climbing book kept at the Wastwater Hotel (today the Wasdale Head Inn) is signed 'A.G.', which is confusing as it was certainly written by Cary Gilson, the man who donated the climbing book to the hotel.

1890 Dec 29 **Eagle's Nest Gully, The Napes** RC Gilson and party
'Ascended the gully to the left (as you face the mountain) of the gully coming down to the left of the Needle. This gully does not seem to have been described before and I have no idea how it goes in summer. On this occasion it presented no particular difficulty except, just above a large boulder about one third of the way up, where a smooth slab was thinly glazed. Near the top we passed to the left onto the arete, and then rushed down Hell Gate screes to escape the blizzard on the ridge.'
Wasdale Hotel Climbing Book, 1890–1919)

1890 Dec 30 **Shamrock Gully, Pillar** JW Robinson, C Hopkinson, G Hastings, RC Ritson and party
'"This has only once been ascended previous to the ascent recorded below and on the first occasion 5 feet of snow gave a good start in surmounting the vertical wall on the right side of the stone... Yesterday Geoffrey Hastings followed by Charles Hopkinson and John W. Robinson succeeded in passing successfully up the gully and taking the right-hand side of the boulder completed the first ascent without the aid of a snowdrift. They afterwards went onto the Pillar Rock which was unusually tedious owing to the iced state of the rocks. JW Robinson." Mr Robinson's note above shows what may be done in the depth of even the severest winter. It is hard to imagine rocks in worse condition for climbing than during the past ten days, though the enormous accumulations of ice have probably rendered some waterfalls possible which are very rarely so.'
RC Gilson, Wasdale Hotel Climbing Book, 1890–1919

Previously climbed in semi-winter conditions, 5th March 1887, by ELW Haskett Smith and G Hastings with the aid of snowdrift (Wasdale Hotel Visitors' Book, 1885–1891).

1890 Dec 30 **Slab and Notch Climb, Pillar** C Hopkinson, JW Robinson, G Hastings

Rounding the Curtain on the so-called Easy Way *Variation to Slab and* Notch Climb *(III), Pillar Rock ca 1900 (Copyright: The Abraham Family)*

'Ice and snow...up over Notch and down Ledge and Chimney Route (this is the **Easy Way** – a variation on Slab and Notch). The Slab one mass of ice, Hopkinson led during the ascent and I was last man in coming down, time 1hr 40mins in ascent, 20mins coming down. Took one hour to cross the Slab.'

JW Robinson's Climbing Diary, FRCC Archive

However an earlier ascent on Feb 6th 1887, by G Hastings and party, may also have been in winter conditions.

'Bright sunny day with hard frost. Ascended Pillar Fell by gully direct from Mosedale. Climbed Pillar Rock by easy way and then descended down the gully to the west side and ascended the rock again, descending again by the easy way. The slab on the rock was coated with ice which had to be cut away.'

Wasdale Hotel Visitors' Book, 1885–1891

1890/1 New Year **Grainy Gill, Lingmell** A Marshall and party
In the Wasdale Hotel Climbing Book 1890–1919 is a somewhat confusing account which clearly describes the narrow ridge between the two branches of the gill, and an ascent of the right branch of Grainy Gill, but has wrongly been ascribed as Greta Gill Right Branch.

'What is marked Grainy Gill in the Ordnance Map (situated between Skew Gill and Greta Gill, the left hand branch of Piers Gill) is, in reality two water courses, distinct though separated in parts by a very narrow ridge. The right hand branch (facing the mountain) which it has been proposed to call Corney Gill, contains two very fine falls, ascended so far as is known for the first time by Prof. Marshall's party this winter.'

Wasdale Hotel Climbing Book, 1890–1919

The exact date of Professor Marshall's ascent is unknown but it was, almost certainly, the first ascent of the gill in winter conditions and quite possibly the first recorded ascent of a pure water-ice climb anywhere in the world.

1891 Easter **Needle Ridge, The Napes** GA Solly, WC Slingsby, M Schintz
In descent.

'It was not till Easter, 1891, that I had a chance of attempting any of the serious courses. I was staying at Seatoller with W.C. Slingsby and M. Schintz, and on our way down from Great Gable, we descended the Needle Ridge. It had then, I think, been only once ascended, and this was the first descent under winter condidtions… Slingsby led and I came last.'

GA Solly, 'Some Early Recollections', *FRCC Journal* (1909)

1891 Apr 1 **Central Gully, Gable Crag** A Marshall, WI Beaumont, HB Dixon.

'Up Central Gully on N. side of Gable. Snow in good order.'

Wasdale Hotel Climbing Book, 1890–1919

The **Smart Exit** was added in 1937 by S Cross, A Nelson, AT Hargreaves, R Hargreaves and A Cooper as a direct finish. The route involved delicate cutting up frozen moss on the crux wall and tenuous moves to reach the top. Albert Hargreaves was due to address the Pinnacle Club's annual dinner in the Sun Hotel at Coniston that evening, and Cross remembers him practising his speech all the way up the climb – a fact which says much for the nonchalance and confidence with which they were approaching technically difficult and serious first ascents (Interviews with Sid and Jammy Cross (nee Nelson), 1996). L Kendall and R McHaffie (alt) added the **Contrived Eliminate**, 10th Dec 1960 and the **Less than Smart Exit** was soloed by B Davison, 31st March 1996.

1891 Apr 3 **Old Professors' Chimney, Scafell** AM Marshall, HB Dixon, WI Beaumont, AG (HA Gwynne?)
First recorded winter ascent, but may have been climbed earlier.
> 'After heavy snow storm of day before Deep Ghyll was nearly full of soft snow. Had to cut a channel 4 – 5 foot deep through the powdery snow. First obstacle quite easy. Second obstacle just impossible to do straight up. Had to return and go up chimney to left. This was very bad owing to the rocks being iced under loose snow. Up Professors Chimney which was comparatively easy. Took 7 hours from Hotel to top of Scawfell.'
> > Wasdale Hotel Climbing Book, 1890–1919

1891 Apr 19 **Mickledore Chimney, Scafell** OG Jones, WE Sumpner, CG Munro
> 'This proved to be very difficult the snow being 6 or 7 feet deep and very rotten. At the obstacle we were brought to a stop for the rocks on the left were ice covered and no handholds seemed available. O.G.J. managed to climb up after a struggle and returned by Broadstand, the others descended the chimney again.'
> > Wasdale Hotel Climbing Book, 1890–1919

There is also a detailed account of this ascent in OG Jones's *Rock Climbing in the English Lake District* (Longmans, 1897). AL Mumm descended the gully in snowy conditions dropping the last few feet into snow, Easter 1881 (*FRCC Journal*, 1922).
> **Variation Icefall Start** and **Finish** added by JJS Allison and L Kendall, 14th Dec 1960.

1891 Apr 21 **New Professors' Chimney, Scafell** OG Jones, WE
Sumpner, CG Monro

'Instead of continuing straight up Deep Ghyll, they turned up the
gully to the left, from which springs Professors Chimney. (This
gully apparently is as yet nameless). There appeared to be too
much snow on the rocks in the Professors Chimney so they
continued their ascent up the nameless gully and reached the top
after cutting through a fine ice cornice.'

Wasdale Hotel Climbing Book, 1890–1919

1891 Dec 25 **Steep Ghyll, Scafell** JN Collie, WLW Brodie, EW Marshall
There are only brief references to this remarkable and futuristic climb,
the first grade V recorded anywhere in the UK, and probably the world.
The history of the ascent remained hidden for many years due to Collie's
reticence in recording it, probably because of its 'unjustifiable' severity.

'My recollection of the latter [Steep Ghyll] in snow and ice, is that
it is one of the most dangerous climbs I have ever made.'

FRCC Journal (1926)

'Another party of three strangers – Dr Norman Collie, Messrs.
Wilfred L.W. Brodie, and E.W. Marshall had arrived, and on
Christmas Day made a desperate climb of Steep Ghyll under
frozen conditions, while Robinson's party climbed on Great End.'

FW Jackson, 'Some Early Climbing at Wasdale and
an Episode', *Rucksack Club Journal* (1925)

The **Direct Start** was added by JJS Allison and L Kendall in January
1963.

1891 Dec 25 **South-East Buttress, Great End** JW Robinson, G Hastings
'Up S. Gully then out onto right hand face and straight up, built
cairn at top with Hastings.'

JW Robinson's Climbing Diary, FRCC Archive

1892 Dec 27 **B (Great) Gully, Wastwater Screes** G Hastings, JW
Robinson, JN Collie
The gullies of the Wasdale Screes were labelled from left to right by
Haskett Smith in 1895, A, B and C; B Gully also being known as Great
Gully. In the original 1979 winter guide to the Lakes only Great and C
Gullies were recorded, but by the second edition of the guide in 1986,

two minor gullies towards the right-hand (west) end of the crag had been climbed and were mistakenly named A and B. In this set-up Great Gully was assumed to be D, and gullies climbed to its left (east) were then labelled E and F (E actually already being A Gully, and F being another gully further left which was actually Seven Pitch Gully, although this may have been wrongly assigned in the 1924 FRCC guide)! Hopefully the situation is now resolved.

> 'It was on a perfect winters morning, many years ago now, that we started for the great gully in the screes. Not a breath of air stirred; hoar frost covered the ground: the trees were a mass of silver, glittering in the morning sun… Perpendicular walls rose on both sides for several hundred feet; above us stretched cascade after cascade of solid ice, always at a very steep angle and sometimes perpendicular. Up these we cut our way with our axes, sometimes being helped by making steps close to the walls and using any small inequalities on the rock face to steady us in our steps.'
>
> JN Collie, *Climbing on the Himalaya and other Mountain Ranges* (David Douglas, 1902)

'Great help was afforded by the waterfall being almost completely ice and the turf also being frozen hard' (Wasdale Hotel Climbing Book, 1890–1919). It is interesting to note that this ascent was made the day after the first ascent of Moss Ghyll, during which no mention is made of ice or winter conditions. This must have been a sustained period of high pressure with hard frosts overnight and little or no snow.

The **Right-Hand Branch** was climbed in 1978 by J Loxham and R Wilson, and also around this time, or possibly earlier, by W Pattison and A Dunn. **Chimney Finish** added by W Pattison and J Arthy, 1984/5.

1892/3 Christmas Vacation **Oblique Chimney, Gable Crag** OG Jones, L Amery and party
A remarkable lead for its day and, in pure technical terms, one of the two most difficult winter climbs undertaken prior to the Great War. Climbed in conditions of heavy snow with Great Gable 'a picture of alpine solitude' and Styhead Tarn frozen over.

> 'There was much ice and fresh snow plastering the rocks…though the gully overhangs too much to prevent any drift snow to settle in it, the smooth walls of the gully were black and shiny with

ice… I had started with my back resting against the left wall, bracing my feet as firmly as the ice would permit…'

> OG Jones, *Rock Climbing in the English Lake District* (Longmans, 1897)

1893 Jan 9 **Moss Ghyll, Scafell** O Jones

An amazing tour de force by Jones, arguably his finest hour. Climbed solo despite the encumbrance of a clinometer and broken ribs sustained by a fall from the Collie Step (luckily he was saved from worse thanks to the backrope he had fixed through a chockstone). OG Jones, *Rock Climbing in the English Lake District* (Longmans, 1897).

The Direct Finish up **Collier's Chimney** was climbed by T Furness and J Fotheringham on 18th Feb 1984, but had probably been done earlier – the *FRCC Journal* (1917) notes that in 1917 GS Bower and Masson made an ascent of the Chimney. 'This was iced but was not rendered appreciably more difficult thereby, since we took the outside route up to the Sentry Box.' The **Mechanical Orange** variation finish was added by B Davison and RAL Jones on 14th Feb 1987, 'Named after a youth club in Puno, Peru. So poorly protected that the second unclipped from the belay and stood on the great chockstone ready to jump in order to prevent a groundfall should the leader come off!'

1894 **Striding Edge, Helvellyn** WP Haskett-Smith

Climbed around this time, and probably before. This was a regular venue during the 1860s and 1870s for the Alpine Club who used it for alpine practice.

1896 Dec 25 **Napes Needle, The Napes** OG Jones and party

The Needle was covered in snow and the fells were very wintery. A photograph of the ascent, taken by the Abraham brothers, was published in the second edition of Jones's *Rock Climbing in the English Lake District* (Abraham, 1900); the date of the ascent and a note identifying Jones as one of the climbers in the picture appeared a few years later in a magazine article written by one of the Abrahams. It is doubtful if the Needle is ever anything more than a snow-covered rock climb, but ascents have been made when full winter conditions embraced the fells; Jones's may have been the first. George Sansom led three others up the Needle on 3rd Jan 1911, finding it 'fairly stiff with snow on it', and the meet report in the *FRCC Journal for Easter 1913* records ascents of the Needle and

Needle Ridge when 'the fells were covered in snow and ice [and] nearly all rock work impossible'.

Prior to 1899 **Needle Gully, The Napes** OG Jones and party
The ascent was photographed by the Abrahams. Jones was killed in the Alps in 1899, so it must have been prior to this.

1899 Jan **The Curtain and the Arete, Pillar** OG Jones, G Abraham
'Though ice and snow masked the rocks insidiously, there seemed a chance of success'.

> G Abraham, *Mountain Adventures at Home and Abroad* (Methuen, 1910)

1899 Apr 8 **North Climb, Scafell** G Barton, C Barton, Cowley, Davey
'The wind had gone due N. & with the snow as well things were moderately alpine...this was our first encounter with snow and ice... North Climb proved moderately hard under the present conditions.'

> Barton Climbing Book, FRCC Archive

1899 Apr 11 **Slingsby's Chimney Route, Scafell** G Barton, C Barton, Cowley, Davey
Along with Jones' Oblique Chimney, this was technically the hardest winter route achieved prior to the Great War. They were three and a half hours on the climb, which they describe as an 'encounter with snow and ice on difficult rocks with an "entirely incompetent climber"', and came to the conclusion that the route 'is nowhere really difficult barring the 60 ft in the middle of the climb which includes the Slingsby Chimney'! Nevertheless the Bartons admitted that, 'Our position on the Pinnacle wall was chilling in the extreme.... it was quite by chance we did not get frost bitten' (Barton Climbing Book, FRCC Archive). The exact line they took is not entirely certain, but is quite possibly that claimed in 1995 as **Low Man by the Right Wall of Steep Ghyll**.

1901 Dec 26 **Great Gully, Pavey Ark** Two unknown Climbers' Club members.
'The cave and the small climb immediately above were successfully passed: then came a steep snow slope of 40 to 50 feet, and a short vertical climb, beyond which lay another slope terminating in what was considered the Mauvais Pas of the ascent,

The Barton brothers and one other member of their team after their historic first ascent of Slingsby's Chimney Route *(IV), Scafell, in 1899 (FRCC Archives)*

an almost "A.P." wall of 20 to 30 feet securely encased in ice… The leader…had got up some twenty feet…when hearing a rush of snow below he turned his head and was astonished and dismayed to behold his companion disappearing down the gully on his back.

A bundle of Harris Tweed, enveloped in a cloud of snow, shot over the pitch immediately beneath, and the leader waited for the jerk, which he knew he would be powerless of withstand. But the jerk never came, for the second man, during his enforced idleness, noticing a large rock tooth on the left side of the gully, had swung the rope round it in a loop. When the platform of snow…gave way… the rope so jammed that it never even tightened between the leader and the tooth.'

'Christmas at Langdale Head', *Climbers Club Journal* (1902)

1903 New Year **New West Climb, Pillar** WF Wright, L Meryon and two others

An epic to say the least!

'They started about midday but found the conditions very icy… Eventually they arrived at the (final) slabs and found them glazed with ice. The leader attempted in vain to make progress further than a ledge 15 feet above the shattered rocks. Prolonged effort led to a sudden and unexpected descent. The second climber apparently possessed no belay, but when the fall occurred he instantly hitched the rope around a slight excrescence and braced himself for the strain. The leader went flying out over the ledge; the rope held and he hung suspended in the darkness over the abyss. The last man on the rope, anchored by his companion in front, was just traversing around the sensational corner from the chimney at the time. The sight of the flying leader so startled him that he also lost his balance and swung pendulum-like into a crack in the cliff where fortunately he became wedged, in a more or less dazed condition… The second climber, with commendable courage, undertook to lead them up the disastrous slabs; and after many attempts he was at last successful'.

Amalgam of quotes from George Abraham writing in *British Mountain Climbs* (Routledge, 1908) and *Mountain Adventures at Home and Abroad* (Methuen, 1910)

Three of the party were killed in the Alps a year later.

1905 Feb 1 **Mare's Nest Gully, Pike Crag Scafell Pike** GH Almond, CT Oulton, CT Beecroft, WI Cumberlidge, PR Parkinson

Sometimes known as E Gully. Although not the first ascent, the details of the previous party are unknown.

'Climbed this gully completely in ice and snow. It afforded interesting climbing and has one difficult pitch which was turned by a previous party. The pitch was ascended by backing up the left wall with the aid of shoulders and ice axe from below and jamming the left knee in between this wall and the chockstone. Probably the gully is uninteresting in summer but in winter it is worth a visit.'

Wasdale Hotel Climbing Book, 1890–1919

1906/7 **West Wall Traverse, Scafell** A large party of Climbers' Club members.
Over twenty climbers – including George Seatree, Geoffrey Hastings, the Abraham brothers, Lehmann Oppenheimer and AE Field – were staying at the Wastwater Hotel; the majority as part of a Climbers' Club meet. Heavy snow had fallen recently and large teams struggled up Skew Ghyll, Deep Ghyll, Lord's Rake and the West Wall Traverse. This is the first recorded winter passage of the last of these routes, but it had certainly been done earlier, possibly in the 1880s.

1907 **Easy Terrace, Dow Crag** SH Gordon, H Goodier
'Easy Terrace. Finish up Intermediate in ice and snow.'

Coniston Parkgate Climbing Book, FRCC Archive

1908 **Rake's Progress, Scafell**, and **AB Buttress, Pike Crag Scafell Pike**
FRCC parties
'There was an unusually large quantity of snow on the fells, particularly on the North face of Scafell Pike. Ice and frozen snow abounded… Rakes Progress…presented genuine difficulties, being so choked with ice and ice covered snow that a party of three took over two hours to traverse it, cutting steps nearly the whole way from the foot of Lord's Rake to Mickledore Ridge. At the same time another party were experiencing a good deal of trouble with the buttress between A and B gullies on Pikes Crag.'

FRCC Journal (1908)

Pre-1909 **Angle Tarn Gully, Hanging Knott** G Abraham
'In wintertime…Hanging Knott is well worth a visit'.

G Abraham, *British Mountain Climbs* (Routledge, 1909)
Although the gully is not mentioned by name, it seems a very likely target, and possibly the icefalls too.

1910 Easter **Keswick Brothers' Climb, Scafell** TC Ormiston-Chant, Scantlebury

'I lost my axe when half way up Keswick Brothers Climb. It was nearly dark and Scantlebury and I spent a weary hour in chipping steps with a wedge of rock in a huge fringe of ice above Botterill's Slab, hoping to avoid a descent. A cheery hail from Hollow Stones brought two good Samaritans to the top of the climb, and the ring of their axes in the hard ice kept us company for another hour whilst they cut down to within a rope length of us. The rescuers were Worthington and Gemmel.'

TC Ormiston-Chant, 'In Memoriam: Claude Swanwick Worthington', *FRCC Journal* (1919)

However, they may have not completed the ascent by fair means!

'Easter 1910 – Scantlebury and I started up Keswick Brothers Climb as dusk came on and found the finish so badly iced as to make it impossible. We were hauled out by two kind hearted companions.'

FRCC Wasdale Climbing Book, 1907–1938

1910 Easter **Engineer's Chimney, Gable Crag** CS Worthington and JD Gemmel

The third of the quartet of Grade V climbs to be achieved by pre-Great War Lakeland climbers.

'During this Easter holiday the two (Worthington and Gemmel) did nearly all the severe and very difficult climbs in the Pillar, Gable and Scafell crags. A notable climb was Engineer's Chimney with a considerable amount of ice in it.'

TC Ormiston-Chant, 'In Memoriam: Claude Swanwick Worthington', *FRCC Journal* (1919)

1910 Easter **North Gully, Bowfell** SF Jeffcoat, TW Oliver, J Wilding

Actually a descent of the gully after ascending the continuation at the other side of the buttress. Probably climbed before. The party

'set out with the intention of climbing Bowfell Buttress by Oppenheimer's route, but returned with an account of a traverse of the buttress on snow. On arriving at the climb, they were unable to distinguish the route owing to mist. They therefore took to the snow in the gully to the left of the buttress, and by this reached the top… It was therefore, decided to descend the gully on the right

side of the buttress which contained steep snow, in which good steps could be kicked all the way down.'
'Easter Meet 1910 Langdale', *Rucksack Club Journal* (1911)

1911 Jan 5 **Arrowhead Ridge Direct, The Napes** GS Sansom, JC Brunskill, A Woodsend
'There was a great deal of snow on the ridge and we had a very fine climb. At my "mauvais pas" below the Arrowhead I used my knee on the little holds and found them distinctly safer under icy conditions.'

George Sansom, *Climbing at Wasdale Head before the First World War* (Castle Cary Press, 1982)

1911 **Great Gully, Dow Crag** TC Ormiston-Chant, Balfour, Smith, Parker, Huntley, Pidcock, Lyon
'Fells snowbound, rocks about Great Gully badly glazed with ice… Two thermos flasks were smashed during the climb.' [The start of a great Lakeland tradition.]

Coniston Parkgate Climbing Book,
FRCC Archive and *FRCC Journal* (1913)

Traverse and Slab Variation was added by J Ashcroft and C Bett, 9th Feb 1986.

1912 **Black Chimney, Dow Crag** L Hardy, G Milligan, HC Diss
'Black chimney (snow).'
Coniston Parkgate Climbing Book, FRCC Archive

1912 **Woodhouse's Route, Dow Crag** D Murray, Miss Eckland, L Hardy
'Woodhouse's Route of B Buttress (ice)' (Coniston Parkgate Climbing Book, FRCC Archive). Climbed on the same day that Rosalind Murray climbed North Gully, so the route was almost certainly in winter condition (Rosalind Murray, 'A Blizzard on Doe Crags', *FRCC Journal* (1913)).

1912 **North Gully, Dow Crag** Miss R Murray and party
'It was only my fourth attempt at climbing, and I had never climbed in snow… It was I was assured a very easy climb under ordinary conditions… This time, however, the "under ordinary conditions" was a saving clause, for our conditions were not ordinary. The rocks were covered with two inches of solid ice;

Rosalind Murray and other members of her party on their way to Dow in 1912 on the day they made first winter ascents of Woodhouse's Route *(IV) and* North Gully *(III/IV) (Len Hardy, FRCC Archive)*

genuine ice that had to be cut through with an ice axe before any hand or foot holds could be found.'
Rosalind Murray, 'A Blizzard on Doe Crags', *FRCC Journal* (1913)

1913 Mar 24 **Central Jordan Climb, Pillar** FRCC party
'A large gathering of climbers, the fells covered with snow and ice, a heavy fall taking place on Easter Saturday night and Sunday...plenty of step cutting...'

FRCC Journal (1913)

West Jordan Climb was descended the same day.

1913 Mar 24 **The Old West Route, Pillar** FRCC party
Almost certainly done earlier, but this is the earliest definite recorded ascent discovered to date. However, there is a reference to climbing Pillar Rock from the west side on Feb 6th 1887, by G Hastings and party, when it seems to have been in winter conditions. Realistically this is likely to have been by the Old West.

'Bright sunny day with hard frost. Ascended Pillar Fell by gully direct from Mosedale. Climbed Pillar Rock by easy way and then descended down the gully to the west side and ascended the rock again, descending again by the easy way. The slab on the rock was coated with ice which had to be cut away.'

Wasdale Hotel Visitors' Book, 1885–1891

1913 Mar 24 North Climb, Pillar S Herford, G Sansom
Another impressive futuristic lead by this strong team which was to tragically end with Herford's death in World War I.

'Herford was a very efficient leader under icy conditions. I well remember him leading over the Nose of the North Climb on Pillar when the rocks were covered in snow, and also up Walker's Gully on a New Year's Day when it was covered in ice.'

GS Sansom, 'Goodbye To All That', *FRCC Journal* (1974)

'Fells covered in snow and ice…nearly all rock work was impossible… North on Pillar was ascended by a party of two, a very fine performance under the conditions.'

'Easter at Wasdale Head', *FRCC Journal* (1913)

1913 Mar 25 Kern Knotts Chimney, Kern Knotts FRCC party

1913 Easter Overbeck Chimneys, Overbeck S Herford, G Sansom
'North on Pillar was ascended by a party of two, a very fine performance under the conditions, the same two also visited Overbeck Chimneys.'

'Easter at Wasdale Head', *FRCC Journal* (1913)

1914 New Year Walker's Gully, Pillar SW Herford, GS Sansom, CF Holland
'The gully was reached about noon and promised to be difficult as the lower reaches were draped with ice… For the next three quarters of an hour threading operations ensued, but at last an object appeared. It proved to be Herford's head: soon the rest of his body joined it from the bowels of the earth and he commenced a devastating assault on the upper icefall… The leader, after much toil, succeeded in attaining a somewhat doubtful position on a slope of ice below the top boulder. Here he found further progress impossible without imbedding the axe in frozen scree and using it

as a handhold. The first attempt failed, as the scree went on strike and the leader's quiet remark, "I am coming off now," was immediately justified. The thread did its work and a second shot was successful. The writer now joined Sansom in a horrible ice well which exuded much moisture. Sansom had been immured here for about an hour and a half, and was a "demned damp moist unpleasant body." The next two pitches were speedily routed, though the writer has stirring memories of backing up with his right ear on one wall and his left toe on the other, with a ruck-sack possessed of at least seven devils on his back. This rucksack turned out to be really an octopus disguised as a rucksack, and by way of retarding prowess apparently attached suckers to the rocks when its bearer was not looking. When viewed from below the top pitch had appeared tolerably free from ice, but a closer inspection revealed the unpleasant fact that all the rock was covered with what the writer believes the Germans call 'Verglas.' (He hopes it isn't swearing.) For the next hour or so important threading operations ensued. Finally Herford performed marvellously on the right wall, assumed a backing up position and disappeared. Now it was Sansom's turn to do surprising things on the wall, apparently preserving his *statu quo* by sticking his head into ante-chambers in the rock while he unthreaded. Meantime, he who tells the tale had retired into the recesses of the cave and kept the octopus quiet by sitting on it. Subsequently this went aloft guarded by the ice-axe, which throughout displayed great strength of character.'

CF Holland, 'Walker's Gully', *FRCC Journal* (1914)

OG Jones, GD Abrahams and AE Field made the first ascent of this route in semi-winter conditions in 1899. There is a fine account of his epic ascent in his book *Rock Climbing in the English Lake District* (2nd ed., Abraham, 1900).

1914 Feb 21 **South Chimney**, **Jones's Route** and **Blizzard Chimney, Dow Crag** CS Worthington, SW Herford, GS Sansom, AR Thompson, WB Gourden

This large party climbed these and Black Chimney. Although the record is not sufficiently detailed to prove that these climbs were in true winter condition, the fact that 'six inches of snow lay on the fells' that day suggests that there was a good chance that they were, and, given their previous record, the climbers were certainly capable of tackling the climbs in this condition, some of which would probably merit grade V today (Coniston Parkgate Climbing Book, FRCC Archive).

Pre-1915 **Tarn Crag Gully, Thirlmere** GD Abraham
'Worth a visit, especially in snow time' GD Abraham, *FRCC Journal* (1915)

1918 **Easter Gully** and **Scoop Route, Dow Crag** Mr and Mrs Murray, Mr and Mrs Ormiston-Chant, WA, JPR and one other
'Easter 1st pitch, traverse west... S. Chimney... good scramble in hard snow.'

Coniston Parkgate Climbing Book, FRCC Archive

1919 Jan **North Gully, Low Water Crag** JJ Bower, RP Vickers
'Snow gully from Low Water to Old Man Ridge (gully slopes up to L just to right of crags). Much step cutting... Time c. 4 hrs.'

Coniston Parkgate Climbing Book, FRCC Archive

1919 Feb **'C' Ordinary Route, Dow Crag** TC Ormiston-Chant, G Wilson, D Pilley and party
'Dorothy Pilley and I will never forget Ormiston-Chant's astonishing lead of 'C' Buttress on Dow when it was a solid mass of ice, about half the climb being made in pitch darkness owing to the time spent in lowering various members of the party who had succumbed to the cold.'

Graham Wilson, 'In Memoriam: TC Ormiston-Chant',
FRCC Journal (1957)

Graham Wilson's obituary, published a few years later, mentions that he attended his first FRCC meet at Coniston in Feb 1919, and the meet report says 'the weather was delightful, beautiful fine and cold, while the mountains glittered under a vesture of snow, frozen so hard as to support the boot, but not so hard as to prevent the delightful crunch which only the nails of a climbing boot can make on hard snow.' This strongly suggests it may have been the same meet during which the 'C' Buttress ascent took place, especially as the February Coniston meets in the following two years recorded mild weather.

1919 **Intermediate Gully, Dow Crag** PR Masson, C Alexander, G Bower
'Very badly iced' (Coniston Parkgate Climbing Book, FRCC Archive).

Bower and Borrowman also record that they climbed Intermediate Gully in 1918 'in snow'. Unfortunately, the entry in the Parkgate Book is rather too vague to ascertain whether the gully was in true winter condition, or simply that snow was falling.

1925 Jan 4 **Mitre Ridge, Grey Crag** RST Chorley, KC Hopkinson, M Barber, GS Adair and 'another'
Ascended 'under snow'. However it seems likely this meant sweeping aside the powder to uncover rock, as the log records the snow's arrival occurring shortly before this, on the 3rd January, after three days of gales (FRCC Buttermere Climbing Book).

1926 **Hiatus, Gimmer Crag**
'Hiatus – the whole course has been traversed under ice and snow…'. George Basterfield, *FRCC Journal* (1926) – though it may only have been top-roped.

1928 Jan **Fleetwith Gully** Chorley, KC Chorley, Pilkington, G Adair
'Climbed under alpine condition' (FRCC Buttermere Climbing Book). 'Chorley' was Lord Theo Chorley, husband of Katherine (nee Hopkinson). Early 1928 seems to have been one of the few periods of the decade when good conditions obtained, allowing skating to take place on Bleaberry Tarn. Despite this, nothing else of note was recorded during the 20s – a stark contrast to the activity before the Great War.

1933 **Pisgah from Jordan Gap, Pillar Rock** J Carswell, F Carruthers
'Completely iced up' (Interview with Jack Carswell, 2006).

1935 **The Barn Door, Birkness Combe** J Carswell, B Beck
The ascent was filmed by Austin Barton, and the film survives: a copy is held in the FRCC Archives.

1936/7 **Dollywaggon Gully** and **Chock Gully, Helvellyn** S Cross, A Nelson

1937 **Pisgah Buttress Direct, Scafell** AT Hargreaves, S Cross, A Nelson
Hargreaves led the hardest pitches, after they had tossed a coin for the privilege (Interviews with Sid and Jammy Cross (nee Nelson), 1996).

1937/8 Bowfell Buttress, **Bowfell** S Cross, A Nelson
Cross recalled tackling the crux crack pitch using Nelson's axe as a foothold while torqueing his own axe (an ancient implement given to him by the famous Lakes pioneer George Bower) higher up the crack. Later on in the climb (on which the pair led through) he displayed even more prescient technical skills when he used a Scout knife, which he carried on climbs for splicing hemp rope, as an ice-dagger. The winter ascent of Bowfell Buttress is especially significant in two ways. It regained the heights of technical difficulty which had been achieved before the First World War. Secondly, the co-equal role of a woman is remarkable on a route of this difficulty during the late 1930s (Interviews with Sid and Jammy Cross (nee Nelson), 1996).

1930s Little Gully, Pavey Ark S Cross A Nelson

1930s Pier's Gill, Lingmell S Cross, A Nelson

1930s Angle Tarn Icefalls, Langdale S Cross, A Nelson

c.1940 Inaccessible Gully, Dove Crag J Birkett
An ascent which went unnoticed for many years thanks to Jim Birkett's famously reticent habit when discussing his activities, and his opinion that Lakes' winter climbing was 'cold and nasty'. Hence, the exact dating is still vague. An impressive achievement, especially as Birkett climbed this steep, technical route 'wearing tricounis and sporting a single long ice-axe' (Bill Birkett, *Lakeland's Greatest Pioneers* (Hale, 1983)).

1941 Apr Birkness Chimney, Eagle Crag W Peascod, B Beck
Famously climbed using rocks as ice daggers.

> 'I had asked Bert to bring up with him a suitable stone for hacking purposes and when he saw my belay he went back down the snow slope to find a larger one. Just above me was a small chockstone completely iced into the parent rock. With our primitive tools I attacked the ice, hoping to break a hole through behind the chock to form a thread belay. Hacking at ice, frozen pebbles and clay is painful work, particularly without gloves. Soon the gore from cut fingers mingled with the ice and clay to form an unpleasant melange.'
>
> Bill Peascod, *Journey after Dawn* (Cicerone Press, 1985)

Other Info

1947 Pinnacle Ridge, Gable Crag CR Wilson, B Williamson
'A severe winter with many roads blocked but with few routes climbed
due to the scarcity of petrol and austerity of rationing after the war'.

Memories passed on to Les Kendall from
Charlie Wilson, notes from Les Kendall (2006)

1940s Low Water Beck, Coniston

1954 Goat Gill, Buttermere Raffles Alpine Club
The Raffles Alpine Club was a small group of Carlisle Climbers led by
the indefatigable Ray McHaffie; and at one time the only other member
was Les Kendall.

1959 Central Gully, Raven Tor Barrow MCC

1950s Trough Gully and **Carrock Fell Icefall, Carrock Fell** Raffles Alpine
Club
Notes from Les Kendall (2006). **Trough Gully Icicle Start** was probably
added in 1986.

1960 Jan 8 Harrow Buttress, Grey Crag T Greenbank, Diggery, J Quinn

1960 Jan 21 Sergeant Crag Gully, Sergeant Crag L Kendall, J Curry
'Heavy snow' (Notes from Les Kendall, 2006).

1960 Feb 20 Great Gable Traverse, Gable Crag R McHaffie, L Kendall
(both solo)
'Also known as Traverse of the Gods as a result of Mac's wild antics.
He had high hopes for the line and had pre-christened it. He did his
best to make that grand name appropriate by taking some hair-raising
variations while I plodded along the obvious easy way'.

Notes from Les Kendall (2006)

1960 Feb 22 Tophet Bastion, Tophet Wall L Kendall, H Sumner
'Very exceptionally deep consolidated snow gathers on the Napes
ridges to give alpine style climbing of some quality. Good signs are
the formation of a bergschrund along the foot of Tophet Wall and
distinct cornices on the wall tops. Tophet Bastion was done in just
such conditions.'

Notes from Les Kendall (2006)

Les Kendall on the first known winter ascent of Sergeant Crag Gully *(II/III), Borrowdale, in 1960. Note the slater's hammer. (Photo: Les Kendall Collection)*

1960 Mar **Greenhow Gully, Deepdale** N Hewett, C Hewett
Variation Finish CA Usher, M Humphries, 28th Jan 2003

1960 Dec 10 **Moses's Back Door, Gable Crag** L Kendall, R McHaffie (alt)

1960 Dec 11 **North-West Climb, Pillar** L Kendall, R McHaffie (alt)
The pair soloed up the initial slabs of North-by-North-West, kicking steps in the deep snow, until they got to a ledge just below the top of the Bounding Buttress, where they stopped to rope up and McHaffie took a photo of Kendall.

> 'Above the rock seemed free of all but a sprinkling of ice, a sad deception as we were soon to discover. Mac set off on the initial groove which was Very Severe. Now followed the first of the main pitches, Le Coin, which went nicely though I had to clear every hold of snow and chop one hold in the ice. As we made height, it became readily apparent that things were becoming increasingly severe. Where we had been able to avoid or clear ice below, it now became impossible to advance without painstakingly chipping away verglas. At Lamb's Chimney we found the crux.

Les Kendall having stopped to put on the rope after soloing up two pitches on the first winter ascent of North-West Climb *(V), Pillar Rock, in 1960 (Photo: Ray McHaffie/Les Kendall Collection)*

Half an hour's chopping holds from an ice bulge, combined tactics, and a piton for direct aid, finally saw us up with stick-like fingers to a safe stance near the final chimney.'

Les Kendall's Climbing Diary

It was repeated in January 1961. 'This was in difficult conditions with a foot of ice in the chimney, where a piton had to be used for aid (6 hours)' (JJS Allison, 'Winter Climbing in the English Lake District', *Nottingham University Climbing Club Journal* (1962/3)).

1960 Dec 12 **Columba's Gully, Borrowdale** JJS Allison, D Moya

1960 Dec 12 **Great Eastern Route, Scafell East Buttress** L Kendall, J Douglas
Climbed in nailed boots with an axe and slater's hammer. When the going got too hard, the latter was used to knock the ice off so the rock could be used.

Variation Direct Start, January 12th 1999, B Davison, N Hewitt.

1960 Dec **Chapel Crag Gully, Chapel Crags** L Kendall
Also climbed by D Greenop and party about this time in conditions when the gully was completely banked out. Almost certainly climbed previously, as Greenop had been told about it by Bill Peascod. **Direct Start**: SJH Reid, S Prior, 5th Feb 2003 (but may well have been climbed before in banked-out conditions); **Pitch 2 Variation** and **Right-Hand Variation on Second Chockstone**, B Davison, 1st March 1998.

1960 Dec **Bleaberry Chimney, Chapel Crags** L Kendall

1960 Dec **Gillercombe Buttress, Gillercombe** L Kendal, R McHaffie, J Douglas

1960 Dec **Clark Gable, Gable Crag** J Douglas, J Currie

1960 Dec 18 **Gable End, Gable Crag** R McHaffie, L Kendall (both solo)

1961 Dec 8 **Little Chamonix, Shepherd's Crag** AH Greenbank and party

Pre-1962 **Aira Force, Ullswater** JJS Allison
JJS Allison (JJS Allison, 'Winter Climbing in the English Lake District', *Nottingham University Climbing Club Journal* (1962/3)).

Pre-1962 **Scale Force, Buttermere** JJS Allison
Although not claimed as the first ascent, this is the earliest record so far found (JJS Allison, 'Winter Climbing in the English Lake District', *Nottingham University Climbing Club Journal* (1962/3)).

Pre-1962 **Taylor Gill Force, Borrowdale** JJS Allison

Other Info

Although not claimed as the first ascent this is the earliest record so far found (JJS Allison, 'Winter Climbing in the English Lake District', *Nottingham University Climbing Club Journal* (1962/3)).

Pre-1962 **Sour Milk Gill, Borrowdale** JJS Allison
Although not claimed as the first ascent this is the earliest record so far found (JJS Allison, 'Winter Climbing in the English Lake District', *Nottingham University Climbing Club Journal* (1962/3)).

1962 **Summit Route, Low Water Crag** JF Hool
Climbed previously by Barrow MCC.

1962 **South Gully, Low Water Crag** JF Hool
Climbed previously by Barrow MCC.

1962/3 **Doctor's Chimney, Gable Crag** J Douglas, J Currie

1963 Jan **Kirk Fell Gill, Kirkfell** L Kendall, A Todd

1963 Jan **Ignition Buttress, Kirkfell** L Kendall, A Todd

1963 Jan **Pigott's Route, Birkness Combe** L Kendall, A Todd

1963 Dec **High Scawdell Gill** and **Scaleclose Gill, Borrowdale** L Kendall

1963 Feb 27 **C Gully, Wasdale Screes** R Blain, R Heatherington.
'Ice all the way. Hampered in upper section by large flows of spin drift powder snow down the ice' (FRCC Brackenclose Hut Book). However a note in the Wasdale Hotel Climbing Book (1895) states: 'This gully is said to have been climbed throughout in winter. As there is no account in the book we shall be glad if our description elicits further information.'

1963 Feb 28 **Cascade, Scafell Shamrock** R Byfleet, R Blain, C Whalley
'Scafell Shamrock Tower by right hand flank. 3 ice pitches – rest snow and rock. Previous parties steps had filled in. Enjoyable route of no great difficulty.'

FRCC Brackenclose Hut Book

LAKE DISTRICT WINTER CLIMBS – FIRST ASCENTS

It is not known who the previous party were, but JR Lees and a group from Ullswater Outward Bound were also at the hut and did several routes.

1963 Apr 14 **Boneyard Wall, St Sunday Crag** N Allinson, B Bullivant
'Plastered in snow.'

1963 **Y Gully, Haystacks** R McHaffie, A Liddell, M Burbage, A Todd

1963 **Ill Gill, Kirkfell** Raffles Alpine Club

1963 **Lorton Gully, Buttermere** L Kendall

1963 **Buttermere Gully, Grasmoor** L Kendall

1963 **Stack Gill, Haystacks** L Kendall, J Douglas
'500 feet of gleaming blue water ice' (from a conversation with Les Kendall).

1963 **Eagle Front, Birkness Combe** R McHaffie, S Bradshaw
'Mac had persuaded a large Carlisle party up to Birkness Combe. Eagle Crag was completely plastered in snow and ice and Mac was very enthusiastic, but, by the time they got to the foot of the climb, most of the rest of the team were so intimidated that they had drifted off to Grey Crags to go rock-climbing instead. Only Stan, who was a bit slower on the uptake, remained.'

> From a conversation with Les Kendall

'I was one of the team that opted out – we went and did West Gully and then waited for Mac and Stan. The entire buttress was encased in ice and verglas, and how Mac got up it I just don't know. He was wearing so little clothing that he was absolutely frozen and when he finally got to the top his arms were numb to the elbows!'

> From a conversation with Alan Ferguson

1963 **Central Chimney, Birkness Combe** R McHaffie, J Holliwell, A Quey
Probably its only other ascent occurred when Brian Davison soloed it in 1988 having mistaken it for Birkness Chimney.

1963 **Warnscale Beck, Buttermere** L Kendall

1963 **Combe Gill, Combe Head** L Kendall

1963 **Hind Gill, Borrowdale** L Kendall

1963 **Grains Gill, Borrowdale** L Kendall

1963 **Ruddy Gill, Borrowdale** L Kendall

1963 **Goat Crag Icefall, Goat Crag** L Kendall

1963 **Portcullis Ridge, Black Buttress** N Allinson, B Bullivant

1964 **Grey Crag Icefall, Grey Crag, Coniston** Barrow MCC

Early 1960s **Black Crag Icefall, Dovedale** N Allinson, J McReady
A step-cutting tour de force – one axe, no ice screws, and l-o-o-o-ng run outs! Dachstein Mitts had just appeared in the UK that winter, and Jim bought Neil Allinson a pair as a reward for getting him up the route in one piece.

Early 1960s **Sleet Wall, Hutaple Crag** N Allinson and party
Originally graded IV, the climb was reassessed as VII on Feb 26th 1989 by B Davison and B Attwood – as the main difficulties lie on the first pitch, it is quite possible that different starts were taken by the teams involved. **Variation Start** added by A Phizacklea, R Graham, 29th Dec 1999.

1966 Feb **Dove Crag Gully, Buttermere** W Freeland, JJS Allison

c.1966 Dec **East Wall Route, Hutaple Crag** N Allinson, J Soper
The original line of ascent may have been closer to *East Wall* as described in the current FRCC Eastern Crags guidebook.

1966/67 **Force Crag Waterfall, Coledale** WA Barnes, S Clark, A Jackman
'Barney' had been watching the fall through binoculars for several winters waiting for it to come into condition.

1967 Feb **Percy's Passage, Low Water Crag** J F Hool, C McGreath

1967 Feb Cautley Spout, Howgills W Pattison, A Robson

'May have been done before, but no-one I knew then knew of
anyone who had climbed it earlier. My gear consisted of one axe,
a Commando knife, one corkscrew ice-screw, and ex-army
crampons with all the rigidity of lead sheet – you had to stop every
few moves to knock them back into shape!'

Conversation with Bill Pattison (2006)

*Bill Pattison and Angus Robson on the first known ascent of Cautley Spout
(III), Howgills (Photo: Dave Thompson, Bill Pattison Collection)*

The **Brussels Spout Variation** was added by C Wells and M Hill, 29th
Dec 1995.

1969 Jan 30 The Direct Route, Scafell Shamrock R Bennett, R Lavender
Lost Arrow Traverse Variation added by R Bennett and R Lavender in
1972; **Pillar Variation** added by W Pattison and A Dunn, early 1970s.

1969 Feb Honister Crag Gully, Honister Crag E Cleasby, N Bulmer

1969 Mar 1 Dandle Buttress, Buckbarrow Crag M Lynch, D Jewell

Other Info

1969 March West Waterfall Gully, Pillar BJ Clarke, J Stanger
A banked-out grade II at the time – and in fact they followed someone else's footprints up it. The big ice pitch was first know to have been climbed by R Wilson, J Loxham and C Downer in March 1978, though it was almost climbed by JW Robinson and T Creak, January 1887!

> 'The deeply drifted snow gave us easy passage over the first fall, and in a few minutes the upper fall was before us, a solid column of hard ice. This was so vertical, and as no opportunity presented itself of gaining support from the wall of the ghyll, progress was no easy matter. Steadily cutting step over step with a deep notch for hand holds, we were able to get within six feet of the top – when down came darkness, and we quickly realised that we must make tracks at once or spend the night in that uncanny place.'
>
> JW Robinson, 'A Novice in Snow', *FRCC Journal* (1907)
> (NB The date in this article is incorrect, but it is right in his diary.)

1960s Curving Gully, Hutaple Crag N Allinson, K Harrison

1960s Curving Gully, Chapel Crags D Greenop and party
Originally known as Central Chimney. Probably climbed previously, as Greenop had been told of the crag by Bill Peascod. **Direct Variation** added by J Martin and D Wilkinson, 20th Jan 2001.

1960s Troutdale Pinnacle, Black Crag AH Greenbank and party, also R McHaffie and party

1960s Corvus, Raven Crag R McHaffie and party

1960s Western Gully and **Variation Finishes, Steeple** D Greenop

1970 Jan Spiral Gully, Dove Crag D Roberts, A Austin
'Austin forgot his crampons and followed cutting steps' (*FRCC Journal* (1970)).

1970 Feb 16 Eliminate A, Dow Crag WF Hurford, M Wragg
> 'Fells covered in snow down to the valley floor. A sunny day. The first two pitches were mainly rock with ice in the cracks, the upper pitches well iced. A peg was used for aid higher up.'
>
> From a conversation with Wil Hurford

The route awaits a true winter ascent.

1970 Dec 20 **Grooved Arete, Scafell Pike** C Read, J Adams

1970 **Hen Crag Buttress, Hen Crag, Wetherlam** C Brown
The **Left-hand Finish** was added in 1980 by G Cock and D Andrews, and the **Direct Start** by A Hyslop and AH Greenbank, 26th Dec 1993. The **Direct Finish** was added by D Birkett (solo) in 2000.

1970/1971 **Westmorland's Route, Dove Crag** N Allinson, D Shakeshaft

1972 Mar 12 **Stoat's Crack, Pavey Ark** AH Greenbank, C Bacon

1972 **Great Doup Buttress, Pillar** R Bennet, R Lavender
1972 **Long Ledge Entry and Exit, Scrubby Crag** J Loxham, D Noels

1973 **Grossbuttock, Great End** A Rutherford, P Denny
However, concerning this and all later first ascent claims on Great End, it is worth recording Les Kendall's comments:
> 'In the exceptional conditions of 1960–1963 much then new ground was climbed on Great End by Geoff Oliver, Jeff Allison, Ray McHaffie, Les Kendall and others. Little was left untouched. In general it was found possible to climb anywhere, the standard rarely exceeding III to IV+.'
>
> Notes from Les Kendall (2006)

1973 Feb **Birkett's Gully, Mardale** TW Birkett, M Myres
Rumoured to have been climbed previously.

1974 **Window Gully Icefall, Great End** R Bennett and party

Early 1970s **Greathall Gill, Wasdale Screes** W Pattison, A Dunn, D Barras, K Thompson

Early 1970s **A Gully, D Gully, E Gully, Wasdale Screes** W Pattison (solo)

Early 1970s **Greathall Gill, Wasdale Screes** W Pattison, A Dunn, D Barras, K Thompson

Early 1970s **The Ramp, The Ramp Left-Hand, Wasdale Screes** W Pattison, A Dunn

Early 1970s **Seven Pitch Gully, Wasdale Screes** W Pattison (solo)
Variation Icefall added by W Pattison and A Dunn around the same time.

Early 1970s **Juniper Ridge, Wasdale Screes** W Pattison (solo)

Early 1970s **Lost World Gully, Lingmell** W Pattison, A Dunn

Early 1970s **Stanley Force, Eskdale** W Pattison, D Barras

Early 1970s **Birker Force, Eskdale** W Pattison, D Barras

Early 1970s **Harter Fell Gill, Eskdale** W Pattison, D Barras

Early 1970s **Scale Force Gill, Eskdale** W Pattison, D Barras

1976 **Shoulthwaite Gill, Thirlmere** C Downer, C Samuels

1976 **Bramcrag Quarry Fall, Thirlmere** C Downer, S Kysow

1977 Feb 24 **Pinnacle Ridge, St Sunday Crag** I Wall, S Parr

1978 **Girdle Traverse, St Sunday Crag** N Kekus, R Cox

1978 **Gully of the Plods, Green Gable Crag** C Read
However, when considering this and other Green Gable Crag ascents it is worth noting,

'In the early '60s New Year parties were held at Dubbs Hut high on Fleetwith Pike. The proximity of Green Gable Crag ensured its popularity with those who were less hungover. Members of the Keswick, Carlisle and Raffles Alpine Clubs did everything imaginable. Notably some of the easier slopes were done by a dog which would bark for a top-rope if things became too difficult.'

Notes from Les Kendall (2006)

1978 **Robinson's Gully, Dove Crag** CM Wornham, G Bradshaw

1978 **Left and Right-Hand Grooves, Great End** B Jenkins and party
The direct version of Left-Hand Groove was added later by persons unknown.

1978 **Girdle Traverse, Great End** R Bennett and party

1978 **Walla Crag Gully, Walla Crag** N Kekus, R Cox

1979 Jan 21 **Cambridge Crag Climb, Cambridge Crag** R Bennett, D Mounsey

1979 Dec **Southern Corner, Pikes Crag** E Cleasby, A Phizacklea

1979 Dec **Gwynne's Chimney, Pavey Ark** A Phizacklea, B McKinley, P Fleming
Direct Finish added by M Thomas, 14th March 2006.

1970s **Cable Gully, Left-Hand Gantry Curtain, Right-Hand Gantry Curtain** and **Right Gantry Icefall, Honister Crag** R McHaffie, P Hirst

1970s **Western Gully** and **Left Gully, Haskett Buttress** D Greenop
However Greenop is certain that they had been climber earlier. The **Variation Finishes** were soloed by B Davison, 29th Dec 2003.

1970s **Terrace Ice, Ruthwaite Cove** N Allinson, J Loxham
The pair climbed several other lines in this area.

1980 **Little Stanger Gill, Borrowdale** C Downer and party

1980 **Nexus, Raven Crag** I Conway, C Bacon

1980s **AB Buttress, Ruthwaite Cove** N Allinson, J Loxham

1981 Dec 13 **Crinkle Cut, Crinkle Gill** A Phizacklea, B McKinley, P Fleming

1981 Dec 28 **Cook's Tour, Pavey Ark** A Phizacklea, D Geere

1981 **Module, Grey Crag, Coniston** A Phizacklea, B McKinley

1982 Jan 16 **Pudding Beck, Coledale** M Lynch R Wightman

1982 Jan 16 **Tranearth Quarry Icefall** A Phizacklea, Ed Cleasby

1982 Jan 16 **Parrock Quarry Icefalls** A Phizacklea , Ed Cleasby (solo). The same team top-roped **Sasquatch** (8) in Hodge Close Quarry – it has still to be led.

1982 Dec 23 **White Ghyll Chimney, White Ghyll** A Hyslop, S Hubbard

1982 Dec 26 **Tilberthwaite Trundle, Tilberthwaite Gill** A Phizacklea

1982 Dec 26 **Side Show Icefall, Hodge Close Quarry** A Phizacklea. Top-roped the day before, after Christmas Dinner, by R Graham and A Hyslop.

1982 Dec **Mere Gill, Thirlmere** L Kendall

1982 Dec **Galeforth Gill Fall, Longsleddale** L Kendall

1982 Dec **Cleft Gill, Buckbarrow Crag** L Kendall, P Kendall

1983 Jan **Born Free, Great End** P Hirst, R McHaffie

1983 Feb 9 **Photon Corner, Pillar** D Kay, R Andrews

1983 Feb 14 **Raven Crag Left-Hand Gully** and **Kirkstone Curtain, Kirkstone Pass** P Dowthwaite, J Dowthwaite

1983 Feb 18 **Cave Route, Hobcarton Crag** M Armitage

1983 **Horse and Man Rock, Pikes Crag**

1983 **Crenation Ridge, Pikes Crag**

1983 **Steeplechase Groove, Pikes Crag**

1984 Jan 20 **Birkness Gully Wall, Eagle Crag** J Fotheringham, C Bonnington

1984 Jan 21 **Jones's Route Direct, Scafell** A Phizacklea, E Cleasby

1984 Jan 29 **Border Buttress, Eagle Crag** M Armitage, T Daly

1984 Feb 15 **Botterill's Slab, Scafell** A Phizacklea, D Kay
Although unlikely, it is perhaps worth noting the following mention of a possible much earlier ascent by Geoffrey Winthrop Young:

> 'A little later another lesson was driven home, when we came upon Fred Botterill, upon whose eponymous slab on Scafell H.V. Reade and I had just made the first winter ascent cautiously and admiringly, much adrift upon the iced holds of the Professor's Chimney, which gave our Alpine technique no pause.'
>
> GW Young, *Mountains with a Difference*
> (Eyre & Spottiswood, 1951)

The reference to this alleged first winter ascent is, however, a little puzzling. The mention of the 'Professor's Chimney' which lies at the head of Deep Ghyll, for example, is confusing, but it is possible that he meant the chimney up which Botterill's Slab finishes. In addition, the tone suggests that they first met Botterill shortly after their ascent. It is known that Young met Botterill at Wasdale Christmas 1907 ('The Club Meets', *FRCC Journal,* 1908), and he may have met him still earlier, yet the records credit Herford and Sansom with the second ascent of the route in 1913. Young wrote this brief account many years later, so we may never know what really happened, but the reference remains intriguing. If he really did make the first winter ascent around 1907 of what is now regarded as a modern winter classic, it would have been a remarkable achievement by England's finest Edwardian alpinist.

1984 Feb 18 **May Day Direct, Scafell** A Phizacklea, E Cleasby, S Swindells

1984 Feb 18 **White Slab, Scafell** E Cleasby, A Phizacklea

1984 Mar 1 **Minotaur, Scafell** A Phizacklea, D Geere

1984 Mar 24 **Slime Chimney, Scafell** J Fotheringham, S Howe

1984 Dec 21 **Sod's Law, Scafell** A Phizacklea, G Smith

1984 **Central Groove, Kirkfell**

Other Info

1984 **Urchin's Groove, Pikes Crag** J Fotheringham and party

1984 **Sinister Ridge, Black Crag** W Pattison

1984 **Dexter Slab, Black Crag** W Pattison

1984 **Black Crag Gully, Black Crag** W Pattison

1984 **Straight Gill – Right Hand Arete**, **Lingmell** W Pattison

1984 **Castor, Scafell**

1984 **The Wrinkled Crinkle, Crinkle Gill** J White

1985 Jan 19 **Moss Ghyll Grooves, Scafell** B Davison, R Jones, A Perkins
Several parties were vying for the first winter ascent. On the successful ascent the slab pitches were covered in unconsolidated snow with thin ribbons of ice in the corners.

1985 Jan 20 **Mosedale Gully, East Gully** B Davison, R Jones

1985 Jan 27 **The Eagle's Claw, Eagle Crag** S Clark, J Rigg, A Wardropper

1985 Jan 27 **Central Icefall, Spout Head** FRCC party

1985 Jan 27 **Shamrock Chimneys, Pillar** D Kay, M Lynch

1985 Jan **Sledate Ridge, Gable Crag** B Davison, P Herrold

1985 Feb 16 **Engineer's Slabs, Gable Crag** B Davison, R Durran, M Phillips
The **Arete Finish** was added by D Hetherington and D Donovan, 8th Jan 1997.

1985 Nov 27 **Pendulum Ridge, Scrubby Crag** S Miller, D Kay (alt)

1985 Nov 28 **Overhanging Wall, Scafell** J Fotheringham, G Bonington

1985 **Intermittent Chimneys, Scafell Shamrock**

1985 **Sandbed Gill Crag, Thirlmere** E Cleasby, M Lynch

1985 **Bleawater Gill** and **Icefall, Bleawater Crag** M Duxbury, C Clarkson, JD Kitchig

1985/86 **Dungeon Ghyll, Langdale** J White, I Williamson
Although portions had been climbed numerous times before, this is the earliest recorded ascent of the entire gill.

1986 Jan 3 **Great Chimney, Scafell** J Fotheringham, G Bonington

1986 Jan 4 **Tricouni Slab, Scafell** A Phizacklea, G Smith
Also climbed about the same time by J Fotheringham and V Saunders.

1986 Jan 5 **Left-Hand Route**, **Cambridge Crag** A Hyslop, R Graham

1986 Jan 5 **Right-Hand Route, Cambridge Crag** R Wightman, D Seddon
One nut was used for aid on the crux pitch due to soggy turf.
The **Direct Start** was added by R Graham and L Steer, 13th Jan 1991.

1986 Jan 7 **Deception, Pavey Ark** A Hyslop, R Graham

1986 Jan 7 **Gomorrah, Pillar** D Kay, J Grinbergs

1986 Jan 25 **Duncan's Groove, Great End** D Richards, TW Birkett

1986 Jan 27 **Left-Hand Climb, Black Crag, Dovedale** M Cocker, R Andrews

1986 Jan 31 **Middling Buttress, Pavey Ark** T Walkington, B Rogers

1986 Jan **Plaque Route, Bowfell Buttress** D Sanderson, M Halsey

1986 Feb 9 **Age Concern, Scafell** S Howe, J Grinbergs, D Kay, M Lynch

1986 Feb 9 **Steep Ghyll Grooves, Scafell** T Stephenson, K Murphy, L Rutland

1986 Feb 13 **Sinister Slabs, Bowfell Buttress** R Graham, SJH Reid

1986 Early Feb **Whiteout, Crinkle Gill** J White, SJH Reid
A bold lead on rotting ice by John White.

1986 Feb 16 **Hopkinson's Gully, Scafell** R Wightman, M Lynch

1986 Feb 16 **West Wall Climb, Scafell** D Kay, S Lowe

1986 Feb 18 **Ray of Sunshine, Crinkle Gill** J White, J Thorpe

1986 Feb 19 **Restless Natives, Scafell** D Kay, J Grinbergs. Repeated by R Graham

1986 Feb 19 **Bridge of Sighs, Scafell** S Howe, T Stephenson, P Andrews

1986 Feb 20 **Siamese Chimneys, North Buttress** R Wightman, R Graham

1986 Feb 20 **Wight-Out, Crinkle Gill** R Graham, R Wightman

1986 Feb 22 **Moonbathing, Scafell** A Phizacklea, D Richards

1986 Feb 26 **Midnight Special, Scrubby Crag** A Phizacklea, M Halsey
The **Ringway Finish** was added by A Phizacklea and A Rowell, 2nd Jan 1995.

1986 Feb 26 **Accidental Discharge, Hutaple Crag** D Kay, J Grinbergs

1986 Feb **West Buttress, Steeple** J Loxham, M Mills

1986 Feb **Steeple East Buttress, Steeple** J Loxham, J Coradice

1986 Feb **Border Buttress Gully, Eagle Crag** P Dowthwaite, G Phillips, D Liddy

1986 Feb **Oxford and Cambridge Ordinary Route, Grey Crag** P Dowthwaite, G Phillips, D Liddy

1986 Feb **Viking Buttress, Red Tarn Cove, Helvellyn** W Freeland, A James. The **Thor's Corner** variation was added by S Ashworth, 1st March 2002

Duncan Richards on first ascent of Moonbathing *(VI), Scafell, in the excellent conditions of 1986 (Photo: Al Phizacklea)*

1986 Mar 1&2 **Central Buttress, Scafell** A Moore, T Brindle
An imperfect ascent of the classic summer line which took place over two separate days. The Flake Crack was climbed without crampons as Moore had insisted he did not want to damage such an historical pitch. For the same reason he refused to carry pitons – much to the annoyance of Brindle who felt the climb would have been a lot safer with them. The party had gone with the intention of bivying out in duvet jackets on Jeffcoat's Ledge, but as the temperature plummeted they realised that hypothermia was highly likely if they stayed put, and they beat a hasty retreat to the valley, whereupon they were whisked round to a party at the Old Dungeon Ghyll. The next morning the pair walked in from Langdale, abseiled in and completed the route – an epic two days that immediately aroused a storm of controversy.

1986 Mar 2 **Impunity Slabs, Scafell** A Phizacklea

1986 Mar 2 **Sod All, Scafell** M Lynch, A Phizacklea
However a similar line was climbed c.1972 by R Bennett and R Lavender.

1986 Mar 16 **Upper Deep Ghyll Route, Scafell** A Phizacklea

1986 Dec 20 **Dollywaggon Great Chimney, Falcon Crag** J Grinbergs, R Kenyon, S Ely

1986 Dec 22 **Huckleberry Grooves, Nethermost Cove** M Halsey, S Coxon

1986 Dec 27 **Goat Scar Gully, Longsleddale** I Waller, O Turnbull, SJH Reid. It was Ivan Waller's 80th birthday.

1986 **Hope Head Icefall, High Ashgill – Alston** J Fotheringham

1986 **Birkside Gill, Thirlmere**

1986 **East Hutaple Groove, Hutaple Crag**

1987 Jan 9 **Wall Climb, Scrubby Crag** J Grinbergs, D Kay

1987 Jan 10 **Tic Tac Man, Falcon Crag** S Miller (solo)

1987 Jan 11 **Harvest Crunch, Scafell** B Davison, R Mulvaney

1987 Jan 11 **Ginny Clegg, Scrubby Crag** J Grinbergs, D Kay
The **Firedragon Finish** was added by R Graham and I Weetman on 3rd Jan 1995 during an early repeat of Grendel.

1987 Jan 17 **Left of Centre, Pikes Crag** A Phizacklea, D Kirby

1987 Jan 18 **Heorot, Scrubby Crag** A Phizacklea, B McKinley

1987 Jan 18 **Slate Cap, Honister Crag** C Downer, M Armitage

1987 Feb 21 **V-Corner, Red Tarn Cove** B Davison (solo)
Extended Finish added prior to 1995 by persons unknown.

1987 Feb 21 **Aspirant, Great End** B Davison, A Wells

1987 Mar 21 **Slanting Groove, Pikes Crag** B Davison, A Atkinson

1987 **Pollux, Scafell** A Phizacklea, A Rowell, P Plowright

1987 **Scabbard, North Buttress** P Cornforth
An impressive solo of which not much is known. Even the first ascentionist can't remember anything about it!

1988 Nov 22 **Cofa Wall, Black Buttress** N Kekus, S Kekus, J Fotheringham

1989 Feb 25 **Horizon Climb, Boat Howe Crag** A Phizacklea, D. Kirby

1989 Feb 25 **Right of Centre, Pikes Crag** B Davison, B Attwood

1990 Jan 28 **Deep Ghyll Integrale, Scafell** A Phizacklea, J Holden

1990 Feb **Starboard Chimney, Boat Howe Crag** N Kekus, J Fotheringham

1990 Nov 28 **Sodom, Scafell** A Phizacklea, A Rowell, P Plowright

1991 Jan 6 **Grendel, Scrubby Crag** B Davison, B Attwood

1991 Jan 10 **Dollywaggon Chimney Right-Hand Finish, Tarn Crag** J Bumby, M Curtis

1991 Jan 10 **Ledge and Groove, Bowfell Buttress** R Graham, L Steer

1991 Jan 10 **Halcyon, Scrubby Crag** J Rigg, N Hewitt, B Davison

1991 Jan 12 **Kirkby's Folly, Lonscale Fell** M Kirkby, A Archer, M Robinson

1991 Feb 1 **Central Route, Bowfell Buttress** R Graham, L Steer

1991 Feb 12 **Diagonal Gully, Dead Crag** J Coyle, C Moyle

1991 Feb 13 **Central Ice Fall, Dead Crag** C Moyle, J Coyle

1991 Feb 16 **Broad Crag Gully – Left Wall, Broad Crag** J Daly, K Phizacklea, J Hudson

1991 Feb 16 **Left Branch Greta Gill** J Daly, K Phizacklea, J Hudson

1991 Feb **Blea Water Buttress, Blea Water** J Loxham, A Loxham, J Morgan

Other Info

1991 Feb **Arlecdon Aquarian, Great End** G Wilks, J Loxham

1991 **Fisherplace Gill, Thirlmere** P Yardley and party

1991 **Rigghead Quarry Icefalls, Borrowdale** R McHaffie, J Pierson, K Woolsoncroft

c.1991 **The Enforcer, Coledale** P Wright, T Bryden, G Lee, D Nichol, A Hall

1991/92 **Dob Gill, Thirlmere** S Fletcher, J Metcalfe
Almost certainly done before.

1993 Nov 24 **Evening Buttress, Angle Tarn** D Wright, J Bean

1993 **Isaac Gill, Langdale** J White

1994 Jan 2 **Overhanging Wall – Original Finish, Scafell** A Phizacklea, D Donnini
Dom Donnini was heard to utter 'He's mad! He's going to kill himself! There's no ice!' In fact, according to Al, there was plenty of ice, just not as thick as Dom liked it.

1994 Jan 8 **Right Wall Eliminate, Bowfell Buttress** B Attwood, B Davison

1994 Jan 16 **Right Buttress Crack, Brown Cove Crag** B Davison (solo)

1994 Jan16 **Central Route, Cock Cove Crag** B Davison (solo)

1994 **Eel Crag Gully** and **Eel Crag Main Ridge, Eel Crag** S Miller

1994 **Scott Gully, Scott Crag** S Miller

1995 Jan 25 **Vegiburger, Foule Crag** O Ross
However, Bill Freeland and the FRCC had been climbing on Foule Crag since the 1960s without putting pen to paper.

1995 Jan 30 **Traverse of the Sods, Foule Crag** O Ross

1995 Jan 30 **Wowzers, Foule Crag** O Ross

1995 Jan **East Gully, Scoat Fell Crag** N Kekus, T Mather

1995 Feb 25 **Corner and Rib, Bowfell Buttress** B Davison, B Attwood

1995 Feb 26 **Tarn Crag Buttress I, Tarn Crag** B Davison (solo)

1995 Feb **Oblique Reference, Gable Crag** J Fotheringham

1995 Feb **Jeffrey's Mount Escarpment** P Dowthwaite, M Taylor

1995 Mar 4 **North-West Gully, Pike of Stickle** B Davison, C Ottley, C Wells (solo)

1995 Mar 5 **Base Brown – Left Fork, Base Brown** B Davison, C Wells (solo)

1995 Mar 9 **Calculator, Parallel G, Garden of Eden, Arjuna, Green Gable Crag** B Davison, C Wells

1995 Mar 9 **Beta Hammer Belter, Epsilon Chimney, Ride the Wild Turf, Green Gable Crag** C Wells, B Davison

1995 Mar 9 **Sod-U-Like, North Gully, Green Gable Crag** B Davison, C Wells (solo)

1995 Mar 12 **Low Man by the Right Wall of Steep Ghyll, Scafell** B Davison, C Wells
However may previously have been climbed by the Barton brothers and friends as a start to Slingsby's Chimney Route on April 11th 1899.

1995 Mar 16 **Chockstone Gully, Traverse Crag** M Cocker, P Cocker

1995 Mar 19 **Buttress Right of Right-Hand Groove, Buttress Left of Left-Hand Groove, Great End** R Graham

1995 Mar 19 **Green Gable End, Green Gable Crag** C Wells, B Davison.

1995 Mar 19 **East of Eden, Green Gable Crag** B Davison, C Wells

1995 Mar 19 **North Face, Green Gable Crag** B Davison

1995 Mar 21 **Great Western, Scafell** B Davison, C Wells

1995 Mar 27 **Summer Time Blues, Gable Crag** B Davison, C Wells

1995 Mar **Turf At The Top, Honister Crag** C Downer, C Bacon

1995 Mar **Captain Patience, Honister Crag** C Downer, D Sanderson, A Stockford

1995 Dec 21 **Pulse, Foule Crag** O Ross
Pulse Direct, O Ross Dec 21 1996

1995 Dec 24 **Bottlescrue, Gable Crag** D Bodecott, P Bunting

1995 Dec 24 **Secondhand, Foule Crag** O Ross

1995 Dec 24 **Blunt Gully, Sharp Edge** O Ross

1995 Dec 28 **Crowdless Raven, Raven Crag** B Poll, F Dooley

1995 Dec 28 **Raven Crag Grooves, Raven Crag** N Clement, D White

1995 Dec 28 **Hopkinson's Crack, Dow Crag** B Davison, P Clay
However, although open to interpretation, John Jackson's description of his and his brother Ron's solo ascents of a frosty and verglassed Hopkinson's Crack sounds very much like the condition in which the route might be tackled using crampons and axes in the modern era, though they were climbing in nailed boots and without axes (J Jackson, 'The Iron Lung', *FRCC Journal* (2002)). They certainly had the ability – Ron was known to have soloed Eliminates A, B and C on Dow in a morning wearing nails, and John notched up over fifty Himalayan expeditions during his lifetime. There is also an intriguing reference to George Basterfield:

> 'In his very early days, he found himself in the arena of Eastern Gully. Hopkinson's Crack, snow filled, seemed to him the easiest way out, and knowing or caring nothing of its reputation, he forced a way up it.'

'In Memorium: George Bower', *FRCC Journal* (1950)

Colin Downer making the first ascent of Turf at the Top (V), Honister Icefalls, in 1995 (Colin Downer Collection)

Basterfield lived from 1877 to 1949. His first new route on Dow was in 1917, so presumably this ascent would date from about that time.

1995 Dec 29 **Threshwaite Gully, Threshwaite Cove** B Davison, P Clay

1995 Dec 29 **Far West Rib, Western Avenue, Hutaple Crag** R Graham

1995 Dec **Mill Gill, St Johns in the Vale** P Ramsden, S Barker

1995 **Rob's Icefall** and **Lower Icefall, Red Screes Northern Cove** R Lee, R Lee

1996 Jan 13 **Blake Rigg Ice Fall, Langdale** TW Birkett, J White

1996 Jan 27 **Hell Gill, Langdale** N Green, B Davison, C Spark, N Lewis (solo)

1996 Jan 27 **Hole in One, Bowfell Links** B Davison, N Green, N Lewis, C Spark

1996 Jan 28 **Hidden Gully, Bowfell Links** B Davison (solo)

1996 Jan 28 **Chimney Crack, Bowfell Links** B Davison (solo)

1996 Jan 28 **Pitch and Putt, Bowfell Links** N Lewis, N Green, B Davison

1996 Jan 28 **The Caddy, Bowfell Link** C Spark, N Lewis

1996 Jan 28 **Half Way Up, Bowfell Links** B Davison, N Green, N Lewis

1996 Jan 28 **Sunday Special, Bowfell Links** N Green, B Davison

1996 Jan 28 **Green Buttress, Bowfell Links** B Davison, N Green

1996 Jan 28 **Two Under Par, Bowfell Links** N Lewis, C Spark (solo) **Direct Finish** added by B Davison (solo), 21st Feb 1996

1996 Jan **Hobgrumble Gill, Swindale** J Lowther, J Fotheringham

1996 Jan **Silver Screen, Greta Gill** P Kennet and party

1996 Feb 3 **Beckthorns Gill, St Johns in the Vale** P Dowthwaite, R Pearson, S Umpleby, A Plimmer

1996 Feb 20 **Dandle Face Direct, Buckbarrow Crag** B Davison, C Wells

1996 Feb 21 **No. 1 Gully, Tower Buttress, Twisting Turf, Great Gully, Great Gully Wall, Vulcan Buttress, Bowfell Links** B Davison (solo)

1996 Feb 21 **Shelter Corner, Shelter Icefall, Central Chimney, A Gully, B Gully, Gully Icefall, Shelter Crag, Langdale** B Davison (solo)

1996 Feb 24 **Tia Maria, Scafell** K Phizacklea, S Merry

1996 Feb 25 **Combe Head** B Davison, P Clay
However, the crag was climbed on extensively by the Raffles Alpine Club in the early 1960s and there is little doubt that this route would have been done then.

1996 Feb 27 **Arete, Chimney and Crack, Dow Crag** D Sanderson, J Coe

1996 Feb 27 **Broadrick's Crack, Dow Crag** B Davison, C Wells
C Read and B Robinson climbed Broadrick's Crack to the Bandstand and finished via Hopkinson's Crack, 9th March 1974.

1996 Feb 28 **Smoken, Foule Crag** O Ross

1996 Feb 28 **Centre Route, Scafell** B Davison, N Green

1996 Feb **South-East Gully Left-Hand Buttress, Great End** P Kennet and party

1996 Mar 2 **Zero Gully, Gladstone Knott** B Davison, P Clay

1996 Mar 2 **Left Corner, Y Route One, First Chimney, Second Chimney, Fifth Chimney, Gladstone Knott** B Davison (solo)

1996 Mar 2 **Y Route Two, Third Chimney, Gladstone Knott** P Clay (solo)

Other Info

1996 Mar **Arctic Spring, Scott Crag** S Miller, J Lowther

1996 Mar **Ema Ho, Chamber's Crag** J Fotheringham, D Hayward

1996 Mar **Big Question, Ill Crag** J Fotheringham, D Hayward

1996 Mar **Pier Review, Piers Gill** J Fotheringham, D Hayward

1996 Nov 24 **Twisting Gully, Scafell** P Dowthwaite, S Edmondson

1996 Nov 28 **Fourth Chimney, Gladstone Knott** B Davison

1996 Dec 29 **Blea Water Cleft, Blea Water** D Scott, P Braithwaite

1996 Dec 31 **Black Crag Grooves, Black Crag** C Wells, M Hill

1996 **Quarryman's Falls, Honister Crag** C Downer, G Lee

1996 **Left Wall of Greta Gill Left-Hand Branch**, **Lingmell** P Kennet and party

1997 Jan 1 **Scorpion, Hutaple Crag** B Davison, N Hewitt

1997 Jan 1 **The Main Ridge Climb by the Lower Slabs Ordinary Route, Black Crag** C Wells, M Hill
Variation Gully Finish added by A Clifford 15th Feb 2003

1997 Jan 2 **Gone with the Wind, Gable Crag** P Kennet and party

1997 Jan 2 **Eye Spy, Scafell** B Davison, N Hewitt

1997 Jan 2 **Dharma Armour, Scafell** N Hewitt, B Davison

1997 Jan 2 **Chimney Stack, Scafell** B Davison, N Hewitt

1997 Jan 4 **Mallory's Corner, Gable Crag** D Bodecott, R Johnson
Direct Start added by S Ashworth and P Ashworth, 27th Dec 1999.

1997 Jan 4 **Lesser Fall, Honister Crag** B Davison (solo)

1997 Jan 5 **Tunnel Vision, Honister Crag** B Davison (solo)

1997 Jan 5 **Y-Gully Left Branch, Harter Fell Crag** D Scott, P Braithwaite **Right Branch**, B Davison, 1st Feb 2003

1997 Jan 11 **High Beck, Ennerdale** N Kekus, B Davison

1997 Jan 11 **Savage Gully, Pillar** B Davison, N Kekus
An epic ascent that finished in a thunderstorm in the dark as all true epic ascents should – the struggle down through the forest was equally gruelling:

'We had one poor head-torch between the two of us which only worked for 3 or 4 seconds at a time, and wasn't good enough for us to find our way off the crag so we resorted to abseiling down the route by feel. Pulling down the ropes dislodged a block and we could hear it in the dark, rattling down the groove towards us – fortunately it missed. We got separated in the woods and I walked into a tree and got a foot long piece of branch stuck in my eye. I managed to pull it out, and thought I was blinded when I couldn't see anything, but it was just so dark. We finally reached the car at 3am.'

Interview with Brian Davison

The **Direct Finish** was added by SJH Reid and S Prior, 30th Jan 2004 during the second ascent.

1997 Jan 22 **Bottleneck Blues, Gable Crag** C Bonnington, D Bodecott

1997 **Greta Garbo, Greta Gill** P Kennet and party

1998 Feb 28 **Left-hand Buttress, Great Carrs** S Parson

1998 Feb 28 **Central Buttress, Great Carrs** R Jarvis

1998 Dec 6 **Slab and Groove**, **Right-Hand Gully**, **Left-Hand Gully**, **Middle Gully, Hobcarton Crag** B Davison (solo)

1998 Dec 7 **Black Shiver, Black Crag** A Hyslop, J Burrell

1998/1999 **Vestry Wall, Scafell Pike** P Kennet and party

Other Info

1999 Jan 16 **Straight Gully, Chapel Crags** B Davison (solo)

1999 Jan 17 **Sunday Chimney, Chapel Crags** B Davison, D Wilkinson

1999 Jan 17 **Narrow Gully, Chapel Crags** B Davison, D Wilkinson (solo)

1999 Jan 17 **Straight Buttress, Chapel Crags** B Davison (solo)
Climbed via its right-hand side. Climbed via its left-hand side by N Kekus, S Kekus, 19th Dec 2004.

1999 Jan 17 **Bootlegger's Groove, Gable Crag** M Armitage, D Bodecott

1999 Feb 19 **Flying Buttress, Chapel Crags** B Davison, P Bartlett, D Wilkinson
Right Hand Start added by B Davison (solo), 27th Dec 1999.

1999 Mar 6 **Big Answer, Ill Crag** D Hayward, I Armstrong

1999 Mar **Crack Magic, Flat Crag** A Nelhams, D Mounsey

1999 Dec 11 **Jacob's Ladder, Scafell** P Dowthwaite, P Smalley

1999 Dec 26 **Hind Cove Gully** and **Rib and Gully Climb, Hind Cove** B Davison (solo)
However, RC Gilson left a short note of his ascent of Hind Cove Gully on 1st January 1897 in the Wasdale Climbing Book, remarking only that 'the pitch at the bottom is of the cave type and presents no difficulty'. He makes no mention of snow or ice, but as it is known that winter conditions were present three days earlier (the Abraham brothers recorded an icy and somewhat epic ascent of Shamrock Gully on 29th December) so it seems likely that this ascent was made in winter or at least semi-winter conditions.

1999 Dec 27 **Monday Chimney, Chapel Crags** B Davison (solo)

1999 Dec 29 **Mary Ann, Flat Crag** B Davison, N Turton

1990s **Chicken Out, Dove Crag** P Dowthwaite, S MaCallum

2000 Mar 4 **Hooch, Gable Crag** D Bodecott, R Kenyon

2000 Dec 20 **Pinnacle Crack, Gable Crag** S Ashworth, D Noddings

2000 Dec 26 **West Hutaple Edge, Hutaple Crag** A Hyslop, S Wood

2000 Dec 30 **Master of Torquing, Neckband Crag** D Birkett, A Hyslop

2000 Dec 30 **The Neckband, Neckband Crag** A Hyslop, J Hughes

2000 Dec 30 **Groove and Ramp, Neckband Crag** D Birkett, M Jenner

2001 Jan 18 **A Carton of Hobnobs, Sheep Buttress, Hobcarton Crag** D Wilkinson, J Martin

2001 Jan 19 **Sodomy, Turf Accountant, Chapel Crags** D Wilkinson, J Martin

2001 Jan 20 **West Hutaple Variations, Hutaple Crag** B Davison
An unsatisfactory day soloing.

2001 Jan 20 **Little Sod, Chapel Crags** J Martin, D Wilkinson

2001 Dec 29 **Rape and Pillage, Red Tarn Cove** S Ashworth, D Davies.
Pitch 1 was originally named Prince of Darkness and was climbed by S Ashworth and B Malcolm at night after work.
Variation Finish added by M Thomas and C Badcock, 2nd Jan 2002.

2001 Dec 30 **Warn Gill, Haystacks** B Davison, D Wilkinson
In lean conditions – best left until the next ice age.

2001 Dec 31 **Right-Hand Gully, Parallel Gully Right** and **Left, Brant Bield Crags** B Davison, D Wilkinson

2002 Jan 1 **Grass Corner, Gully Arete, Chapel Crags** B Davison (solo)

2002 Jan 1 **Bear Left, Right Frog, Chapel Crags** B Davison, D Wilkinson

2002 Jan 2 **Mutley's Icy Wait, Green Gable Crag** A Clifford (solo)

Other Info

2002 Jan 3 **Skint and Single, North Buttress** M Thomas, D Almond

2002 Feb 2 **Close to the Edge, Steel Edge** S Harvey

2002 Feb 2 **South South Gully** and **South South Groove, South Hen Crag** S Harvey, P Bardsley

2002 Feb 2 **Hen's Teeth, Hen Crag** S Harvey, P Bradsley

2002 Feb 2 **North Buttress, Hen Crag** S Harvey

2002 Feb 28 **Torquers are no Good Doers, Gable Crag** S Ashworth, M Fryer

2002 Feb **Hollyway, Penny Lane, Twopenny Crag** C Dandridge

2002 Mar 2 **Windy Ridge, Gable Crag** H Davies, I Vermeulen
First claimed ascent, however climbed numerous times in the past.
Variation Finish B Davison (solo), Dec 30th 2003 – also probably
climbed before.

2002 Dec 8 **Blade Runner, Red Tarn Cove** S Wood, J Corrie

2002 Dec 20 **Bobbins Route, Ramp Route, Cock Cove Crag** S Wood, A Hyslop
Direct Start added by M Thomas and C Ensoll, 20th March 2006.

2002 Dec 21 **Thanks for the Tip, Cock Cove Crag** A Clifford

2003 Jan 3 **Snicker Snack, Gable Crag** S Ashworth, S Wood
The winter ascent of this classic summer E3 aroused considerable controversy at the time, mainly revolving around whether it was in winter
condition or not, whether aid had been used, and whether it would seri-
ously damage a fine summer climb. The first was refuted by photographic evidence, the second vehemently denied, and only time will tell
regarding the third. It certainly was a fine achievement, despite an abseil
inspection immediately prior to the ascent, and it inspired a wave of
development of modern winter routes on the crag.
   'A lot of people must have been quite relieved when I finally
climbed Snicker Snack as I had been obsessed by it for at least a

Steve Ashworth on the first ascent of the main pitch of Snicker Snack, Great Gable *(Photo: Stuart Wood)*

year. Captured by the photo in the summer guide and knowing that the crag offers great winter conditions, this 40m, pick-width crack seemed like a dream line for the winter climber. My first attempt ended in failure, it was after work and the crag was in the best condition I have ever seen it in, I got carried away and decided to set off up it, with hindsight this was pretty foolish, even with 4 headtorches (1 on each ankle, one pointing up and one pointing down) I still couldn't see enough to begin unlocking the sequency climbing. All too soon the climbing became too hard and to add insult to injury I snapped the head unit off my axe. Route 1: Climber 0. With an air of healthy competition permeating the Lakes' winter scene I headed up to Gable yet again, aware that conditions were building and that a strong team knew about my route and were heading up to do it the next day. I rapped the line on the day to try and persuade myself that it was possible and that my previous struggles were merely due to darkness, this didn't really help and I just had to get on with it. The climbing was fantastic, very thin and sequency for your feet but near perfect hooks all the way. The top pitch was surprisingly good with excellent positions. Snicker Snack was climbed with leashes, I think a more modern leashless approach will take at least a grade off the difficulty and make the whole experience more enjoyable. The route received a very impressive on sight second ascent the following day at the hands of Nick Bullock.'

Steve Ashworth 2006

2003 Jan 3 **Ramp It Up, South Gully, Ruthwaite Cove** A Hyslop

2003 Jan 4 **Troll, Gable Crag** D Birkett, M Jenner

2003 Jan 4 **Turf Wars, Turfs Up, New Turf, Deep Cut Chimney, Turf Walls, Pinnacle Groove, Turf Time, Black Chimney, No 2 Buttress Traverse, Chapel Crags** B Davison (solo)
However Black Chimney was probably climbed by Don Greenop c.1960, and is likely to have had earlier ascents.

2003 Jan 4 **Coco-Tara Direct, Cock Cove Crag** A Clifford, P Newton

2003 Jan 4 **East Hutaple Gully Devious Exit, Hutaple Crag** W Walker, M Blackburn

2003 Jan 5 **Sheltered Accommodation, Shelter Crag** B Davison (solo)

2003 Jan 5 **Thrash Corner, Rescue Groove, Dolly Mixture, Ruthwaite Cove** A Hyslop, J Lagoe

2003 Jan 5 **Swallow Gully, Nethermost Cove** P Jackson and party
However this area was extensively climbed on by N Allinson and friends in the 1960s and 1970s.

2003 Jan 6 **Jabberwock, Gable Crag** D Birkett, P Deady
J Cartwright and M Dickinson repeated the route and added the **Left-Hand Finish** the following day, not without excitement as Dickinson had left his crampons behind but managed without!

2003 Jan 7 **Back Off, Trundle Ridge, Gable Crag** S Wood, S Ashworth
'Woody and myself were convinced that an elaborate conspiracy was taking place against us with various collaborators trying to send us to crags that weren't in condition. Gable was clearly the place to go. We were disappointed to hear that Dave Birkett had beaten us to the brilliant winter line of Jabberwock the previous day, so we had to pick another objective. With an early start we were already half way up Trundle Ridge when one of the teams who had been trying to throw us off the scent arrived at the crag. We finished the day with a second new route, Back Off, so called because both me and Woody failed to lead our respective pitches, I led Woody's pitch and he led mine.'

Steve Ashworth 2006

2003 Jan 7 **That 'ard, Bason Crag** J Fotheringham, D Hayward

2003 Jan 7 **White Russian, First Cut, Whelter Crag** J Fotheringham, D Hayward

2003 Jan 8 **Mono Culture, Ruthwaite Cove** J Lagoe, A Hyslop

2003 Jan 8 **Die Another Day, North Buttress** S Ashworth, M Panton

2003 Jan 8 **Gimps to the Left of Them, The Flying Gimp Trick, North Buttress Bowfell** S Wood, D Kells

2003 Jan 10 **Browney Gill** and **Variations, Great Knott Langdale** B Davison (solo)

Other Info

433

2003 Jan 11 **Bus Shelter, Shelter Ridge, Thirty Nine Steps, Central Chimney Left Finish, Shelter Crag** B Davison, N Hewitt

2003 Jan 11 **Anderson, Morrison, Shelter Crag** S Muir, D Wilkinson

2003 Jan 11 **Turf Corner, Cock Cove Crag** A Clifford

2003 Jan 11 **Swallow Rake, Nethermost Cove** P Jackson, M Would, R Rushworth
However this area was extensively climbed on by N Allinson and friends in the 1960s and 1970s.

2003 Jan 11 **Turf-tastic, Ruthwaite Cove** P Sanday, C Pope

2003 Jan 12 **Big Issue, Shelter Crag** B Davison, N Hewitt

2003 Jan 12 **In Her Mouth, Gable Crag** K Williams, R Horton

2003 Jan 17 **West Gully Tunnel Route, Black Crag** A Clifford

2003 Jan **Juniper Crack, Scrubby Crag** A Hyslop, H Davies, D Hunter

2003 Feb 1 **Little Harter Gully, Arrowhead Buttress, Harter Fell** B Davison (solo)

2003 Feb 4 **Fibre Tube, Wimp's Route, Flypaper, Bason Crag** J Fotheringham, D Hayward

2003 Feb 5 **Further from the Edge, Steel Edge, Wetherlam** R Jones, R Jones

2003 Feb 22 **Easy Gully** and **West Gully Cave Route, Black Crag** A Clifford, C Thistlethwaite

2003 Mar **Acceleration due to Gravity, Terminal Velocity, Dollywaggon North Crag** S Ashworth, A Hyslop

2003 Dec 22 **Wild World, Low Water Crag** S Harvey, R Jones

2003 Dec 28 **Tongue and Groove, Scrubby Crag** T Marshall, G Marshall

2003 Dec 31 **Dollymixture, Ruthwaite Cove** A Clifford (back rope solo)

2004 Jan 2 **Haskett Gully, Haskett Buttress** B Davison (solo)

2004 Jan 2 **West Chimney Route**, **North Gully, Steeple West Buttress** B Davison (solo)

2004 Jan 4 **Hen Pecked, Hen Crag,** S Harvey, P Bardsley

2004 Jan 17 **Threepenny Bit, Twopenny Crag** B Davison

2004 Jan 18 **Loki, Red Tarn Cove** K Telfer, P Morgan

2004 Jan 18 **Scoating for Boys, Scoat Fell Crag** C Wells, M Twomey

2004 Jan 29 **Soul Vacation**, **North Buttress** D Almond, M Thomas

2004 Jan 29 **Gimpsuit Fall**, **Bowfell** S Keenor, I Almond

2004 Feb 29 **Green Ledge Icefall, Pillar** SJH Reid, D Bodecott (solo)

2004 Feb 29 **Incline Fall, Honister Crag** A Cannon, N Smith

2004 Mar 12 **First Cut is the Deepest, Great End** S Ashworth, M Fryer, G Howarth

2004 Mar 13 **Pinnacle Climb, Falcon Crag** H Davies, I Vermeulen, R Bilton

2004 Dec 19 **Icy Chimney, Ramp Line**, **North Buttress** B Davison (solo)

2004 Dec 19 **Left Gully, Buttress Gully**, **Traverse Buttress** B Davison (solo)

2004 Dec 19 **Ramparts Chimney, Black Crag** Harvey, P Bardsley

2004 Dec 19 **Heirloom, Heirloom Crag** A Nelhams, T Lofthouse

2004 Dec 27 **Mulled Wine, Low Water Crag** S Harvey

2004 Dec 28 **Serendipity Ridge, Scoat Fell Crag** SJH Reid, C Wells

2004 Dec 28 **Scoathanger, Scoat Fell Crag** C Wells, SJH Reid
Finished via Scoating for Boys. The **Direct Finish** was added by SJH Reid
and C Wells 16th Feb 2005.

2004 Dec 29 **Professor, Cambridge Crag** A Nelhams, P Yardley

2005 Feb 2 **Racecourse Hill Recourse, Blea Tarn** A Phizacklea

2005 Feb 2 **Racecourse Gully, Blea Tarn** A Phizacklea, K Phizacklea

2005 Feb 16 **Turf Wars, Scoat Fell Crag** SJH Reid, C Wells

2005 Feb 16 **Sod this for a Lark, Scoat Fell Crag** C Wells, SJH Reid

2005 Feb 26 **Original Route, Rampsgill Head Crag** B Davison, D
Wilkinson

2005 Feb 26 **South South Gully, Rampsgill Head Crag** B Davison, D
Wilkinson (solo)

2005 Feb 26 **South Pinnacle Ridge, Rampsgill Head Crag** D Wilkinson,
B Davison,

2005 Feb 26 **South Gully, Rampsgill Head Crag** B Davison, D
Wilkinson
Left-Hand Variation added by B Davison and D Wilkinson, 6th March
2005.

2005 Feb 26 **Butterfingers, Westmorland Crag** A J Huddart, JA
Stevenson

2005 Feb 26 **Drop Out, Dropping Crag** A Phizacklea, K Phizacklea

2005 Feb 26 **Middleboot Gill** A Phizacklea, K Phizacklea (probably
done before)

2005 Feb 27 **Follow Your Nose, Westmorland Crag** AJ Huddart, JA
Stevenson

2005 Feb 27 **Central Gully, Rampsgill Head Crag** B Davison (solo)
Escape Exit B Davison (solo), **North Pinnacle Exit** B Davison and D Wilkinson, the same day.

2005 Feb 27 **North Gully, Rampsgill Head Crag** B Davison, D Wilkinson

2005 Mar 5 **Central Ridge, Rampsgill Head Crag** B Davison, D Wilkinson

2005 Mar 5 **Left Gully, Rampsgill Head Crag** B Davison, D Wilkinson

2005 Mar 5 **Right Gully, Rampsgill Head Crag** B Davison (solo)

2005 Mar 6 **Buttress Groove, Rampsgill Head Crag**, B Davison, D Wilkinson

2005 Mar 6 **Friends Above, Rampsgill Head Crag** B Davison, D Wilkinson
So called because the first ascentionists were buzzed by friends in a helicopter during the climb – taking photographs for this guidebook.

2005 Mar 6 **Central Pinnacle Gully, Rampsgill Head Crag** B Davison (solo)

2005 Mar 6 **Evolution, Great End** S Ashworth (unseconded)
'After a hard spell of training in the previous autumn, and fired up by two weeks of climbing in Scotland, it was time to climb something at home. Having stood underneath it on a number of occasions, I knew that this route wouldn't suit my style of climbing (hence a concentration on more explosive moves in my training), so it was going to be a challenge, and I wanted to climb it ground up and on sight. I took one impressive clattering whipper onto a Friend 5 which I had placed before committing to the crux, dropping an axe in the process. I descended, pulled the ropes and set off again. The route was very pumpy, pulling on quite tenuous hooks. Even with both axes in the turf over the top I still felt that I might fall off.'
Steve Ashworth 2006

2005 Mar 6 **Central Buttress Variation to Curving Gully, Chapel Crags** N Kekus, S Kekus

2005 Mar 6 **No Way Out, Cambridge Crag** A van Lopik, T Fish

2005 Mar 8 **The Girdle Traverse, Scafell** S Ashworth, B Davison
'A route that had been in the back of my mind for some time, I just needed someone to climb it with. Brian had been in touch with me over the production of the new guidebook, saying that he felt a crag had matured once it had a girdle traverse. He agreed to come along. I felt like some young pretender with my leashless axes and monopoints standing next to Brian in with his slightly more dated gear. It was a great route, one of the best I have done, the conditions were so good that it all seemed to pass in quite a relaxed manner. Neither of us had a camera that worked with us, so you'll just have to picture the temperature inversion, alpenglow picking out Gable in the early evening and glistening neve on the crest of the pinnacle.'
Steve Ashworth 2006

2005 Mar 12 **Blow Out, Rampsgill Head Crag** D Wilkinson, D Williams (alt), R Gray

2005 Mar 12 **Windy Buttress, Rampsgill Head Crag** D Wilkinson, D Williams, R Gray

2005 Mar 12 **Wind Up, Rampsgill Head Crag** D Wilkinson, D Williams, R Gray

2005 Mar 13 **Gendarmerie, Rampsgill Head Crag** D Wilkinson, R Gray

2005 Mar 13 **Umbrella Gully, Rampsgill Head Crag** D Wilkinson, R Gray

2005 Mar 13 **Easy Buttress, Rampsgill Head Crag** D Wilkinson, R Gray

2005 Mar 13 **Long Walk, Crinkle Gill Area** B Davison, D Donnini, N Wharton

2005 Nov 26 **Band on the Run, Traverse Crag** S Ashworth
Soloed during his lunch hour from work!

2005 Nov 26 **Misty Mountain Hop, Cambridge Crags** S Ashworth
Also soloed during his lunch hour from work.

2005 Nov 27 **B.B. Corner, Flat Crags** S Ashworth, J Kelly

2005 Nov 29 **Into the Groove, Traverse Crag** S Ashworth B Davison

2005 Nov 29 **Big Groove, Traverse Crag** B Davison, S Ashworth
During this cold snap Ashworth climbed five new routes during four days at work!

2005 Nov 30 **First of Many, Black Crag** W Sim, E Booth

2005 Dec 29 **Buttress Gully, Red Screes Northern Cove** B Davison (solo)

2006 Feb 25 **Solo Symphony, Dollywaggon North Crag** H Worsnop

2006 Feb 26 **Dolly Daydream, Dollywaggon North Crag** D Bell, R McGibbon

2006 Mar 3 **Cambridge Girdle, Cambridge Crag** S Ashworth, B Davison

2006 Mar 3 **Bowfell Girdle, Bowfell Buttress** B Davison, S Ashworth
The second traverse of a snowy day.

2006 Mar 4 **Southern Cross, Scafell Pike** N Kekus, S Kekus

2006 Mar 4 **Buttress Route and Gully Arete, Red Screes North Cove** B Davison (solo)

2006 Mar 5 **The Memo, Hutaple Crag** R McGibbon, D Bell

2006 Mar 5 **Riboletto Groove, Cambridge Crag** A van Lopik, S Normington

2006 Mar 5 **Two Grooves, Brown Crag Cove** B Davison, N Wharton, D Donnini

2006 Mar 13 **The Crack Direct, Gimmer Crag** D Birkett, M Edwards
The Crack was recorded as having been climbed in winter prior to 1962 but it is not known exactly what the conditions were or what route was taken (JJS Allison, 'Winter Climbing in the English Lake District',

Nottingham University Climbing Club Journal (1962/3). It was also climbed on 9th March 1969 by WF Hurford and S Town. The pair avoided the first pitch by starting up Hiatus. Conditions were described as 'Lots of snow, but not full-blown iced up' (*Interview with Wil Hurford*).

2006 Mar 15 **Turfed Out, Green Gable Crag** BJ Clarke (solo)

2006 Mar 16 **The Gnomon, North Buttress** M Thomas, D Almond

2006 Mar 17 **Salvation, Neckband Crag,** M Thomas
A nerve-wracking rope solo.

2006 Mar 17 **Antarctic Monkeys, Lingmell** H Worsnop, M Balmer

2006 Mar 18 **Ill Gully, Ill Crag** B Davison, S Ashworth (solo)

2006 Mar 18 **Chambers Ramp, Chambers Crag** B Davison, S Ashworth (solo)

2006 Mar 18 **Chambers Pinnacle, Chambers Crag** B Davison, S Ashworth

2006 Mar 19 **Rib and Groove, Cambridge Crag** M Thomas, D Drown

2006 Mar 19 **Late Season Flurry, Gable Crag** BJ Clarke (solo)

2006 Mar 20 **Equinox, Cock Cove Crag** M Thomas, C Ensoll

2006 Mar 20 **SOS, Scafell East Buttress** D Birkett, M Edwards
A considerable achievement, but it still awaits a complete ascent to the top of the crag.

2006 Mar 22 **Unsullied Gully, High Cup Nick** C Harrison (solo)
However F Stevenson has done many unrecorded routes here in winter.

2006 Mar 22 **Grotty Gully, High Cup Nick** D Bailey (solo)

2006 Mar 22 **Black Gully, Black Groove, Black Chimney, Black Buttress** B Davison (solo)

MOUNTAIN ACCIDENTS

by Dr John Ellerton (an LDSAMRA team doctor)

Procedure for climbers in the Lake District

Mountain rescue in the Lake District is well served by 13 voluntary teams backed up by special search and cave/mine rescue units. They are equipped to a high standard and work closely with the RAF helicopters and Air Ambulance services. Consequently, only minor casualties should come within the scope of treatment and evacuation by the climber's companions. The rule for all other cases is to make the casualty safe, start first aid and send for a Mountain Rescue Team.

Sending for help

A reliable member of the party, with full information about the nature of the injuries and the position of the incident (including, if possible, the map reference), should use a mobile phone (which can save a considerable amount of time) or be sent to find the nearest telephone. He should dial 122 from a mobile or 999 from a landline and ask for the Police, who will notify the appropriate mountain rescue team. The sender of the message should keep his mobile phone on and keep within reception range (reception is often better on the tops or ridges of the mountains), or stay by the landline phone, as the rescue team leader will call back to give instructions.

Lack of help

You have a difficult decision to make when the casualty is severely injured, possibly unconscious, and you are alone. You should try to summon help from nearby climbers or walkers by shouting, giving the distress call on a whistle (6 blasts spread over one minute and repeated regularly), flashing a torch (6 flashes spread over one minute repeated regularly) or sending up a red flare. If there is no response then assess the relative dangers of leaving the casualty, and of failing to get help, and then act decisively in the interest of the casualty.

Emergency precautions and first aid

While waiting for the rescue team, you should check for further danger, and then carry out basic first-aid treatment.

Safety first

Are you and the casualty safe from further danger? If not try and make yourselves safe: either by moving, or anchoring yourselves, or both. Check whether the casualty is responsive.

A Is the casualty's **A**irway open? If necessary, open it by a simple jaw thrust or lift. If possible, avoid moving the neck after trauma. An open airway is essential if the casualty is unconscious or semi-conscious as reduced consciousness can cause death from asphyxia as the tongue falls back blocking the airway. The position of the casualty, in particular his head and tongue, should be adjusted to open the airway and be continually reassessed.

B Is the casualty **B**reathing? Look, feel and listen for breathing. Basic life support should be started, if you are trained, when the casualty is unconscious and shows no signs of breathing, and it can be continued until help arrives and where there is a chance of recovery (lightning, drowning, heart attack). It is usually futile in casualties with internal injuries, and it is probably best to defer in cases of severe exposure/hypothermia until expert help is available. An unconscious and breathing casualty should be put in the recovery position if possible. Check the airway is still open.

C Is the casualty's **C**irculation adequate? Stop any bleeding from wounds by elevation and direct pressure with dressings or clothing. The pressure needs to be applied continuously for at least 10 minutes. Raising the legs and/or lowering the head may be appropriate. Internal haemorrhage should be suspected if the casualty has sustained blows to the chest or abdomen or broken the femur (thigh bone). The condition often deteriorates and all steps should be taken to facilitate the rapid arrival of the mountain rescue team and, if possible, a helicopter. A record of the pulse rate and consciousness level is very helpful.

D Is the casualty **D**isabled due to damage to his head or spine? Record the casualty's consciousness level – alert, responsive to voice, responsive to pain or unresponsive? Has the spine been damaged? If so, do not move the casualty unless essential for safety reasons. Maintain the head in the normal straight position using your hands.

Prevent hypothermia (exposure). Hypothermia occurs when a person's heat loss exceeds their heat generation. To avoid hypothermia yourself, use a two-pronged approach by dressing appropriately and avoiding exhaustion. Modern mountain clothing is very effective at conserving heat in a wide range of climates; wind resistance and keeping the surface of the body dry are important factors when choosing clothing. The best way of generating heat is muscular exercise. Bear in mind that to maintain this you should eat carbohydrate snacks and drink regularly during the day. Alcohol, even the previous night, can significantly reduce your exercise endurance.

The symptoms of hypothermia start with feeling cold, apathy, clumsiness and stumbling, followed by shivering. More severe hypothermia is recognised by confusion, lack of shivering, an inability to walk and finally coma. In the early stages, increased insulation, warm drinks and 'carbs' should allow a retreat to safety by walking.

Established, more severe hypothermia, is more difficult to manage as sudden movements of the casualty can precipitate a cardiac arrest.

- Insulate the casualty as best as you can without disturbing the casualty's position too much.
- Shelter the casualty from wind and rain.
- Wrap them in as many layers of clothing as possible and encase them in a 'poly bag' or other impermeable barrier.
- Do not forget to insulate the head and the area underneath the casualty.
- Then call for a mountain rescue team.

Even people with severe hypothermia showing 'no signs of life' have been resuscitated successfully, but when to start basic life support is complex and best discussed with the mountain rescue team before you start.

Check the limbs for fractures. In cases of fracture, immobilise the limb by the simplest method available. For a fracture of the arm, pad it and bandage it to the chest; and in the case of the leg, pad it and bandage it to the other leg.

Helicopter rescue. A helicopter may arrive before the mountain rescue team. Extinguish all flames and secure all equipment. The downdraught can knock you over, so get in a safe position. Do not approach the helicopter until clearly signalled to do so by the pilot.

Other Info

*An RAF rescue helicopter hovers over Red Tarn, Helvellyn
(Photo: Stephen Reid)*

Further Points to Consider

Large, **organised groups** should bear in mind that mountain rescue teams are a finite resource and it is wrong to assume their availability.

The majority of climbers killed in the Lake District as a result of a climbing accident die from a head injury. A **helmet**, whilst not being 100% effective, can make the difference between living and dying. This would seem particularly pertinent in winter where falling ice and long tumbling falls add to the hazards.

Whilst **mobile phones** can be very useful in emergencies, any temptation to use them in the hills to call the emergency services in non-emergency circumstances should be resisted. If you are not sure whether it is an emergency or not, please investigate a little yourself first before reaching for your phone.

GPS systems, whilst also useful, are no substitute for carrying a **map** and **compass** and knowing how to use them.

The routine carrying of a suitable **head-torch** would save many needless call-outs.

Lake District mountain rescue teams are made up of unpaid volunteers and rely on charitable contributions. Your consideration and a 'Thank you' go a long way to ensure the service continues.

The Lake District Search and Mountain Rescue Association (LDSAMRA) acts as an umbrella body for the Lakeland mountain rescue teams. It has a website at: http://homepages.enterprise.net/ldsamra which gives contact details for the individual teams.

INDEX

Other Info

445

OTHER INFORMATION

OTHER INFORMATION

Other Info

INDEX OF DIAGRAMS AND MAPS

Other Info

Stephen Reid silhouetted on the icefall of Curving Gully Direct *(III), Chapel* Crags *(Photo: Steve Prior)*

PUBLICATION INFORMATION

About the Author

Brian Davison has been winter climbing for some 30 years and has notched up an impressive list of first ascents in Scotland, Wales and the Lake District. These include Big Daddy (VIII, 8) in Coire Sneachda, Mort (IX, 9) at Lochnagar, and Moss Gill Grooves (V, 6), Harvest (VII, 9) and Mechanical Orange (VIII, 8) all on Scafell. He has also made many expeditions overseas to such diverse areas as the Himalayas, Morocco, Greenland, Alaska and South Georgia. His intimate knowledge of the Lake District has further been enhanced by endurance feats such as completing an unsupported Bob Graham Round, and climbing all the Lakes' routes in *Classic Rock* in a day without use of a vehicle. He lives in Lancaster with his family and is a researcher at Lancaster University.

Previous Winter Climbing Guides to the Lake District

1972	A Guide to Winter Climbs in the Lake District
	Wyndham MC Journal, Bob Bennett
1974/5	Climbing in the Wasdale Area
	Wyndham MC, Bob Bennett
1979/80	Winter Climbs in the Lake District
	Cicerone, R Bennett, W Birkett, A Hyslop
1985/6	Winter Climbs in the Lake District
	Cicerone, R Bennett, W Birkett
1997	Winter Climbs in the Lake District
	Cicerone, R Bennett, W Birkett, B Davison

FRCC Guidebooks

Langdale (1999)
Dow, Duddon and Slate (1993)
Scafell, Wasdale and Eskdale (1996)
Borrowdale (2000)
Lake District Rock (2003) (selected routes)
Gable, Pillar, Buttermere and St Bees (due 2007)
Eastern Crags and Outcrops (due 2008)

Other Info

Two Moors Way
Walking in Dorset
A Walker's Guide to the Isle of Wight
Walking in Somerset
The Thames Path
Channel Island Walks
Walking in Buckinghamshire
The Isles of Scilly
Walking in Hampshire
Walking in Bedfordshire
The Lea Valley Walk
Walking in Berkshire
The Definitive Guide to
    Walking in London
The Greater Ridgeway
Walking on Dartmoor
The South West Coast Path
Walking in Sussex
The North Downs Way
The South Downs Way

SCOTLAND

Scottish Glens 1 – Cairngorm Glens
Scottish Glens 2 – Atholl Glens
Scottish Glens 3 – Glens of Rannoch
Scottish Glens 4 – Glens of Trossach
Scottish Glens 5 – Glens of Argyll
Scottish Glens 6 – The Great Glen
Scottish Glens 7 – The Angus Glens
Scottish Glens 8 – Knoydart
    to Morvern
Scottish Glens 9 – The Glens
    of Ross-shire
The Island of Rhum
Torridon – A Walker's Guide
Walking the Galloway Hills
Border Pubs & Inns –
    A Walkers' Guide
Scrambles in Lochaber
Walking in the Hebrides
Central Highlands: 6 Long
    Distance Walks
Walking in the Isle of Arran
Walking in the Lowther Hills
North to the Cape
The Border Country –
    A Walker's Guide
Winter Climbs – Cairngorms
The Speyside Way
Winter Climbs – Ben Nevis & Glencoe
The Isle of Skye, A Walker's Guide
The West Highland Way
Scotland's Far North
Walking the Munros Vol 1 – Southern,
    Central
Walking the Munros Vol 2 –
    Northern & Cairngorms
Scotland's Far West
Walking in the Cairngorms
Walking in the Ochils, Campsie Fells and
    Lomond Hills
Scotland's Mountain Ridges
The Great Glen Way

The Pentland Hills: A Walker's Guide
The Southern Upland Way

IRELAND

The Mountains of Ireland
Irish Coastal Walks
The Irish Coast to Coast

INTERNATIONAL CYCLE GUIDES

The Way of St James – Le Puy to Santiago
    cyclist's guide
The Danube Cycle Way
Cycle Tours in Spain
Cycling the River Loire – The Way
    of St Martin
Cycle Touring in France
Cycling in the French Alps

WALKING AND TREKKING
IN THE ALPS

Tour of Monte Rosa
Walking in the Alps (all Alpine areas)
100 Hut Walks in the Alps
Chamonix to Zermatt
Tour of Mont Blanc
Alpine Ski Mountaineering
    Vol 1 Western Alps
Alpine Ski Mountaineering
    Vol 2 Eastern Alps
Snowshoeing: Techniques and Routes in the
    Western Alps
Alpine Points of View
Tour of the Matterhorn
Through the Eastern Alps: E5

FRANCE, BELGIUM AND
LUXEMBOURG

RLS (Robert Louis Stevenson) Trail
Walks in Volcano Country
French Rock
Walking the French Gorges
Rock Climbs Belgium & Luxembourg
Tour of the Oisans: GR54
Walking in the Tarentaise and Beaufortain
    Alps
Walking in the Haute Savoie, vol. 1
Walking in the Haute Savoie, vol. 2
Tour of the Vanoise
GR20 Corsica – The High Level Route
The Ecrins National Park
Walking the French Alps: GR5
Walking in the Cevennes
Vanoise Ski Touring
Walking in Provence
Walking on Corsica
Mont Blanc Walks
Walking in the Cathar region
    of south west France
Walking in the Dordogne
Trekking in the Vosges and Jura
The Cathar Way

PYRENEES AND FRANCE / SPAIN

Rock Climbs in the Pyrenees
Walks & Climbs in the Pyrenees

LISTING OF CICERONE GUIDES

ABOUT THIS GUIDE

This guide is a collaboration between Cicerone and the Fell and Rock Club of the English Lake District (FRCC).

Cicerone, based on the edge of the Lake District, is one of the UK's leading and most respected publishers of guides for walkers, trekkers, mountaineers and climbers, and currently has more than 250 guides in print covering the UK, Europe and worldwide. Over the past 40 years, Cicerone has published several guides and editions on winter climbing in the Lake District.

The FRCC is one of the UK's oldest and most revered climbing clubs, and for many years has published a definitive series of guides to rock climbing in the Lake District. With over 1000 members and a range of huts and other facilities throughout the Lake District, the FRCC has been at the forefront of exploring winter climbing in the fells and retaining the records, and in many cases the history, of these climbs.

This collaboration is intended to bring together the best of Cicerone and the FRCC – combining resources, talents and even styles – to develop what is, for now anyway, the best and most comprehensive guide to Lake District Winter Climbs.

The core text in the guide was written by Brian Davison, and combines his long experience of Lake District winter climbing and his knowledge as co-author of earlier Cicerone guides. Maps were developed by Al Phizacklea.

A guide such as this has many parents, who contribute the knowledge and understanding, background and history, and maps and photographs. A full list of these is included in the Acknowlegements, but mention must be made of Stephen Reid who, in his role as FRCC Guidebooks Editor, has brought together a wide range of materials and contributors and created a guide that will reward climbers in the Lake District for many years to come.

Cicerone Press
Milnthorpe, Cumbria, October 2006